THE WRITINGS OF RABASH

ASSORTED NOTES

Volume Six

LAITMAN
KABBALAH
PUBLISHERS

Rav Baruch Shalom HaLevi Ashlag

The Writings of RABASH
Volume Six—Assorted Notes

Copyright © 2023 by Michael Laitman All rights reserved
Published by Laitman Kabbalah Publishers

Contact Information
E-mail: info@kabbalah.info
Website: www.kabbalah.info
Toll free in USA and Canada: 1-866-LAITMAN

1057 Steeles Avenue West, Suite 532, Toronto, ON, M2R 3X1, Canada

No part of this book may be used or reproduced in any manner without written permission of the publisher, except in the case of brief quotations embodied in critical articles or reviews.

ISBN: 978-1-77228-143-9

Translation: Chaim Ratz, Rinah Shalom
Translation Assistance: Mickey Cohen, Moshe Eisenberg
Content Editing: Noga Bar Noye
Editing and Proofreading: Mary Pennock, Mary Miesem, Joseph Donnelly, Michael Kellogg, Debbie Wood
Internal Design: Gill Zahavi
Cover Design: Baruch Khovov/Inna Smirnova
Executive Editor: Chaim Ratz
Printing and Post Production: Uri Laitman

SECOND EDITION: SEPTEMBER 2023

Table of Contents

1- *Atzilut* Is Private Providence 15
2- The Striking of Thoughts upon Man 16
3- Against Your Will - 1 17
4- If There Is a Virgin Maiden 18
5- The Meaning of Sins Becoming as Merits 20
6- A Gentile Who Observes the Sabbath Must Die 21
7- The Correction of Lines 24
8- This Is the Path of Torah - 1 25
9- A Hedge for Wisdom - Silence - 1 25
10- He Whom the Lord Loves He Admonishes 26
11- The Fear of You and the Dread of You Shall Be
 upon All the Animals of the Earth 26
12- The Whole World Is Nourished by My Son Hanina - 1 ... 27
13- A Hand on the Throne of the Lord - 1 28
14- Thus You Shall Say to the House of Jacob 29
15- Ordinances 31
16- The Numbered Things of the Tabernacle - 1 33
17- Concerning the *Shechina* [Divinity] 34
18- The Garments of the Soul 36
19- Beginning to Speak from the Connection with the Creator 37
20- Concerning the Will to Receive 37
21- Sanctification of the Month 39
22- And You, Israel 41
23- Behold, I Am Setting Before You 43
24- The Main Thing We Need 44
25- The Summoning for the Blessing on the Food 45
26- Who Will Not Lift Up the Face 47
27- Three Lines - 1 48
28- The Earth Feared and Was Still 49
29- The Creator Observed Their Works 51
30- Turn Away from Evil and Do Good - 1 52
31- How I Love Your Teaching 54
32- Man's Greatness Is According to His Work 56
33- What Is Amalek, Whose Memory We Must Blot Out 59
34- TANTA [*Taamim, Nekudot, Tagin, Otiot*] 60
35- Find Favor and a Good Mind 60
36- Who Hears a Prayer 61
37- Fish Means Worries 61

38- The Blessing of the Torah 61
39- Anyone with Whom the Spirit of the People Is Pleased – 1 62
40- Concerning Two Witnesses 62
41- Raising the Hands 63
42- Serve the Creator with Joy 64
43- The Discernments of "Woman" and "Sons" in the Torah 64
44- Ruin by Elders—Construction; Construction by Youths—Ruin 66
45- Sons of Wise Disciples 66
46- This Moment and the Next Moment 67
47- Worse than Everyone 67
48- Right, Wholeness, and Truth 67
49- Our Faith in Books and Authors 68
50- Man's Sensation of Time 68
51- The State of Shabbat [Sabbath] 69
52- God Made It so that He Would Be Feared 69
53- The Voice, the Voice of Jacob, but the Hands, the Hands of Esau 70
54- Everlasting Salvation 70
55- Delight Them with a Complete Structure – 1 71
56- Questions in the Work 71
57- A *Kli* [Vessel] that Holds a Blessing 72
58- *Ani* [I] and *Ein* [Nothing/Null] 72
59- Anyone Who Is Angry, It Is as though He Commits Idol-Worship ... 73
60- A Request for Help 73
61- Right and Left 74
62- Reward and Punishment 75
63- You Stand Today – 1 75
64- All Is Done by His Word 76
65- Turn Away from Evil and Do Good – 2 77
66- Woe unto You Who Await the Day of the Lord 77
67- What Is Truth? 79
68- The Order of the Work 81
69- The Reward for Work in Spirituality 82
70- The Difference between *Kedusha* [Holiness] and
    Sitra Achra [Other Side] 83
71- The Meaning of Exile 84
72- Concealed and Revealed in His Providence 85
73- Flavors of Torah 86
74- Father and Mother 87
75- The Work of the Greatest in the Nation 87
76- The Works Go Up 88
77- Greeks Have Gathered Around Me 88
78- The War of the Inclination 89
79- What Is Handsome In the Work? 90

80- Man's Receptions..91
81- Against Your Will You Live; Against Your Will You Die..................93
82- A Horse to Ride On 93
83- A Prayer for Life and Nourishments 94
84- Touching the *Tefillin* [Phylacteries] 95
85- Observing Torah Only in the Land of Israel....................................95
86- The Degree of "Wicked"...95
87- Jerusalem 96
88- The War Against Amalek 96
89- Joy and Fear..97
90- The Difference between Money and Honor 97
91- All Bitter Herb [*Maror*]..98
92- Old and New...98
93- A King Who Breaks through a Fence..98
94- A Groom Is Akin to a King 98
95- The Kingdom of Heaven Begins with *Hesed*................................. 99
96- Affliction Precedes Mercy..99
97- The Torah Must Be Received with Both Hands...........................100
98- Midnight Correction 101
99- Wholeness and Deficiency – 1 102
100- Faith and Reason 102
101- Faith Above Reason 103
102- Good Deeds Are Called Sons..103
103- The Unification of ZON...104
104- The Prohibition to Teach a Gentile Torah 104
105- Blessed Is Our God, Who Has Created Us for His Glory...........105
106- The Ruin of *Kedusha* [Holiness]..105
107- And Golan in the Bashan 106
108- Man Determines 106
109- The Reason Why People Go to the Graves of the Patriarchs........106
110- The Path of Torah 107
111- Nothing New Under the Sun..107
112- Returning a Theft...107
113- The Old Man Looks for Fear of Heaven 107
114- Three Partners 108
115- The Meaning of "Torah *Lishma* [for Her Sake]" 108
116- Who Are the Wicked?..109
117- The Light in It Reforms Him 109
118- Except for "Leave!" 109
119- From *Lo Lishma* to *Lishma* 109
120- Joy that Comes from Dancing 110
121- Two Forces within Man...111
122- Being Rewarded with Life...111

123- Without Hands and Without Legs 112
124- To Serve Me 112
125- Definitions – 1 113
126- Visiting the Sick 113
127- Happy Is He 113
128- Exalt the Lord Our God 114
129- Knowledge and Faith 115
130- The Testimony of the Creator 115
131- See a Life with a Woman that You Love 116
132- Upper and Lower 117
133- It Is All Corrections 117
134- Repentance Does Not Help in GAR 118
135- Righteous Take by Force 119
136- The Binding of Isaac 120
137- The Lack Is the *Kli* [Vessel] 120
138- A Near Road and a Faraway Road 121
139- A Foot and a Shoe 122
140- The Difference between Envy and Lust 122
141- The Spirit of the Wise Is Displeased with Him 123
142- The Sorrow of the *Shechina* [Divinity] – 1 124
143- The Need for Recognition of Evil 124
144- Revealed and Concealed 125
145- Passion for Knowledge 125
146- Suffering and Joy 125
147- The Line of the Work 126
148- Faith Is Called "Action" 127
149- "Land" Is the Kingdom of Heaven 127
150- A Knife for Slaughter 128
151- The Desire to Bestow – 1 128
152- Walk Discreetly 129
153- Torah with the Manner of the Land 129
154- Sitting in Corners 130
155- You Have Chosen Us – 1 130
156- Sanctification of the Moon 130
157- What Comes First—the Blessing or the Peace? 132
158- According to the Sorrow Is the Reward 132
159- The Need and Importance of Teaching Faith 133
160- And All the People Stand Over You 151
161- Awakening – 1 159
162- Love of Others 160
163- Colors in the Work 160
164- What to Ask of the Creator—to Be His Servant 160
165- The Matter of Keeping 161

#	Title	Page
166	Which Repentance Helps?	162
167	Strict with Himself and Blesses	162
168	Blessed Is the Man Who Puts His Trust in the Lord	163
169	The Meaning of the Bed	163
170	Faith Within Reason	164
171	How Good Are Your Tents, Jacob – 1	164
172	Man and the Torah	165
173	*Tefillin*	165
174	The Commandments Are from the Mouth of the Creator	166
175	Three Degrees of Man	166
176	Faith Is Regarded as Above Nature	166
177	The Fruit of Torah	167
178	Father Ejected Mother Because of Her Son	168
179	*Ibur* [Conception] – 1	168
180	King David Has No Life	169
181	The Quality of *Adam HaRishon* – 1	169
182	Heresy Is the Punishment	170
183	Work Is the Most Important	170
184	The Time of Wearing the *Tefillin* [Phylacteries]	171
185	Concerning *Shekalim* – 1	171
186	Return, Israel – 1	171
187	The Greatness of the Creator Is His Humbleness	172
188	Covering a Portion, Revealing Two Portions – 1	173
189	Concerning Learning the Wisdom of Kabbalah	173
190	The Place of Repentants	173
191	The Roles of Light of Wisdom	174
192	Foundations	174
193	The Meaning of the Second Restriction	175
194	Why Was David Punished?	176
195	The Association of the Quality of Judgment with Mercy	177
196	Devotion	179
197	Concerning Suffering – 1	179
198	*Hochma* and *Hassadim*	180
199	Oral Torah	180
200	Receiving Pleasure from Three *Kelim* [Vessels]	180
201	Raising MAN – 1	182
202	Concerning Fear	182
203	The Torah Is Acquired through Suffering	183
204	Two Kinds of Repentance	183
205	Action and Intention	184
206	Three Things in the World	184
207	For Your Crimes, Your Mother Was Sent Away	185
208	The Meaning of Dust	185

209- A Groom and a Bride 186
210- Man's Actions 187
211- Man 188
212- A Palace 189
213- Darkness, Fire, and Shadow 190
214- He Who Robs His Father and His Mother 190
215- Having Guests - 1 191
216- Concerning Women 191
217- Run My Beloved 192
218- Israel Are the Sons of Kings 195
219- Seek Peace and Pursue It 197
220- Good Taste in Small, Corporeal Things 199
221- What Is Life? 200
222- Scrutinies in the Work 200
223- Entry into the Work 201
224- The Reason for the Faith 202
225- Names Are Given only According to the Lower One ... 203
226- The Ark Carries Its Carriers 204
227- In *Katnut*, *Gevurot* Appear First 206
228- Moses Is the Quality of Faith 206
229- She Opened Her Mouth with Wisdom 206
230- Am I In the Place of God? 207
231- Aza and Azael 207
232- Bribing the *Sitra Achra* 208
233- Concerning *Yenika* [Suction/Nursing] 208
234- Reality and the Existence of Reality 210
235- The Forms of the Light 211
236- The Whole Earth Is Full of His Glory 212
237- Mind and Heart 214
238- The Joy of the Groom and Bride 215
239- Widows 217
240- Discernments in States 218
241- When Wicked Are Lost, There Is Singing 219
242- As He is merciful, So You Are Merciful 220
243- Finding Grace 220
244- Repentance 220
245- The Help of the Creator 220
246- Concerning *Shekalim* - 2 221
247- He Who Is Meticulous about Turning His Gown 223
248- He Who Delights the Shabbat 224
249- I Will Sin and Repent 225
250- Anyone in Whom There Is Fear of Heaven - 1 227
251- Concerning the *Minyan* [Ten in the Synagogue] 229

252- A Broken Heart - 1 231
253- Do Not Eat the Bread of an Evil-Eyed Man 231
254- Work Means Faith 232
255- Words of a Dead Man 232
256- The Light that Was Created on the First Day 234
257- Idol Worship 235
258- Who Is Rich? 236
259- Building the Temple 236
260- Great Is He Who Is Commanded and Does 237
261- Hear, My Son, Your Father's Morals - 1 238
262- We Have Forgotten the Good 239
263- The Merit of the Bride 240
264- Ascend in Degree, Choose a Bridesmaid 241
265- Inner Keys and Outer Keys 241
266- Anyone Who Is Settled in His Wine 245
267- Man Was Created in the Torah 249
268- One Learns Only Where One's Heart Desires 250
269- One Does Not Toil Over a Meal and Misses It 252
270- Anyone with Whom the Spirit of the People Is Pleased - 2 253
271- Any Person Who Is Favored 254
272- Anyone Who Associates the Aim for the Creator
    with Another Thing 255
273- The Mightiest of the Mighty 256
274- Specifically through a Man and a Woman 256
275- I Wish They Left Me and Kept My Law 257
276- If a Human Being Has on the Skin of His Flesh 257
277- When One of the Members of the Group Dies 259
278- The Light that Was Created on the First Day 259
279- Why Israel Are Compared to an Olive Tree 260
280- This World and the Next World - 1 261
281- Be Mindful with a Minor Commandment as with a Major One - 1 ... 263
282- Be Mindful with a Minor Commandment as with a Major One - 2 .. 264
283- Be Mindful with a Minor Commandment as with a Major One - 3 ... 265
284- I Have a Minor *Mitzva* [Commandment], Whose Name Is *Sukkah* 267
285- A Person Builds a Building 268
286- Truth and Peace Loved 270
287- Turning His Ear from Hearing Torah 270
288- With Me, from Lebanon, Bride 272
289- The Creator Is Meticulous with the Righteous 272
290- A Righteous Shall Live by His Faith 273
291- Man and His Role 274
292- One Who Restrains Himself in Strife 276

293- Anyone Who Observes the Shabbat [Sabbath] Properly, Desecrates It 278
294- We Will Do and We Will Hear - 1 279
295- Anyone Who Sanctifies the Seventh - 1 280
296- The Core of Creation and the Correction of Creation 283
297- He Raises the Poor from the Dust, Lifts the Indigent from the Trash . 285
298- Associating the Quality of Mercy with Judgment 286
299- Having a Clean Mind 287
300- A Land Where You Will Eat Bread Without Scarcity 288
301- The General Public and the Chosen Few 290
302- For the Lord Chose Jacob for Himself 291
303- Delight Them with a Complete Building - 2 293
304- Fear and Love 294
305- The Meaning of Evil 295
306- If the Rav Is Similar to an Angel of the Lord 296
307- You Have Not a Blade of Grass Below 297
308- You Have Chosen Us - 2 298
309- Concerning Walking in Secrecy 299
310- The Righteous Perishes and No One Notices 300
311- The Tree from which *Adam HaRishon* Ate Was Wheat 300
312- If You Go to War - 1 301
313- When the Lord Rejoices Over You 302
314- Smallness and Greatness 303
315- Three Souls 304
316- *Adam HaRishon* - 2 305
317- Faith - 1 306
318- Seeing and Hearing 307
319- Anyone Who Is Proud, It Is as though He Commits Idol-Worship 307
320- It Is Not the Shy Who Learns 308
321- Eating from the Waste 308
322- Concerning Choice 308
323- Discernments in a Spiritual *Kli* [Vessel] 309
324- The Preparation Period 311
325- The Light of *Hassadim* on which There Was No *Tzimtzum* 312
326- Man's Work 313
327- The Merit of Having Guests 314
328- Their Idols Are Silver and Gold, the Work of Man's Hands 315
329- Prayer 316
330- Lowliness 317
331- The Voice Is Good for Perfumes 318
332- Concerning Equivalence of Form 319
333- He Who Begins a *Mitzva* [Commandment] 321
334- The Difference between Charity and a Gift 322

335- A Messenger of the Public 322
336- He Who Cries over a Fitting Person 324
337- Happy Is the Man 325
338- A Cure before the Blow 326
339- Let the Earth Put Forth Grass 327
340- In the Beginning [God] Created 330
341- And the Lord Saw 331
342- Noah Was a Righteous Man 333
343- Gopher Wood 334
344- Go Forth 334
345- Anyone with Whom the Spirit of the Creator Is Pleased 337
346- Mind and Heart 338
347- Passed By Your Servant 338
348- When the Creator Loves a Person 339
349- The Tree of Knowledge of Good and Evil 340
350- The Lord Appeared to Him by the Oaks of Mamre 343
351- How to Draw Near Him 344
352- Before I Was Circumcised - 1 345
353- Abraham Arose 347
354- Abraham Gave All that He Had 349
355- He Who Has No Sons 351
356- A Son Makes the Father Worthy 352
357- Abraham Begot Isaac 352
358- And Isaac Was Forty Years Old 354
359- Isaac Sowed in That Land 357
360- I Did Not Find My Hands or Legs in the Seminary 359
361- Your Good Treasure 359
362- Jacob Saw that There Was Grain 360
363- Four Angels 361
364- All Who Are Violent, Prevail - 1 363
365- And Judah Approached Him - 1 364
366- Hard on Himself and Easy on Others 365
367- To Benjamin He Gave Three Hundred Pieces of Silver 366
368- And Behold, the Lord Stood Over Him 367
369- Joy While Learning Torah 369
370- The Way of the Land Preceded the Torah 370
371- A Ladder Set on the Earth 372
372- It Came to Pass as That Day 374
373- He Saw that He Could Not Prevail Over Him 377
374- He Touched the Hollow of His Thigh 379
375- Jacob Sent 380
376- Jacob Was Very Frightened 382
377- Better a Poor Child 384

378- Jacob Lived in the Land Where His Father Dwelled 387
379- Miracle and Choice... 389
380- Anyone Who Sanctifies the Seventh - 2 390
381- The Lord Hears the Poor 393
382- When Pharaoh Sent the People 395
383- They Stood at the Foot of the Mountain 396
384- Observing Shabbat [Sabbath] 397
385- I Will Carry You on the Wings of Eagles.............................397
386- This Is the Day that the Lord Has Made 399
387- A Decent Judge and an Indecent Judge 399
388- These Are the Ordinances 401
389- Raise a Contribution for Me - 1 402
390- Coercion and Inversion 404
391- The Creator Did Not Try Job 406
392- A Hand on the Throne of the Lord - 2 408
393- Carrier of Iniquity... 409
394- When You Count the Heads of the Children of Israel
to Number Them 410
395- The Quality of "Still" and the Quality of "Vegetative" 411
396- Behold, the Lord Has Called the Name Bezalel.................... 412
397- Take from Among You a Contribution to the Lord............. 414
398- The Numbered Things of the Tabernacle - 2 416
399- The Tabernacle of the Testimony 418
400- Half a *Shekel* - 1 419
401- Hear, O Israel... 420
402- If a Woman Inseminates - 1.. 422
403- This Shall Be the Law of the Leper 426
404- And Say a Matter 427
405- When an Ox or a Sheep or a Goat Is Born 427
406- Six Days You Shall Work.. 428
407- If You Buy a Hebrew Slave... 430
408- Count the Heads of the Whole Congregation of Israel 430
409- Concerning Suffering - 2 431
410- Self-Love and Love of the Creator......................................434
411- All Who Are Violent, Prevail - 2 435
412- The Vow of a Hermit, to Dedicate Himself to the Lord 435
413- The Difference between Books of Ethics and
the Books of the Baal Shem Tov..437
414- The Rabble Who Were Among Them Had Greedy Desires 437
415- When You Raise the Candles - 1 439
416- This Is the Making of the Menorah [Temple Lamp] - 1 440
417- And Aaron Did So 441
418- Poverty Becomes Israel 443

419- Spies 444
420- Send Forth 444
421- Concerning the Spies 445
422- From Afar the Lord Appeared to Me 447
423- Three Lines - 2 447
424- The Dispute between Korah and Moses 448
425- Korah Took 450
426- The Prayer of a Righteous, Son of a Righteous,
       and a Righteous, Son of a Wicked 451
427- This Is the Constitution of the Torah [Law] - 1 452
428- This Is the Constitution of the Torah [Law] - 2 453
429- Make Everything in Order to Bestow 458
430- A Higher Soul 460
431- A Shoe for His Foot 462
432- The Making of the Calf 463
433- The Lord Your God Was Unwilling to Listen 464
434- How Good Are Your Tents, Jacob - 2 465
435- When Balak Took Counsel 467
436- Three Prayers 471
437- Great Priesthood 473
438- Save Your Servant, You, My God 475
439- Why Was Pinhas Awarded the Priesthood? 477
440- Pinhas Saw 477
441- Avenge the Vengeance of the Children of Israel 479
442- Your Children, Whom You Said 480
443- The Writing Is in the Labor 482
444- Darkness Precedes Light 482
445- No *Masach* [Screen] in *Keter* 483
446- The Meaning of Dry Land 484
447- Peace with the Creator 485
448- The Sensation of Wholeness 487
449- The Drop Is Declared 488
450- Forces that Induce the Development of the Heart and the Mind 488
451- Pure Eyed 489
452- Just as I Am Dancing before You 489
453- The Eyes of Both of Them Opened 491
454- He Who Prays for His Friend 492
455- Because You Hear 493
456- Small Talents 494
457- The Counsel of the Lord Ever Stands 494
458- And It Came to Pass because You Hear 495
459- Because of Humbleness and Fear of the Lord 496
460- Will Keep His Promise to You 498

461- "See" in Singular Form 499
462- Blessed Is the Place [Creator] 500
463- You Became Rich; You Are in the Evening; Light the Candle 501
464- If You Go to War - 2 502
465- The Work of the General Public and the Work of the Individual ... 504
466- Optional War and a War of *Mitzva* [Commandment] 505
467- All the Peoples of the Earth Shall See 506
468- This Day, the Lord Your God Commands You 509
469- Each Day They Will Be as New in Your Eyes 510
470- When You Come 511
471- You Stand Today - 2 513
472- The Concealed Things Belong to the Lord Our God 514
473- Sins Become for Him as Merits 515
474- And the Canaanite, King of Arad, Heard 517
475- Lend Ear, O Heavens 518
476- The Rich Shall Not Give More and the Poor Shall Not Give Less ... 519
477- What Do You Have in the House? 520
478- What Was the Sin of Korah? 521
479- You Shall Not Distort Justice 522
480- The Place Where the Lord Will Choose 523
481- The Whole World Is Nourished by My Son Hanina - 2 524
482- This Is the Path of Torah - 2 525
483- A Hedge for Wisdom - Silence - 2 526
484- He Whom the Lord Loves He Admonishes 526
485- The Fear of You and the Dread of You Shall Be
upon All the Animals of the Earth 526
486- The Beginning of Speech Is from *Ein Sof* 527
487- Concerning the Will to Receive 528
488- The Garments of the Soul 528
489- Against Your Will - 2 529
490- Adornments of the Bride 529
491- Raising MAN - 2 529
492- The Reward for a *Mitzva* 530
493- A Righteous Son and a Wicked Son 530
494- There Is Fear Only in a Place of Wholeness 531
495- The Creator Ascended 532
496- The Path of Truth 532
497- Blessed Are You 534
498- It Shall Come to Pass That If You Surely Hear 534
499- "I" is the *Malchut* 535
500- When You Raise the Candles - 2 536

Assorted Notes

1- *Atzilut* Is Private Providence

It is written in *The Study of the Ten Sefirot* (Part 3, Chapter 3, Items 4-5) that in the world of *Atzilut*, it is the light itself. It seems to me that his intention is that this is not so with the light that shines in the world of *Beria*, which is called "a light of *Tolada* [result/offspring]," and not the actual light.

We should interpret that *Atzilut* is called "private Providence," where it is considered that "He alone does and will do all the deeds." For this reason, the light that shines there is essential light, without any participation of the lower one. But in the separated BYA, where there is the sorting of good from bad, it is called "reward and punishment."

Hence, the light that shines is through the association of the Emanator and the emanated, which is a partnership. This is why it is called "a light of *Tolada*," as it is born out of two causes. This is unlike the world of *Atzilut*, where there is no partnership, meaning the lower one does not assist in anything. This is called "Evil will not dwell with you," where there is no sorting; this is why it is called "private Providence."

This is the meaning of what is written there, that the *Masach* [screen] makes a *Parsa* [slicing/partition] between *Atzilut* and *Beria*, so that BYA are below the *Masach*, while in *Atzilut*, there is no *Masach* at all.

At the same time, it is explained in several places that there are *Masachim* [pl. of *Masach*] in *Atzilut*, as well—a removing *Masach* in *Bina*, and a window and a narrow crevice. The explanation is that this is only with respect to BYA, but with respect to *Atzilut*, there is no distinction whatsoever.

The meaning is that with regard to the souls in BYA, which is reward and punishment, they feel that there are *Masachim*, but when BYA ascends to *Atzilut* and they are rewarded with private Providence, they see that everything is unity and there are no *Masachim* at all there.

2- The Striking of Thoughts upon Man

"Because of the striking of upper light, which strikes that curtain, lights sparkled from them and went through that *Masach* [screen]" (*The Study of the Ten Sefirot*, Part 3, Chapter 4, Item 6).

We can interpret that striking is the thoughts that strike a person, trouble him and tire him, and he has thoughts this way and that way. And all this is because he has a *Masach*.

If he keeps the *Masach* and agrees to walk on the path of the Creator, which is regarded as "mind," as "scrutiny," when he comprehends that it is good for him to accept faith above reason, it is considered that he causes an addition of light in the upper degree, for the joy comes specifically through the scrutiny.

We see that when two people love each other, when one of them has another friend who wants to join the other, too, the first one does not like it, and the first one sits and waits to see whom he will pick as a loyal friend, and he begins to compare one to the other. He begins to measure the importance and benefits he receives from the two of them, and thoughts begin to run about within him. This is called "striking with his views."

In the end, he decides on the first one, that it is worth bonding with him. He scrutinizes only as a force above reason. This means that although he does not really feel the importance of the upper one, the scrutiny is through a *Masach*, called "an attempt," regarded as "concealment."

But when he overcomes the *Masach* and sustains it, meaning he does not cancel the *Masach*, this causes joy above, and then the upper one also gives him joy. That is, to the extent that he received the importance of the upper one above reason, that same measure of greatness of the upper one extends to him within reason, not less and not more.

3- Against Your Will – 1

"Against your will you are born; against your will you live; and against your will you die."

Birth is as the verse, "A proselyte who converted is as a newly born child." That is, each time we reacquire the quality of faith, it is considered a "new birth." And the reception of the quality of "mind" is above reason.

Since the body cannot do anything that is against reason, he must accept the quality of "mind" against its will, meaning the body disagrees. But if one's work is in a manner of reception and knowledge, the body will obey any order.

This is the meaning of "Against your will you are born," that birth in *Kedusha* [holiness] is only against one's will, until one is rewarded with "will bring it near [also sacrifice] to His will," as our sages said, "He is forced until he says, 'I want'" (*Kidushin* 50a).

By accepting faith, we are rewarded with a life of *Kedusha* through Torah and work, and the vitality he receives must also be against his will. That is, he does not want to receive the pleasure, but because the Creator wants to delight him, he must receive, and not because of his own desire.

"And against your will you die" when you engage in corporeal matters, as these actions are only self-reception, called "death." It should be "against his will," meaning that he would enjoy more if he did not have to do all the corporeal things.

It is as Baal HaSulam said, this is like a person who suffers from boils [disease] and scratches. Although it gives him pleasure, he would be happier if he did not have boils and would not have to scratch and enjoy.

4- If There Is a Virgin Maiden

"If there is a virgin maiden engaged to a man, and a man finds her in town and lies with her."

We can interpret that the holy *Shechina* [Divinity] is called "maiden." There are three states: available, engaged, and married.

In the state of "still of *Kedusha* [holiness]," she is called "available," since everything he does for her is only in order to receive reward—either this world or the next world. However, he knows that the holy *Shechina* is enslaved to him, meaning to self-reception. Hence, she is called "available," since she has no one to need.

At that time, he wants her to need him. Therefore, then, in the state of "still," he can continue his work without blemishing anything.

But when he begins the work of the "vegetative," when he already knows that one must engage in Torah and *Mitzvot* [commandments] in order to bestow, the holy *Shechina* is considered "engaged to a man," meaning to the Creator, and one should work to make the unification of the Creator and the *Shechina*.

Therefore, one who lies with her, meaning who wants to take pleasure in her, who begins to work in reception while knowing that reception is already forbidden, since to him, she is already regarded as "engaged to the Creator," then "you shall stone them both."

The holy *Shechina* herself is regarded as "there is no thought or perception of Him at all." Rather, it is all with respect to the attaining individual. For this reason, man is sentenced to stoning, meaning that foreign thoughts shatter his brain and he dies. That is, he loses all the vitality of *Kedusha*, and the *Shechina*, too, falls within him to a state of "dust." In other words, he sees that there is no life in her, meaning no one for whom to work.

This is the meaning of the verse, "the maiden, because she did not cry out in the city" (this is the meaning of "Wicked! Do not touch me!"). "In the city" means when he had a great awakening and worked with a huge flame. At that time, "the maiden did not cry out," meaning that no sin was sensed in this work. Rather, he wanted to continue this work in self-reception forever. This is why he blemished her, herself.

Hence, now he sees that there is no vitality in her and it is not worth working for her. Our sages said, "The serpent came over Eve and cast filth within her." Baal HaSulam explained that *Zuhama* [filth] comes from *Zu-Ma* [what is this?], meaning he said, "What is this work for you?" This is called "and they both died."

"And if the man finds her in the field…" Work in the field means that during the work he lied with her. That is, he engaged in Torah and *Mitzvot* in order to receive and knew it was forbidden since she was engaged to a man. In that case, "And to the maiden you shall do nothing… since he found her in the field, the maiden cried out… and there was no one to save her." That is, he feels that she is crying out, "Wicked! Do not touch me!" meaning that it is forbidden to work in a manner of reception.

"And there was no one to save her," meaning that a person cannot overcome his manner of reception, which is called "a field." That is, during the work, when he wants to overcome reception, the holy *Shechina* remains alive, meaning he sees her greatness and importance.

Anyone who clings to this work to bestow, she has life but he dies because he received for himself the vitality that he extended from her, so he dies and claims that he cannot continue the work.

Only one who was born with a keen mind and virtues, and upright qualities, but one who is born with ignoble qualities cannot continue this work. This is considered that he died, that he no longer has fuel to continue his work and have life.

But the Creator, with His great mercies, revives the dead with great mercy and a person is resurrected until he undergoes several reincarnations, whether in one body or in several bodies, as in "No outcast shall be cast out from Him," and he is rewarded with adhering to the level for eternity.

5- The Meaning of Sins Becoming as Merits

We can understand the meaning of sins becoming as merits, that if a person has a question, which is certainly a great iniquity because this question might cause him to fall into the *Klipa* [shell/peel] called "pondering the beginning." If he repents from fear, meaning strengthens himself and is not impressed by this thought, then they become to him as mistakes. That is, it is not a sin but a mistake. In other words, it would be better had no foreign thought come to him, but now that it came, he did not have a choice but to strengthen himself with acceptance of the burden of the kingdom of heaven.

Also, there is repentance from love, when he receives the burden of faith anew because of love, meaning he accepts the work with love. That is, he is happy that the Creator has given him this foreign thought by which he can observe this *Mitzva* [commandment].

This is similar to a flame that is tied to the wick. The foreign thought is considered the wick, which wants to install a flaw in his work. That is, the foreign thought makes him think that from the perspective of the mind and reason, he has nothing to do in His work. And when he gets the foreign thought, he says that he does not want to make any excuses, but everything that the reason says is correct except he is walking on the path of faith, which is above reason.

It follows that the flame of faith is tied to the wick of the foreign thought. Thus, only now can he observe the *Mitzva* of faith properly. It follows that the questions have become to him as merits, since otherwise he would not be able to accept any merits from faith.

This is called "rejoicing in suffering." Although he suffers from the foreign thoughts that afflict him and cause him to slander and gossip and speak badly about His work, he is nonetheless happy about it for only now, at such a time, he can observe in a manner of faith above reason. This is called "the joy of *Mitzva*."

"It is forbidden to raise one's hands without a prayer and litany." Also, we should understand the meaning of "why he reveals sins." The scrutiny of the quality of "mind," he should first be ready for battle, meaning he must have weapons prepared for this, so he can win the battle. If he is not prepared for it, he must not do any scrutinies that will reveal the sin, meaning that it will be revealed that he is not ready to take upon himself the quality of "mind." Thus, he must prepare himself, for if the body does not want to accept the "mind," he should immediately extend over it a prayer that the Creator will help him accept the burden of the kingdom of heaven.

This is the meaning of "It is forbidden to raise one's hand." "Hands" are attainment and reception. Raising the hands is when he pulls himself without prayer from being a receiver, whether in mind or in heart, so there will be no hold to the *Sitra Achra* [other side]. Rather, as soon as he sees that he cannot walk in this path, he will pray.

In other words, if he cannot overcome with labor, he will overcome with prayer. But if he is not ready for prayer, he must not make the scrutiny.

6- A Gentile Who Observes the Sabbath Must Die

"A gentile who observes Shabbat [Sabbath] must die." "Make your Shabbat a weekday and do not be needy of people." "Welcoming the Shabbat should be while it is still day." The curse of the serpent is that dust will be his food. "A wise disciple is as the Shabbat." "An uneducated person has the fear of Shabbat over him."

There is "weekday" and there is "Shabbat." A weekday is the six workdays, which is the time of work, when we must sort and separate holy from worldly, meaning which is *Kedusha* [holiness], and which is the opposite.

During the acceptance of the burden of the kingdom of heaven permanently, when he should no longer think and contemplate, this is called "welcoming the Shabbat." The holy *Shechina* [Divinity] is called Queen Shabbat, meaning that during the work, she is called "*Shechina* in the dust," but after the scrutiny she is called "a queen."

This is the meaning of "Go my beloved, toward the bride," which is the unification of the Creator with the *Shechina*. But when she is in the dust, it is impossible to say, "Go my beloved," for the person himself makes the separation, as he himself says that it is unbecoming of the Creator to unite with such work, whose entire foundation hangs on nothing, as in, "She has nothing of her own," but rather everything is above reason.

For this reason, when a person comes to welcome the Shabbat, it is certainly still a weekday for him. But after he welcomes the Shabbat, it is called "Shabbat." That is, now it is forbidden to make any scrutinies, which is the time of rest, for with respect to the sanctity of the day itself, it is forbidden to do any work of scrutinies.

If, by chance, a person sees that he has no fear of heaven, and thinks that it is forbidden to make scrutinies on Shabbat, since it is forbidden to work on Shabbat, it was said about this, "A gentile who observes Shabbat must die," meaning he puts himself to death by not engaging in the work of accepting the burden of the kingdom of heaven, since it is written that "he lives in them" and not that he dies.

That is, saving a life takes precedence over Shabbat. If a person sees that he has no fear, then he has no life, for only acceptance of the burden of the kingdom of heaven attaches him to the Life of Lives. Hence, if he feels that he is still a gentile and wants to rest, he must die.

Although he has the option to accept faith from the environment, for he can say, "I see that all the townspeople engage in Torah and *Mitzvot* [commandments], so why should I engage in scrutinies?"

They said about this, "Make your Shabbat a weekday and do not need people" (*Shabbat* 118a). This means that it is forbidden to receive the foundation of faith from people, but he must rather sort out the foundation of faith so it comes only from the heaven, as in "that his nourishments will come by heaven."

Then he is called "a wise disciple." "Wise" means the Creator, meaning he receives the construction from the Creator. He should not be a disciple of people, learning the "one letter," called "faith," from people.

This is the meaning of a wise disciple being Shabbat. One who is rewarded with permanent faith, rests from his work. At that time, the uneducated one, meaning his body, the fear of Shabbat is upon him. That is, "An evil angel will answer 'Amen' against his will."

But as for the serpent, dust will be his food. Therefore, he always has nourishments and never needs the Creator, meaning with his work that is *Lo Lishma* [not for Her sake], when the whole foundation is built on people, which is dust from the earth. At that time, he only needs people, and this he can always receive and will always stay in the quality of "still."

But if a person does not agree to remain in the state of a serpent, which is the will to receive, when he wants to engage in bestowal, then he needs the Creator.

Conversely, the serpent, who was cursed that he would not need the Creator's help, will naturally always remain in his lowliness and the words, "If the Creator did not help him, he would not overcome it," will not come true in him, as in "The Lord will finish for me," will not come true in him. Rather, the whole world will provide for him and he will always be needy of people.

But one who walks in the path of the Creator and not in the path of the world, is rewarded with being favored by the Creator.

This is specifically one who needs the help of the Creator, as it is written, "He who comes to purify is aided" (*Shabbat* 104a). It was interpreted in *The Zohar*, "With what? With a holy soul." The

Creator gives him a soul of *Kedusha*, and with this force he can purify himself.

This is the meaning of "Rewarded more? He is given *Ruach*..." meaning that if he wants to be cleansed each time, meaning to be purer, and the assisting power of the soul is not enough for him for the purity that he thinks he needs before he received the soul of *Kedusha*.

But after he receives the soul of *Kedusha*, he feels that there is more room to work on purity, and the assisting power he received is not enough to determine to the side of purity. Hence, he prays and asks once more for help from above. At that time, he must be given greater force than he was given before. Therefore, now he is given *Ruach*, etc., until he is given all the *NRNHY* in his soul.

7- The Correction of Lines

The correction of lines. The right line is the white of *Abba* [father]. Through the appearance of light of *Hochma* [wisdom] into the 320 sparks, the *Malchut* of each *Melech* [king] descends back to her place since there is a *Tzimtzum* [restriction] on the *Aviut* [thickness], and when the *Aviut* is incompatible, she must descend.

We can interpret that by the light of *Hochma* lowering the *Aviut*, meaning that person feels that there is nothing lowlier than working for himself, but he is still powerless to work for the sake of others, meaning to bestow, this is why we need a left line, which is regarded as "the red of *Ima* [mother]."

Hence, the core of the *Sefirot* extends from the right line, like a person who has five senses—sight, hearing, smell, speech, and touch—but in order for them to be activated, we need an objective.

For this reason, when the white of *Abba* comes, he sees that it is not worthwhile to work with the "sight, hearing, smell, and speech" for his own sake. Thus, he sits idle and seems asleep, as though his senses are inactive because they have no fuel. But to work with the senses in order to bestow, he has still not achieved this knowledge, which is also an objective.

In order to obtain the power to bestow, he must receive from the left line, called "red of *Ima*," which is *Malchut* that is sweetened with *Bina*, meaning that his will to receive will agree to the work of bestowal, which is the quality of *Bina*.

Afterward, when he has the fuel from bestowal, when he makes a *Zivug* [coupling] on this quality, meaning when he performs actions with this quality, the verse, "I will bless you in all that you do" comes true. That is, the upper light becomes unified over this quality, and this is called "the middle line," when the light is on the unification of the two lines, right and left, and this is already wholeness.

8- This Is the Path of Torah – 1

"This is the path of Torah: Lead a sorrowful life."

Because he works for the sake of the Creator, the body has no pleasure because it is not receiving anything. But when accustoming the body to work in bestowal, against its will, we are rewarded with "Then shall you delight in the Lord." That is, when we work for the sake of the Creator, we receive pleasure, and this is called "Her ways are ways of pleasantness."

9- A Hedge for Wisdom – Silence – 1

"A hedge for wisdom - silence." That is, in order to be rewarded with *Hochma* [wisdom], one must first correct the *Kelim* [vessels] so they have the quality of bestowal. Hence, the correction is "silence," meaning that in every matter, he shall answer himself as in "Silence! Such was My thought."

10- He Whom the Lord Loves He Admonishes

"He whom the Lord loves He admonishes." That is, the Creator sends suffering to those He loves, meaning that they will suffer that they are not walking on the path of the Creator. Conversely, one who does not feel any suffering at not walking in the path of the Creator, never received any counsels how to be saved from it.

11- The Fear of You and the Dread of You Shall Be upon All the Animals of the Earth

"The fear of you and the dread of you shall be upon all the animals of the earth." RASHI interprets that "as long as a day old infant is alive, there is no need to guard him from the mice. When Og, King of Bashan, is dead, he must be guarded" (Sanhedrin 98).

Vitality means that all the war against the inclination is only in that it shows a person that there is vitality in corporeal matters in this world. It argues that it is not worthwhile to relinquish them in order to be rewarded with the next world. When a person is rewarded, all the corporeal animals become annulled before him because all the corporeal vitality is that which pertains to the will to receive, but when a person is rewarded with walking in the desire to bestow, they are naturally annulled.

It is a rule that the will to receive is called "death," and the desire to bestow is called "life," since it is adhered to the Life of Lives. Hence, if a person is rewarded with walking in the ways of bestowal, even though he is still an infant, he is nonetheless considered alive, and the animals of the earth surrender before him, meaning all the bad animals are vitality that is dependent on the will to receive.

12- The Whole World Is Nourished by My Son Hanina – 1

"The whole world is nourished by my son Hanina, and Hanina my son suffices himself with 102 carobs [meager food] from one eve of Shabbat [Sabbath] to another."

In the work, we should interpret that one who walks on the path of the Creator, during the work, which is called "weekdays," as in "He who did not toil on the eve of Shabbat," it is enough for him to feel the taste of carobs. He will rest from his work. And yet, through his labor, when he feels no taste in his work, he wants only the discernment of carobs.

It is known that if "You labored but did not find, do not believe" (*Megillah* 6b). At that time, he wants that through his work and labor, abundance and blessing will extend to the entire world, meaning that all the vitality and attainments of the light of Torah will reach the whole world.

This is the meaning of the words, "The whole world is nourished by my son Hanina" (*Taanit* 24b). Why does he do so? It is because he has the grace of *Kedusha* [holiness], after which he is called Hanina, from the word *Hen* [grace]. At that time, he is rewarded with the quality of Shabbat. Hence, one who did not toil in the eve of Shabbat, what will he eat on Shabbat?

We could ask, If Hanina extended the light of Torah to the entire world, why are they not perceiving the light of pleasure, and only Hanina was rewarded with the quality of Shabbat? It is because they haven't the *Kelim* [vessels] to receive, for the labor is the correction, the making of the *Kelim* into which the lights pour.

It was said about this (*Avoda Zara* 3a), "He who did not toil on the eve of Shabbat, what will he eat on Shabbat?" Although Hanina extended the light of Shabbat to the entire world, they do not have the *Kelim* in which to receive. Nevertheless, the servant of the Creator himself must walk on the path of not receiving anything, and this is called "carobs."

13- A Hand on the Throne of the Lord – 1

"And he said, 'A hand on the throne of the Lord; the Lord has war against Amalek from generation to generation.'" RASHI interprets, "The Creator swore that His name will not be whole and His throne will not be whole until He blots out the name of Amalek," meaning that the name is split in half.

To understand this, we must first present the verse, "In *Yod-Hey* [the Lord], the Lord is an everlasting rock." That is, He depicted the worlds with the two letters *Yod-Hey*. In the Mishnah: "The world was created with ten utterances. What does that mean? After all, it could have been created with one utterance. Yet, it was created in ten utterances in order to avenge the wicked who are destroying the world" (*Avot*, Chapter 5).

There is a famous question: Does the Creator complain against His creations? It is like one who gives to his friend a cup that is worth one pound to watch over it. If he loses it, he must pay only one pound, but the landlord paid ten pounds. Should he have paid ten pounds for this?

The thing is that in the beginning, He created the world with the quality of judgment. When He saw that the world cannot exist, He associated with it the quality of mercy, for by this, man will be able to achieve his completion. Conversely, when it was in the quality of judgment, it was impossible for man to be able to emerge from his evil inclination.

This is the meaning of "to give a good reward to the righteous." In other words, by the correction of the quality of mercy, called "ten utterances," there is existence to the world.

"And to avenge the wicked," meaning now that they have been given the chance to emerge from the control of the inclination, they still do not want to. For this they deserve to lose the world, although there is the correction of ten utterances there, which is easier than before the correction, meaning in one utterance.

14- Thus You Shall Say to the House of Jacob

"Thus you shall say to the house of Jacob" are the women; tell them the matters in general, for they can listen; "and tell the sons of Israel" are the men. He told him, "Tell them the precisions of the matters, for they can listen.

Another explanation: Why to the women first? For they hurry with *Mitzvot* [commandments]. Another explanation: Why to the women? So they will lead their sons to the Torah.

Rabbi Tachlifa deKeisarin said, "The Creator said, 'When I created the world, I commanded only *Adam HaRishon*. Afterward, Eve was commanded, and she transgressed and corrupted the world. Now, if I do not call the women first, they will cancel the Torah.'" This is why it was said, "Thus you shall say to the house of Jacob."

We should understand the following:

1) Why do women hurry with *Mitzvot* more than men?

2) Why should women be addressed first so they will lead their sons to the Torah? If the men are approached before them, will they not agree to lead their sons to the Torah?

3) It is as though He is afraid of the women, that they might spoil the world unless He gives them the honor of preceding the men.

4) How can it be said that because of the honor that the Creator gave when he commanded *Adam HaRishon* before Eve, she transgressed and corrupted the world? It is as though Eve avenged it.

In the work, we can interpret that man and woman are within the same person. When one works in order to receive and satisfy his own lack, meaning his femaleness, a person is called "woman." When he acts in order to bestow, he is called a "man."

It is known that man is but a desire to receive. The order of the beginning of the work is that we start with the will to receive, which is called *Lo Lishma* [not for Her sake], and afterward we come to *Lishma* [for Her sake].

Therefore, the order, "Thus you shall say to the house of Jacob," are the women. "Tell them the matters in general," meaning the beginning of the work, when He forbade them to say that we must work *Lishma* because a person cannot begin with *Lishma*.

Afterward, "and tell the sons of Israel" are the men, who can already work *Lishma*, meaning to bestow. "Tell them the precisions of the matters, for they can listen," meaning that they can already hear about *Lishma* and should already be meticulous that everything will be only *Lishma*. This is the meaning of "the precisions of the matters."

"Another explanation: Why to the women first? For they hurry with *Mitzvot*," meaning in *Lo Lishma*. When one's intention is to receive reward in return for his work, the body rushes the person. Conversely, the body does not agree that a person will work in order to bestow, and will certainly not rush him.

Hence, when a person begins the work in order to receive, he accustoms himself to be quick in the work, and later he can use this habit when he begins to work in order to bestow, as well, since he has already acquired the tool of quickness at the time of *Lo Lishma*.

"Another explanation: So they will lead their sons to the Torah." Father and son are cause and consequence. That is, if first there is a cause for reception, this reason causes him to want to do more things in Torah and *Mitzvot*. But in bestowal, it is hard for the body to make efforts to add. Rather, each time requires a new overcoming. Conversely, *Lo Lishma* constantly gives more power to add.

By a person being accustomed to work during the preparation period, he already has tools that are ready for work while he marches on the path of bestowal. At the time of the creation of the world, *Adam HaRishon* was commanded first. This is according to what *The Zohar* wrote, that *Adam HaRishon* had nothing of this world, meaning he was devoid of any reception whatsoever; he was only *VAK*, in the quality of the upper nine (see "Introduction to the Book Panim Meirot uMasbirot").

In that respect, everything was fine. However, through his mingling with the will to receive, called Eve, since he did not have the preparation of *Lo Lishma* for reception—since only then can one bring in the will to receive so it is reception in order to bestow—so when he approached the will to receive, called "woman," and he already attained the *Lishma* on his own quality, for his root is vessels of bestowal, she therefore transgressed and corrupted the world, since she lacked the practice in *Lo Lishma* on the will to receive, as Maimonides wrote, that the matter of *Lishma* must not be revealed at once, but gradually.

Therefore, when he revealed the *Lishma* to the woman, she immediately transgressed and corrupted the world. Therefore, we must start with the women and tell them only the matters in general, meaning the *Lo Lishma*.

15- Ordinances

It is written in *Midrash Rabbah*, "Another explanation: 'These are the ordinances.' Idol-worshippers have judges and Israel have judges, and you do not know the difference between them."

There is an allegory about a patient that a doctor came to see. He told his family, "Feed him anything he wants." He went to another patient and told them, "Be sure that he does not eat this or that food." They said to him: "You said to the first one that he can eat whatever he wants, but to the other one you said that he should not eat this or that food." He replied, "The first one will not live; this is why I said that he can eat whatever he wants. But as for the one who will live, I said, 'Be careful with him.'"

Likewise, idol-worshippers have judges and they do not engage in Torah and do not do it, as was said, "And I also gave them laws that are not good and ordinances that they will not live in" (Ezekiel 20). But what is it written about the *Mitzvot* [commandments]? "The one who does them will live by them" (Leviticus 18).

We should understand: 1) The verse that the *Midrash* brings from Ezekiel, that the meaning of the verse about the judges of the idol-worshippers, that verse concerns the people of Israel! 2) The allegory about the doctor who said "Feed him anything he wants," meaning he has no limitations, but the verse, "laws that are not good and ordinances that they will not live in," implies that there are rules and limitations contradicting the allegory.

We should interpret that the intention of the *Midrash* when it says that idol-worshippers have judges, it is not the nations of the world. Rather, it concerns Israel. When he calls them "judges of idol-worshippers," it means that all the *Mitzvot* that they do and that the mind obligates them to, and which do not follow the path of faith, to achieve *Lishma* [for Her sake], that mind is called "a judge of idol-worshippers."

Since all that the judge obligates is on the path of *Lo Lishma* [not for Her sake], meaning that his aim is not to thereby achieve *Dvekut* [adhesion] in life, it follows that he is not intended for life.

To this one he said, "Feed him," meaning his nourishments of life is anything he asks and he has no special conditions because he will not survive. Thus, what he does is of little consequence.

This is not so with the judges of Israel, when the power to judge is because of Israel, meaning because of faith to achieve *Dvekut*. At that time, he has special conditions, for not from everything is he permitted to receive vitality. Rather, with every thing, he must be careful not to eat this or that food. In other words, he must not receive vitality even of *Mitzvot* and good deeds, unless it brings him to *Dvekut*.

This is the meaning of the prohibition not to eat certain things, meaning not to draw vitality from something specific: from the will to receive.

This settles the two questions: 1) His intention is Israel and not the nations of the world. 2) Even in a state of *Lo Lishma*, there are *Mitzvot* and rules, but they are not good, as our sages said, "If he is not rewarded, it becomes to him a potion of death" (*Yoma* 72b).

However, we must try to make the judge be from Israel, and then we will cling to the Life of Lives.

16- The Numbered Things of the Tabernacle – 1

"These are the numbered things of the tabernacle, the tabernacle of the testimony."

It is written in *Midrash Rabbah*, "Why does it write 'tabernacle' twice? Rabbi Shmuel said that it was mortgaged twice ["mortgage" and "tabernacle" have the same root in Hebrew]. This is why the members of the great assembly say 'We have acted very corruptly,' and corruption is mortgaging, as it is said, 'he will not corrupt [take mortgage].' What is the testimony? Rabbi Shimon said, 'It is a testimony to all the people of the world that there is forgiveness to Israel.'"

We should understand what is a mortgage. Normally, one who lends money to his friend and wants to be certain that he will repay his debt, receives from him a mortgage. Thus, what does a tabernacle mean here? that the Creator reclaimed the Temple? What should Israel pay that they did not pay, and for which He took the tabernacle so He could be certain that we will pay the mortgage? Also, what is the testimony, and why does it immediately imply that the tabernacle was mortgaged twice?

It is written in *The Zohar*, "'These are the numbered things of the tabernacle.' Rabbi Shimon started, 'In the beginning God created.'" What is the conjunction between the "In the beginning" and the counted things of the tabernacle? It is written in *The Great Midrash*, "In the beginning... created... created from where?" We should understand the meaning of existence from absence.

But first we must understand what is "we," who must pay the debt and redeem the tabernacle, the purpose of creation. Creation is called "will to receive," and this is called "existence from absence," and the need for concealment is because of the bread of shame.

Rabbi Yohanan and Rabbi Elazar both said, "When one needs people, his face changes as chrome. It was said, 'as when vile things become high in the eyes of people.' What is 'become high'? There is a bird in the coastal cities whose name is *Ke-Rum* [become high]. When the sun shines on it, it changes into several colors" (*Berachot* 6b).

The sun refers to abundance. "The coastal cities" are those on the seashore. The "sea" is called *Hochma* [wisdom].

A "bird" is when a person lifts himself from worldliness, for it is the conduct of the bird that when it flies, it conceals its legs and spreads its wings. Legs means spies, and wings are coverings, as it is written "And with two, it covers its face." Covering means faith.

When the abundance appears over it, he is ashamed, meaning he feels the bread of shame. The Temple means the revelation of pleasures called the "instilling of the *Shechina* [Divinity]."

The payments mean that it will be reception in order to bestow, and the reception of the mortgage, as is implied right in the beginning, is that this is a testimony that there is forgiveness. The reason why the Creator did not take the Temple back is that it was only as collateral, but He is destined to return it to us soon in our days, amen.

Thus, there is a testimony that there is forgiveness, meaning that He intends to return to us when we have paid our debt, meaning when we have the power of bestowal, at which time there will be *Dvekut* [adhesion].

17- Concerning the *Shechina* [Divinity]

The *Shechina* is the place where the *Shochen* [dweller] is revealed. It is written, "The whole earth is full of His glory," "There is not a place vacant of Him," yet there is concealment.

Where there is revelation of His Godliness, that place is called *Shechina*, meaning that here the *Shochen* is revealed. It follows that when speaking of the *Shechina*, meaning when speaking of the *Shochen*, meaning the Creator, when we call Him *Shechina*, it is the place of revelation.

That which is revealed in *Malchut* is what is bestowed upon the lower ones. This means that the measure of His Godliness that is revealed, that revealed measure is only from the perspective of the lower ones, for with respect to the upper ones, there is no such matter as revealing or concealing.

For example, it is impossible to say with respect to the person himself that he is revealed or concealed. Rather, revealing or concealing pertains only to others. Likewise, in spirituality, revealing and concealing pertain only to creation.

It therefore follows that when speaking of the *Shechina*, meaning when speaking of the measure to which the Creator reveals Himself to the lower ones, it follows that whether we call Him "Creator" or *Shechina*, it is all one. But the meaning is that the Creator is regarded as concealment, and the *Shechina* is considered revealing, meaning that the *Shochen* is revealed, meaning that here the *Shochen* is apparent and revealed.

When we say, "For the sake of the unification of the Creator with His *Shechina*," it means that the concealed will become revealed. It follows that everything is spirituality. Hence, when we say that the person has been rewarded with the installing of the *Shechina*, it means that the person has been rewarded with the revelation of the *Shochen*, and any measure of revelation is called *Shechina*.

When we say that the holy *Shechina* is called "the common soul of Israel," it means that the revelation is only toward others. It follows that the *Shechina* means the revelation that is revealed to the lower ones. It follows that she is the overall of the revelation to the lower ones, meaning that she dresses in the desire of the lower ones.

The desire is the created beings. For this reason, the soul is called "a part of God." The meaning of "part" is explained in the

Sulam [Ladder commentary on *The Zohar*], and means that there is a will to receive and through the correction in the desire to bestow, the light of the Creator appears to the creature, and to the lower one, only a part of it is revealed—the measure that the Creator wanted the creatures to attain of Him.

It follows that the meaning of "soul" is that there is a revelation of His Godliness here to a certain extent, which the lower ones can receive. It follows that a soul is only a part of the holy *Shechina*, who is called "the common soul of Israel."

This means that the full measure that the Creator wants to be attained, this is called "His desire to do good to His creations," and a soul is called "part of the *Shechina*," meaning a part that the lower one can attain according to the measure of the purity.

This is why our sages said, "Moses is tantamount to 600,000" (Song of Songs 1), meaning that Moses was rewarded with the revelation of Godliness that was ready to be revealed to the whole of Israel. This is the meaning of the words, "The *Shechina* speaks from Moses' throat," meaning that Moses was rewarded with the general revelation called *Shechina*.

18- The Garments of the Soul

Concerning the garments of the soul, "Rabbi Shimon says, 'To the extent that a person exerts in observing Torah and *Mitzvot* [commandments], a garment is made for him above in that palace (the palace of the essence of heaven, *Hod*), to wear in that world'" (*The Zohar*, *Pekudei*, Item 166).

We should understand the meaning of clothing. It is known that nothing can be attained in spirituality except by clothing, which is like a *Kli* [vessel] that is suitable for revealing light. Hence, if a person exerts, the exertion makes the *Kli* for him, meaning the desire and the need for the filling of light, since nothing is given from above before there is a need for that illumination.

The labor that a person exerts causes him a need and a desire, meaning he becomes needy of the Creator's help to emerge from the strait in which he finds himself during the labor. Were it not for the labor, he would have no need for His help. It follows that precisely the labor provides him with the clothing of the soul, so there will be revelation of Godliness.

19- Beginning to Speak from the Connection with the Creator

According to the rule that we begin to speak only by actions, the connection between the Creator and the creatures, which is called *Ein Sof* [infinity], which is the desire to do good to His creations and not before, it follows that we should not ask about the reason that the Creator wants to do good, meaning what is the reason that caused it, since we begin from the desire to do good downward, and not preceding the desire.

If we ask, What is the point? meaning what is the reason that it emerged before the quality of doing good, then we are asking about prior to the connection, and there we do not attain. Even the quality of doing good that we attain is in the manner of "By Your actions we know You," meaning that by receiving the benefit, we grasp the desire to do good.

20- Concerning the Will to Receive

We should understand concerning the matter that it is explained that the purpose of creation is for man to come to a state where he receives in order to bestow, and that this pleasure is permitted, while pleasure for oneself is forbidden. We should understand this, since in the end he enjoys this, for otherwise there is no way he can bestow, for it is impossible for man to be able to do anything at all if he derives no pleasure from the act.

For example, if a murderer comes to a person and asks him to give him his money, and he grants his request and gives him what he asked for, we must say that the person had pleasure in giving him his money, for otherwise, he would not give him anything. After all, what difference does it make if a person gives his money in return for a house or for garments, since he enjoys this because through the money he obtains things that are more important to him than money, for when a person needs a house, the house is more important to him than money; otherwise, he would not give the money.

It is likewise here with the murderer. Receiving his life in return for the money is more important to him now, meaning he exchanges a small pleasure for a greater one. It follows that there is not a single action in the world that a person does unless he receives pleasure.

Hence, when one bestows upon the Creator, he certainly enjoys this. Otherwise, he would not bestow. Thus, what is the difference if a person receives pleasure from reception or from bestowal?

The thing is that the prohibition that there is in reception is for the known reason, which is the bread of shame. On this comes the correction that he will receive in order to bestow. At that time, if his pleasure is in bestowing, he no longer has shame.

When a person gives his friend a gift, we must say that the giver enjoys it. But if the pleasure comes by bestowal, then there is no shame because the rich is not ashamed when he gives to the poor although he enjoys it.

What is the difference in the division of the soul of *Adam HaRishon* into 600,000 souls? In *Panim Masbirot*, he brings an allegory about this, that it is like a king who wanted to transfer a great treasure but was afraid that if he gave it to one person he would steal. What did he do? He divided it into pennies and gave it to many people by whom he transferred the treasure to a different place.

We should understand the difference between a person having a great desire that he cannot overcome, or a small desire that he cannot overcome. We should say that in the end, we see that a person can overcome a small passion, but it is hard for him with a great one. When we say that he is always fifty-fifty, it is precisely after the soul was divided into parts, and for this reason the tree of knowledge was forbidden for him, since there is more than half there and he would have no room for choice. Hence, now each one has a part of the desire, so there is room for choice.

The will to receive is the essence of man. It is considered an innovation "existence from absence." But the rest of the things, meaning all the fillings, extend "existence from existence," called "creation," meaning existence from existence. However, all the kinds of fillings in the world extend existence from existence, meaning that they are included in the Creator. Conversely, the negative things, the lacks and the sufferings, are something new.

21- Sanctification of the Month

"This month shall be the beginning of months for you" (Exodus 12).

RASHI interpreted: "Moses was perplexed over the birth of the moon: To what extent should it be seen in order to be fit for sanctification? He showed him with the finger the moon in the firmament and said to him, 'This you shall see and sanctify.'"

The interprets asked, What was so perplexing to Moses concerning the sanctification of the moon? Also, what is the connection to showing him with the finger? What does the word "finger" imply to us?

Baal HaSulam said that the moon implies *Malchut*, which pertains to the acceptance of the burden of the kingdom of heaven. It was difficult for Moses to tell the people of Israel to take upon themselves the burden of the kingdom of heaven when they feel concealment. It stands to reason that if he approached the people of Israel to take upon themselves the kingdom of heaven with some revelation of Godliness, there would be something with which to speak to them. But with the intention that the moon is still not full and should be sanctified at the time of its birth, when it is still not apparent how she receives the light of the sun, and when it still does not shine, yet at that time it must be sanctified?

The meaning is that a person must take upon himself the burden of the kingdom of heaven on the lowest quality, and say about it that to him, even that state, the lowest that can be, meaning one that is entirely above reason, when he has no support from the mind or the feeling so he can build its foundations on it.

At that time, he is seemingly standing between heaven and earth and has no support, for then everything is above reason.

Then a person says that the Creator sent him this state, where he is in utter lowliness, since the Creator wants him to take upon himself the burden of the kingdom of heaven in this manner of lowliness.

At that time, he takes upon himself because he believes above reason that the situation he is in now comes to him from the Creator, meaning that the Creator wants him to see the lowest possible state that can be in the world.

And yet, he must say that he believes in the Creator in all manners. This is considered that he has made an unconditional surrender. That is, a person does not say to the Creator, "If You give me a good feeling, to feel that 'The whole earth is full of His glory,' I will be willing to believe."

Rather, when he has no knowledge or sensation of spirituality, he cannot accept the burden of the kingdom of heaven and observe the Torah and *Mitzvot* [commandments]. Rather, he must accept the kingdom of heaven unconditionally.

This is what perplexed Moses: How could he come to the people of Israel with such lowliness? It is about this that the Creator showed him with the finger and said, "This you shall see and sanctify," meaning the moon at the time of its birth, when its merit is still not apparent.

Precisely accepting the kingdom of heaven in lowliness will reveal what our sages said, "Rabbi Elazar said, 'The Creator is destined to pardon the righteous and dwell among them in the Garden of Eden, and each one will point with his finger, as was said, 'And he said on that day, 'Behold, this is our God for whom we have waited and He will save us. This is the Lord for whom we have waited; let us rejoice and be glad in His salvation''''" (*Taanit* 31).

It follows that the hint that the Creator points to the moon with the finger and says, "This," by this we are rewarded with each one pointing with his finger, "Behold, this is our God."

22- *And You, Israel*

"And you, Israel, listen to the laws and the judgments... You shall not add to the matter that I command you, nor take away from it, to keep the commandments of the Lord your God that I command you."

We should understand what is a law and what is a judgment. The verse makes a precision, "You shall not add... nor take away... that I command you." In both addition and reduction, everything must be only precisely as He commands.

There is a difference between those who walk in the work in order to bestow or in order to receive reward. Those who walk in order to bestow begin the work anew each day in both mind and heart. They cannot receive any support from "the day before, for it has passed." Rather, they truly have no choice, but each day they must return to the foundations of the work, to the reasons that compel them to walk on the path of truth.

It is as though each day he should speak with himself that it is worthwhile to be a servant of the Creator, and the body asks him every day when he begins the work, "Give me the reasons why you are forcing me to give all my powers for the sake of the Creator." And if it asks, we must answer; otherwise, it does not want to work. Thus, each day there are the same arguments and the same questions and the same answers.

When a person is drawn to work in the Torah and prayer and good deeds, but does not remember the purpose of the work, which is in order to bestow, the work is easier for him, since at that time he follows the general public. But when he remembers the goal, which is mind and heart, "the world darkens for him" because it is against the body, which is called "self-love."

At that time, he has nothing to answer to the body, but it is a law that the Creator wants us to believe him that it is for His sake, that specifically through work in mind and heart, a person is rewarded with achieving his wholeness, and then his enemies, too, become his friends. This is called "with all your heart, with both your inclinations, the good inclination and the evil inclination."

It is written about this, "You shall not add," meaning to increase mind and reason in a place that should be specifically above reason. It follows that if he tries to understand and learn it within reason, if he thinks that by this he will be able to do more work because the body agrees where it understands within reason, this is called "You shall not add."

Instead, we must believe in the Creator, that precisely through Him we will achieve completion, called "faith above reason."

However, there is the matter of "judgment," which is the opposite. There, a person must try to understand the Torah within reason. A person should try to understand the Torah that the Creator gave him as much as he can. If he sees that he does not understand the words of Torah, he should increase the prayers and litanies, where there is the matter of "understanding, growing knowledgeable, hearing, to learn and to teach."

Here comes the second matter, "Do not take away," but rather increase the Torah, as is explained about the hand *Tefillin*, called "faith," as it is written, "And it will be a token on your hand." Our sages said, "A token for you and not for others," meaning that the hand *Tefillin* should be covered because it implies faith above reason, called "kingdom of heaven."

Conversely, the head *Tefillin* represents the Torah, called *Zeir Anpin*. Our sages said about it the verse, "And all the peoples of the earth shall see that the name of the Lord is called upon you and will fear you." These are the head *Tefillin*, where there is revelation, as it is written, "shall see."

Torah is called "revealing," when the peoples of the earth within a person feel the quality of the Torah that they extended, they "will fear you," for then the evil surrenders and the good governs. This is call "judgment," for "judgment" is revealing, and we must not take away from it but increase the knowledge of Torah. Conversely, a "law" means covering, which is above reason, when it is forbidden to increase knowledge.

23- *Behold, I Am Setting Before You*

"Behold, I am setting before you." He begins with singular form [in Hebrew] and ends in plural form. Also, we should understand the meaning of "Behold," as in "seeing."

Singular form means that each one should be rewarded with seeing, as in, "And you shall love the Lord your God," singular form. This speaks to the whole of Israel, meaning that each individual in the collective must be rewarded with the discernment, "the Lord your God," in singular form. That is, one should not rely on the other, but each one must be a foundation, and on this foundation he builds all of his servitude.

Also, a person must be rewarded with seeing, as our sages said, that when a person says, "were completed," he testifies to the work of creation.

We should understand, 1) This testimony, for whom must he testifies, 2) Testimony is only by seeing, and not by hearing, so what evidence is it when he says "were complete"?

The testimony that one should make is that it is true that the work of creation that the Creator created was in order to do good to

His creations. This is precisely when they were rewarded with seeing, meaning the light of *Hochma*. When this is revealed, he testifies to the work of creation, which is to do good to His creations. This is regarded as Shabbat [Sabbath], the end of the work, when the goal—to do good to His creations—is revealed. This is called "Who rested from all His work," since the goal has been revealed.

24- The Main Thing We Need

The main thing we need, and for which we have no fuel for the work, is that we are lacking importance of the goal. That is, we do not know how to appreciate our service so as to know to whom we are bestowing. Also, we are lacking the awareness of the greatness of the Creator, to know how happy we are that we have the privilege of serving the King, since we have nothing with which to be able to understand His greatness.

In the words of *The Zohar*, this is called "*Shechina* [Divinity] in the dust," meaning that bestowal upon Him is as important to us as dust. Naturally, we have no fuel to work, since without pleasure, there is no energy to work.

Where self-love shines, the body derives vitality from this. But in the work of bestowal, the body does not feel any pleasure in this and must naturally "collapse under its weight."

Conversely, when one feels that he is serving an important King, to the extent of the importance of the King, so is his delight and pleasure from serving Him. Hence, at that time he has fuel that can give him the power to go forward each time, since he feels that he is serving an important King.

Then, when he knows and feels to whom he bestows, to the extent that he had the strength to work with the intention of self-love, now he has the strength to work in order to bestow, since one who bestows upon an important person is regarded as receiving from him. And since the body has the strength to work for reception, in order to receive reward, likewise, in bestowing upon an important King he derives pleasure in this.

By this we will understand what is written in the "Introduction to The Study of the Ten Sefirot" concerning the matter that if she gives, and he is an important person, she is sanctified because of the pleasure of receiving from him. We are seeing something new: Bestowing upon an important person is tantamount to receiving, although there he references the essay about matrimony in the context of reception in order to bestow, at which time reception means bestowal.

From this we can understand the other side of the coin—that bestowal is called reception, and because of this he already has fuel, for if he bestows upon an important person, it is to him as though he is receiving. Therefore, he already has the power to work.

It follows that all we need is to believe in the greatness of the Creator, and then we will have the energy to work in bestowal.

25- The Summoning for the Blessing on the Food

When we summon for the blessing on the food, when we say, "*Rabotai* [great ones], let us bless," it is as though we are preparing and summoning to bless over the food.

Baal HaSulam said that we see that sometimes someone does something good to another, although he does not hear that the beneficiary blesses him, he is certain that he blesses him in his heart even if he does not hear. Likewise to the contrary: If a person does something bad to another, even if he does not hear him curse him, he is certain that he is cursing him because such is nature.

It follows that when do we need to see and hear that he blesses or curses another? When the bad or good are not evident, he must show his intention, how he feels about his friend's act, whether it is bad or good.

The Torah said, "And you shall eat, and be satiated, and bless." Our sages said that the Torah states that we must bless only for eating that is satiating, but our sages were stricter saying that even when a meal is not satisfying, we should still bless.

This is as they explained about the verse, "The Lord will lift up His face to you." They asked, "It is written, 'who will not lift up the face or take a bribe.'" They replied that the Creator—"And you shall eat, and be satiated, and bless," and made it stricter on themselves, "even as much as an olive and as much as an egg."

Baal HaSulam explained that the meaning of "as an olive" is as that the dove said, "I would prefer my nourishments to be as bitter as an olive from the hand of the Creator than as sweet as honey from the hands of flesh and blood."

The explanation of the "egg" is that when we look at an egg, we say that an animal might emerge from it, meaning a chick. But before the chick has hatched, there is still no life in the egg.

This is why our sages made it stricter on themselves to bless the Creator even when they do not taste the flavor of Torah and work, and still do not feel any vitality in it. Nevertheless, they make it even stricter on themselves. For this reason, He will lift up His face for them, meaning that the work they are doing with the austerity is just as though they did a good deed.

We should understand the answer, "How will I not lift up My face, since they are so strict on themselves?" It sounds as though the austerity that they took upon themselves is like a bribe, and by receiving the bribe He does something called "lifting up the face," which brings back the question, "The God... who will not lift up the face or take a bribe."

However, we must say that it is an eye for an eye: "As they say about everything I give them that it is a good, I will lift up My face, too, and I, too, will say about the work they do that it is good, that they deserve reward as though they did good deeds."

Therefore, we need preparation so we can bless even though we still feel that we are lacking good bestowals.

26- Who Will Not Lift Up the Face

In the verse, "who will not lift up the face or take a bribe," we should understand the meaning of the words, "who will not take a bribe." How can the Creator be bribed, for the verse tells us that He "will not take a bribe"?

The thing is that all the qualities we attribute to the Creator are in fact those of man. If a person is used to receiving a bribe, meaning for his own delight, he has no ability to adhere to Him, since it is "cling unto His attributes."

It follows that the meaning of the verse, "who will not take a bribe" is that a person must not take a bribe when he wants to scrutinize some matter in a manner of truth and falsehood, for if there is some intention there for his own pleasure, he can no longer see the truth, "for bribe blinds the eyes of the wise," since the light of *Hochma* [wisdom] can expand only where there are *Kelim* [vessels] that are completely cleansed of self-reception.

Conversely, *Hassadim* [mercies] can be done even while he is not completely cleansed, since while performing *Hassadim*, he cannot blemish because the act is one of giving. However, when the light of *Hochma* expands, it is knowing and receiving, and therefore it is possible to blemish. For this reason, as long as one is not purified of self-love, there is a correction that he cannot see anything of the quality of *Hochma*.

27- Three Lines – 1

There are two lines, and there is a dispute between them: Each one wants to cancel the other.

Three manners extend from this: 1) One cancels the other. 2) Each one wants to cancel but cannot cancel, so they remain disputed. 3) Peace is made between them.

"Right" is called "wholeness." In other words, a person depicts to himself that he is the most complete and happiest person in the world because he concludes that he is a simple person who has no advantage over others, but the Creator has chosen only him to serve the King. Although this service is not continuous, but once a month or once a week, when he sees that there aren't many people who serve the King even once in their lives, this alone gives him vitality. And if he has vitality, he can engage in Torah and *Mitzvot* [commandments] with joy and increase his good deeds.

However, ascending the degrees also requires walking on the left line, which is *Hochma* [wisdom], where there is criticism over the acts and the thoughts—whether they are truly in order to serve the King, to bestow contentment upon his Maker, or for himself. At that time, the left wants to cancel the right and go specifically in a manner of criticism. It does not let a person do anything good. It follows that "His wisdom is greater than his deeds."

However, one should mainly walk on the right line, meaning do good deeds and feel himself as complete, and serving the king. One must believe that everything he does brings contentment to Him.

At the same time, he should dedicate time to walking on the left line, meaning to criticize, but the left should surrender before the right. That is, he walks on the left not because he wants the quality of the left, but in order to improve the right, to show that despite all his criticism and knowledge, he is going above reason, meaning in the "right," which is called "faith."

This is called the "middle line," which decides between the two lines and leans toward the right. This is also called *Achoraim* [posterior].

Through this unification, one is later rewarded with receiving the quality of *Panim* [face/anterior] of the degree. At that time there is clothing of *Hochma* in *Hassadim*, which cause a *Zivug* [coupling] *Panim be Panim* [face-to-face] above, in ZON.

28- *The Earth Feared and Was Still*

Rabbi Hizkiya said, "Why is it written, 'You caused judgment to be heard from heaven; the earth feared and was still.' If it feared, why was it still, and if it was still, why did it fear? Indeed, first it feared, and finally it was still."

Why was it afraid? In accordance with Rish Lakish, as Rish Lakish said, "Why is it written, 'And there was evening and there was morning, the sixth day,' What is the purpose of the additional 'the'? This teaches that the Creator stipulated with the works of creation and said to them: 'If Israel accept the Torah, you shall exist; but if not, I will return you to *Tohu ve Bohu* [emptiness and formlessness]'" (*Shabbat* 88a).

We should understand the judgment that says, "From the heaven You sound judgment," what is the meaning of "judgment"? It is known that the purpose of creation is because of His desire to do good to His creations. However, in order to have *Dvekut* [adhesion], which is equivalence of form, there was the *Tzimtzum* [restriction], which is a concealment. Thus, in the place of reception, a judgment was passed that the abundance will not be drawn in full unless one can aim in order to bestow.

This is the meaning of "From the heaven You sound judgment," and because of it, the earth feared.

Eretz [earth/land] is called *Malchut*, which is a vessel of reception. *Eretz* comes from the word *Ratzon* [desire], as our sages said about the verse, "Let the *Eretz* [earth] put forth grass," that she wanted to do her Maker's will. And what is her fear? It is that she might not be able to aim in order to bestow, since *Malchut* is called "the assembly of Israel," which means she includes the whole of Israel, for all the souls extend from *Malchut*.

By all creations being extended from reception and the judgment that was sounded from heaven—that it is forbidden to receive in order to receive, but only in order to bestow—how can the lower ones aim in order to bestow?

It follows that all the works of creation that were with the aim to do good to His creations, the creatures cannot receive from this *Kelim* [vessels]. This means that all the works of creation will be in the manner of *Tohu ve Bohu*.

We should understand the meaning of "If not, I will return you to *Tohu ve Bohu* [emptiness and formlessness]." To which *Tohu ve Bohu* will He return them? According to what the ARI wrote, the breaking that took place in the world of *Nekudim*, when the *Kelim* [vessels] broke, was because they received in order to receive. Afterward came the World of Correction, called *ABYA*, and corrected the *Kelim* so they work in order to bestow.

The creatures must make all those corrections, which are in order to bestow, so they can receive the delight and pleasure. However, how can the lower ones, who were created with a nature only to receive, how can they go against their nature? This is why the earth, which is *Malchut*, feared that she would not be able to bestow anything upon the lower ones, due to the separation and disparity of form of the lower ones.

Thus, in order for the lower ones to have a way by which to turn the vessels of reception to work in order to bestow, He created the Torah, as our sages said, "I have created the evil inclination; I have created the Torah as a spice" (*Kidushin* 30b). There is a way in the Torah to subdue the evil, as our sages said, "The light in it reforms him."

This is the meaning that He stipulated with the works of creation that if Israel receive the Torah, they will exist, meaning that then the purpose of creation to do good to His creations will come true, and if not, He will return them to *Tohu ve Bohu*, as it was in the world of *Nekudim*.

Hence, when Israel received the Torah, she became still, since through the Torah they could correct the vessels of reception to work in order to bestow. She was still because now the delight and pleasure will come true, namely the purpose of creation to do good to His creations.

29- The Creator Observed Their Works

"The Creator observed the works of the righteous and the works of the wicked, and did not know which the Creator wanted, whether their works"—when he says, "And the Lord saw the light, that it was good, and divided"—it means the works of the righteous.

We should understand how there can be doubt and say, "He does not know what the Creator wants." Is it conceivable that the Creator wants the works of the wicked?

According to the explained rule, that before one is rewarded with emerging from self-love, while he is still controlled by the will to receive, all the good deeds that a person does, if he wants to aim in order to bestow, he sees that the body disagrees with it because it is against its nature.

It follows that in every single act that one does in Torah and *Mitzvot* [commandments] he has tremendous efforts because the bad in him resists it. At that time, that state is called "the works of the wicked," when the bad is still within him and overcomes him every day.

But afterward, when he is rewarded with correcting the evil in him and becomes righteous, his works are effortless because the bad in him no longer objects to his aiming all his actions in order to bestow, since he implements "And you shall love the Lord your God with all your heart," with both your inclinations. It follows that his works are called "the works of the righteous."

Then the question is, Which does the Creator want? That which a person labors and must constantly exert. It follows that the person shows his effort, meaning that a person does according to what he is. But with the works of the righteous, he no longer has any effort. Instead, at that time he is in a state of peace of mind.

Thus, the question, Which does the Creator want, whether the work where a person exerts or the work of the righteous, although then he has no labor, as it is written in *The Zohar*, "In a place where there is labor there is the *Sitra Achra* [other side]," meaning that as long as one has not corrected the evil in him to be good, he has labor.

Hence, he brings evidence from "And the Lord saw the light and divided," meaning the work of the righteous, since from the Creator's perspective, the goal is for the created beings to attain the thought of creation, which is to do good to His creations.

However, since it is impossible to obtain this without equivalence of form, when a person engages in equivalence of form he has labor. This is from the perspective of the Creator. However, for man's part, he should always yearn for labor.

Thus, when one is rewarded with *Dvekut* [adhesion] with the Creator, there is no *Sitra Achra* and no labor. At that time, a person should yearn for labor. However, at that time he cannot have labor.

Therefore, the advice for this is as it is written in *The Zohar*, that his fear is from the past ("Introduction of The Book of Zohar," Item 118), meaning that when he has no work and labor, he must yearn for labor from the time when he was in a state of the works of the wicked, and then he has wholeness.

30- *Turn Away from Evil and Do Good – 1*

Man's work begins with "Do good," and then he can keep the "Turn away from evil," since by education he cannot perceive the bad as bad. Rather, man yearns to satisfy his wishes because he feels great pleasure is satisfying his passions.

When one is told that satisfying his desires is bad, he does not know why. Instead, he must believe above reason that this is bad and he must turn away from this path.

Also, when one comes to engage in doing good, such as to wear a *Tzitzit* [a Jewish fringed undergarment], he does not feel anything good about it because he feels no pleasure when wearing the *Tzitzit* so he can say about it that it is good. Instead, he must believe above reason that it is good.

But later, when he walks in this way above reason, whether in good or in bad, he is given from above some taste of "Do good." To the extent that he feels good when doing the commandment to do, he begins to taste a bad taste in bad things. At that time, he has a good feeling in "Do good," and a bad feeling in "Turn away from evil." In that state, he has reward and punishment in this world.

But for those who work in order to receive reward, through faith in reward and punishment they observe the "Turn away from evil," even though they feel a passion for pleasure. Nevertheless, they turn away from the pleasures because they cannot tolerate punishments in the next world.

Also, when one observes "Do good," he can also observe the commandments to do although he does not feel any flavor in it, but he believes that he will be paid a reward for this, so he has the strength to observe.

But when he wants to engage not in order to receive reward, the question is, Why does he observe the "Turn away from evil and do good"? Clearly, he must understand that this is the King's commandment. Yet, why does the King need it? After all, He is not deficient, lacking the Torah and *Mitzvot* [commandments] of the lower ones.

Evidently, this is for us, so we may correct ourselves. At that time, a person begins to scrutinize the benefit that he derives from this.

For this reason, the first work is in faith above reason, and then he gets help from above, which is called an "illumination from above," until he obtains the NRNHY of his soul.

31- How I Love Your Teaching

"How I love Your Torah [law/teaching], it is my conversation all day long. Your commandments make me wiser than my enemies."

There are many kinds of "What": 1) "What is this work for you?" 2) "What does the Lord your God require of you?"

The "Whats" contradict one another. One "What" speaks of moving away from the Creator and the other "What" speaks of nearing to the Creator. *Doresh* [requires] comes from the words *Doresh be Shlomcha* [sends His regards]. Yet, both are regarded as Torah, meaning both come to teach us one thing, which a person must learn in practice.

We can understand that "What does the Lord your God require of you" means that one must learn and understand so as to know what to do. But what does "What is this work?" come to teach us?

Since the verse says it, clearly, one must feel this state in all its lowliness. Why do I need all this? Ostensibly, it would be better if man never entered that state, and if such thoughts come to him, it would be better if he did not pay attention to them.

We see that there is no answer to the question of the wicked one other than "Blunt his teeth," which is as our sages said, "And you shall memorize them, so that the words of Torah will be sharp within your mouth, so that if someone were to ask you something, do not hesitate before you speak but tell him right away" (*Kidushin* 30a). What can one tell him about this "What"? The other "What," meaning "What does the Lord your God require of you? Only to fear Me?"

In other words, we must know that the first "What," the Lord your God asked, and not you, meaning that the Creator brought this "What" into your mind, since there is no other force in the world, as it is written, "There is none else besides Him."

Clearly, the Creator will not create a creation that is against Him. Rather, He created this thought so as to fear Him, which is the acceptance of the burden of the kingdom of heaven above reason, for through the wicked one's question, he must take upon himself a new acceptance of the burden of the kingdom of heaven, called "fear," each time anew.

The power to be able to overcome and take upon himself the burden of the kingdom of heaven is through Torah and *Mitzvot* [commandments], whereby observing them, a person is cleansed from his evil, for only then will he be able to accept the burden of the kingdom of heaven.

This is the meaning of "God has made it that He will be feared," that all the bad situation that we feel is only so that man will not remain in the state he is in. That is, unless a person rises on the degrees of greatness of the Creator, he will not be able to overcome, and only when one feels the greatness of the Creator does his heart surrender. This is regarded as having to climb the degrees of fear of the Creator.

It follows that these questions cause him to need the Creator to open his heart and eyes to be rewarded with the greatness for the Creator. Otherwise, he suffices for the fear of heaven he has acquired through his upbringing. But when the wicked one's question keeps coming to him, it is not enough for him and he needs to constantly ascend up the degrees of greatness of the Creator.

This is the meaning of "How I love Your Torah [teaching]." Through the "What" question, there is a cause and a reason to be rewarded with the love of the Torah, since otherwise, we cannot answer the "What" question, but only to the extent of the acceptance of the burden of the kingdom of heaven in *Ohr Yashar* [direct light], and we can be rewarded with this only though the light in Torah and *Mitzvot*. Therefore, "it is always my conversation," since the "What" question always comes.

32- Man's Greatness Is According to His Work

It is written that Rabbi Yosi says, "It is not man's place that honors him; it is rather man who honors his place, for we find that on Mount Sinai, as long as the *Shechina* [Divinity] was on it, the Torah said, 'neither shall flocks or cattle graze before that mountain.' When the *Shechina* departed from it, the Torah said, 'When the ram's horn sounds a long blast, they shall come up the mountain.' We also find concerning the Tent of Meeting in the desert that as long as it stood, the Torah said, 'Send away from the camp every leper.' When the curtain was rolled up, the leaking and the lepers were permitted therein" (*Taanit* 21b).

To understand this, we must interpret the meaning of "place," meaning the Creator, as it is written, "Blessed is the Place." *Tzon* [flock] comes from the word *Yetzia* [exit]. *Bakar* [cattle] comes from *Mevaker* [criticizing]. "Shall come up" means ascending in degree.

The explanation is that it is known that the reward is only according to the sorrow, meaning that a person cannot receive the gifts of the Creator before he adjusts his actions to be for the sake of the Creator.

It is known that upon the revelation of the light of the Creator, when the Creator shines to a person and gives him awakening in Torah and work, there is no room for choice because the pleasure forces a person to engage in that which gives him pleasure. For this reason, at that time there is no place for choice.

In such a state, he is not obligated to believe in the Creator to such an extent that he says that without faith he will not do this, since what affirms the matter is another cause, which is the pleasure. This is called *Lo Lishma* [not for Her sake], since it is not faith that causes this action, but the pleasure determines it for him and motivates him to work and increase his good deeds.

Hence, although the Creator has given him a great awakening for Torah and work, he cannot ascend in degrees of truth by this, since "he acquired truth," meaning that the degree of truth must be acquired. Only by labor in acceptance of the burden of the kingdom of heaven voluntarily is one rewarded with climbing the degrees of truth, each time to a higher level. This is the meaning of "It is all according to the action."

By this we can understand the words, "It is not man's place that honors him." That is, it is not for this, if a person has been rewarded with some awakening. It follows that the Creator honored him; by this a person becomes respected, since an awakening that comes from above will finally depart from him because he still lacks the qualification to be fit to receive for the sake of the Creator and not for his own pleasure.

"It is rather man who honors His place." Specifically by this, when one makes an effort during the choice and wants to honor His place, meaning the Creator, only then does one become honored. That is, through his work, a person becomes a vehicle for the throne. However, it is not during an awakening from above, which is regarded as the Creator honoring the person.

He brings evidence from Mount Sinai, that as long as the *Shechina* was on it, "neither shall flocks or cattle graze before that mountain." The exits, when a person exits the work, is because of his criticism of Providence. At that time he should make a choice on these states. During the awakening there is not ascent because he is not making any effort of his own, since now he is in an awakening from above, and he is not making any effort to ascend to states where he should make a choice.

This is why it is written, "When the ram's horn sounds a long blast," meaning after the departure of the *Shechina*, "they shall come up the mountain." Precisely after this there is a place for the "What," meaning places where he could not endure the test and could not enter the *Kedusha* [holiness]. Now he has a place where he can overcome them because he can make a choice.

This clarifies the evidence from the Tent of Meeting, "When the curtain was rolled up, the leaking and the lepers were permitted therein." RASHI interpreted "the curtain was rolled up," that they were rolling along as they were traveling. A "leper" pertains to slander. In ethics, "slander" pertains to slandering Providence.

Also, in ethics, "leaking" is as they said, "a cemented cistern that does not lose a drop." This means that as long as one has not completed the measure of labor that he must exert, as much as he may take upon himself the burden of Torah, he immediately forgets and turns astray again.

It follows that any drop of fear of heaven that he takes upon himself leaks off from him. But once he is rewarded with permanent faith, he is called "a cemented cistern that does not lose a drop."

Man's heart is called "a cistern." *Sud* [lime] is from the word *Yasad* [established], as in "for so the King established." (RASHI interprets it as *Yesod* [foundation], so he established and commanded.) When man's heart is corrected with the foundation of faith, when all he wants is because "for so the King established," the King of the world, at that time the heart is called "a cemented cistern that does not lose a drop" of fear of heaven.

It is called "a drop" because man was created from this drop, since "You are called 'man'" pertains to one who has fear of heaven, as it is written, "Fear God and observe His commandments" (*Berachot* 6b).

Precisely when the curtain was rolled up, the leaking and lepers were permitted in there. This means that then they were given an opportunity, since precisely at the time of concealment there is room for work, and one can make a choice and take upon himself the burden of the kingdom of heaven permanently to be rewarded with the quality of "a cemented cistern that does not lose a drop."

It follows from all the above that only a person himself must work in order to make a choice. Afterward, the Creator gives him everything that was intended in creation, which is to do good to His creations.

33- What Is Amalek, Whose Memory We Must Blot Out

"To the wicked, it seems like a hairsbreadth" (*Sukkah* 52). That is, they are shown that Amalek does not have so much power that he cannot be defeated.

"To the righteous—as a high mountain," since they are powerful in that they want to be righteous and work in this manner for the sake of the Creator. Hence, they are given more evil each time, in order to overcome it and admit it into *Kedusha* [holiness]. In other words, each time, they take the aim for themselves, and instead of the aim for themselves, they work for the sake of the Creator.

For example, when they began the work they felt ten grams of pleasure in eating and drinking and so forth, and had the strength to relinquish this. Afterward, they are given fifteen grams of pleasure in corporeal pleasures. Then, a new work begins, and they feel that they have become worse, meaning that they lost their power to overcome because they see that now there is more work to overcome.

At that time, they must say that this is not the truth, but that previously, they felt the taste of ten grams of pleasure, and prevailed, and now they cannot overcome fifteen grams.

Afterward, through work and prayer, they can overcome fifteen grams, and they are given twenty grams of flavor in corporeality, and they see that they cannot overcome. When they look back, they ask themselves, "Why could we overcome sleep and other things before, and we see that now we have become worse than then?"

Also, we should understand that this is not the truth, but that previously, when they felt ten grams, they were able to overcome. But now that they are given twenty grams of pleasure, of course they are as yet unable to overcome, since they never had the work of relinquishing twenty grams of flavor, since even their whole lives were not worth as much as ten grams of pleasure in their eyes, and now they feel that living is worth more than ten grams, so the dedication they had had before is difficult for them.

34- TANTA [Taamim, Nekudot, Tagin, Otiot]

Taamim [flavors] means one who wants to taste a good taste in life should pay attention to his point in the heart.

Every person has a point in the heart, except it does not shine. Rather, it is like a black dot. The point in the heart is a discernment of *Nefesh* [soul] of *Kedusha* [holiness], whose nature is a vessel of bestowal.

However, she is in a state of *Shechina* [Divinity] in the dust, meaning that a person regards her as nothing. Instead, to him she is as important as dust. This is called *Nekudot* [dots/points].

The solution is to increase her importance and make its importance as *Tagin* [crowns], like a "Crown on his head." That is, instead of being dust, as before, he should raise her importance to be as a *Keter* [crown] on his head.

At that time, the *Nefesh* of *Kedusha* expands in *Otiot* [letters], meaning in the *Guf* [body], for the *Guf* is called *Otiot*. In other words, the *Kedusha* spreads from potential to actual, called *Otiot* and *Guf*.

35- Find Favor and a Good Mind

"Find favor and a good mind in the eyes of God and man" (Proverbs 3).

We should understand what it means to be favored by the Creator, meaning to do things by which man's actions are approvable in the eyes of the Creator. How can man, who is deficient, perform complete actions? For this reason, we asked to be found in favor.

Being favored is as our sages said, "How does one dance before the bride? The House of Hillel say... no blue paint and no rouge and no braiding, and still a graceful gazelle" (*Ketubot* 16b), or as our sages said about Ester, "Esther was greenish" (*Megillah* 15a), "And Esther found favor in the eyes of all who saw her."

It follows that when we want to be favored, it is because in terms of actions, we cannot say that we can perform complete actions; this is why we want to be favored.

36- Who Hears a Prayer

"Hears a prayer." There is a question: Why is prayer written in singular form if the Creator hears prayers, as it is written, "For you hear the prayer of every mouth of Your people Israel with mercy"?

We should interpret that we have only one prayer to pray—to raise the *Shechina* [Divinity] from the dust, and by this all the salvations will come.

37- Fish Means Worries

Dagim [fish] means *Daagot* [worries/concerns] about spirituality, meaning deficiencies. On Shabbat [Sabbath], when everything is corrected, the worries become food. In Egypt, the worries were for nothing, meaning without *Mitzvot* [commandments]. If the worries concern self-reception, the body is worried and we do not need to do much work. But if the worry is for the purpose of a *Mitzva* [sing. of *Mitzvot*], the body does not let us worry.

38- The Blessing of the Torah

"The blessing of the Torah" means that the body obligates him to bless. That is, the body that the Creator created with a nature that if he receives something good from someone, he blesses him, and this is called "the blessing of the food" from the Torah.

"Is not commanded" means that the body does not obligate him to bless because he feels he needs a few more things that the other one could give him but is not giving him. At that time, the body says that it is still not satisfied with Him and cannot say that He is good and does good, since I still need a few things so why is He not giving me? And yet, he is strict with himself and blesses. It follows that he is "not commanded but does."

39- Anyone with Whom the Spirit of the People Is Pleased – 1

"Anyone with whom the spirit of the people is pleased."

He asked, We find that the greatest and most renowned were disputed, so the spirit of the people is not pleased with him. He explained that that they did not say "Anyone with whom the people," but rather "the spirit of the people," meaning that only the bodies were disputed, meaning that each one uses only the will to receive, but the spirit of the people, this is already spirituality.

"Pleased with him" means that when the righteous extends abundance, he extends for the whole generation. Only because he still did not clothe their spirit, they are still unable to attain and feel the abundance that the righteous extends.

40- Concerning Two Witnesses

SAM seeks to accuse Israel, so the Creator tells him to bring witnesses, so he brings with it the sun. He went to bring the moon, and he followed her. He went up to the place where he was told, "In that which is inconceivable to you, do not inquire." The "sun" means the Torah, and the moon is a *Mitzva* [commandment], which is faith above reason.

There are two times in *Malchut*: 1) The time of *Katnut* [smallness/infancy], when she has only the point of *Keter* and the light of *Malchut*. When she is in *Katnut*, she ascends to *Keter*, and then the *Sitra Achra* [other side] has no hold on *Malchut* because above reason, there is no grip to the outer ones. It follows that when he wants to slander Israel and brings with him the sun, which is the Torah, he has no witnesses because they are not witnesses unless they are two, which are Torah and *Mitzva*, and wholeness means that there are two things: Torah and *Mitzvot* [commandments].

Conversely, if they are adhered in the form of a *Mitzva*, which is faith above reason, called *Aviut* [thickness] of *Keter*, the *Sitra Achra* has nothing with which to grip on to Israel.

41- Raising the Hands

It is written, "Raise your hands of holiness and bless the Lord." Also, a prayer is by raising the hands, as it is written, "And it came to pass that when Moses lifted up his hands, Israel prevailed."

Raising the hands is regarded as "surrender," since when one sees that he cannot get what he wants, he raises his hands and says that here he cannot achieve anything with his own hands.

Therefore, when praying to the Creator, we should raise our hands, as it is written (Psalms 63:5), "In Your name I will lift up my hands," that only the Creator can help him.

Likewise, in blessing, he raises his hands and blesses the Creator for everything that He has given him, since for himself, he is incapable of anything and only the Creator has given him, so he is thankful to the Creator for all that He has given him.

42- Serve the Creator with Joy

The Zohar asks, It is written, "The Lord is near to the brokenhearted." A servant of the Creator, whose intention is to bestow, should be happy when he is serving the King. If he has no joy during this work, it is a sign that he lacks appreciation of the greatness of the King.

Therefore, if one sees that he has no joy he should make amendments, meaning think about the greatness of the King. If he still does not feel, he should pray to the Creator to open his eyes and heart to feel the greatness of the Creator.

Here the two discernments develop: 1) He should regret not having a sensation of the greatness of the King. 2) He should be happy that his regrets are about spirituality and not like the rest of the people, whose regrets are only in order to receive.

We should know who it is who gave us the awareness that our regrets should be over spirituality, and we should be happy that the Creator has sent us thoughts of spiritual deficiency, which in itself is regarded as the salvation of the Creator. For this reason, we should be happy.

43- The Discernments of "Woman" and "Sons" in the Torah

"A woman is only for beauty; a woman is only for sons; a woman is only for a woman's adornments," and RASHI interprets that adornments should be bought for her to make her beautiful (*Ketubot* 59b).

Good days imply the ascent of the worlds, when each one ascends in degree and rises a little higher than the state he is in. This is the time when each one examines the reason for which he is taking upon himself the kingdom of heaven, who is called "a woman."

He brings three elements here, meaning we should discern three reasons that cause one to take upon himself the burden of the kingdom of heaven:

1) **Beauty**: Baal HaSulam said that beauty means *Hochma* [wisdom], meaning that by taking upon himself the kingdom of heaven he will later be rewarded with the light of Torah. It follows that the light of Torah, called "wisdom" or "beauty," is what causes him to take upon himself the burden of the kingdom of heaven.

2) **Sons**: In other words, he takes upon himself the burden of the kingdom of heaven in order to be rewarded with multiplication in the Torah. This is also called "attributing," meaning that when he learns Torah, he wants to attribute the Torah to the Creator. This is called "attributing," which means that through the burden of the kingdom of heaven he will have the strength to attribute the Torah to the Creator. In other words, during the study of Torah, he will have the strength, for the Torah is the names of the Creator.

Accordingly, we should interpret "A woman is only for sons," since through the kingdom of heaven he will have the power to *Lehavin* [understand]—called *Banim* [sons]—that the Torah is the names of the Creator. But in the absence of the kingdom of heaven, it is impossible to aim while learning Torah, that the Torah is the names of the Creator.

3) **For a woman's adornments**. This is as RASHI interpreted, that jewels should be bought for her to make her beautiful. Here it means that a person needs Torah and *Mitzvot* [commandments] so as to honor the kingdom of heaven, for Torah and *Mitzvot* are called "the bride's adornments," and by them we see that the bride is beautiful (and we should understand the difference from "Cast your eyes on beauty").

44- Ruin by Elders—Construction; Construction by Youths—Ruin

"Ruin by elders—construction; construction by youths—ruin" (*Megillah* 31b).

Elders are those who are accustomed to the work of the Creator. Youths are those who are in the beginning of their work. "Ruin" means a descent or a fall, where previously they had some ascent in the work, which is regarded as building, meaning that they appreciated the ascent, but the ruin is when they felt some fall, which comes from the concealment of the Creator, that the Creator hides Himself from them. This is called "ruin."

"Ruin by elders" means that they say that the Creator sent them the concealment. It follows that they are already building, since they believe that the Creator is tending to them, and from this they derive vitality.

Faith is apparent primarily during the descent, when it does not shine for a person. At that time, he faces a dilemma: Either he says, "I do not need any benefits. Rather, I want to bring contentment above and I do not care what I feel," or it is otherwise.

45- Sons of Wise Disciples

Our sages said, "Why are the sons of wise disciples not wise disciples? It is because they did not bless in the Torah first" (*Nedarim* 81b).

A wise disciple is one who learns Torah. "Their sons" are the offshoots born to them after the learning. Not blessing in the Torah first means that they did not give thanks in the beginning. That is, before they began to learn, they did not give thanks that they were given a desire to learn, for even for this one should be thankful, and by learning and understanding something, he gives greater thanks.

But one who is not thankful for the desire he was given to come to the seminary, it means that he does not appreciate the whole matter.

46- This Moment and the Next Moment

"This moment" is called *Ohr Pnimi* [inner light], and the "next moment" is called *Ohr Makif* [surrounding light]. A person who is dissatisfied with the present begins to think "When will the next moment come?" for then he will have satisfaction.

In the work, this is called "extending *Ohr Makif* inside," employing tactics to be happy at this moment.

47- Worse than Everyone

A person should feel that he is worse than everyone because he feels that no person has the faults that he has, although he sees that they engage in the work less than he does.

48- Right, Wholeness, and Truth

If a person believes in the greatness and importance of the Creator, and believes that the Creator enjoys his observing His commandments because he is serving Him, this applies when a person feels that compared to the Creator, he is like a little one compared to the greatest in the generation.

Because there is a law in nature that the small annuls before the great, even the smallest service he does for the Creator, believing that everything comes from the Creator, that everything is under Providence, he is therefore happy and content with even the shortest moment that he has the opportunity to serve the King. This is called "right, wholeness, and truth."

49- Our Faith in Books and Authors

The townspeople bought a diamond and everyone were happy that they bought the diamond for so little money. But one of them asked if the diamond they had bought was real.

However, none among the townspeople knew about diamonds, so they went to an expert dealer to tell them if the diamond was real or fake. They were happy with his reply that the diamond was real.

But one of them asked if they could trust the dealer, since he could be a crook. Therefore, he himself wants to learn the trade and be an expert in his own right, and he learns and succeeds.

The lesson is that we can believe our engagement in Torah and *Mitzvot* [commandments] when we rely on faith that we received from books and authors.

50- Man's Sensation of Time

When a person enjoys something, it extends from the *Ohr Pnimi* [inner light], when the light shines within the *Kli* [vessel]. When a person enjoys the past, he enjoys the *Reshimot* [recollections/memories] that remained from the *Ohr Pnimi*. When a person enjoys what illuminates for him, that he is destined to receive in the future, this extends from the *Ohr Makif* [surrounding light].

It follows that those three things speak of a person's sensation in the present in those three *Kelim* [vessels] called "past," "present," and "future." The past can exist only if the *Ohr Pnimi* called "present" precedes it. Afterward there is a "past," and then we come to enjoy the future.

It follows that the light that shines in the present extends from the *Ohr Pnimi*, and the light from the past is named after the *Reshimot* that remained from the past. The light of the "future" is called *Makif* [surrounding] and is called "light of confidence." That is, to the extent that his confidence shines for him, to that extent he can enjoy. Also, *Ohr Makif* is called "the light of the end of correction."

51- The State of Shabbat [Sabbath]

A Shabbat addition: Good things are given additions before and after. But bad things remain as they are, meaning no additions are attached to them, and we choose the least bad.

Since Shabbat is a good thing, there are additions to Shabbat before it and after it. What is good about Shabbat? The writing says, "It is good to thank the Lord." If a person can thank the Creator, this is called Shabbat. Accordingly, if one can thank the Creator in the middle of the week, that person is in a state of Shabbat, as our sages said, "A wise disciple is regarded as Shabbat." That is, if he can thank the Creator, this is called "the state of Shabbat."

52- God Made It so that He Would Be Feared

"God made it so that he would be feared," for otherwise there is no demand to draw the lights. This is the meaning of the door that must be shut to prevent the entry of uninvited guests, but to make this door is very difficult!

53- The Voice, the Voice of Jacob, but the Hands, the Hands of Esau

Our sages said that Esau was going to receive Isaac's blessing because Jacob did not have *Kelim* [vessels], but once Jacob received the hands of Esau, meaning Esau's vessels of reception, and spoke with the voice of Jacob, it was a correction. Through the correction that Jacob made, he did not know him, for he had vessels of reception through the *Hitkalelut* [merging/mingling].

"The voice, the voice of Jacob, but the hands, the hands of Esau." He did not know him because Jacob has the quality of a smooth man, having no deficiencies. For this reason, he had no *Kelim* in which to receive the blessings, since there is no light without a *Kli* [vessel].

"And Rebecca heard" and gave him the advice to borrow the clothing of the hairy one only so he would have *Kelim* to receive the blessing, and immediately after, return it.

54- Everlasting Salvation

Everlasting salvation: This world is in the present, and the next world is in the future.

Within reason is in the present. Above reason is called "in the future," when he believes in what he will have later as though he has it now.

55- Delight Them with a Complete Structure – 1

"Delight them with a complete structure." We should understand the meaning of an incomplete structure. After all, an incomplete structure is unfit for anything.

We should interpret that a time of *Kedusha* [holiness] is a structure, when a person builds in his heart a place for installing *Kedusha*. There are two forces in man's heart: the good inclination and the evil inclination. An incomplete structure means that one can be a servant of the Creator only with the good inclination, which is vessels of bestowal, while a complete structure means that he can serve the Creator also with the evil inclination, as our sages said, "with all your heart, with both your inclinations" (*Berachot* 54a).

56- Questions in the Work

How come after a whole year of corporeal work that a person does, he does not ask himself, What have I gained in this year? But in spirituality, a person does ask what he gained during this past year. Does the question about what he gained come from the side of *Kedusha* [holiness] or from the side of the *Sitra Achra* [other side]?

It is known that this world is called "the world of falsehood." Hence, one does not ask what he gained when it comes to falsehood, such as to say that this work was worthwhile. But in spirituality, which is truth, a question comes each time from the side of *Kedusha*, to awaken him to know what he gains, so as to make corrections.

We see that if a person makes a deal from which he intends to profit, meaning what he should get out of the deal, he does calculate. If it does not pay off, he changes the business for another business, since the profits he wants to make are on his mind. In this, he is not deceiving himself, meaning if this is the reward he wants, namely money or power. By this one measures oneself.

This is not so with the permitted corporeal life in general. In general, all pleasures are false. Hence, there is no point asking what he has to gain from making money or power, since this was made from the beginning so as to be false. However, it is called "a helpful lie." That is, before one can walk on the spiritual path, from where will he take vitality? Therefore, he is given a life that is called "falsehood."

57- A *Kli* [Vessel] that Holds a Blessing

Concerning a *Kli* that holds a blessing, a blessing is called "the light," and "peace" means the *Kli*. Peace is made by wanting to bestow, and this comes through the light. Thus, who comes first, the light or the blessing?

Answer: the light.

When the light comes, we must first think about the correction of the *Kli*. It follows that the light comes first for the purpose of the *Kli*, and then for the purpose of the light.

58- *Ani* [I] and *Ein* [Nothing/Null]

Ani is our desire. *Ein* is the annulment of our desire. Our desire is to receive, and it is called *Nukva* [Aramaic: female]. The Creator's desire is to bestow. It follows that when one cancels the *Ani*, the *Ani* and *Ein* are conjoined. This implies that our work is to make the *Ani* into *Ein*, meaning the desire of *Nukva* into a desire to bestow. But without a desire, there is nothing.

59- Anyone Who Is Angry, It Is as though He Commits Idol-Worship

"Anyone who is angry, it is as though he commits idol-worship," since in all the transgressions, there is only one transgression: lust. However, there is no pride in them because one is not proud about one's inability to overcome lust.

This is not so with anger. Besides enjoying the lust of anger, he also takes pride in being angry, for he knows that justice is on his side. Otherwise, he would not be able to take pride.

It follows that there are two transgressions here: 1) lust, which he enjoys, 2) taking pride, and "Anyone who is proud, he and I cannot dwell in the same abode and his soul departs" (*The Zohar, Tetzaveh*, Item 55).

60- A Request for Help

When a person suffers from some corporeal affliction, he should be sorry that the Creator punished him, that he is afflicted. If he is not sorry, it is not a punishment, since a punishment is that which hurts a person and he cannot tolerate his situation, whether sorrow over provision or sorrow over illness.

If he says that he does not feel the sorrow, then he did not receive the punishment that the Creator has given him. We must know that the punishment is a correction for his soul. Thus, if he is not sorry, he has lost the correction.

One should pray to the Creator to take away from him the suffering and sorrow that he feels, since a prayer that stems from suffering is a greater correction than the correction of the punishment.

As I heard from Baal HaSulam, the Creator punishes a person not as a revenge, punishing him for not obeying Him, as do people. Rather, the punishment is a correction.

When one prays to the Creator to take away from him the punishment, it is as though he is asking the Creator to take away from him the correction. He asked, How can a person ask the Creator to take away from him the correction, if the correction is in man's favor? And he explained that through the prayer when one asks the Creator to help him, he acquires connection with the Creator, and this is a greater correction than the correction that a person receives through the punishment.

61- Right and Left

A *Zivug* [coupling] to sustain the worlds, a *Zivug* that does not stop, which is covered *Hassadim*. A *Zivug* for engendering souls, a *Zivug* that stops, and it is considered *Hochma*.

On the right, it is possible to live but not to engender, but on the left, which is *Hochma*, called "deficiency," it is possible to engender the next state. Conversely, one who desires mercy is content with his share and has life but not for engendering because he is happy the way he is, so why should he want a different state?

A unification (*Zivug*) to sustain the worlds is a continuous unification and it gives life. A unification for engendering souls is a unification that stops, meaning intermittent. We must engage in unification in both.

A corporeal example is that in order to live, we cannot say, When do we not have to live? This comes from the quality of desiring mercy, when one is content with his share. But to engender, this is something in which we do not always need to engage, since engendering a new state is specifically through a deficiency, and a person should not constantly engage in deficiencies.

62- Reward and Punishment

In the work, we use reward and punishment in this world. In the next world, we do not use it although it exists. However, the general public uses reward and punishment primarily in the next world, and not reward and punishment in this world.

"Reward" means pleasure, and "punishment" means suffering. For the general public, who work for their own sake, they use reward and punishment of the next world because only in the next world will they feel the pleasure of observing Torah and *Mitzvot* [commandments], and the suffering for not observing Torah and *Mitzvot*. In this world, they do not feel pleasures or suffering from observing Torah and *Mitzvot* or vice-versa. Therefore, they must use only with regard to the next world.

But those who work in the individual manner feel a punishment if they have no faith in the Creator, meaning they suffer because they have no faith. Also, they derive pleasure, meaning reward, from being able to believe that the Creator leads the world in a manner of good and doing good, which is called "reward and punishment in this world."

63- You Stand Today – 1

"You stand today all of you." This means that he gathered them... to admit them into the covenant (RASHI). "All of you" means that everyone entered into the *Arvut* [mutual responsibility] (*Ohr HaChaim*).

There is a question why he begins with plural form, "all of you," then shifts to singular form, "every man from Israel." It means that "all of you" permeates everyone in Israel, meaning that every person from Israel will be included with "all of you," as it is written, "And the people camped at the bottom of the mountain," as one man with one heart. In other words, when there is love of Israel, they can succeed, as it is written, "Ephraim is joined to idols; let him be."

Man is a small world and comprises the entire world. He should achieve the degree of being singular, as it is written, "Rewarded, he sentences himself and the entire world to the side of merit" (*Kidushin* 40b).

Therefore, when a person admits all the individuals, "your heads and your tribes," for everyone must join in the covenant, meaning to come to be a worker of the Creator "with all your heart—with both your inclinations." In other words, even the lowly attributes in man should undergo correction.

"So that He may establish you today as His people and He will be a God unto you." That is, a person will achieve this attainment, that he is in the singular authority.

64- All Is Done by His Word

Concerning the blessing, "All is done by His word," the rule is that if he had to stop, he must bless again.

We should interpret that in the rest of blessings over delights, even though he had to stop, he can still bless, since he has something to bless for within reason. This is not so with "All is done by His word," meaning both what makes him feel good, and what makes him feel bad, "All is done by His word," as it is written, "And by the breath of His mouth is all their hosts," meaning over the desire to do good to His creations.

This can be only above reason. And when the building is above reason, for any stop, we must begin the work anew. This is why we must bless once more.

65- Turn Away from Evil and Do Good – 2

If a person wants to turn away from evil, he need not take any action in order to remove the evil from himself, since there is a rule in nature that a person cannot stand something bad about himself.

Rather, when a person realizes that something is harmful and bad for him, that it could make him lose his life, he immediately turns away from it and stays far from its reach. It follows that turning away from something bad comes to him without any work.

Rather, the work is to come to realize that this thing is so harmful that he cannot go on with it in his life. To come to this, we need "good." By engaging in Torah and *Mitzvot* [commandments] and wanting to achieve the complete spiritual life, one can come to the recognition of evil. When he achieves this recognition, he naturally turns away from evil. This is the meaning of "do good."

66- Woe unto You Who Await the Day of the Lord

"'Woe unto you who await the day of the Lord; it is darkness and not light.' There is an allegory about a rooster and a bat, who both waited for the light of day. The rooster said to the bat, 'I can see why I wait, for her light is mine'" (Gemara, Sanhedrin 98a).

Explanation: The bat does not have eyes to see, so what does he gain from sunlight?

We should understand the following:

1) What is the connection between eyes and looking at the light of the Creator? Clearly, sunlight requires eyes. But how is this connected to the light of the Creator, to the point that the verse

calls it "the day of the Lord," implying that one who has no eyes remains devoid of the light of the Creator?

2) What is the day of the Lord and what is the night of the Lord? What is the difference between them? Evidently, man's eye detects the rising of the sun. Yet, how does one detect the day of the Lord?

The thing is that with respect to the Creator, we discern night from day by revealing and concealing. The day of the Lord is called "revelation of the face," meaning that a matter becomes as clear as day.

It is as our sages said about the verse, "By the light of day, a murderer will rise and slay the poor and the indigent, and at night, he will be as a thief." The Gemara argues, "But it is written, 'At night, he is as a thief.' Does this mean that 'light' is 'day'? The meaning there is this: If the matter is as clear as light to you that he comes to take life, he is a murderer, and he [the victim] may be saved at the cost of his [the thief's] life. But if you are doubtful about it, like the night, he will be in your eyes as a thief, and he [the victim] cannot be saved at the cost of his [the thief's] life" (*Pesachim* 2a-b).

It follows that "day" means that he has revelation of the face, that the face of the Creator is revealed, meaning that the Creator reveals to Him a face of good and doing good. For example, when he prays, his prayer is immediately answered, and he has wealth, and sons, and contentment, and wherever he turns he succeeds.

"Night" means concealment of the face, when he has doubts and foreign thoughts concerning Providence, for the concealments bring him doubts. This is called "night."

One who waits for the light of the Creator has a feeling and clear knowledge in the form of faith above reason, that the Creator watches over creation with the name, The Good Who Does Good, but he does not feel the open Providence in plain sight for his own sake, as it is a correction, so he will not blemish the light of the Creator with the vessels of reception within him, which cause separation.

Therefore, he must do a lot of work before he turns the will to receive to work in order to bestow. Through persistence, a second nature forms in man. Previously, he had the nature of receiving only for himself, even while performing acts of bestowal, since through the act of bestowal he will receive something in return. That is, it is impossible to do anything without receiving something for his own sake in return, and any pleasure he receives separates him from *Dvekut* [adhesion] with the Creator, since *Dvekut* is measured by equivalence of form.

We should say that what the Creator wants, namely to do good, to bestow, is not because of a deficiency. Rather, it is regarded as "playing," and playing is not regarded as deficiency. Our sages said about it that the Queen asked, What does the Creator do once He has created the world? And the final answer that the Gemara brings is that the Creator sits and plays with a whale (*Avoda Zarah* 3b).

A "whale" means connection (from the words, "to the clear space on each, with wreaths"), meaning that the purpose of the connection of the Creator with the created beings is like playing, and not a matter of a desire of a deficiency.

67- What Is Truth?

For the most part, beauty is determined by what the majority decides is beautiful or not beautiful when it comes to clothes and furniture. We see that each generation rejects the depiction of beauty of the previous generation. For example: In the previous generation, people knew that furniture should be made of wood, with all kinds of engravings on them. Today, the closets are wall-closets, as it was in Jerusalem a few generations ago. We see that in old apartments there are wall-closets, but today the wall-closets are nicer than then.

However, who can really say what is beautiful? It is impossible to answer this or give a definition. Instead, anything that the majority agrees on that is beautiful, everyone follows this example. Hence, each time, there is a new trend, meaning new patterns.

It follows that anything that the majority appreciates is considered beautiful and people follow is called "respectable clothes," and what people respect, people can exert in order to acquire.

Therefore, in spirituality, called "in order to bestow," which people do not respect because the majority does not appreciate spirituality, it is difficult to work and labor to obtain spiritual things. But here, too, the question is, Which is the truth? Is it important or not?

The answer to this is that although spirituality is very important, but in order not to spoil spiritual matters, there was a correction that we cannot see who appreciates it. Instead, a person must believe that there is great importance in being among those who see the King's face.

It follows that in truth, it is very important and very honorable, but it was given in a manner of correction so that the creatures will not see the importance of the matter. Hence, there is no general consensus over it. For this reason, spirituality is regarded as being in the dust, meaning that nothing can be more despised than dust. It follows that internally, it is truly important and honorable. But on the outside, it seems like dust.

Conversely, in corporeality, on the outside, a different form is defined as beautiful, and each time we respect things. But internally, meaning in truth, it is all a lie, except people determined that this is beauty.

But each time, they regret and say about something else that it is beautiful, and about the previous form, that it is not beautiful. But in truth, inside there is no beauty; it is all a lie. However, according to the view of the majority, they say that this is important and that is unimportant, but fundamentally, it is all a lie. This is not so with spirituality.

68- The Order of the Work

In the beginning, one must believe above reason that the Creator wanted to do good to His creations. For this reason, He created His creations and installed in them the desire and yearning to receive pleasure. The reason is that this is the only *Kli* [vessel] to receive pleasure, since man enjoys only that for which he yearns. He can receive something to which he does not yearn, but he cannot enjoy it because the *Kli* for enjoyment is called "coveting," "yearning," etc.

However, this should be above reason, since when he looks within reason, he does not find His Providence over the world as benevolent. On the contrary, this is why it is said that we must believe above reason that this is so.

But in truth, if His guidance is only in a manner of good and doing good, why is this not felt within reason? We learned that it is because of the correction of the bread of shame. Therefore, as long as the created beings have no vessels of bestowal, they cannot see light and remain in the dark.

When one believes in the delight and pleasure that exists in above reason, he comes to consciously feel, to know the evil within him. That is, he believes that the Creator imparts such delight and pleasure, and although he sees all the good above reason, he achieves recognition. That is, he feels in all the organs the power of the evil that is found in receiving for oneself, which prevents him from receiving the abundance.

It follows that faith above reason causes him to feel his enemy within reason—who obstructs him from reaching the good. This is his standard. That is, to the extent that he believes in the delight and pleasure above reason, to that extent he can come to feel the recognition of evil.

Later, sensing the bad yields the sensation of delight and pleasure, since the recognition of evil in the sensation of the organs causes him to correct the bad.

This is done primarily through prayer, when he asks the Creator to give everything in bestowal, called *Dvekut* [adhesion]. Through these *Kelim* [vessels], the goal will be revealed in open Providence, meaning that there will be no need for the concealment because there will already be *Kelim* that are able to receive.

69- The Reward for Work in Spirituality

Generally, there are three things in the world: 1) the Creator, 2) the created beings, 3) the delight and pleasure that the Creator gives to the created beings.

In that sense, we discern the world of *Ein Sof* [infinity] filling all of reality. There is no beginning or end there. Here, there is no room for work because there is nothing to add.

The first receiver, called *Malchut*, wanted equivalence of form. She said she did not want to receive in a manner where she is the recipient. Thus, the first *Tzimtzum* [restriction] took place, and the many worlds and *Partzufim* [pl. of *Partzuf*] and souls and angels were made over *Behina Dalet* [4th Phase/Discernment].

In other words, *Behina Dalet* became the root of all the corruptions and the place of corrections, which did not exist before *Behina Dalet* emerged, when *Malchut*, who is called "receiver," did not want to receive in her own quality.

Since the new vessels of reception, called in order to bestow, are attributed to the created being, this unfolds slowly because we are going against nature, meaning against the will to receive that emanated from the Creator, for the lower one to receive. For this reason, the desire that comes from the Creator, everyone wants to work with this desire.

That is, with the desire to bestow, all of our work is that we must go against the nature that the Creator created. The end of correction is when the general will to receive will be corrected to work in order to bestow. At that time, there will be no work.

It follows that there are only four *Behinot* [discernments]: 1) Creator, 2) created beings, 3) the gift that the Creator gives to the created beings, 4) the created beings wanting to give to the Creator.

Thus, the labor is because we must work against nature. Conversely, in the will to receive that comes from nature, from His desire to do good to His creations, there is nothing to work on. Instead, work is only on the desire to bestow.

70- The Difference between *Kedusha* [Holiness] and *Sitra Achra* [Other Side]

The difference between the will to receive that is in *Kedusha* [holiness] and the will to receive that is in the *Sitra Achra* [other side] is that in *Kedusha*, we use only the part of the desire we can aim in order to bestow. The part that works in order to receive is not in *Kedusha*. Naturally, we cannot say that the will to receive in order to receive will be corrected because it has no contact with *Kedusha*, so how can one correct that which he does not have?

In the *Sitra Achra*, there is the will to receive in order to receive. However, how can it be corrected, since light of *Kedusha* cannot reach there because the *Kelim* [vessels] drew away from the abundance and are regarded as a space that is vacant of the light of abundance. Thus, how can there be correction, since correcting these *Kelim* requires light and abundance, for the lights correct the *Kelim*, and here, where they have no light, who will correct them?

Therefore, man was created so that until he is thirteen, he acquires vessels of reception that work in order to receive. But when he still does not have light, he acquires *Kelim* that separate him from the *Kedusha*. After thirteen years, when he begins to work with the point in the heart, and observes Torah and *Mitzvot* [commandments] with the aim to bestow, he is rewarded with some degree of *Kedusha*. At that time, he can be begin to correct the *Kelim* he has acquired from the *Sitra Achra*.

71- The Meaning of Exile

"When Israel are in exile, the *Shechina* [Divinity] is with them." This means that if one falls into a descent, spirituality is also descended in him. But according to the rule, "a *Mitzva* [commandment] induces a *Mitzva*," why does he come into a descent? Answer: He is given a descent from above so as to feel that he is in exile and ask for mercy, to be delivered from exile. This is called "redemption," and there cannot be redemption if there is no exile there, first.

What is exile? It is that he is under the rule of self-love and cannot work for the sake of the Creator. When is self-love considered exile? It is only when he wants to emerge from this control because he suffers from not being able to do anything for the sake of the Creator.

It follows that when he began to work, there had to be some pleasure and reward for which the body agreed to this work. Afterward, when he was permitted to see that there is the matter of "for the sake of the Creator," because a *Mitzva* induces a *Mitzva*, and he had to ask to be delivered from exile, then he runs from the exile.

How does he run from the exile? It is by saying that he will not succeed in this work. Thus, what does he do? He commits suicide, meaning leaves the work and returns to corporeal life, which is regarded as "The wicked in their lives are called 'dead.'"

It follows that where he should have asked for redemption from exile, he runs from the exile and commits suicide. This is as it is written, "The ways of the Lord are straight; the righteous will walk in them, and transgressors will fail in them." However, he should go above reason.

A descent in spirituality does not mean that now he has no faith. Rather, now he must do more work, and the previous faith is considered a descent compared to this work.

72- Concealed and Revealed in His Providence

For the world in general, His Providence is concealed from the public. That is, the world does not believe that there is guidance over the world, and thinks that everything is happening without any leader.

Therefore, the Creator leads the world with revealed reward and punishment. This means that the creatures must keep the Creator's laws, which are called "nature," or they are punished on the spot. This is called "revealed reward and punishment."

For example, the Creator created the creatures as a fusion of four elements: air, wind, water, and earth, and all have to be blended in.

If a person breaks nature's laws and adds, for example, more heat than the Creator determined, such as by entering a very hot place, the person is punished for breaking nature's laws and he pays with his life because he dies from excessive heat. Or to the contrary, if a person goes into a place that is colder than what nature determined, his punishment is to pay with his life and he freezes to death. Thus, the reward and punishment are revealed.

He, however, is still concealed and they do not say that there is a leader. Rather, they say that nature is not the Creator but rather a force without leadership.

For this reason, it follows that in the corporeal world, He Himself is concealed, and the reward and punishment are revealed in this world on the spot without any compassion, and anyone who breaks nature's laws suffers the punishment right away. Likewise the reward: When he observes nature's laws, he immediately receives.

73- Flavors of Torah

We eat in order to have strength to work, and we work in order to have something to eat, then we eat in order to have strength to work, and so on.

We should understand which is important and which is unimportant. It is simple: If you ask a person which of them he wants to relinquish, meaning we would like to give you one of them, and not that you will bind one with the other, of course he will say that he relinquishes the work and not the food, since he finds a good taste in eating, whereas in work, he finds a bad taste. Hence, if he could relinquish one act, he would relinquish work and choose food.

But sometimes people feel no taste in eating and eat only because it is necessary, for otherwise the body would not persist and they would not be able to work.

Why do they need to work? It is because they derive satisfaction from the work. In the work, they find a good taste because they see that they are doing something, whereas in eating, they feel no taste. This happens because of some illness or old age, as our sages said, "There is no flavor in an old man."

Likewise, in the work of the Creator, eating is called Torah. There are those who eat in order to have the strength to work, or work in order to be able to eat, meaning to taste the taste of Torah. If they see that they still have no understanding in the Torah, they must learn Torah as a *Segula* [virtue/remedy/cure], meaning that through the power of the Torah they will have the strength to work, since "the light in it reforms him."

It follows that he eats from the Torah in order to have strength to work. Accordingly, he then works in order to be rewarded with eating, meaning to understand the Torah, as in the flavors of Torah. And if he still finds no taste in it, he learns Torah in order to be able to work. It follows that the Torah is only a means to be able to work, while work is the main thing. And sometimes, the Torah is the main thing—when one is rewarded with the flavors of the Torah.

74- Father and Mother

"Father gives the white." The male brings down the vessels of reception of *Behina Dalet* [Fourth Phase], called "self-love." "Mother gives the red." The female gives the *Kelim* [vessels]. However, they are vessels of bestowal.

It follows that it is impossible to obtain vessels of bestowal prior to deciding that the vessels of reception are unfit to use. That is, it is impossible to obtain vessels of bestowal, which is the love of the Creator, before we know that self-love is wrong, that it is forbidden to use these *Kelim*.

Conversely, the order of the work of the general public is that in addition to self-love, they want to add love of the Creator. But these two matters cannot be in the same carrier, so they must remain in self-love and do not achieve love of the Creator. Instead, it is ascending and descending.

75- The Work of the Greatest in the Nation

Baal HaSulam made it so that if an ordinary person follows his way, he can achieve *Dvekut* [adhesion] with the Creator just like a dedicated wise disciple. Before him, one had to be a great wise disciple in order to be rewarded with *Dvekut* with the Creator. Before the Baal Shem Tov, one even had to be among the greatest in the world, or he would not be able to attain Godliness.

76- The Works Go Up

When we walk on the path of bestowal, nothing of one's good deeds remains with him. Instead, everything goes up, as it is written in *The Zohar*, the acts of fear and love fly to the world, go up. Conversely, an act in *Lo Lishma* [not for Her sake], remains below, meaning that at that time a person feels he has a possession of Torah and good deeds.

77- Greeks Have Gathered Around Me

"Greeks have gathered around me, then in the days of the Hasmoneans."

The Greeks are the *Klipa* [shell/peel] opposite from the *Kedusha* [holiness]. *Kedusha* is the quality of faith above reason, and the Greeks go explicitly within reason. The Greeks come specifically in the days of the Hasmoneans, meaning right when one wants to walk on the path of *Kedusha*. Before this, there is no room for the Greeks because "God has made them one opposite the other." This is the meaning of "Anyone who is greater than his friend, his inclination is greater than him" (*Sukkah* 52).

This is as it is written, "He who comes to purify is aided" (*Shabbat* 104a). Why is one not assisted from above before he comes? The answer is that before he comes to purify himself of his vessels of reception, although he believes that the Creator helps, as our sages said, "Man's inclination overcomes him every day, and unless the Creator helps him, he cannot overcome it" (*Kidushin* 30b), and one must believe that this is so, but within reason, he sees that man does everything anyhow.

But one who comes to purify himself of vessels of reception sees that it is not within man's power. Rather, there needs to be a miracle from above, and if this miracle does not happen, he is lost. He sees this within reason—that he needs assistance from above—and within reason, there is no way that he will emerge from the control of the will to receive.

It follows that when one wants to walk on the path of *Kedusha* [holiness], the Greeks come and ask as it is written, "Why should the nations say, 'Where is their God?'" At that time, it is forbidden to answer within reason, but rather above reason, meaning that only the Creator, who is above our reason, for He created our reason, He can answer all the "Where?" questions that they ask.

We see that on Shabbat [Sabbath], in the *Kedusha* of *Keter* [part of a prayer], the ARI says there that in the word "Where?" shines the light of Shabbat, which is called *Mochin de Haya*, for precisely over the above reason over the Greeks, when we hear the "Where?" comes the answer of the light of Shabbat, which shines and cancels all the judgments, as it is written, "And the Judgments are removed from her."

It follows that through Greece, meaning the *Klipa* [shell/peel] of Greece, who go according to reason, we descend into the abyss and it is impossible to rise, as it is written, "I have drowned in the abyss of Greece" (Psalms 69), and only from above is it possible to lift up.

78- *The War of the Inclination*

The war of the inclination is internal and external. It is like a boxing match, where each one wants the other to surrender. In other words, he does not want to kill the other. At that time, the war is without clothing, but a war of strength: The one with more strength subdues the other.

Likewise, in the war of the inclination, there is no need to kill it. Rather, as our sages said, "One should not pray that the wicked will die, but that they will repent" (*Berachot* 10), meaning that it will surrender under the rule of the good inclination.

79- What Is Handsome In the Work?

The soul, which is a part of God above, is captive among the nations. That is, every person is a small world and consists of the seventy nations of the world, and they all govern his soul, which is called "a point in the heart." For this reason, "If you go"—to an optional war, which is the place to reveal the intention to bestow, for through the war appears the point in the heart.

This is the meaning of the words, "And the Lord your God delivers them into your hands and you take them away captive." That is, the point in the heart was captive among the nations of the world, so you would prevail over the nations of the world and liberate her.

She must undergo the explained corrections before you take her in order to bestow, or she will return to her captivity among the nations, meaning she will depart. This is regarded as the nations governing the daughter of Israel. That is, we do not see the beauty, but on the contrary, we see that the beauty is in the nations. In other words, if a person is poor in knowledge of *Kedusha* [holiness], it covers the daughter of Israel, meaning the soul of Israel.

80- Man's Receptions

We should distinguish seven manners in man's receptions, and in each manner there are special conditions:

1) Reception of charity,

2) Reception of a gift,

3) Reception by acquisition with money,

4) Reception by exchange,

5) Reception of a salary for work,

6) Reception by a return of a debt,

7) Reception of a loan.

Concerning "reception by a return of a debt," we should discern not necessarily the debt that comes to him from the borrower, but also the harm, for one who does harm must pay the one whom he damaged in how he damaged him. Concerning an acquisition, we should discern that one receives an object in return for money or in an exchange, unlike charity or a gift, where there is no return.

The drawback about charity is that one is ashamed when he receives it and would be happy if he did not have to receive the charity. Nevertheless, he bargains.

Conversely, a receiver of a gift is happy when he receives it, but the drawback is that he does not bargain, saying, "Give me a greater gift," since usually, we measure a gift and the greatness of the gift according to the greatness of its giver. With charity, however, the measurement is the greatness of the object, regardless of the greatness of the giver.

One who receives one's debt has no consideration of the giver or the object. Rather, if he returns his debt to him without any profits, he is content. Otherwise, if there is something more than he has given him, it is considered interest, which is forbidden in the Torah.

One who receives by exchange, the two things may not be of equal value in the market, but if one needs what the other has, and the other needs what the first one has, we cannot say that one deceived the other because the need for the matter determines and not the value of the object.

An object might be of little value in the market, but he needs it, so he agrees wholeheartedly to be given it because of the need of the owner for this object. In other words, the necessity is involved in evaluating the object.

Purchase through exchange, as Rabbi Yitzhak of Berditchev wrote, is when one gives the Creator iniquities, sins, and transgressions in return for forgiveness, absolution, and atonement. These are *Kli* [vessel] and light, since there cannot be forgiveness if there is no iniquity.

A person who receives an object or money should distinguish whether he enjoys the reception, meaning if he would be happier if he did not need to receive. This pertains to one who receives charity or a loan. This is not so in reception of a gift, returning of a debt, salary for work, or reception by acquisition.

With an exchange, it can be said that he would be happier if he did not need the exchange, but would have everything in his possession and would not need his friend, who gave him the object in the exchange.

Likewise, we should discern in the reception of a person and not in the reception of an object of a person, such as when welcoming guests, greeting a person, or welcoming a sage.

In welcoming a sage, the person enjoys. In welcoming guests there is already labor, since he must serve them, which he does only because it is a *Mitzva* [commandment], and also because "welcome every person with a bright face." Also, the body does not always enjoy it, since sometimes a person that he cannot stand comes over to him, and yet he must welcome him with a bright face.

In the work, faith is called "charity." A person would be happy if he had knowledge. A gift is called "Torah," called "knowledge," and from this a person enjoys. However, a gift must not be requested, since a gift is given to one we love. Hence, after the faith, when one comes to love the Creator, he receives from the Creator the Torah, which is called a "gift."

The Torah is also called "possession," for it is a payment for the labor, as it is written, "If you labored and found, believe" (*Megillah* 6b). The labor was that he wanted only to bestow in a manner of faith, and by this he later found the gift, since the exertion he made in order to acquire the Torah is like money that is paid for something that is bought through acquisition with money.

81- Against Your Will You Live; Against Your Will You Die

"Against your will you live." If a person does not want to receive life for himself, then he is alive.

"Against your will you die." If a person does not want to die, as our sages said, "The wicked in their lives are called 'dead,'" the more he does not want to be wicked, the more he is dead. That is, he achieves recognition of evil, which is called "dead." Otherwise, he is in the life of the wicked.

82- A Horse to Ride On

The fathers are the *Merkava* [chariot/structure], as it is written, "And the Lord rose above Abraham." The horse thinks that the owner gives it all its needs because he loves it like his sons. So why are the sons at home while it is in the stable? It is because it will make the house dirty. This is why the owner places it outside the house in its designated place.

However, the fact that the owner provides for the horse's needs is not because of love, but in order for the horse to serve it. Otherwise, he would not pay attention to the horse.

The lesson is that when a person feels that he is the owner of the body, he tells the body, "I give you everything you need not because I love you. Rather, I give you everything so that you can serve the Creator. Everything that you receive is only to the extent that I can aim that it will benefit the Creator. Otherwise, I would not receive anything for you."

This is the meaning of the *Masach* [screen] and *Ohr Hozer* [reflected light], when we receive all the pleasures to the extent that it benefits the Creator. This is called "in order to bestow."

83- A Prayer for Life and Nourishments

Our sages asked, "If we need life and nourishments, we should pray for nourishments because nourishments are given to those who are alive" (*Taanit* 8b). "Life" is called "necessity," meaning faith. "Nourishments" are the flavors of Torah and *Mitzvot* [commandments], called "commandment of the upper one."

When we pray for the commandment of the upper one, we give faith, since it is forbidden to teach Torah to idol-worshippers, as it is written, "He did not do so for any nation and they did not know the judgments" (*Hagiga* 13a).

In other words, when one should ask for life and for nourishments, one should ask for nourishments, since nourishments can be given only to the living. Faith is called "life." Nourishments are called "Torah." One should ask that the Creator will open his heart in the Torah, and then he will have faith anyhow, since the Torah is given only to the quality of Israel, and Israel are those who have faith in the Creator.

84- Touching the *Tefillin* [Phylacteries]

"One should touch the *Tefillin* so as not to get distracted."

It seems as though it would be better for distraction if he looked at the *Tefillin*. However, distraction means that we should remember that the *Tefillin* are a *Segula* [remedy/power], and touching is called "an act." Action is called "faith," which is the opposite of reason; it is against reason.

85- Observing Torah Only in the Land of Israel

The Torah in its entirety is found only in the land of Israel (*The Zohar, Haazinu*).

There is the quality of "desert," "settlement," "world," and "land of Israel." This means that all the *Mitzvot* [commandments] can be observed even when one is abroad, meaning even though he has not entered the *Kedusha* [holiness] of the land of Israel, called "kingdom of heaven." However, the *Mitzvot* of fear and love cannot be observed abroad, since before one has the kingdom of heaven, he can observe only by compulsion, and not out of love and of one's own volition.

86- The Degree of "Wicked"

"And to the wicked, God said, 'Why do you need My book of laws?'" "The world was created only for the [complete] righteous ... and the complete wicked." To the complete wicked, when he feels, he is using the 613 *Eitin* [Aramaic: counsels], which are *Mitzvot* [commandments]. To the righteous—613 *Pekudin* [Aramaic: deposits].

87- Jerusalem

Jeru-Salem: "Fear" means a lack, which is the reason for fear. "Complete fear" is one who has no fear.

"Right" is called "whole." "Left" is called "fear," such as the "fear of Isaac."

Making the middle line is both together, meaning when they unite, it becomes joined—Jeru [from the word *Yiraa* (fear)] Salem [from the word *Shalem* (complete)].

"They have eyes and do not see" is right, whole. Wherever you turn, it should be to the right, *Hesed*.

88- The War Against Amalek

"And it came to pass that when Moses raised his hands, Israel prevailed." They asked, "Do Moses' hands make war?" Answer: "When Israel look up, they prevail" (*Rosh Hashanah* 29a).

Interpretation: "Looking up" means to bestow. "Looking" means seeing that the matter is fine, as it is written about Joseph and Benjamin, "And I shall cast my eyes," meaning watch over him and benefit him.

It is as Nachmanides wrote, that when looking toward the heaven, when wanting to please the heaven, called "in order to bestow," it means "This one rises." In other words, if everything is for the sake of the Creator, Amalek, which is the will to receive, falls, when they look up and enslave their hearts to their Father in heaven.

89- Joy and Fear

It is written, "Serve the Lord with gladness," "Serve the Lord with fear."

When a person comes to pray for a lack of spirituality, he should be happy that now he realizes that what he needs is spirituality, for previously, he was as an unconscious patient. Afterward, there is room to pray, and then he should have fear.

90- The Difference between Money and Honor

Kesef [money/silver] comes from the lower one, who *Kosef* [yearns] and exerts to obtain what he wants. Honor does not depend on the lower one. Rather, it comes from outside of him, as in our world, when people understand that they should respect him.

Hence, once a person has money, it is time to work for honor.

When one begins to yearn for the nearness of the Creator, that the Creator will bring him closer, although he is repeatedly rejected by the Creator, he should believe that all the disturbances come from the Creator, and yet he does not rest, like a child asking something of his father.

Likewise, when a person yearns for the Creator, although he is ejected, every time he stands up after his fall, he begins to pray once more to be brought closer.

Afterward, the Creator gives him the honor, which settles a *Kli* [vessel] of *Kesef* [silver/money]. That is, the Creator gives him the light of Torah, for "The Lord's candle is man's soul."

It follows that *Kesef* is an awakening from below, and honor is an awakening from above.

91- All Bitter Herb [*Maror*]

At the time of redemption, one feels that the exile was all bitter. But before the redemption, we still cannot know that the exile is so bitter. This is the meaning of "As the advantage of the light from within the darkness." When we see the light, we can see the darkness. This is the meaning of "If there is no knowledge (for reason is still in exile), from where is there distinction?"

92- Old and New

Old *Kelim* [vessels] that were broken, if the cause of the shattering is vessels of reception, you will be careful next time, meaning you will receive new *Kelim* to work in order to bestow.

93- A King Who Breaks through a Fence

"A king breaks through a fence and no one protests against him." "A King" is the Creator. "Breaks through a fence" is that which separates between reception and bestowal. "No one protests against him" means that the body, called the "will to receive," surrenders.

94- A Groom Is Akin to a King

A groom is akin to a king in that his iniquities are absolved. In that, he is akin to a king, meaning he has the power of bestowal. This is precisely when the groom feels that he is of inferior degree, and that he annuls before the King. At that time, he is akin to a king who has no authority. See the results from here.

95- The Kingdom of Heaven Begins with *Hesed*

"The kingdom of heaven begins with *Hesed* [mercy]," meaning covered *Hassadim* [mercies]. Memories are *Gevura*, when we know that the Creator remembers his son. *Shofarot* [pl. of *Shofar*, a ram's horn] is the middle line. *Shofar* means *Shapru* [improve] your actions. If the initial aim is to improve the actions so they are in order to bestow, we begin with *Hassadim*, and finally achieve the improvement of the actions so they are in order to bestow.

96- Affliction Precedes Mercy

"When preceding Torah to *Mitzva* [commandment], or wisdom to fear... likewise will be the redemption. If they are rewarded, they will come out with mercy... and if he does not precede mercy, they will come out in affliction, and it is good that he preceded affliction and judgment to extend mercy... according to the sorrow is the reward" (*The Zohar, Ki Tezte*, Item 52).

We should understand the following:

1) Why must there be affliction and judgment first in order to extend mercy?

2) What is the meaning of "According to the sorrow is the reward?" After all, we should work without a reward.

To understand the above, we must know what are affliction, labor, and judgment, and what is the reward that was promised, "According to the sorrow is the reward." It is known that there is no light without a *Kli* [vessel]. This means that there cannot be filling if there is no place of deficiency there. Since for the creatures to receive the delight and pleasure without shame there was a correction called "*Tzimtzum* [restriction] and concealment," where we do not feel the Creator, in order to be able to know the Creator we must obtain the vessels of bestowal. This takes a lot of work, sorrow, and labor, since by nature, we are born in vessels of reception. We cannot grasp with our minds that *Kelim* [vessels], meaning deficiencies, will work only in order to bestow and not for self-benefit.

For this reason, when we want to walk on the path of bestowal, it is called "above reason" because the mind cannot understand this. When a person wants to purify himself from vessels of reception, this is called "purity."

The question is, Who gives man the thought and desire to want to purify himself from vessels of reception? It comes to him through books and authors, when he hears and sees what they are telling him, that the life he yearns for according to the desire of his body is called "death" and not "life."

97- The Torah Must Be Received with Both Hands

It is said that we must receive the Torah with both hands. The verse says, "Long life on her right, and wealth and honor on her left."

Long life means that one should not stop the work of the Creator, but always be in *Dvekut* [adhesion] with the Creator. The reason why right is called *Hesed* [mercy] is the annulment of reality—that he wants only to bring contentment to the Creator.

Reality is interpreted in two manners: 1) in corporeality, 2) in spirituality.

"In corporeality" simply means that one is serving the Creator devotedly. In spirituality, reality means the vitality and pleasure that one feels during the work.

When one's intention is for the sake of the Creator, he wants the annulment of reality. That is, he agrees to serve the Creator without any vitality or pleasure, a complete annulment of the spiritual reality, for then it is certain that he has no reward for his work. For this reason, he is certain that he is serving the Creator only in order to bestow, which is called "the quality of *Hesed*."

Naturally, he will not be able to have any descent in his work because all the descents come because he has no pleasure or vitality, for which reason he cannot continue with his work. But if he agrees to work in such a state, and even yearns for it, he cannot have any cessation in the work. This is regarded as "long life."

By this we should interpret "My soul shall be as dust to all," meaning that his soul, the vitality clothed in him in Torah and *Mitzvot* [commandments], will be in the annulment of reality, which is regarded as "dust," completely tasteless.

"To all" means for both the Torah and the *Mitzva* [sing. of *Mitzvot*]. He agrees to come to such annulment, and one who achieves such a degree cannot have stops in serving the Creator, which is called "day," and this is regarded as long life.

"Wealth and honor on her left" is the left line. This is the meaning of the persistence of reality. Honor is called *Neshama* [soul], as it is written in *Shaar HaKavanot* about the verse, "Hence, give glory to Your people." "Wealth" is regarded as the quality of the Torah. It is as our sages said, "There is none who is poor except in knowledge" (*Nedarim* 41a). This is called "with both hands," and then the Torah is his middle line.

98- Midnight Correction

"Midnight" is called "half and half," meaning in the middle of the night. "Night" is called "darkness," and in the middle there is darkness, called "half and half," half good and half bad, meaning that the light of *Kedusha* [holiness] shines for him a little bit and he also feels a little bit like he is in the darkness. This is the time for him to mourn the ruin of the Temple in general.

And specifically, man's heart is called a "house," as it is written, "Three things broaden one's mind: a handsome woman, a handsome abode, and handsome *Kelim* [vessels]" (*Berachot* 57b). *The Zohar* interprets, "A handsome woman is his soul; a handsome abode is his heart." Man's heart is the house where he lives. It should be a house of *Kedusha* [holiness], which is to bestow upon the Creator. But this was ruined and in its stead came a structure of self-love.

99- Wholeness and Deficiency – 1

In a place of deficiency, there is a grip to the *Sitra Achra* [other side]. Hence, when criticizing, a person is deficient, and then there is a grip to the *Sitra Achra*. At that time, although one does not feel it, he is nonetheless separated.

But on the right line, when one is in a state of wholeness, there is no grip to the *Sitra Achra*. At that time, a person is in *Kedusha* [holiness]. Although it is a small degree, it is nonetheless *Kedusha*. But on the left line he is deficient and separated.

100- Faith and Reason

Adar 22, Tav-Shin-Yod-Gimel, Tel-Aviv, March 9, 1953

He asked, "Why must we draw *Hochma* [wisdom], which is knowledge, if all of our work is in faith above reason?" He answered, "If the righteous of the generation were not in the state of knowing, the whole of Israel would not be able to work in the manner of faith above reason." Specifically when the righteous of the generation extends illumination of *Hochma*, his *Daat* [reason/knowledge] illuminates in the whole of Israel.

This is like a person. If his brain understands and knows what it wants, the organs work and do not need any brains. Rather, the hand and the leg and the rest of the organs work and do what they must.

No sensible person would consider asking or saying that if the hand and the leg had brains, their work would be better. Rather, the brain does not change the organs, for the organs are evaluated according to the greatness of the brain. This means that if the brain is a great mind, all the organs are named after it and are considered great organs.

It is likewise here: If the public adheres to a true righteous, who has already been rewarded with knowledge, the public can act in faith and will have complete satisfaction, and they do not need any knowledge.

101- Faith Above Reason

For example, we learned that below *Tabur de AK* there are ten *Sefirot* of the *Sium*. In other words, as long as he says that he does not want to receive because he cannot aim in order to bestow, he has light of *Hassadim* and illumination of *Hochma*. But when a matter of reception comes into his mind, he promptly falls from the degree of *Kedusha* [holiness].

102- Good Deeds Are Called Sons

Good deeds are called "sons." Sons are also called "understanding" and "knowing." Fathers are called the "reasons" that engender the understanding. Therefore, when we engage in Torah, we want to have understanding and knowledge by engaging in Torah and *Mitzvot* [commandments].

...This is not so with righteous ... the sons of ... good deeds, as RASHI interpreted, "to teach you that the primary offshoots of the righteous are good deeds."

103- The Unification of ZON

"'And Judah approached him.' Rabbi Elazar started, 'For You are our Father, though Abraham does not know us and Israel does not recognize us; You, Lord, are our Father, our Redeemer from of old is Your name.' In the *Sulam* [Ladder commentary on *The Zohar*], 'You are our father' means *Malchut*. It means You are our root, for *Malchut* is called 'You are our root.'"

"'Abraham does not know us,' for although the existence of the world is in him, for he is the meaning of *Hesed* [mercy], as it is written, 'A world of mercy shall be built,' he did not entreat for us as he entreated for Ishmael, when he said, 'Oh that Ishmael might live before You?' 'And Israel does not recognize us ... our Redeemer from of old is Your name.'" *Malchut* is called "redeemer," and she is also called "the redeeming angel." This is the meaning of "our Redeemer from of old is Your name."

We learned that there is no cessation between redemption and prayer, and between the hand *Tefillin* and the head *Tefillin*.

Judah is called *Malchut*, a prayer. Joseph is called *Yesod*, who is the giver. For this reason, he is called "redeemer," and there is no cessation between redemption and prayer. Rather, they must be united. There must not be a stop between the hand *Tefillin*, called *Malchut*, and the head *Tefillin*, called "the giver," and we must make the unification.

104- The Prohibition to Teach a Gentile Torah

"It is forbidden to teach a gentile Torah, as was said, 'He did not do so for any nation'" (*Hagigah* 13a).

According to what Baal HaSulam interprets concerning prohibitions, wherever it is written "forbidden," it means impossible.

It follows that the prohibition to teach a gentile Torah, even if he has been circumcised but does not observe the commandments of the Torah, is that he cannot learn Torah.

The thing is that there is Torah and there is wisdom.

105- Blessed Is Our God, Who Has Created Us for His Glory

One thanks the Creator when the Creator gives him that feeling and he can work in this way, meaning that everything he does is to increase the glory of heaven, and not for his own sake.

106- The Ruin of *Kedusha* [Holiness]

One should pray for the ruin of the Temple, that the *Kedusha* is ruined and in lowliness, and no one pays attention to this lowliness, that the *Kedusha* is placed in the earth and must be lifted from its lowliness.

In other words, each one recognizes his own benefit and knows that this is something very important and worth working for. But to bestow, this is not worthwhile. This is considered that the *Kedusha* is placed in the earth, unused and unwanted.

However, one must not ask the Creator to bring him closer to Him, as it is insolence on the part of man, for in what is he more important than others? However, when he prays for the collective—which is *Malchut*, called "assembly of Israel," the sum of the souls—that the *Shechina* [Divinity] is in the dust, and he prays that she will rise, meaning that the Creator will light up her darkness, then all of Israel will rise in degree, too, including the beseeching person, who is included in the collective.

Also, *Malchut* is regarded as inferior, meaning of inferior importance, since no one feels the importance of the matter of above reason.

107- And Golan in the Bashan
Adar 1, Tav-Shin-Zayin, February 21, 1947

Bashan comes from the word *Busha* [shame]. *Golan* comes from *Geula* [redemption]. That is, through the shame we are redeemed.

"The Hermon and the Tavor will sing." *Tavor* comes from the word *Vatar*, as in "the mountains of Vatar" (Song of Songs 2). *Harim* [mountains] are called *Hirhurim* [reflections], meaning thoughts that come to a person. *Vatar* comes from the verse, "and he cut them in the *Tavech* [middle]" (Genesis 15:10), where through reflections, they are cut in two, the head from the neck, and then the body loses its life.

108- Man Determines

It is man who determines the form, whether it is good or bad. That is, if the suffering comes to mitigate him, it is called "good." But if he does not say this sincerely, he feels them as suffering.

109- The Reason Why People Go to the Graves of the Patriarchs

Once, Baal HaSulam went to Hebron before he moved to Tel-Aviv. When he returned from the Cave of Machpelah, he said why people go to the graves of the patriarchs: It is to say, "When will my deeds come to be as my fathers' deeds?"

110- The Path of Torah

The path of suffering is when a person suffers. The path of Torah is when he can depict to himself the suffering he experienced, and then his benefit is that he does not need new suffering.

111- Nothing New Under the Sun

"There is nothing new under the sun." "Novelty" means something new, which did not exist until now. "Under the sun" is not regarded as a novelty, since it is natural that one must work for one's own sake. Above the sun, which is above reason, is novelty, as it is against nature.

112- Returning a Theft

"He shall return the theft that he had robbed." A "robbery" is when he receives by force, against the giver's will. The upper one wants the lower one to receive only when he pays in return, meaning so the seller will enjoy. In corporeality, he gives him money, and in spirituality, a reward is called "in order to bestow." This is the meaning of "returning," when everything he had received in order to receive is corrected into working in order to bestow.

113- The Old Man Looks for Fear of Heaven

"Before I lose, I search." That is, the old man who walks always looks at the ground, as though searching for something (*Shabbat* 152).

We should understand what this comes to tell us. An old man is one who has acquired wisdom. Before he loses the fear of heaven, he searches in the earth, for earth is an intimation of the fear of heaven. He does not wait until he loses his fear of heaven, and then he searches, but rather "The wise sees the future" and searches in advance.

114- Three Partners

"There are three partners in man: the Creator, his father, and his mother" (*Kiddushin* 30b).

"Right" is called "father," who gives the white. Man should give an awakening from below, since this is the *Kli* [vessel], meaning the lack. This is the meaning of "As the advantage of the light from within the darkness." Mother gives the red, meaning the "left," meaning a red light, when we see that we cannot walk on this path. This is called "the left rejects," when he sees that he is being rejected from the path of reaching the Creator.

Conversely, "The right pulls near," when he believes that he can walk, and he is content with whatever grip he has on *Kedusha* [holiness], and he thanks the Creator.

When he has "right" and "left" and he sees the distance between them, he comes to the state of "essence," when he comes only to purify. However, he cannot. At that time, the Creator gives the soul, and then he achieves the degree of "man."

115- The Meaning of "Torah Lishma [for Her Sake]"

"If he is rewarded, the Torah *Lishma* [for Her sake] becomes to him a potion of life" (*Yoma* 72b). That is, he tastes the flavor of Torah, which is regarded as "life." "If he is not rewarded, it becomes to him a potion of death." In other words, he feels the taste of death in the work of bestowal.

116- Who Are the Wicked?

The wicked are those who cannot say that they have an order of good and doing good.

117- The Light in It Reforms Him

This means that when one engages in Torah and *Mitzvot* [commandments] and does not feel good, the light in it reforms him so he will feel good. That is, when he feels bad, he cannot thank the One who reforms him, so he can be thankful for being happy.

118- Except for "Leave!"

Man is but a guest, and the Creator is the Host. It is known that our sages said, "Anything that the landlord tells you, do," for so is the custom, "except for 'Leave!'" This is so because when one leaves the domain of the landlord, he is no longer his host, so as to listen to His voice.

119- From *Lo Lishma* to *Lishma*

There must always be a beginning; otherwise, it is impossible to achieve *Lishma* [for Her sake]. That is, one must believe that in all the corporeal lusts, meaning eating, drinking, and the rest of the lusts, as well as in pleasures found in learning external teachings, control, vengeance, and so forth, as it is written in general, "Envy, lust, and honor take a person out of the world," in those pleasures there is nothing more than a thin light, as *The Zohar* says.

Conversely, great lights are deposited in Torah and *Mitzvot* [commandments], unlike corporeal pleasures, in which only sparks of the light of *Kedusha* fell.

Hence, *Klipot* [shells/peels] give one an awakening to enter *Kedusha* because they want to be rewarded with great lights. This is called *Lo Lishma* [not for Her sake]. Afterward, from this *Lo Lishma*, he can be rewarded with *Lishma*.

120- Joy that Comes from Dancing

In corporeality, we see that raising the feet off the ground implies vitality, for *Raglayim* [legs] imply *Meraglim* [spies], who went to tour the land. They went to see if it was worthwhile to make an effort to be rewarded with the land of *Kedusha* [holiness]. Within reason, there are always views that are opposite from *Kedusha*, but we need to believe above reason that it is a land flowing with milk and honey.

Therefore, when lifting the feet off the ground and going above reason, there can be joy, even though there are ups and downs.

However, the broken is not more than the standing; rather, the ascents and descents change rapidly, so the periods of joy never go away.

121- Two Forces within Man

Man detects two forces in the world: 1) The rejecting force, so one will move from the state he is in. 2) The attracting force, which draws a person, for which reason he must move from the state he is in.

The rejecting force is called "suffering." The fact that he suffers in the state he is in makes him leave that place and go look for a place where he can enjoy life.

The pulling force is called "pleasure." If a person sees that there is a place that if he went there he would receive more pleasure than he has in this place, although he has pleasures here, if he sees that he can enjoy life more in another place, he leaves his place and goes there.

However, one force is not enough, since there is a possibility where he will be dissatisfied with the situation he is in, but will not see where he will be better off. Our sages bring an allegory about a pigeon that had a snake under the rock and a hawk up in the sky, so where could it go? While Israel came out of Egypt, the sea was before them and Pharaoh and the Egyptians were behind them.

Sometimes we can receive more pleasure, but we must make an effort. Hence, a person is afraid to leave his place so he will not be left empty handed on either side.

But when there are the rejecting force and the pulling force, a person can move from his place. That is, when one feels suffering where he is, and believes that there is a place to go and receive pleasure, he goes forward. This is called "Turn away from evil and do good."

122- Being Rewarded with Life

"Rewarded" means that if a person says that he has a desire to learn Torah although he finds in it no flavor, still, he considers it a great privilege that he sits and delves in the book and was given a thought and desire to come to the seminary, and he thanks the Creator for this. This is called "rewarded," when he says that it is a great privilege for him.

By this, the Torah becomes to him a potion of life and he receives vitality from above.

"Not rewarded" is if he does not appreciate the fact that he could come to the seminary because he was rewarded from above and was given a thought and desire. Therefore, when he comes to learn, the Torah becomes for him a potion of death, meaning that he dies and has no vitality of the Torah. This is as it is written, "How good are your tents, Jacob, ...and I, by Your great mercy, will come into Your house."

123- Without Hands and Without Legs

It is possible to live without hands and not feel an absence, like birds. Also, it is possible to live without legs, like the snake, of whom it was said, "On your belly you shall walk." "Hands" are the *Kelim* [vessels] that obtain positivity. "Legs" are criticism and negativity. "Above reason" is without hands and without legs.

124- To Serve Me

"The whole world was created only to serve me." According to the interpretation of Baal HaSulam, it means that all the faults that a person sees in others, he believes that they are his. Therefore, he has what to correct. It follows that the whole world serves him by providing him with his faults, and he does not need to look by himself. Instead, they are doing him a big favor by providing him with his flaws.

125- Definitions – 1

The "good side" is called "support." He has what to count on, meaning he has a foundation.

The "side of the harsh judgment" means that he has no foundation on which to build the structure of the kingdom of heaven. At that time, he is in a state of "hangs the earth on nothing."

The "middle line" is the Creator, meaning that He helps.

"Grateful for the past" is the "right line," and "that which You are destined to do with me" means the "left line," which is also in the future, which is what he still does not have, which is called "a lack." And yet, he is thankful and praises as though he has already received a filling for his lack and does not stay separated during his criticism.

"Desiring mercy" means he is not looking at himself, at what he has, but looks at the Creator, at what the Creator has. The Creator has wholeness; therefore, he is serving the Whole One.

The *Kli* [vessel] in which to feel spirituality is generally called *Neshama* [soul], and the *Neshama* comprises five qualities called NRNHY.

126- Visiting the Sick

The Creator is above the sick person's head. "Sick" means his head aches, meaning foreign thoughts, and sick in his abdomen means in the vessels of reception. Also, the Creator gives the awareness that one is sick.

127- Happy Is He

"Happy is he for whom the Creator does not attribute iniquity and whose spirit does not contain deceit" (*The Zohar, Nasso*, Item 1).

That is, why should the Creator not attribute iniquity to him although he has iniquities? It is because there is no deceit in his spirit.

"Exalted" means greatness. He is not great because he has iniquities, for sometimes a person is proud; he has grievances against the Creator but thinks that he himself is fine.

This is considered that there is deceit in his spirit, that he deceives himself thinking that he is fine because he is deceiving himself. For this reason, with pride he pretends to be observing Torah and *Mitzvot* [commandments], and by keeping the covenant, he then feels as though he did not circumcise himself at all.

128- Exalt the Lord Our God

"Exalt the Lord our God and bow before His holy mountain, for the Lord our God is holy."

"Exalt" means that if one wants to know the exaltedness and greatness of the Creator, we can obtain this only through *Dvekut* [adhesion] and equivalence of form. Thus, what is "equivalence of form" and how does one achieve equivalence of form?

"Bow before His holy mountain." Bowing means surrendering. It is when one lowers his reason and says that what the reason understands or does not understand, I annul and subjugate it. Before which quality do I subjugate it? Before "His holy mountain."

Har [mountain] means *Hirhurim* [reflections], meaning thoughts. "His holy," for "holy" means separated from the matter. This means that he removes himself from the desire of reception. "Bow" means submitting the body, even though it disagrees, and taking upon oneself only thoughts of *Kedusha* [holiness]. This is the meaning "Bow before His holy mountain."

Why must we submit ourselves to thoughts of *Kedusha*, meaning retire from receiving in order to receive? It is because "The Lord our God is holy," for the Creator only bestows. For this reason, one must be in equivalence of form with the Creator, and by this we can obtain the exaltedness of the Creator. Afterward, we can achieve the attainment of the exaltedness of the Lord our God.

129- Knowledge and Faith

Man works and toils in order to keep the laws of the nourishments of the body whether knowingly or unknowingly, since the reward and punishment are revealed. For this reason, even if a person does not feel the taste of eating or drinking, such as when he is sick, he still forces himself to eat and drink, even though he does not enjoy these foods, since if he does not observe these laws he will be punished, and not merely punished, but will be punished by death.

This is not so with nourishments of the soul, which are Torah and *Mitzvot* [commandments]. When one does not find flavor in them, he cannot observe them by force. Rather, to the extent that he believes in reward and punishment, to that extent he observes them. However, the reward and punishment are not revealed to the person, but the nourishments of the soul depend on faith and the measure of faith, and a person cannot always go with faith. Conversely, when the reward and punishment are known, they are strong and clear, and it cannot be said that he has ascents and descents.

130- The Testimony of the Creator

"The testimony of the Creator makes the unwise wise." If a person knows that he is not wise, the Torah makes him wise.

The meaning of "The teaching of the Lord is whole" is that sometimes a person learns Torah, but is the intention that this is the teaching of the Creator, meaning that the whole Torah is His names?

There is the Torah of the Creator, meaning that the whole Torah speaks only of His holy names, since there is the *PARDESS* [*Peshat* (literal), *Remez* (implied), *Drush* (interpreted), *Sod* (secret)] in the Torah, that everything was given from the Creator's mouth through Moses. However, the three qualities that are *Peshat*, *Remez*, and *Drush*, His dresses, are of matters of people, meaning what one must observe.

Yes, *Sod* is that which the Creator must reveal. This is called "The secrets of Torah are revealed to him," pertaining only to the holy names. When a person wants to be rewarded with "The Torah of the Creator is whole," meaning that it includes *PARDESS*, when he feels that he is in a state of "unwise," for this reason, the answer comes—the testimony of the Creator.

In other words, the testimony, when the Creator testifies that he has "The Torah of the Creator is whole," is if he has been rewarded with "makes the unwise wise." That is, where he was previously unwise, he is then rewarded with wisdom.

Baal HaSulam said the true meaning of "unwise." It is as our sages said, "Who is unwise, let him come here—this is Moses," pertaining to faith. That is, one who walks on the path of faith is called "unwise," as it is considered that he is walking on the path of *Lishma* [for Her sake], and then the secrets of Torah are revealed to him.

131- See a Life with a Woman that You Love

This means that one should include life from the tree of life, which is *Zeir Anpin*, in this place, which is *Malchut*, who is called a "woman." One without the other, *Zeir Anpin* without *Malchut*, does not work. One should include the quality of day in the night, since life, which is illumination of *Hochma*, is present only on *Malchut*.

Explanation: A "woman" means the kingdom of heaven. "That you love" means that the acceptance of the kingdom of heaven should be as it is written, "And you will love the Lord your God." "Day" is called "right line," which is "For he desires mercy," and he is content with his share, and "night" means a deficiency. "Know-Him" means that all the work is to unify the *HaVaYaH*.

132- Upper and Lower

Kelim [vessels] of one who acquires, and *Kelim* of one who gives. The upper one is the one who gives, and the lower one is the one who acquires. The *Masach* [screen] of the lower one that he has in the *Eynaim* [eyes] is called "shutting of the eyes," so he sees that the upper one, too, has not more than *Galgalta* and *Eynaim*. It follows that the *Masach* of the lower one covers the upper one.

When the upper one gives the *Masach* that covers the upper one from the lower one, meaning he removes the *Masach* from himself and leaves it with the lower one, by this the lower one acquires *Gadlut* [adulthood/greatness].

It follows that the *Masach* and concealment of the upper one, which he left in the lower one, at that time the lower one sees that there is no concealment whatsoever on the upper one. He asks, Who made the concealment before? It is only the upper one himself. This is considered that the upper one gives the *Masach* to the lower one. He sees this now that the upper one has removed from himself the concealment of his importance.

133- It Is All Corrections

"All the illnesses that I had placed on Egypt, I will not place on you, for I the Lord am your healer" (Exodus 15:26).

Our sages ask, "If I do not place the illness, what is the need for a healer?" (Sanhedrin 101a).

We should interpret that since I am the healer, why should I place on you an illness if I must heal the illness? What do I gain by placing an illness? It must be as a punishment, and if I must heal the illness, what kind of punishment is it? It is as though I work for nothing.

For this reason, I will not place illness upon you, and what you think is illness, you are wrong about it. Rather, all the states you feel, if you attribute them to Me, are all corrections by which you will approach Me in *Dvekut* [adhesion].

134- Repentance Does Not Help in GAR

When the light shines in the *Kelim* [vessels], there is no difference between the light and the *Kli* [vessel]. When the light departs, the difference becomes apparent.

Therefore, when rewarded with repentance from love, the sins become merits because the upper light shines to all the *Kelim*, meaning to all the actions that have been done. It follows that all the actions become *Kelim* for the light. Thus, even the sins become merits, meaning *Kelim* to receive the upper light.

This is so because the sins come only from the vessels of reception in order to receive. When one repents, meaning corrects them to work in order to bestow, they become *Kelim* for installing the abundance.

Accordingly, what our sages said in several places, that "repentance does not help," becomes perplexing. After all, there is a rule that nothing stands before repentance.

However, wherever our sages said, "Repentance does not help," it refers to a place where he cannot repent, for he can receive in order to bestow only in VAK de Hochma. But in GAR, repentance does not help, meaning that he cannot receive in order to bestow because the GAR cannot illuminate prior to the end of correction.

135- Righteous Take by Force

There are three manners in reception: 1) receiving charity, 2) receiving a gift, 3) receiving by force, meaning demanding because he deserves it.

1) In charity, one is ashamed when receiving charity, but a person demands although he is ashamed.

2) With a gift, it is not customary to ask for a present. Rather, a present is given without a demand from the receiver. Instead, it is customary to give gifts to those we love.

3) Demanding by force, meaning he is not ashamed to ask. Under which discernment can we categorize this? When demanding charity, we are ashamed. We also cannot attribute this to a gift because one does not ask for a gift.

Instead, when one comes to ask for something big, such that he does not aim for his own benefit, but for the sake of the giver, this is not a charity because it is not for his own sake. Hence, there is no shame here. It is also not like a present because it is not for his own sake. Therefore, he can ask and not be ashamed when receiving.

Hence, this is not similar to charity, which is why it is called "reception of the righteous," who take by force, meaning like a debt that they deserve from the purpose of creation, which is to do good to His creations. This is the meaning of "Paying a debt is a commandment."

136- The Binding of Isaac

The binding of Isaac, when Abraham, who is the right line, which is above reason, tied the left line, which is the mind that criticizes everything, it gave him a general picture of the situation he was in. He left all the "left" and took upon himself the quality of "right," which is above reason. By this he was later rewarded with the middle line.

That is, there is a difference between receiving the right line before he sees the left line, to a state where he renews the right line after he has seen the state of the left. "Right," which is above reason, is called "devotion," since he cancels all the reason he acquired from the left line and goes above reason, and then he is rewarded with the middle line.

137- The Lack Is the *Kli* [Vessel]

The lack is the most important, and it is called a *Kli* [vessel] to receive the filling. The amount of the filling is measured by the size of the lack.

It follows that if there is the exact same filling, not more and not less, yet one enjoys the filling and is delighted and happy and cannot find words to express his joy, while the other feels that he has no pleasure whatsoever with which to sustain his soul, and sometimes feels as though he is fed up with life itself because he does not feel any purpose in his life.

For example, a healthy man, whose body is well and all his organs are healthy and well, yearns to receive delight and pleasure so he will have something with which to sustain his soul with some pleasure, but he does not succeed.

At the same time, another person is suffering from some illness and the doctors decided that he needs an operation but they do not know if the operation will succeed and his very life is in danger. He has seen several experts but they did not make any promises that he will be able to go on living.

And then, a wise man came and gave him a cure that helped him. Later, when he came to the doctors to do tests for his illness, they determined that he was completely well and there was nothing wrong with him. Clearly, at that time he is delighted and cannot say that he has nothing from which to derive vitality. Instead, his joy is immense.

At the same time, the first one, although he is healthy, he cannot receive vitality from his health because he does not have a *Kli* of lack of health. Hence, this filling gives him no vitality.

The question is, Is the filling that delights him true or is it imaginary?

138- A Near Road and a Faraway Road

Dvekut [adhesion] is called "life," *Kedusha* [holiness]. "Separation," meaning self-reception, is called "death," separation from the Life of Lives. Also, separation from the *Kedusha* is regarded as *Tuma'a* [impurity].

The question, "Why are we removed?" concerns one who was impure in his soul. The Creator's answer was both on one whose soul is impure, as well as on one who was on a faraway road.

A road that is near to *Kedusha* is when he walks on the path of bestowal. The "faraway road" is when he sees that he is walking on the path of reception, which removes him from *Kedusha*.

"Impure for man's soul" means that when they come to the recognition of evil, they cry out, "Why are we removed?" But the general public does not feel that they are impure for the soul of man. Rather, all their passions concern the body, and with respect to the soul, they do not feel that they are deficient of anything.

Therefore, they are pure, since impure and pure are in one's feeling. A person may be sick, but if he does not feel the illness, he does not go to the doctor to be cured. It follows that in his feeling, he is well although in truth, he is not.

It depends with respect to whom it should be true.

139- A Foot and a Shoe

"How beautiful are your feet in shoes" (*The Zohar, Hukat*). A shoe is on one's foot. We should discern between feet and shoes. In corporeality, the shoes keep the feet from harm. Otherwise, if there are no shoes on the feet when we step on the ground, sometimes there are harmful things that harm a person.

In the work, *Raglaim* [legs] are regarded as *Meraglim* [spies] who go to spy on the holy land—whether it is worthwhile to work and labor in order to enter the holy land. Since the legs come in contact with the outer ones, meaning with external views that remove a person from entering the servitude of the Creator, the correction is *Naalayim* [shoes], from the word *Man'ul* [lock], which closes the thoughts and desires that the spies bring him.

This shoe, called "faith above reason," when he says, "They have eyes but they will not see; they have ears but they will not hear," then it is said, "How beautiful are your feet in shoes," meaning that if there are no feet, it cannot be said that he is wearing shoes. Thus, it requires both feet and shoes, and then it is regarded as beautiful.

140- The Difference between Envy and Lust

The author of the book *Resheet Hochma* (in "Gate of Humbleness," Chapter 7) brings an allegory: There is a story about one who was greedy (meaning he coveted everything he saw), and one who was jealous (who was always jealous of what others had, even though he did not need it, but why does the other one have it?).

They were walking together. The king met them along the way and said to them, "One of you will ask me for something and I will give it to him, but then I will give the other one twice as much as I have given the first." The greedy one wanted both parts, so he did not want to ask first. The other one also did not want to ask first because he would be jealous of the other if he received twice what he was given.

In the end, the greedy persuaded the jealous to ask first. What did the jealous one do? He requested that one of his own eyes would be poked out, so that the other one would receive twice as much, and both his eyes would be poked out.

This is the difference between envy and lust.

141- The Spirit of the Wise Is Displeased with Him

Spirit is called "the spirit of the wise," which shines in the *Kelim* [vessels] of above reason, called *Hassadim* [mercies]. Hence, when one should receive the spirit of the wise, it is displeased with him. That is, it is not according to their spirit and they want to receive the quality of the wise and not the spirit of the wise. In other words, they want to receive within reason.

However, to receive the spirit of the wise, which is that *Hochma* [wisdom] will clothe in *Hassadim*, which is called "the spirit of the wise," they cannot tolerate. This is called "The spirit of the wise is displeased with him."

Although the literal meaning of "The spirit of the wise is displeased with him" means that it is not a good thing, since the wise say that it is wrong, but in the work, we can interpret that "The spirit of the wise is pleased with him" is above reason, whereas "displeased" is when people want to receive everything within reason.

142- The Sorrow of the *Shechina* [Divinity] – 1

The sorrow of the *Shechina*: a king who has a tower filled with abundance but no guests, like one who held a wedding for his son and ordered hundreds of courses, but now he has no guests, for no one wants to come and enjoy the tower.

This is the sorrow of the *Shechina*.

143- The Need for Recognition of Evil

Why do we need recognition of evil, that we are submerged in the mud, unable to come out? This is the allegory. It is all because we must be very thankful. But there is a difference in how He helped him. To the extent of the favor that he received, so he comes to love Him and adhere to Him and can work for Him because He is great and ruling.

That is, the greatness of the Creator becomes evident to a person precisely if He made for him a great miracle. To the extent of the miracle, so the love awakens and His greatness is seen by His ability to help him out of the great trouble. Conversely, the spies said, "The Landlord cannot save His vessels." This is the meaning of the verse, "From the narrow place I called on the Lord; answer me in the broad space, Lord," meaning specifically when one is in a state of trouble.

144- Revealed and Concealed

The Torah divides into two manners: The practice of *Mitzvot* [commandments], which are the revealed part, a visible act. And there is a part of the Torah that is called "hidden," which is unseen. That part of the Torah belongs to the general public, but the part of the Torah that is unrelated to practices is called "hidden" and belongs only to the thought and the desire, meaning the mind and the heart.

145- Passion for Knowledge

The passion for knowledge comes to those who act in order to know, who exert themselves and delve as much as they can. These actions give him the passion to know the Torah. By this, a *Kli* [vessel] forms within him, which is a desire and yearning. However, the knowledge itself comes from above and a person cannot assist the knowledge; he can only assist the *Kli* through the effort to know.

146- Suffering and Joy

Suffering is left line, when a person examines whether his actions are on the path of truth, in order to bestow. At that time, he sees all of his faults. This is called "suffering," meaning that it pains him that he is so weak about bestowal.

At that time he sees the truth, that he is unable to do anything with the aim to bestow and has no way out of his situation, and he sees that only the Creator can help him. Therefore, then he has room for prayer, to pray to the Creator from the bottom of the heart.

When a person engages in Torah and prayer, he should observe "Serve the Lord with gladness," and then he should shift to the right line, called "wholeness."

However, one must be happy with whatever grip he has on *Kedusha* [holiness], that even one moment a day is to him a great possession, for when speaking of important matters—which are *Kedusha*, which is Torah and *Mitzvot* [commandments]—a person cannot evaluate even something small in quantity or quality.

One must be grateful to the Creator for rewarding him by giving him a thought and desire for the least thing in *Kedusha*, since he sees that he is not more worthy or important than the rest of the people, yet the Creator awarded him with this. Hence, such a state commits him to thank the Creator, meaning that this is the time to give singing and praising to the Creator.

147- The Line of the Work

One line is called "wholeness." The general public follows the one line, meaning one way. That is, each one has a part in Torah and *Mitzvot* [commandments], and each one assumes how much labor he must do in order to feel that he has done his duty.

Each one calculates if he has done as he thinks, and then he is satisfied and feels that he is walking on the path of the Creator, and each day he is advancing.

This is not so on the right line: He should do everything the same as those who walk on one line, but the difference is that those who belong to one line do not have any more deficiencies, while those who walk on the right line have difficulties because the left line cancels the right line.

The left line evokes the craving for spirituality, which makes him think that we must walk on the path of *Lishma* [for Her sake], that this is the main thing. Thus, it is hard for him to walk in *Lo Lishma* [not for Her sake], meaning he does not have the satisfaction that makes it worthwhile to go, since the left line evokes the craving and the lack for spirituality.

Conversely, the one line does not evoke any lack within him. Rather, he adds each time because he has what to look at, whereas the left line erases everything.

148- Faith Is Called "Action"

Faith is called "action" and not "intellect." And faith, when the body disagrees, it must go by force, which is above rhyme and reason, but only an act.

This is similar to feeding a child and the parents make him see that it is to his benefit although the child does not find any flavor in this. Thus, as hard as the parents try to make him understand, the child does not want to listen. At that time, the parents go by force against the child's will. That is, they deal with the child by way of action and do not wait for the child to say that he understands that it is worthwhile to eat this food.

It is likewise with faith: We should not wait for the body to agree that it is worthwhile to relinquish self-reception. Rather, we must deal with the body with action, meaning with force, although in the mind, the body disagrees with it.

149- "Land" Is the Kingdom of Heaven

"And I will also establish My covenant with them to give them the land of Canaan." Because they were circumcised, they inherited the land, as it is written, "And Your people are all righteous, they will forever inherit the land" (*The Zohar*, Vaera, Item 20).

We should ask about the connection between circumcision and land. It is written that for the circumcision, meaning because he was circumcised, they inherited the land.

The thing is that "land" is called the "kingdom of heaven," which is the instilling of the *Shechina* [Divinity]. Hence, one who is there, who threw away from himself the foreskin, called "the three impure *Klipot* [shells/peels]" that extend from the will to receive, and took upon himself the *Tzimtzum* [restriction] not to use the vessels of reception, is worthy of the instilling of the *Shechina*, called "land of Israel," meaning the "land of *Kedusha* [holiness]."

There are three discernments in meeting "this villain": draw him to the seminary, read the *Shema* reading, and remind him of the day of death.

150- A Knife for Slaughter

A "knife" is that with which one slaughters. Devotion should be the reason that there will not be any flaw. For example, one who commits suicide is because of a flaw, since he has no point in living for several reasons, and therefore he commits himself to death. Hence, we must see that when one becomes devoted, it is not because of some flaw but because of the love of the Creator. This is why we check the knife, so there will not be any flaw in it.

151- The Desire to Bestow – 1

A question: When we say that His desire is to do good to His creations, and when the creatures receive His benefit, this means that His desire is satisfied, meaning that He receives pleasure from bestowing. But we have a rule that the Creator only gives and does not receive. Thus, two interpretations go hand in hand.

Indeed, one should ask oneself the same question. How does a person, whose quality is to receive, become able to turn the vessels of reception into vessels of bestowal? After all, even when he gives, we must say that he enjoys it, or he would not bestow, since we cannot conceive doing something without reward, as anyone with some sense cannot do anything unless it yields him benefit.

Rather, "Were it not for the help of the Creator, he would not overcome it." This is a miracle above reason and is given only as a gift from the Creator. And as for the Creator, we cannot understand that there is a reality of bestowal without reception, as this is above our intellect, since our root is reception.

152- Walk Discreetly

"Walk discreetly" means that "making judgment and love of mercy" should lead one to an intention. "Intention" is called "Walk discreetly," since one cannot see one's neighbor's aim.

153- Torah with the Manner of the Land

"It is good to have Torah with the manner of the land." "Earth" is called *Malchut*. The way of *Malchut* is faith above reason. "It is good to have Torah with the manner of the land" means that if one has a point that he comes to observe the Torah with faith, otherwise he cannot achieve observance of the Torah, meaning to achieve the quality of the Torah, since it is forbidden to teach Torah to idol-worshippers.

Baal HaSulam said that in general, where it says that it is forbidden, it means that it is impossible even though we want to.

This comes from the corrections that even though he wants to transgress, he cannot.

154- Sitting in Corners

"Sitting in corners." There are wise disciples: A "corner" is called "faith," but they have not been rewarded with the Torah, since the Torah is called "profit," and faith is called "capital" [*Keren* means both "corner" and "seed money" (capital)]. We must try to be rewarded with the quality of the Torah.

155- You Have Chosen Us – 1

Man should make the choice. However, when man makes the choice, the Creator chooses the choice that man has made and gives him the abundance pertaining to his choice, as is explained, "When a woman inseminates, she delivers a male child."

156- Sanctification of the Moon

We should understand why we must sanctify specifically the moon.

It is known that sun and moon imply *Zeir Anpin* and *Malchut*. With respect to branch and root, we pray during the sanctification of the moon, "May it please Him to fill the blemish in the moon." We should understand why we should care if there is a blemish in the moon, that we are told to sanctify the moon and ask the Creator to fill her blemish. Also, what is her blemish?

From the words of our sages, "Bring upon me atonement for I have diminished the moon" (*Hulin* 60b), it is implied that the Creator sinned when He diminished the moon. We should understand what is this sin that we must correct.

The thing is that it is known that the moon implies *Malchut*, meaning the kingdom of heaven. In other words, although we should believe that "The whole earth is full of His glory," there was a *Tzimtzum* [restriction] and concealment so we do not feel it, and we must believe above reason that this is so.

Thus, it is as though the concealment that the Creator has made caused the creatures not to be able to take upon themselves the kingdom of heaven due to the concealment. But who made the concealment? It is the Creator. Hence, this is similar to the prohibition, "Do not place an obstacle before a blind man."

Indeed, why did He make the concealment? It is as Baal HaSulam interpreted, that without the concealment, it would be utterly impossible to make a choice to receive in order to bestow. Instead, all the creatures would be serving the Creator in a manner of receiving in order to receive. But since He made the concealment and *Tzimtzum*, there is room for choice, for the creatures to work in order to bestow.

It follows that if the lower ones bring an offering, meaning they offer themselves to the Creator, meaning equivalence of form, everyone sees that thanks to the concealment it was possible to achieve equivalence of form.

Thus, concealing and restricting *Malchut* was not a sin. On the contrary, only the concealment caused all this. It follows that the flaw passed away. This is the meaning of what he said, "Bring upon me atonement," for atonement comes from the word "bad," "to wipe My hand on that man," meaning that all the flaw was erased.

Therefore, it follows that when we sanctify the moon it is that through the flaw and concealment it became possible to begin to work in order to bestow. Thus, the concealment enters the *Kedusha* [holiness]. It follows that this is not regarded as a flaw and a lack but is regarded as a correction. This is called "the sanctification of the moon," and by this the blemish is filled, meaning that we see that it was not a blemish whatsoever.

157- What Comes First—the Blessing or the Peace?

The blessing comes first but it does not hold. Hence, the blessing departed from him. For this reason, he must use the blessing so there will be peace, meaning so there will not be disparity of form. Thus, each time he receives a blessing, he should use the blessing to be rewarded with peace, for peace is called "equivalence of form."

When he has equivalence of form, called "peace," then when the blessing comes he will be able to exist and not depart.

158- According to the Sorrow Is the Reward

Through the Torah and *Mitzvot* [commandments] that a person does, they bring upon him thoughts and desires to want to purify himself. This is called "He who comes to purify." This is the time when he exerts in order to purify himself from self-love.

At that time, he comes to a state of sorrow and pain at not being able achieve purity, but to the contrary. This is so because each time, he sees more of the truth: He is immersed in self-love and does not see any possibility in the horizon that can bring him out of this.

Then when he regrets this, he acquires a need for the Creator's help. At that time, the help from above comes, as our sages said, "He who comes to purify is aided" (*Shabbat* 104a). This is regarded as "all the light."

At that time, we say, "According to the sorrow is the reward," meaning that which he regrets not having, he can obtain this for his sorrow. It is like a person who regrets not having respect. Therefore, his sorrow makes him do things that will earn him respect.

Therefore, when one regrets not being able to purify himself from vessels of reception, what will be the reward, so he will have the strength to purify himself from vessels of reception? It follows that "According to the sorrow is the reward," meaning on whatever substance he regrets, on that substance he receives the filling.

Thus, the question was, How is it permitted to receive reward? The answer is that the whole prohibition on receiving reward is that he will be a receiver. Yet, here it is to the contrary; he wants the reward of being able to bestow, and this is certainly permitted. It follows that there is no light without a *Kli* [vessel], so it is impossible to draw mercy if there is no sorrow.

"According to the sorrow is the reward" means that he is rewarded for that which he regrets. He is not regretful over money and is given respect. The reward of being able to bestow is permitted because this is the purpose of the work.

159-The Need and Importance of Teaching Faith

"'And choose life.' Tanna Rabbi Ishmael, it is a craft. From here, sages said, One must teach his sons a craft. If he does not teach him, he must teach himself. What is the reason? So you will live, it is written'" (Jerusalem Talmud, *Kidushin*, Chapter 1, Rule 7).

This means that it is a *Mitzva* [commandment] to learn a craft, and it falls in the category of "Choose life." Thus, why is there no such arrangement at the seminary that each of the students at the seminary learns a craft, and why is the management of the seminary not seeing to it?

It is written in *Kidushin* (p 30b), "How do we know about teaching him a craft? Rabbi Hizkiya said, he called 'See a life with a woman you have loved.' If a woman, really a woman. As he must marry him to a wife, so he must teach him a craft. If it is Torah, as he must teach him Torah, so he must teach him a craft." So why are they not minding this?

It is written in the *Tosfot*, Chapter, *Kama de Kidushin*: "Rabbi Yosi, son of Rabbi Eliezer, says in the name of Raban Ben Gamliel, 'Anyone who has mastered a craft is like a fenced vineyard that beasts and animals cannot enter, and passersby cannot enter or see what is inside.'"

We should ask, What is the connection between a craft and a fenced vineyard that animals and beasts cannot enter? Also, what does it mean that passersby cannot enter it? How does craft help in this? Also, the fact that they cannot see what is inside, why would it matter if they did see what is inside, so much so that it is worth engaging in craftsmanship instead of Torah?

It is written in *Kidushin* (29a): "Rabbi Yehuda says, 'Anyone who does not teach his son craftsmanship, teaches him to be a robber. Robbery, can you imagine? Yet, it is as though he teaches him to be a robber.'" It seems from the Jerusalem Talmud that it falls into the category of "Do!" from the verse, "Choose life," and for Rabbi Hizkiya it is from the verse, "See a life," and from Rabbi Yehuda it seems that he will transgress the "Do not rob," as he said, "It is as though he teaches him to rob."

Concerning craftsmanship, we find a dispute in the words of our sages: "Bar Kafra said, 'One should always teach one's son clean and easy craftsmanship.' Which is it? Rabbi Yehuda said, 'a needle of furrows.'" RASHI interprets, "A needle of furrows, whose stitches are made in furrows, lines, like the furrows of a plow" (*Kidushin* 82a).

Later in the Gemara, "Tania Rabbi says, 'No craft passes from the world (meaning that everything is for a purpose). Happy is one who sees his parents in fine craftsmanship; woe unto one who sees his parents in flawed craftsmanship.'"

The world cannot be without perfume and without tanning [foul smelling craft]. Happy is he whose craft is a perfume; woe unto one whose craft is tanning. The world cannot be without males or without females. Happy is he whose children are males; woe unto he children sons are females.

We should ask, 1) Why does he begin with his parents, then with himself, and finally with his sons? 2) What does it mean when he says, "Happy is he whose parents..."? What does it come to teach us? After all, he cannot correct his parents. It follows that he is crying out about the past, while our sages teach us that what we should correct pertains only to the present and the future, and not to the past.

"Rabbi Nehorai says, 'I forego every craft in the world and I teach my son only Torah, for any craft in the world stands only during his youth, but when he is old, he is thrown to hunger. But the Torah is not so; it stands by man when he is young, and gives him a purpose and hope when he is old.'"

RASHI interprets that any craft does not yield reward after some time, but their reward is at that time. But the reward of Torah comes by itself over time, and even a sick or an old man who cannot engage in it now, eats from the past (*Kidushin* 82a).

We should ask, What is the reward that one has if he engages in Torah when he is a child the same as when he is old, that we can say that it sustain him? Moreover, according to the above said, it implies that he is exploiting the Torah, against the words of our sages (*Avot* 4). We should interpret all the above, as our sages teach us how to walk in the ways of the work.

But before we elucidate all the above, we must understand the matter of the purpose of creation for which man was created. It is explained in the holy books that the reason is in order to delight His creatures, since it is the way of the good to do good.

Also, it is explained in *Midrash Rabbah* (*Beresheet*, Chapter 8), "The ministering angels said to the Creator, "What is man that you should remember him, and the son of man that you should care for him?' Why do You need this trouble?' There is an allegory about a king who had a tower filled with abundance but no guests. What pleasure does the king have? They said to Him, 'Master of the world, do that which pleases You.'"

This explains that the reason for man's creation was that the Creator wanted to do good to them. This is why He created the creatures, and it is about this that they asked, If the purpose is to do good, why are the creatures suffering torments and sorrow and are not receiving the delight and pleasure that the Creator wishes to give them?

The Zohar explains, "He who eats that which is not his is afraid to look at his face." That is, in every free gift there is the flaw of shame.

In order not to have the bread of shame, meaning that for the Creator's gift to be complete and without any flaw, He has given us a place of work, which is called "the work of choice." Through it, we can receive all our abundance from the Creator without any shame.

When a person observes Torah and *Mitzvot* [commandments], when he still does not feel any flavor in the work, he must observe everything only by way of faith, since when the guidance of the world is in concealment of the face, it is possible to observe the Torah and *Mitzvot* on the basis of faith.

At such a time, there is the matter of choice, to loathe the bad and choose the good. By making the choice, a person can correct himself so he can do all his work not in order to receive reward, but only with the aim for the sake of the Creator.

When one does not feel any flavor in the work, he becomes accustomed to doing things even without a reward. Hence, afterward, when he is rewarded with receiving the interior of the Torah and is rewarded with the light of pleasure, when he will be in a state of revelation of the face, he will still be able to receive these pleasures only because of a *Mitzva* [sing. of *Mitzvot*].

That is, it is the aim of the Creator that man will receive the upper pleasures, as this is the purpose of creation, but not for his own benefit. That is, he does not want to receive the pleasures in order to please himself. Rather, his aim is to receive in order to bestow. This was the whole purpose for making a place of concealment.

Hence, during the concealment there is room to work to take upon himself the fear of heaven "as an ox to the burden and as a donkey to the load" in order to accustom himself to serve the Creator not in order to receive reward.

According to the above, the main work we were given is faith, which is the quality of the fear of heaven. Obtaining fear of heaven is a great thing, as our sages said, "Is the fear of heaven such a little thing?" (*Berachot* 33b).

This means that first we must learn what is fear of heaven, and then there is work to take upon oneself the fear of heaven. As was said, they said that "To Moses, it was a small thing," meaning a little smaller than the degree of Moses is a great thing although we cannot understand how it can be that fear of heaven is such a great thing.

After all, who does not have fear of heaven? Even if a person prays only once a day and eats kosher food, we already say about him that he has fear of heaven. Hence, here we should say that our sages knew what real fear of heaven was; therefore, they determined and said that this is a great thing, whereas we must first learn what is the fear of heaven, that it is such a great thing that our sages said, "In the end, after all is heard, fear God and keep His commandments, for this is the whole of man." What is "for this is the whole of man"? "Rabbi Elazar said, 'The Creator said, 'The whole world was created only for this; this is equal to the entire world—the whole world was created only to command this''" (*Berachot* 6b).

This means that all of our life depends on faith in the Creator, since this is called the *Kli* [vessel] by which we can acquire everything in our world, where we were given the work in Torah and *Mitzvot*. Everything depends on the measure of faith that we acquire.

By this we will understand what our sages said, and as RASHI interpreted, "The Creator considered it for Abraham as a merit and *Tzedakah* [righteousness/charity]," for the faith that he had in Him. We must understand why faith is called *Tzedakah*, and what is the connection between *Tzedakah* and faith.

If a person works in order to bestow and not in order to receive for his own pleasure, it is similar to one who gives to his friend a hundred pounds without wanting anything in return for the one hundred pounds, or to someone who gives to his friend a hundred pounds and in return wants a suit or a closet. No one will say about the one who gives the one hundred pounds in return for a suit that he is very generous and has a kind heart that he can give to the merchant a hundred pounds, since he receives a reward in return for the effort.

But when one gives to his friend a hundred pounds and does not want anything in return, he certainly has a kind heart and wants to give *Tzedakah*.

Therefore, one who serves the Creator on the basis of faith, his work is not in order to receive reward. Otherwise, if his basis is not faith, then he belongs specifically to those who want to receive reward for the labor, since he always wants to be rid of the faith and work only on knowledge.

By serving the Creator in bestowal and not in order to receive any reward, this is called *Dvekut* [adhesion] with the Creator, meaning that by this we become adhered to the Life of Lives, as our sages said, "Cling unto His attributes, as He is merciful, so you are merciful" (*Shabbat* 133b). That is, as the Creator bestows upon the lower ones, so man should work in order to bestow.

When one has come to a state where he can serve the Creator with this aim, he is rewarded with the spiritual pleasures that the Creator contemplated by His aim to do good to His creations, for then the gift that the Creator gives is whole, without the flaw of bread of shame in it. It is as our sages said, "Rabbi Meir says, 'He who learns Torah *Lishma* [for Her sake] (with the aim to bestow) is rewarded with many things'" (*Pirkei Avot*, Chapter 6).

Faith is also called a *Mitzva*. There is Torah, and there is *Mitzva*, as Baal HaSulam interpreted the words of our sages, "If he performs one *Mitzva*, happy is he, for he has sentenced himself and the world to the side of merit" (*Kidushin* 40b), and one *Mitzva* means faith. According to the above, faith, fear of heaven, and one *Mitzva* are the same thing, but each one points to a different form.

Now we can interpret the above-said, that what the Jerusalem Talmud brings in the name of Rabbi Ishmael, "Choose life—this is craftsmanship," that he must teach his son craftsmanship, that it refers to faith. This matter is called "craftsmanship," since this is great learning, as our sages said, "Is fear a trivial matter?"

The term "craftsmanship" pertains primarily to something that depends on actions, but one who learns some science, medicine, or engineering, or a quality, this is called "wisdom" and not "craftsmanship," since it pertains to the brain and not to the rest of the organs.

Hence, since the matter of faith is the quality of above reason, which is against the mind, for one can speak of faith precisely where the mind does not reach, and this is only a force, which is acceptance of the burden of the kingdom of heaven by force, "as an ox to the burden and as a donkey to the load." For this reason, faith is called "craftsmanship."

Here comes the matter of choice in the verse, "Choose life." The father must teach his son this craft, and if he does not, he must teach himself. What is the reason? "So that you may live," meaning that it is impossible to receive the life of Torah without faith.

Also, in this way we can interpret what Rabbi Hizkiya said, that the obligation to teach his son is from the verse, "See a life with a wife," meaning that it is impossible to be rewarded with life without the commandment of faith, since specifically through faith he is rewarded with adhering to the Life of Lives. Naturally, he has life by adhering to life, since Torah without faith is not regarded as life.

This is why he said that as he must teach him Torah, so he must teach him craftsmanship, since when the Torah is on the basis of faith, it is possible to feel the life in it and then we see that it is in the manner of "for this is your life and the length of your days."

According to the above, we can interpret what is written in the aforementioned *Tosfot*, which says, "Anyone who has mastered a craft is like a fenced vineyard." We asked what is the connection between a fence and a craft. We should interpret that craftsmanship is faith, since one who has faith, it is as though he has a fenced vineyard, where "vineyard" refers to the "vineyard of the Lord of Hosts," meaning the spirituality in a person.

At that time, if he has faith, it is like a fence that guards him from all the things that can harm him, since the things that harm a person's spirituality are the foreign thoughts and ill wills, which is considered that a beast and an animal have entered him.

The faith keeps him from all the questions and from all the evil lusts, which is called "a beast"; it is matters that are the work of a beast. Also, bad animals, which are not of *Kedusha* [holiness], cannot enter when a person has taken upon himself the burden of faith, "passersby cannot enter it."

That is, those are the people who always breach the *Mitzvot* and repent. They cannot grip to a person who has faith because they do not see what is inside him, since one who is careful that his work will always be in faith, works in concealment, and then his intention is unseen.

When a person works *Lo Lishma*, it is possible to see his intention because he wants reward for the labor. But one whose work is on the basis of faith, his thought is covered and not revealed to anyone, so there cannot be a grip to the outer ones in his work.

We should interpret similarly what Rabbi Yehuda said, "Anyone who does not teach his son craftsmanship, it is as though he teaches him to be a robber." Our sages said, "Anyone who enjoys in this world without a blessing, it is as though he robs the Creator and the assembly of Israel, as was said, "One who robs his father and mother and says, 'there is no crime,' is a friend to a destructive man." Rabbi Hanina son of Rabbi Papa said, "He is a friend of Jeroboam son of Navat, who destroyed the world to their father in heaven" (*Berachot* 35).

We should understand the connection between a robber and Jeroboam son of Navat, and why he who enjoys without a blessing is considered a robber. What is the connection between robbing and blessing? The thing is that the purpose of creation is to do good to His creations. In order not to have the bread of shame, the place of concealment was made, so that man would be able to receive the pleasure in order to bestow upon the Creator. In this manner, there will not be any flaw in the present of the Creator, as our sages said, "The cow wants to feed more than the calf wants to eat" (*Pesachim* 112a).

However, as longs as a person is not ready to receive, the abundance does not come to the lower ones. Hence, one who enjoys in this world should do so with the aim to bless the Creator. That is, the aim should not be that he wants to enjoy, but that he wants to bless the Creator.

At that time, the Creator gives the upper abundance to the assembly of Israel, as our sages said, "He who performs one *Mitzva*, happy is he, for he has sentenced himself and the entire world to the side of merit" (*Kidushin* 40b). In other words, by performing the *Mitzva*, he causes the Creator to bestow upon the assembly of Israel. This is the meaning of "sentences the entire world to the side of merit."

It follows that when one enjoys in this world without a blessing, without the aim to bless the Creator, because of this, the Creator does not bestow upon the assembly of Israel, since the aim for the sake of the Creator is missing.

Thus, this person robs the Creator and the assembly of Israel by not blessing and by wanting to enjoy only for himself and not for the sake of the Creator. For this reason, he becomes a "friend to a destructive man," Jeroboam son of Navat, who "destroyed the world to their father in heaven."

All this is because they lacked faith in the Creator. This is why Rabbi Yehuda said, "Anyone who does not teach his son a craft, it is as though he teaches him to be a robber," meaning it is as though he teaches him to rob the Creator and the assembly of Israel. Hence, there is a strict obligation to teach the matter of faith, since only by this is it possible to achieve the complete wholeness.

From all the above, we can explain the measure that they gave to learning the craft itself. Bar Kafra says, "One should always teach one's son a clean and easy craft." Rabbi Yehuda interprets that it is "a needle of furrows." In RASHI's interpretation, "A needle of furrows, whose stitches are made in furrows, lines, like the furrows of a plow."

We therefore see that the stitching is in order to connect two separate things so they become one. This means that one should achieve equivalence with the Creator, meaning *Dvekut* [adhesion], as it is written, "And to cleave unto Him," as he interpreted, as the furrows of a plow, meaning to turn the dust that was below and make it on top, and that which was on top to be underneath.

So is man. There are two desires in him: 1) a good will, to bestow, to have faith, and 2) an ill will, when he wants only to receive for his own sake and to have no faith in the Creator. When a person is born, by nature, the good will is of inferior importance to him and he does not want to use it, since it is loathsome to use such a desire.

Conversely, the ill will is of superior importance, and whenever he can use it, he is in utter elation. That is, when he can satisfy the ill will in him, he has no higher state than this, since all he wishes is to satisfy the bad within him.

Hence, a person who wants to cling unto his Maker must equalize the qualities, as our sages said, "Cling unto His attributes, as He is merciful, so you are merciful" (*Shabbat* 133b). In other words, as the Creator wants only to bestow upon the lower ones, man, too, should see that he wants only to bestow upon the Creator and does not want to receive for his own pleasure. This is all of man's purpose in his work in equivalence of qualities.

Hence, man must invert the qualities within him, similar to plowing, so that what was previously above, meaning the ill will, will now be below, and every time he is about to use the ill will in him, he will feel that he regards it as loathsome and base.

Conversely, the good will, which was previously of inferior importance, will now be in a state of "above," so that each time he can do things for the sake of the Creator, he should feel that such a state is an ascent for him, since by this he comes to cling unto Him.

This is only by faith. This is why faith is called "clean and easy craft." It is "clean" because there must not be any mixture of self-benefit there, but only for the sake of the Creator, since when one believes in the greatness of the Creator, a person has no desire or yearning other than to adhere to Him all day and all night. This is why it is called "clean," meaning only for the sake of the Creator.

However, before a person is rewarded with his body's consent to the work of faith, this work is regarded as lowliness, since he does not see anyone respects him when he works only for the sake of the Creator.

At that time, he must see that his work is in concealment, since otherwise his work cannot be clean because while his work is with excitement, his actions will certainly be praised and by this, the matter of respect will interfere, that others will respect him for this.

Therefore, when he wants to have no mixtures, he must work in concealment and then he will not get any respect from this. This is why clean work is despicable in his eyes. Also, *Kalah* [easy/light] comes from the word *Nikleh* [despicable], meaning despised.

Also, clean work is despised because a person cannot tolerate faith above reason, since by nature, a person appreciates what he grasps in the mind when reason obligates him.

Conversely, going against reason is despicable because such work is called "gullible," as our sages said about the verse, "Who is gullible? Let him come here." This is Moses, pertaining to faith, since Moses is called "the faithful shepherd," who has faith and planted the faith in the whole of Israel.

In this way, we should interpret the words of Rabbi, "No craft passes from the world." As RASHI interpreted, whether it is loathsome or clean, since the view of Rabbi is that the whole world cannot do clean work, meaning that specifically one who is inclined to the work of truth is capable of doing clean work where there are no mixtures of *Lo Lishma* [not for Her sake] there.

Conversely, the thoughts of the majority of the world revolve around the view of the world. They do not have a strong mind or a strong desire so they can exert and have the power to get what they want. Rather, they work for the general public, and what the public obligates, they do. They have no permission to do in the world what they understand and want, but are rather dependent on the view of the public.

For this reason, when some *Mitzva* is given to the general public, we must see that the general public can observe it.

This is why Rabbi says, "No craft passes from the world," but the most important is for a person to take upon himself the burden of the kingdom of heaven whether it is clean, meaning entirely for the sake of the Creator, or loathsome, meaning with mixtures of not for the sake of the Creator, since any craft is needed because from *Lo Lishma* we come to *Lishma*.

Our sages said, "A thousand people come to the Bible [Pentateuch]... and one to teach" (*VaYikra Rabbah*, Chapter 2:1). This means that by a thousand coming in, it makes it possible for one to come out to teach. This is why Rabbi says, "No craft passes from the world."

However, "Happy is he who sees his parents in fine craft." "His parents" means thoughts, since before every act, there must be a preceding thought and cause that is the reason that makes him do this thing. Hence, "his parents" are the thought that causes him to observe Torah and *Mitzvot*.

"Fine craft" means one that brings a person to the goal for which he was created—to engage in Torah and *Mitzvot* for the sake of the

Creator—by which he will be rewarded with receiving the delight and pleasure that the Creator contemplated giving.

At that time, he will feel happy because of all that he has acquired through his labor in Torah and *Mitzvot*. But if the thought is not for the sake of the Creator, he cannot achieve the goal, and it turns out that his craft is flawed.

This is why Rabbi said, "Woe unto one who sees his parents in flawed craft." Because his faith is mixed with *Lo Lishma*, this faith is flawed. Therefore, we must try to make the parents, meaning the cause, be for the sake of the Creator.

By this we will understand the words of our sages, "Happy is one who sees his parents in fine craftsmanship." We asked, But this is something that he cannot correct, since if he is born to such parents, what can he do? According to the above, it is all well, as it pertains to himself, that he should try that the thought and the cause of Torah and *Mitzvot* will be with the aim for the sake of the Creator.

In this manner, it is written in *The Zohar, Shemot*, "The world exists only on the smell." And in this manner, we should interpret, "The world cannot be without perfume and without tanning."

"Perfume" refers to perfumes, whose fragrance ascends from below upward. His craftsmanship should be with the aim to bestow contentment above, for the person is regarded as below and the Creator as above. It follows that the man sends all his pleasures to the Creator, who is above.

"Tanning" is the processing of leather, which emits a great stench. This means that when he sees that his work will be *Lo Lishma*, yet he must engage in work only for the sake of the Creator, the work becomes loathsome to him and stinks in his eyes.

In a place where there should be pleasure, when he sees that now he has a chance to work for the sake of the Creator, he cannot do this. Hence, in a state where he does not see the return for his work, he feels heaviness and idleness and lowliness, and his heart is angry and upset.

For this reason, although his work is not with the aim not for the sake of the Creator, he still lacks the joy and merriment from giving contentment to the Creator.

Although "it is impossible without tanning," meaning that man must come to such a state, since this place is the passage between *Lishma* and *Lo Lishma*, but woe unto he who stays in that place, which is a midway stop, and does not continue toward the goal of wanting to please the Creator.

He interprets further and says, "The world cannot be without males and females." "Happy is he whose children are males, and woe unto he whose children are females." The famous question is, What does it mean that his children are females?

We should say that we know from books of those who have fear that the giver and bestower are called "male," and the receiver and deficient are called "female." This is the meaning of what he says, that the world cannot be without males and females, meaning that there must be the state of *Lo Lishma* in the world, regarded as taking pleasure for self-benefit. Otherwise, it is impossible to begin to engage in Torah and *Mitzvot*.

Sometimes the reason is the *Lo Lishma*, but during the act, he comes to thoughts of repentance and performs the *Mitzva* with the aim for the sake of the Creator, meaning his aim is to bestow contentment upon his Maker. This is regarded as "his children are males." For this reason, he says, "Woe unto he whose children are females," meaning that the things he does are also with the aim to receive reward, which is regarded as his children being females.

"Rabbi Nehorai says, 'I forego every craft in the world and I teach my son only Torah.'" He is not referring to the way by which the general public should behave, but rather speaks of his own degree, that he has been rewarded with permanent fear of heaven. This is why he says that he foregoes all the crafts, meaning that now he is leaving the flawed faith and the fine faith, since he has left both kinds of faith. Instead, now he teaches his son, meaning his action, called "son," only the Torah.

He explains that the reason is that "Any craft in the world stands only during his youth." RASHI interprets that "Any craft does not yield reward after some time, but their reward is at that time."

Faith is called Mitzva, and the acceptance of the burden of the kingdom of heaven is a Mitzva. Our sages said, "A Mitzva protects and saves while engaging in it. Torah protects and saves when engaging in it, and when not engaging in it" (Sotah 21b). The difference between Torah and Mitzva is that we see that in the Torah, a person can remember and use what he learned the previous day or even before, or repeat the rules he learned so as to know how to behave according to what he learned before. For this reason, the Torah protects and saves even while not engaging in it, since he can remember what he learned a while ago.

But faith, which is a Mitzva, pertains only when engaging in it, since each time a person takes upon himself the burden of accepting the kingdom of heaven, it is a Mitzva, and a Mitzva is an act. There is no remembering here, as with the Torah; rather, each act stands on its own.

Hence, during the fact, it protects and saves, and he cannot say that he remembers that he took upon himself the burden of accepting the kingdom of heaven a while ago, since this will not help him. Instead, at any given moment, he needs faith, and it cannot be said that now he does not need the burden of faith.

Thus, each acceptance is a new Mitzva. This is why faith is called "youth" and "childhood," since "old age" pertains where something took place a while ago. But since the burden of faith must always be renewed, there cannot be old age in it, and it is always called a "youth."

This is why he says, "forego," since it is with him only in his youth, since faith protects and saves only while engaging in it. As RASHI interpreted, "Any craft does not yield reward after some time, but their reward is at that time," meaning it protects and saves only while engaging in it.

But the Torah is not so. Rather, it assists a person in his youth and gives him hope when he is old. As RASHI interpreted, "But the reward of Torah comes by itself over time, and even a sick or an old man who cannot engage in it, eats from the past."

In other words, the Torah protects and saves even while not engaging in it. This is why he interprets that it helps him in his youth, meaning when he engages, and gives him hope when he is old, when he does not engage in it.

"Even a sick or an old man who cannot engage in it, eats from the past." This means that it protects and saves even while not engaging in it. This is why Rabbi Nehorai says that he himself is doing so, since he has already taken upon himself the matter of permanent faith. For this reason, he says, "I forego every craft," since he has been rewarded with this degree permanently, unlike the rest of the people.

* * *

Rabbi Elazar said, "All the craftsmen in the world are destined to stand on the ground, as was said, 'And they will come down from their ships and all the oarsmen will stand on the earth.' Rabbi Elazar said, 'There is not craftsmanship more inferior to the earth, as was said, and they came down'" (Yevamot 63).

We should ask, If the work of the earth is an inferior craft, why did Rabbi Elazar say, "destined to," meaning that in the end, they will have good craftsmanship, yet he deduces that it will be an inferior craftsmanship?

We should interpret that faith is called "light" [or "easy"], meaning inferior, because to man, faith above reason is not important. This is why it is difficult to work. But in the future, they will be rewarded with this clean faith.

Our sages said, "In the days of the Messiah, proselytes will not be accepted, just as proselytes were not accepted in the days of David and in the days of Solomon. Rabbi Eliezer said, 'What does the verse say? For he will surely fear (he who comes to convert), 'he who is not with Me' (while we are not with you, he will convert, meaning in this world). 'Whoever assails you will fall because of you' (whoever attacks you while you are poor will fall because of you in the next world) (Isaiah 54), but another will not'" (*Yevamot* 24b).

The *Tosfot* ask, "They did not accept proselytes in the days of David? What about Ittai the Gittite and Pharaoh's daughter, for in the days of Solomon there isn't the question; he is the reason, and they do not need the king's table.

And the Gibeonites converted by themselves, as in the days of Esther, "And many of the peoples of the earth became Jews," and from that one who came to Hillel ... Hillel was certain that even if it is for the sake of the Creator, and that one who came and said, "Convert me so that I may marry that disciple, it was also for the sake of the Creator."

From all the above, it seems that one who wants to convert in order to receive the good reward that the people of Israel have is not accepted. This is the meaning of "no proselytes are accepted in the days of the Messiah." Rather, they must convert only for the sake of the Creator and not for the sake of reward.

In other words, one who wants to take upon himself to be a Jew and convert the gentile within him, cannot be a Jew and adhere to the people of Israel unless he does not aim for the good reward, which is called "for the days of the Messiah." Rather, as it is written, "Who dwells with you in the days of your poverty," as our sages said, "Rabbi Yonatan says, 'Anyone who observes the Torah from poverty will eventually observe it from wealth" (*Avot*, Chapter 4).

That is, he who is poor in knowledge yet observes the Torah will eventually observe it from wealth, meaning he will be rewarded with understanding. Conversely, anyone who cancels the Torah because of wealth will eventually cancel it because of poverty, meaning that the knowledge of Torah will depart from him.

Yevamot 63: "Rabbi Elazar said, 'Anyone who does not have a soil is not a man, as was said, 'The heaven are the heaven of the Lord, and the earth, He has given to the sons of man.'"" We should ask, accordingly, each person should strive to have a piece of land.

The *Tania* also asks, So would Rashbi say, "The graves of idol-worshippers are not to be defiled in a tent, as was said, 'You are My flock, the flock of My pasture, you are man. You are called 'man,' and the idol-worshippers are not called 'man'"" (*Yevamot* 61a). This means that specifically a man from Israel is called "man." But how can it be said that if he has no land, he does not fall into the category, "You are called 'man'"?

We can interpret that "land" means earth, as the evidence he brings from the verse, "The heavens are the heavens of the Lord, and the earth, He has given to the sons of man."

The Torah is called "heaven," since the Torah was given to Moses from heaven. Moses received the Torah from Sinai. The earth is called *Malchut*, "faith," "fear of heaven," as our sages said, "everything is in the hands of heaven but the fear of heaven" (*Berachot* 33b).

This is the meaning of "One who has no faith," which is the fear of heaven, called "earth," "is not regarded among "you are called 'man.'"

Yevamot 63: "Rabbi Elazar said, 'There is not craftsmanship more inferior than the earth, as was said, and they came down.' Rabbi Ami said, 'Rains come down only for the faithful, as was said, 'Truth will spring forth from the earth, and justice reflects from heaven.'"" RASHI interprets, when truth springs forth from the earth, when there is faith in negotiation, justice reflects from heaven, meaning rains, which are *Tzedakah* [righteousness/charity].

We should understand why it is specifically because the negotiation is not with faith that *Tzedakah* is not given from above, and the matter of faith, where earth is a desire, which is the heart, where one engages in the matter of faith, called *Tzedakah*, as it is written, "and he believed in the Lord and He considered it for him as righteousness."

Therefore, in a corresponding measure, they cause righteousness, which is faith, to come from above. This is the meaning of the prayer for the rains in order to invoke faith.

"And He smelled him in the fear of the Lord, and He will not judge by what His eyes see, nor make a decision by what His ears hear" (Isaiah 11). This means that the Messiah King, meaning one who wants to walk on the path toward being rewarded with the purpose, which is the quality of the messiah, should not judge anything by what he sees or by what his ears hear, but by the scent of the fear of heaven, which is faith. According to this line, he should determine all his ways.

As it is written afterward, "Justice will be his belt around his waist, and faith, his belt around his loins." In other words, his faith should be justice, regarded as righteousness, not in order to receive reward, and this will be his support that he can walk in the work of the Creator, since the light strengthens his waist so he can walk and not stumble as he walks, meaning not to grow tired from walking.

160- And All the People Stand Over You

Yitro [Jethro], Beer Sheba, *Tav-Shin-Chaf-Bet* [1962]

"And all the people stand over you from morning until evening."

Can this be said so? But any judge who judges in complete truth, even for one hour, the text regards him as though he engages in Torah all day long, and as though he has become a partner of the Creator in the work of creation, as was said about it, "And there was evening," etc. RASHI: "Can you imagine that Moses sat all day long and discussed? When His law is made? Rather, it is to tell you, 'Any judge who judges in complete truth'" (*Shabbat* 10).

It is written in Sanhedrin (7a): "Rabbi Shmuel Bar Nachmani said, 'Rabbi Yonatan said, 'Any judge who judges in complete truth installs His *Shechina* [Divinity] in Israel, as was said, 'God stands in the congregation of God; among gods He will judge,' and any judge who does not judge in complete truth causes the *Shechina* [Divinity] to depart from Israel, as was said, 'For the robbing of the poor, for the groaning of the indigent, now I will arise,' says the Lord.'"

And in *Baba Batra* (8b), "And the enlightened ones will shine as the brightness of the firmament," this is a judge who judges in complete truth. And in the Mishnah it is different, "And the enlightened ones will shine as the brightness of the firmament" is a judge who judges in complete truth, and a collector of righteousness. RASHI interpreted, "a collector of righteousness—who enlighten the poor."

It is written in the *Megillah* (15b), "Rabbi Elazar said, 'Rabbi Hanina said, 'The Creator is destined to be a crown on the head of each and every righteous, as was said, 'In that day, the Lord of hosts will be the crown of a gazelle...'"'"

What is the connection between the crown of a gazelle and a glorious diadem, to those who do His will and hides His glory? Is it true for all? Indeed, it is "to the remnant of His people," to those who make themselves the residue." "A spirit of justice" is one who judges his inclination (and RASHI interpreted, "forces it to repent"). "For him who sits in judgment" is one who judges in complete truth. "And for strength" is one who overcomes his inclination (and RASHI interpreted, he does not follow it to commit a transgression).

We see four manners concerning one who judges in complete truth: 1) On Shabbat [Sabbath], it is as though he becomes a partner of the Creator in the work of creation. 2) In Sanhedrin, he installs the *Shechina* in Israel. 3) In *Baba Batra*, he is "The enlightened ones will shine as the brightness of the firmament." 4) He will be rewarded with what is written, "The Creator is destined to be a crown on the head of every single righteous."

We should understand all the above. Concerning one who judges in complete truth, we should understand what is the precision, "in complete truth." Are there two kinds of truth? And also, what is an incomplete truth?

To understand the above, we must first bring what our sages said, "Our sages said, 'One should always see oneself as half guilty, half innocent. If he performs one *Mitzva* [commandment], happy is he, for he has sentenced himself to the side of merit. If he commits one transgression, woe unto him for he has sentenced himself to the side of fault, as was said, 'and one sinner destroys much good.' For the one sin that he committed, he loses much good" (*Kidushin* 40b).

We should ask, If a person knows that he has few merits and many transgressions, how can it be said that he is half and half? He knows about himself that this is not the truth! Moreover, why do they make a habit out of lying? After all, "the confession of a defendant is as a hundred witnesses," so why did they say that he should see himself as half and half?

In *Sukkah* (52a), the Gemara says, "In the future, the Creator brings the evil inclination and slaughters it before the righteous and before the wicked. To the righteous, it seems like a high mountain; to the wicked, it seems like a hairsbreadth."

We should understand which is the truth; is it as a hairsbreadth or as a high mountain? There, the Gemara brings the story about Abaye: "An old man said to him, 'Anyone who is greater than his friend, his inclination is greater than him.'"

We should ask, Did our sages not say "A *Mitzva* induces a *Mitzva*" (*Avot* 4)? (Rabbi Ovadia from Bartenura interprets that one who makes one *Mitzva* can easily do others.) Yet, here he says that anyone who is greater than his friend (and greatness is certainly in *Mitzvot* [pl. of *Mitzva*], "his inclination is greater than him." If his inclination is greater than him, it is more difficult for him to perform *Mitzvot*, so why did they say, "A *Mitzva* induces a *Mitzva*"?).

It is known that we were given the commandment of choice, that by choice, we can receive the good that the Creator has prepared for the created beings, as this was the purpose of creation—to do good to His creations. In order not to have the bread of shame, we were given the choice during the concealment.

Choice pertains precisely when the bad and the good are equal. At that time, man has the power to subdue them. Conversely, if the bad is more than the good, there cannot be a decision because subduing the bad when it is more than the good, at that time, a person can no longer subdue it.

It is as Maimonides writes, "This matter is a great tenet and is the pillar of the Torah and the *Mitzva*, as was said, 'Behold, I give.' That is, you have the authority, and one can do anything he wants from the acts that people do, for the Creator does not force people or forces them to do bad or good. Rather, everything is given to them" (*Hilchot Teshuva*, Chapter 5). But all this can be said only when the bad is not more powerful than the good.

By this we will explain what was said, "One should always see oneself as half guilty, half innocent." This does not refer to how a person stands before the courthouse of above, for this will be to him a different judgment. When he is sentenced on how much reward and how much punishment he deserves, he will be judged according to the transgressions and the *Mitzvot* he had committed.

Here, in this world, where they said that he must see himself as half guilty, half innocent, it refers to how he should behave in this world, since a person can say that since he has many iniquities, and his bad is greater than the good, he can no longer sentence to the good, since the bad has already subdued the good for the worse.

Instead, he should say that concerning the work, the truth is not as he sees, although it is true that he has many transgressions, but in fact, where it concerns choice, his bad does not have more power than the good. That is, if his good is very small, the bad, too, is not more powerful than the good, since their powers must be equal, or there can be no choice. For this reason, his bad was not given more power than the power of the good.

This is the meaning of "Any judge who judges in complete truth." In ethics, a judge is present in any person from Israel, as is explained (in the essay, "No Calamity Comes to the World But Only because of the Judges of Israel").

When a person should do something, such as to give a big donation to some institution, he has two views before him: One side argues that since this institution is vital, and we must try to sustain it because many people benefit from it, and now this institution needs a lot of support or it could be ruined, and all the effort put into it will all go to waste, and only by his giving a big donation in both body and fortune, it will be able to persist, for this reason, it is worthwhile that he should take upon himself this trouble.

The other side argues that he is very busy with his own business, and if he makes an effort in favor of this institution, his own business will be ruined. He worked so hard to reach his current status, and it cost him so heavily and so much degradation to humiliate himself among relatives and friends so they will help him, and thank God he has succeeded and is now considered among the most respectable people in his town, and by leaving his business, who knows to what state he might come.

And even if he does not decide to take upon himself to become among the managers of the institution, but only give a big donation, meaning participate only with his wealth and not with his body, to be an activist in this institution, how can he spend such a large sum? If he spends such a large sum, he will miss it for his business, for money should be gained, not lost, as it is known that with cash, it is easier to buy merchandise for less.

Also, if he orders goods from some factory, when he pays with cash, he gets the delivery sooner. Therefore, he must not participate even only in money.

Now a person must judge because he has now become a judge deciding between the two sides, who is right and on whose side is justice? Of course, it is a hard decision since there are arguments both ways, and on the face of it, both are correct. For this reason, one must judge in complete truth, meaning to look into the internality of the matters, whether it is worthwhile to annul the individual before the needs of the public.

A decision pertains precisely where they are two equal forces, when one side is not stronger in the necessity to exist than the other side. At that time, it can be said that he must decide whom he should help. But if one side is weaker, he has no negotiation with which to determine justice, since it is natural that one must help the one we believe is more needy of our help.

It is likewise here. When a person can overcome his inclination and sees that he has many transgression and few *Mitzvot*, he thinks that since he has many transgressions and few merits, it follows that the bad in him has the power to control him because the majority prevails.

Accordingly, he need not make any effort to be able to overcome the evil in him, since he cannot overcome the majority. It follows his work will be in vain.

Hence, here our sages came and said that although the truth is what he sees, that it is more bad than good, it seems that way to him because of the good deeds that he had done, and according to the actions, he has more bad deeds than good deeds.

But in truth, if he looks in the internality of the matters, our sages testify that from above they do not place more power in the bad than the amount of good within him, since there must be an equal weight, so he can determine.

For this reason, by doing many bad deeds, he will be sentenced for it in the next world. That is, when they want to punish him for his actions, they will take into consideration the quantity of actions.

But when a person should walk in the ways of the Creator in this world, as long as he is in this world, he has a choice, meaning that the Creator did not place in the evil more power than there is in his good. Hence, they are always in a state of "half and half."

By this we will understand what our sages said, "In the future, the Creator brings the evil inclination and slaughters it before the righteous and before the wicked. To the righteous, it seems like a high mountain; to the wicked, it seems like a hairsbreadth."

We asked, Which is the real form? According to the above, it is clear that since the Creator did not place more power in the bad than the measure of the good, it follows that the righteous, who have many merits, in order to have an equal weight, the bad in them, meaning the evil inclination, must also be equal in size to the good. This is why they said that it seems to them like a high mountain.

But the wicked, whose good is only as a hairsbreadth, their evil inclination is also not more than a hairsbreadth.

By this we will understand what that old man said to Abaye, "Anyone who is greater than his friend, his inclination is greater than him." We asked, But there is a rule that a *Mitzva* induces a *Mitzva*, and one who became great, it is certainly by performing a *Mitzva*, so why did the evil increase in him? According to the above, the good should have increased!

However, since there must be choice, if he does not increase the bad for him to the extent of the measure of the good where he stands now, the good will certainly determine that he will do only good. In that state, he will have no work of choice, and all of man's greatness is expressed in being able to do more in the choice.

This is the meaning of what our sages said, "According to the sorrow is the reward," so the labor is only during the choice. For this reason, more bad must constantly be added to him, so he will have with what to decide.

By this we should interpret what our sages said, "Any judge who judges in complete truth, it as though he has become a partner of the Creator in the work of creation," as it is written in *The Zohar*, "And to say unto Zion, you are My people" (Isaiah 51), do not pronounce it, "My people," but rather "with Me," for you are partners with Me. As I made heaven and earth with My word, as it written, "The heavens were made by the word of the Creator," so you, by your words of wisdom, you made new heaven and earth. Happy are those who labor in the Torah" (*Beresheet* 5a).

This means that by judging in complete truth, a person can make a decision for the better, and then he is rewarded with receiving the delight and pleasure that the Creator has prepared for the creatures, which was the reason for the creation of the world. It follows that a person becomes a partner of the Creator in that the Creator wants to give, and the creatures are able to receive, and by this the partnership is formed.

But if he judges not in complete truth, they will not be able correct their actions and will not be able to receive the benefit that the Creator wants to bestow upon the creatures. As a result, the upper abundance will stay above, and the name, The Good Who Does Good, will not be revealed to the lower ones, and the purpose of creation will not be achieved.

Conversely, when the lower ones can receive the complete benefit, creation is completed. It follows that he has become partners with the Creator by receiving what the Creator wants to give.

In this way, we will understand what our sages said, "Any judge who judges in complete truth installs the *Shechina* in Israel." The explanation is that by correcting his actions, he will cause the *Shechina* to be in Israel. This is as our sages said, "If he performs one *Mitzva*, happy is he for he has sentenced himself and the entire world to the side of merit," for by his actions he causes the revelation of upper abundance to the lower ones.

By this we will also explain what they said, "Any judge who judges, etc., will shine as the brightness of the firmament." That is, by correcting their actions, they are rewarded with the shining of the upper abundance, and this will shine on them as the brightness of the firmament.

Also, he will be rewarded with the Creator being "a crown on the head of each and every righteous," since each one who decides for the better is rewarded with the upper wholeness, which is that the Creator be upon him, and he will see that He is the one covering, surrounding, and protecting him.

It is known that the Creator wants to impart abundance upon the created beings, but we are unable to receive. Because the Creator's wish is that there will not be any deficiency in His gift, He wants us to receive only through our work.

But if we do not make many merits, it will be difficult for us to determine to the side of the good, since the bad in us will have already come to a great amount. For this reason, the Creator made a correction that the bad and the good will always be equal.

161- Awakening – 1

Every religious person has a moment or a time in life when he has some awakening from above, where he feels vitality about being Jewish.

In general, one is in several states where he has no grace of *Kedusha* [holiness], and sometimes altogether forgets that there is *Kedusha* in the world. Even when he remembers, it is only due to upbringing, meaning habit, such as when he blesses the blessing over pleasure. Sometimes, he does not even feel to whom he is speaking or what he is saying, and the blessing he said is only out of habit.

Yet, sometimes in life, a person does feel vitality in *Kedusha*. This can be for a short while, such as a minute of feeling the flavor of *Kedusha*, which comes to him by an awakening from above, and a person can awaken a *Reshimo* [recollection] from this, that once he had an awakening.

It therefore follows that every person has within him a *Reshimo*, and that *Reshimo* contains the *Kli* [vessel], meaning the heart, and by this, one can make an awakening from below.

162- Love of Others

I look at one tiny dot, called "love of others," and I think about it: What can I do in order to benefit people? As I look at the general public, I see the suffering of individuals, illnesses and pains, and the suffering of individuals inflicted by the collective, meaning wars among nations. And besides prayer, there is nothing to give. This is called "He who aches because of the affliction of the public—a medium."

163- Colors in the Work

"Left" is called "red" color, which is illumination of *Hochma*, as in GAR *de Hochma*.

That person is encircled by a black thread, which is the judgments of the *Masach de Hirik* that diminish it from GAR.

Blacker than all blacks: Due to the inversion of the addition of judgment out of her turning in the waters of the sea, due to "The heavens will ascend, will descend to the chasms," that "red" acquired the form of "black," which is regarded that one who is unsound will acquire the form of black, which multiplies the judgments.

She became black, but she is still not regarded as the actual *Malchut*, but rather as mitigated by the red of *Bina*.

164- What to Ask of the Creator—to Be His Servant

When a person sees that he has disturbances in his work of the Creator and he wants to pray to the Creator to have the strength to work, what should he ask?

There are two options:

1) That the Creator will take away from him the disturbances. As a result, he will not need to make great efforts in order to walk in the ways of the Creator.

2) For the Creator to give him a greater taste for the Torah and prayer and good deeds, and by this the disturbances will not be able to detain him because when Torah and *Mitzvot* [commandments] are important, disturbances cannot rule.

For example, a person cannot say that he has many disturbances so he cannot save his life. That is, it is not true if he argued that because his relatives or his environment are disturbing him, he is unable to save his life. Rather, of course, a person will give all that he has for his life, and all the obstacles do not matter to him.

Therefore, he asks the Creator to give him the taste of life in Torah and *Mitzvot*, and against life, one cannot say that he has disturbances because the importance of life does not let him relate to the disturbances.

165- *The Matter of Keeping*

In the tree of knowledge, there is the matter of keeping, meaning that one should know how to keep himself from foreign thoughts. Since the tree of knowledge is called "good and bad," one must know how to keep oneself from the bad that is there. The tree of knowledge is called "*Malchut* of the quality of judgment," called receiving in order to receive," and all the corrections are that he will work in order to bestow. Prior to this, he is in a state of "in order to receive."

166- Which Repentance Helps?

Repentance helps only on *Malchut* that is sweetened in *Bina*, when there is a time of *Katnut* [smallness/infancy]. In *Gadlut* [greatness/adulthood], the *AHP* return to the degree. "Returning" means that they can be used in order to bestow. This is considered that repentance helps, meaning that we can correct, that it is possible to use vessels of reception.

This is not so with the *AHP*, which belong to *GAR*, which can shine only through the correction of *Malchut* in her place. But since *Malchut* was concealed in *RADLA*, here repentance does not help, meaning that he cannot return the *AHP* to the degree before the end of correction.

167- Strict with Himself and Blesses

Obligatory blessing means that the body obligates him to bless. That is, the body that the Creator created with a nature that if he receives good things from another, he blesses him. This is called "The blessing for the food from the Torah." It is not a *Mitzva* [commandment], meaning that the body does not obligate him to bless, since he feels that he still needs a few things that the other could give him but is not. At that time, the body says that it is still not satisfied with him and cannot say that He is good and does good, since he needs a few more things, and why is He not giving them to him? Nonetheless, he is strict with himself and blesses. It follows that he is not commanded yet he does.

168- Blessed Is the Man Who Puts His Trust in the Lord

Explanation: Blessed is a person in whose heart the Creator places the confidence that he will have confidence, for the quality of confidence requires that the Creator will give the confidence. However, there should be light and *Kli* [vessel]. Hence, when a person works and wants to obtain confidence in the Creator, by this the Creator gives it to him as a gift.

169- The Meaning of the Bed

The legs of the bed that the Creator called them, when they would tie it to the legs of the bed.

Mitah [bed] is called *Matah* [low] in importance, meaning faith. Our sages said that when they saw the angels carrying Moses' bed, they made the calf, meaning that the quality of faith of Moses was low among them.

"The legs of the bed" means that on which the bed is placed. Just as a table rests on legs, so a bed rests on legs.

Raglaim [legs] are regarded as *Meraglim* [spies/spying], when they want to see the benefits, if it is worthwhile to work in order to bestow. Reason maintains that it is not worthwhile, so there is room to place on this faith, which is above reason.

This is the meaning of the bed being placed on legs, which tie the offering, meaning that they will approach the Creator through the legs of the bed, where they take the bed, meaning the low importance that is placed on the importance, which is called "reason."

This was on the tenth of the tenth month, which is called *Malchut*, that they took upon themselves the kingdom of heaven on the tenth of the month. This was an awakening from below, and by this they were rewarded with the light of redemption, an awakening from above.

170- Faith Within Reason

Faith within reason is called "A wicked strap with which to strike the wicked." The reason is that through it, we are enslaved within the exile, for were it not for this they would immediately go free.

It is just as Israel were in Egypt 216 years, or as it is written, "And they afflicted them four hundred years." The thing is that what they built would immediately be buried in the ground "and they made their lives bitter with hard work" until "the children of Israel sighed from the work," until they were redeemed.

However, we should ask, Why did they not have a sigh and grief from the work? The reason is that if a person takes faith above reason, his body no longer wants to give him fuel for the work, since where there is no will to receive, there is no body.

The rule is that a body cannot work without any reception for itself. Ten percent, five percent, but no reception whatsoever? This is impossible. But there is an answer to this: One who increases the love of the Creator has the fuel coming from the love of the Creator, and being rewarded with the love of the Creator is specifically through hatred of the body.

171- How Good Are Your Tents, Jacob – 1

"How good are your tents, Jacob." *Yaakov* [Jacob] comes from the word *Akevaim* [heels] and "end." That is, it is the worst state of lowliness that one feels, when he sees that there is nothing in the world from which he can derive pleasure.

He says, "But the purpose of creation is to do good to His creations, and it is written that the delight and pleasure are mainly in Torah and *Mitzvot* [commandments], yet he does not feel any flavor or delight in Torah and *Mitzvot*, although it is written 'for they are your life and the length of your days.'" However, he does not see it.

Likewise, in corporeality, it is written that there is pleasure there because the *Kedusha* [holiness] illuminates in them in a tiny light, yet even this he does not feel now, in corporeality. Thus, he is in a state where he is fed up with life because he has no meaning in life.

At that time, one must believe that he was given this state on purpose from above, so he will have a lack, a reason to pray for the Creator to give him the filling for the lack. This is called "Your dwellings, Israel," for Israel means that he feels that he would like to work for the sake of the Creator, called "Israel," and if there is no deficiency, there is no filling.

172- Man and the Torah

When a person learns Torah, the person is called "low," meaning he is concerned only with his own benefit, and he has no clue concerning *Dvekut* [adhesion] with the Creator, and the Torah that he is learning is from people who were in *Dvekut* with the Creator.

173- Tefillin

The hand *Tefillin* are placed on the weaker hand, which is the left. There are seven bindings there, corresponding to the seven qualities. Each binding is regarded as ascents and descents, but at the same time they advance, meaning that in each wheel, as they go up, there must be a point of descent, or it is impossible to ascend. This is so because if there is no *Kli* [vessel], there is no light; if there is no lack, there is no filling of the lack.

Hence, the hand *Tefillin* are called *Malchut*, which is "faith," in which there are ascents and descents. This is why it was said, "To you as a token and not for others as a token," since there is still no revealing on the outside.

Conversely, the head *Tefillin* are regarded as the Torah, where there is revealing. This is why our sages said, "and they will fear you," for it is already revealed outwards that the light is already clothed in the *Kelim* [vessels].

174- The Commandments Are from the Mouth of the Creator

We were given *Mitzvot* [commandments] from the mouth of the Creator, which are from the Torah, as well as *Mitzvot* of our great sages, and customs of Israel by which we can delight the Creator. Afterward, the light that is found in these *Mitzvot* will be revealed.

175- Three Degrees of Man

"Rabbi said, 'I have learned much Torah from my teachers, more from my friends, and most from my disciples'" (*Makkot* 10a). A teacher to a student is in a manner of bestowal. "More from my friends": A friend asks his friend to learn with him, and by this do him a favor. "And most from my disciples": Disciples are those who want to learn. They want to understand and say, "Teach us, our teacher, where this is from." These are the three degrees in man.

176- Faith Is Regarded as Above Nature

Faith is called "something that is not natural," since it is above reason. Within reason is called "natural," and it is imprinted within man that what he understands and feels, he can do.

Moses is called "faith above reason," and Korah is called "reason," as our sages said, "Korah was clever." Hence, Korah's sin was that he disputed Moses, and not the Creator. Korah said that Moses fabricated and did not speak from the mouth of the Creator.

This is why the sin was so grave, since his view was against the way of faith. This is why Moses asked the Creator to punish him also in a manner of above reason, to show the whole of Israel that the work, the reward, as well as the punishment are all above reason.

Concerning the reward being above reason, it is in the manner of "if you labored and found." That is, after a person exerts himself in accepting the burden of the kingdom of heaven, he is rewarded with things he never thought he would achieve. This is why it is called "finding," since he never thought about it. This is why it is regarded as coming to him absentmindedly, as though he found it, as our sages said (Sanhedrin 97a).

177- The Fruit of Torah

A Sage's Fruit, Part 1

She has nothing of her own except that which others give her. *Malchut*, called "will to receive," is forbidden to receive for herself, meaning into her own quality, due to the *Tzimtzum* [restriction]. By not wanting to receive, to extend into her own quality, she receives from others what they bestow upon her.

This is as it is written, "In return for 'And Moses hid his face for he was afraid to look,' he was rewarded with 'The image of the Lord does he behold'" (*Berachot* 7a). In other words, specifically by not wanting to receive into his own quality and wanting to go above reason, he was rewarded with the *Daat* [reason/knowledge] of *Kedusha* [holiness], and from this comes all the proliferation. However, if he wants to receive into his own quality, this is called "Another God is sterile and does not bear fruit."

178- Father Ejected Mother Because of Her Son

Father means "whole 1." "Ejected mother" pertains to the intellect, outside of the degree, so as not to use the intellect. Why "because of her son"? It is so he can receive the understanding, the knowledge, without blemishing with his vessels of reception.

For this reason, we begin with work above reason, where the vessels of reception cannot grip. Conversely, where the reason agrees with the work, there is a grip to the vessels of reception, or the reason would not agree to work in order to bestow.

"Father" is the first reason in the order of the work. "Ejected *Bina*," meaning his intellect will be outside of his boundaries, so as not to consult with the intellect about the work. "Because of her son," since understanding comes from two opposite things.

This is called "the view of *Kedusha* [holiness]." Her son is considered the purpose, and the purpose of the work is for man to achieve a state where all his actions are for the sake of the Creator. This can be above reason, meaning that if reason agrees, the body evidently feels in this self-benefit, or it would not agree to it.

179- *Ibur* [Conception] – 1

The broken and dead *Kelim* [vessels] arise with the sparks for an *Ibur* through the *Reshimot* [recollections] that received their light.

For example, after the sin of *Adam HaRishon*, the creatures are regarded as broken and dead *Kelim*. That is, their *Kelim* are only in self-reception, separated from the Life of Lives. There is only a spark in them from the *Reshimot* of *Ohr Hozer* [reflected light] that remained and descended in order to sustain the *Kelim* so that through it, they will be able to rise for the revival of the dead.

That spark is a spark of *Kedusha* [holiness] and is a residue of the *Ohr Hozer*. We must raise it, meaning receive it in order to bestow, which is called "raising," meaning raising MAN. By this, a *Masach* [screen] and *Aviut* [thickness] are made, on which comes the filling, when the *Ohr Hozer* fills the *Kelim* to an extent that will clothe the lights (*Ohr Yashar* [direct light]).

180- King David Has No Life

Rabbi Shimon said that King David did not have a life at all, except that *Adam HaRishon* gave him seventy years of his own. Another interpretation: Each of the forefathers, Abraham, Isaac, and Joseph, gave him of their lives. Isaac did not give him because he comes from his side, from the left side. That is, "left" is called "darkness," as it is written, "Abraham begot Isaac" (*The Zohar, VaYishlach*, Item 54).

Accordingly, we should ask why Isaac had life and it is not said that he needed to take life from Abraham's number, as David took life from their number, and with Isaac, it is to the contrary, that he was included with Abraham and has more than Abraham.

In the work, we should interpret that when a person walks on the right, he has vitality because "the blessed cling to the Blessed." This is not so with the left. For this reason, we must always walk on the right, and only a little bit on the left.

181- The Quality of Adam HaRishon – 1

The quality of *Adam HaRishon* is dust, as it is written, "And God created man from the dust of the earth." "Dust" means that he is unfit for sowing. This means that in and of herself, *Malchut*, which is the will to receive on which there was a *Tzimtzum* [restriction], has no life at all. Rather, it is called "a space devoid of light."

182- Heresy Is the Punishment

Heresy is a punishment, that he must look at another body, how it speaks against reason. We must feel sorry for it and evoke mercy on it that it will be reformed.

183- Work Is the Most Important

Man's work should be primarily in order to "raise the *Shechina* [Divinity] from the dust."

This means the matter of the kingdom of heaven, meaning to accept the burden of *Malchut*, which is faith in the Creator, is for the sake of the Creator and not for one's own sake. Since man was created with a will to receive for himself, he is inherently incapable of serving the Creator.

Hence, man's work is to do good deeds, meaning Torah and prayer to the Creator that the Creator will help us raise the *Shechina* from the dust, which is called an "awakening from below," meaning that the lower ones evoke a lack, which is what we say, "May it please You," meaning that there will be a desire above to satisfy our lacks.

This is the meaning of "Let them take Me a donation," which *The Zohar* interprets, to exalt the Creator, which is *Tarum-Hey* ["raise the Creator" or *Trumah* (donation)], meaning *Malchut* that is lowered to the dust, to raise her from her lowliness. However, this requires that the Creator will raise her, as it is written, "The Merciful one will raise for us the fallen hut of David."

184- The Time of Wearing the *Tefillin* [Phylacteries]

The time for wearing *Tefillin* is from the time he begins to see his friend in his four cubits. What does this imply to us in the work? His friend is the Creator, as it is written, "Your friend and the friend of your father, do not leave," "For the sake of my brothers and friends." "Four cubits" are man, who is regarded as "four cubits." If he sees and feels the presence of the Creator within his four cubits, this is called "a day."

At that time, it is considered that he is wearing *Tefillin*, as it is written, "And all the peoples of the earth shall see," for then there is seeing and he is rewarded with *Tefillin*, when he becomes *Tafel* [of no importance] before the Creator.

185- Concerning *Shekalim* – 1

Shekalim: The meaning of *Shekel* is that a person *Shokel* [weighs/considers] what to do. "Half a *Shekel*" comes from the words, "A prayer makes half," when he must pray that the Creator will complement His will.

186- Return, Israel – 1

"Return, Israel, unto the Lord your God." Our sages said, "Great is repentance, for it reaches unto the throne, as was said 'unto the Lord your God'" (*Yoma* 86a).

Kisse [chair] is from the word *Kissui* [cover] and from the word *Kisse* (see in the "Introduction of The Book of Zohar" in the *Sulam* ["Ladder" commentary on *The Zohar*]). "For you have failed in your iniquity," for "One does not grasp words of Torah unless he has failed in them" (*Gitin* 43a). This is so because before one sees that he has failed in the iniquity, it is impossible to repent.

"Take with you words and return to the Lord. Tell Him, 'Take away all iniquity and take good, and we will pay with the bulls of our lips." "Take with you words and return to the Lord," meaning that repentance before the Creator must be by saying words.

Who said to Him, "Take away all iniquity"? These are people who feel that they are carrying iniquities. "Take good" means that they want to receive the good, which is the power of bestowal, as it is written, "My heart overflows with a good thing; I say, 'My work is for the King.'"

And what should they say when they repent? "And we will pay with the bulls of our lips," for *Safah* [lip] is regarded as the *Sof* [end], meaning the kingdom of heaven. It must be for the Creator, and lip, which is important and regarded as wholeness, is as bulls, "For a day in Your courtyard is better than a thousand" (Psalms 84).

187- The Greatness of the Creator Is His Humbleness

To the extent that a person appreciates the greatness of the Creator, to that very extent, he sees His humbleness. That is, the Creator is humble, for He turns to the person. If the Creator is not so great, then He is also not so humble, since man is also great, to an extent. But when a person appreciates the Creator as great, according to the greatness of the Creator, so he sees His humbleness.

188- Covering a Portion, Revealing Two Portions – 1

We should ask why they revealed if afterward they concealed more. We should interpret that it means that to those who were worthy, they revealed a portion, and to those who were not worthy, so they would not see the truth, they had to conceal two portions.

189- Concerning Learning the Wisdom of Kabbalah

In the introduction to the book *Imrei Yosef* by the ADMOR of Spinka, he writes there in the name of Rav Chaim Eliezer the meaning of the verse, "The glory of God is to conceal the matter and the glory of kings is to delve in the matter" (Proverbs 25).

He explained that if a person wants to learn the wisdom of Kabbalah, to know how many worlds and *Sefirot* there are, meaning the glory of God, to know the greatness of His glory, "conceal the matter."

But if one wants to learn the wisdom, to know how to crown the Creator and how to serve Him with intention and sanctify one's 248 organs and make them a vehicle for the *Kedusha* [holiness], this is called "the glory of kings," how to crown and serve Him. In that case, "delve in the matter."

190- The Place of Repentants

"Where repentants stand, complete righteous cannot stand" (*Berachot* 34b).

When a person learns, he is called "complete righteous." When he cannot learn, he is called "wicked." If he overcomes, he is called "repentant." The rule is "According to the sorrow is the reward." Hence, the complete righteous cannot stand where repentants stand.

191- The Roles of Light of Wisdom

There are two roles to the light of wisdom. When it shines, we come to the recognition of evil. Afterward, when one has the recognition of evil, he knows not to use the vessels of reception. Subsequently, it shines and gives strength to the vessels of reception to be able to receive in order to bestow. It follows that there are two actions here for the purpose of the *Kelim* [vessels].

3) This is the abundance of light of wisdom that shines once he has corrected *Kelim* that work in order to bestow.

The light of *Bina* gives the vessels of bestowal so they can aim in order to bestow. Hence, we should discern, 1) unclean 320, 2) 288 without *Malchut*, 3) clean 320 after the giving of the red of *Ima* [Mother], 4) 365 after the light of wisdom shines to the corrected 320 and is called "the bottom *Hey* of *Abba* [Father]."

192- Foundations

"If He brought us near Mt. Sinai and did not give us the Torah, we would be content."

The interpreters asked, "Without the Torah, how can it be said that we would be content? After all, the Creator created the world for the Torah, as our sages said about the verse, 'If My covenant were not day and night, I would not set the ordinances of heaven and earth'" (*Avoda Zara* 3a).

We should ask according to what our sages said, "I have created the evil inclination; I have created the Torah as a spice" (*Kiddushin* 30b). If their filth was removed at the time of Mt. Sinai, meaning that the evil inclination was removed from them, then they no longer need the Torah.

The Torah that was given to them then was from a higher quality, as an essence, and not as a means. That is, they need the Torah not because the Torah is the goal. Rather, the Torah came to help us achieve something else, which cannot be obtained without the Torah.

However, in its higher quality, the Torah is a goal. It follows that the majority of the Torah is as a means for the evil inclination, but there are a chosen few in the generation who are rewarded with the Torah as an essence.

Concerning "Teach me the whole of the Torah on one leg," he said, "That which you hate, do not do unto your neighbor" (*Shabbat* 33a). It is as Rabbi Akiva said, "Love your neighbor as yourself is the great rule of the Torah." The people of Israel were rewarded with this love, as our sages said about the verse, "And the people camped … as one man with one heart."

It follows that the giving of the Torah was as a gift, meaning an essence, and not as 613 *Eitin* [Aramaic: counsels], called *Mitzvot* [commandments].

193- The Meaning of the Second Restriction

Tzimtzum Bet [Second Restriction] in ZAT de Nekudim were separated because there was no correction of lines in them, which is called "connected."

In a place of lack, the abundance does not shine because there is a place of reception called "separation." But if it does not leave abundance because it does not need, since it is in above reason, called "desiring mercy," there is no place for judgments because no deficiency is evident, so there is no place for the grip of the *Sitra Achra* [other side]. This is called "the world of correction," for everyone to be connected.

194- Why Was David Punished?

"Raba said, 'Why was David punished? It is because he called the words of Torah 'songs,' as was said, 'Your laws were songs to me in the house of my dwelling.' The Creator said to him, 'Words of Torah, of which it is written, 'If you blink, it is gone,' you call them 'songs'? I therefore fail you with something that even children know, as it is written, 'But he did not give any to the sons of Kehat because theirs was the work of holiness,' and he came in a wagon.'"

RASHI interpreted "the house of my dwelling": When I ran from my enemies and feared them, I played with Your laws and they were to me songs to entertain me. You make me blink and fold, for if you fold your eyes to inadvertently blink from looking at them, promptly, it is gone.

MAHARSHA: "Songs," since the singing is in one's mouth momentarily, while the words of Torah are never to part from one's mouth so he will not forget them (*Sotah* 35a).

We can interpret that words of Torah are *Malchut*, who is called "speech," which is faith, and faith must be continuous, for about faith it can be said, "If you cast your eyes on it, it is gone," for in a moment, everything disappears from him. Conversely, the Torah is not forgotten in one moment.

Yet, he was using the laws during the escape, meaning when he had fear, then he was using the fear, and the Creator told him that this was a continuous matter.

"Therefore, I fail you," since "One does not grasp words of Torah unless he has failed in them" (*Gitin* 43a). "They shall carry the work of the Temple on their shoulders." This is called "a burden," which they carry on their shoulders, but he placed it in a wagon.

Agala [wagon] comes from the word *Agol* [round], which does not have a top or a bottom, meaning it is an awakening from below. Conversely, straight has top and bottom, depending on man's work. This is called an "awakening from below." A "shoulder" means taking on the burden, which is an awakening from below.

195- The Association of the Quality of Judgment with Mercy

Concerning the association of the quality of judgment with mercy, by which the lower one became worthy of *Mochin*, and concerning the *AHP* of the upper that fell into the lower one.

It is known that the main work is the choice, meaning "choose life," so there will be *Dvekut* [adhesion], which is *Lishma* [for Her sake]. By this, one is rewarded with *Dvekut* with the Life of Lives. When there is open Providence, there is no room for choice. For this reason, the upper one raised the *Malchut*, which is the quality of judgment, to the *Eynaim* [eyes]. This created a concealment, meaning that it seemed to the lower one that there was a drawback in the upper one, that there was no *Gadlut* [greatness/adulthood] in the upper one.

Subsequently, the qualities of the upper one are placed within the lower one, meaning they are deficient. It follows that these *Kelim* [vessels] have equivalence with the lower one, namely that as there is no vitality to the lower one, so there is no vitality in the upper qualities. In other words, he feels no taste in Torah and *Mitzvot* [commandments] for they are lifeless.

At that time, there is room for choice, for the lower one to say that this whole concealment that he feels is because the upper one restricted himself for the sake of the lower one. This is called

"When Israel are in exile, the *Shechina* [Divinity] is with them," that whatever taste he feels, so he says. That is, it is not his fault that he does not feel the taste of vitality. Rather, in his view, there really is no vitality in spirituality.

If a person overcomes and says that the bitter taste he finds in these nourishments are only because he does not have the proper *Kelim* to receive the abundance because his *Kelim* are to receive and not to bestow, and he is sorry that the upper had to hide himself, for which the lower one can slander, this is regarded as MAN that the lower one raises.

By this, the upper raises his *AHP*. "Raising" means that the upper one can show the lower one the merit and the pleasure that exists in the *Kelim* of *AHP* that the upper one can reveal. Thus, from the perspective of the lower one, it follows that he raises the *Galgalta Eynaim* of the lower one, and by this itself, the lower one sees the merit of the upper one. It follows that the lower one ascends together with the *AHP* of the upper one.

Thus, when the lower one sees the greatness of the upper one, by this itself the lower one grows.

However, initially, the lower one is fit to receive only *Katnut* [smallness/infancy]. When *Gadlut* in the upper one appears to the lower one, a dispute between right and left emerges in the lower one, meaning between faith and knowledge.

However, the upper is also diminished later by the lower one. This is regarded as *Masach de Hirik*, meaning that for the lower one to be able to receive the degrees of the upper one, the lower one must receive knowledge only to the extent of the faith, and not more. This is regarded as the lower one restricting the left line of the upper one, meaning that the lower one is the cause.

At that time, the lower one can exist because he comprises knowledge and faith together. This is called "three lines," and specifically in this manner, the lower one acquires wholeness.

196- Devotion

Devotion means that one must sanctify the name of the Creator in public, meaning if the public forces him to commit a transgression that is regarded as "Be killed but do not transgress," meaning if the aim of the public is to be idol-worshippers, then even on shoelaces applies the matter of "Be killed but do not transgress."

In the work, man's desires are called "general public." If the desires are of idol-worshippers, this is called "idol-worshipping general public," who want him to idol-worship. At that time, it is forbidden for him to concede even the shoelaces to the will to receive, if their intention is to thereby remove him from the law of Israel.

197- Concerning Suffering – 1

In the work, suffering cleanses, as our sages said, "I place over you a king such as Haman, who will reform you against your will" (*Berachot* 5a). In other words, the nature of the will to receive is that it wants to enjoy life.

When a person receives into his heart a part of the soul of *Kedusha* [holiness], and the soul wants to be a giver, and the will to receive does not give it the required forces, then the will to receive itself takes no pleasure in life, since the desire to bestow does not let it rest. Each day, it makes it see that if he lives like a beast, this is not a life, when his only needs are worldly lusts.

By this he becomes fed up with life and feels only suffering in life because in everything he does and wants to enjoy, the soul of *Kedusha* does not give him satisfaction in this life. Finally, the will to receive itself says, "I see I have no choice but to obey the desire to bestow, for otherwise I will have no rest." This is called "who will reform you against your will."

198- *Hochma* and *Hassadim*

The light of *Hassadim* [mercies] cannot shine in a place that was restricted. It is like a person who engages all day long in idle things, and when he comes to pray, he wants to pray with intention. And yet, we see that he is given foreign thoughts and cannot aim his mind during the prayer. Although prayer is bestowal, meaning that his *Kli* is light of *Hassadim*, yet why does the light of *Hassadim* not shine for him then?

The reason is that the light of *Hochma* is attached to the light of *Hassadim*, since they are one light. If he is given light of *Hassadim* when all his *Kelim* [vessels] are immersed in reception, he will taste the *Hochma* [wisdom] that is found in the *Hassadim*, and it is impossible to separate the *Hochma* from the *Hassadim*.

199- Oral Torah

"Moses His servant" is called "faith in the sages." Everything that the sages say is called "And they believed in the Lord and in His servant, Moses," meaning that they believed that Moses received the Torah from the Creator and that the expansion of Moses is in every generation. Hence, faith in the sages extends over the continuation of "His servant Moses." This is called "oral Torah," and every teacher gives to the public what he had received from his teacher.

200- Receiving Pleasure from Three *Kelim* [Vessels]

Man receives pleasure from three *Kelim* called "future," "present," and "past."

The greatest pleasure is from the future. For example, when one thinks that he will be invited to a wedding or to an important dinner, where although there are many people in his town, only a few, important people were invited to this dinner, and he is one of them.

1) The meal and the wedding will take place in some time, but he is already enjoying the future, as was said, "Criminal thoughts are worse than a crime" (*Yoma* 29a), since he has much time to enjoy the future.

2) The present—when he is at the dinner and sees that only important people are attending, he is delighted.

3) After the fact, when he remembers the honors he received at the dinner, this also delights him.

One should depict to himself that he will have a gathering of friends, and he should take actions and thoughts concerning how to appreciate the party.

To the extent that he prepares to appreciate the party, he can then enjoy in the present, during the party. To the extent that he enjoys the present, he can then enjoy the past, since as long as he remembers pleasure that he had at the party, he feels pleasure in the present.

It follows that one depends on the other: The future depends on the importance of the surrounding, and the surrounding is regarded as that which is destined to come, and the present is called "internal." The past is called *Reshimot* [recollections], meaning according to the measure of delight he had, to that extent he remains with *Reshimot*. This is regarded as *Reshimot* remaining so as to sustain the *Kelim*. That is, according to the *Reshimot* that remain within him from the pleasure, these *Reshimot* sustain the person.

&&201- Raising *MAN* – 1

Question: Raising MAN is regarded as raising a deficiency upward. Thus, why does he write that raising MAN is called *Mitzvot* [commandments] and good deeds?

MAN is called "a deficiency." But what does the lower one lack by which to add abundance in the world? When one engages in Torah and *Mitzvot*, the Torah and *Mitzvot* first create MAN in a person, meaning he receives a deficiency and sees that he is lacking Torah and fear of heaven because of the concealment and hiding in the world due to the *Tzimtzum* [restriction]. At that time, a person receives a lack, and raises that lack upward so as to be filled. It therefore follows that through the Torah and *Mitzvot*, a person receives MAN, and he elevates that MAN and causes revealing in all the worlds.

202- Concerning Fear

Fear should be that we will not be able to make the correction called "equivalence of form," which is called "because He is great and ruling," where one's only aim is to bestow. Also, the created beings should have the same intention: to bestow.

Conversely, the rest of the fears, whether of punishments in this world or punishments in the next world, are called "reception" and not "bestowal." The purpose of our work is that through the Torah and *Mitzvot* [commandments], we will achieve bestowal. This is the meaning of "God has made it so that He would be feared."

The question is why does He need us to have fear. The idea is that through this fear we will acquire the vessels of bestowal, called "equivalence of form," and then we can complete the purpose of creation.

203- The Torah Is Acquired through Suffering

Why these suffering? There is a rule, "There is no light without a *Kli* [vessel]." That is, there is no pleasure without a prior need for the pleasure, and the need is called "suffering," when one aches at not having pleasure. For this reason, we cannot obtain the light of Torah without a need for the light of Torah, meaning without suffering at not having the light of Torah. Through this suffering, one acquires the light of Torah.

Therefore, when one learns, he should make his Torah into a prayer, to feel a deficiency in the fact that he does not understand the Torah. When one understands, it cannot be said that he is deficient, although he can believe above reason that he does not understand. Nevertheless, above reason we do not feel the lack, since a person feels what comes into his mind.

204- *Two Kinds of Repentance*

1) Repentance in practice. This means that he tries to observe all the practices, meaning the practice of learning and engaging in Torah and *Mitzvot* [commandments] properly.

Repenting means that before he repented, when he still did not observe all the *Mitzvot* as they should be. But after he repented, he observes the whole of Torah and *Mitzvot* as they should be. However, all this is only in the practice. In the intention of the Torah and *Mitzvot*, he still hasn't repented.

2) Repentance in the intention. This means that before he repented in the intention, his aim was to receive reward. Now he regrets the aim he had before, and now he does everything not in order to receive reward, but only in order to bestow.

It follows that there is revealed work, to observe Torah and *Mitzvot* in practice, since a practice is revealed to all, and there is work in intention, which is concealed, since the aim is hidden from people.

205- Action and Intention

An act simply means the things one does—whether he engages in reception, meaning to delight himself, or in bestowal, to bestow upon others.

But there is the matter of intention. That is, when one performs an act of bestowal, such as charity and almsgiving, but one's intention is to receive in return, this is called "in order to receive." Alternately, his intention is to bestow, when he does not want any reward for the act of bestowal. Likewise, when one performs acts of reception, to delight himself, because the aim is that the wants to enjoy, to satisfy the need, the passion that he has to enjoy, or he delights himself because of the desire of the Creator. That is, if the Creator did not want people to enjoy, as it is His desire to do good to His creations, he would not want to receive pleasure.

206- Three Things in the World

There are three things: World, Torah, and man (*The Zohar, Toldot, Item 2*).

The world means *Malchut*.

The Torah is the light of Torah, which reforms a person.

Man is placed under the *Klipot* [shells/peels] for thirteen years, and after thirteen years he enters *Kedusha* [holiness]. By the power of the Torah he can invert the will to receive into a desire to bestow.

207- For Your Crimes, Your Mother Was Sent Away

"For your crimes, your mother was sent away," meaning repentance from both sides. The internality in Torah and Mitzvot [commandments] is called "your mother," meaning she pours on us abundance, as is the nature of a mother who sustains her children.

The question is why do we not feel the internality of the abundance that is clothed in Torah and Mitzvot. The answer is that before a person is qualified to receive, meaning before he can receive in order to bestow, he is placed under the rule of the Tzimtzum [restriction], which is an empty place. Only through repentance, when one obtains the vessels of bestowal, one becomes fit to receive. At that time, the internality that is concealed in Torah and Mitzvot is revealed to him.

This is called "For your crimes, your mother was sent away," through the sins that are governed by reception in order to receive. At that time, one must send and push away the internality in Torah and Mitzvot, and it is regarded as nonexistent.

When one repents, it is called "repentance from both sides": 1) The lower to the upper, when one comes closer to the Creator and wants to bestow upon Him, 2) The upper to the lower, when the Creator is revealed to a person and it is considered that He returns Himself, after being far.

208- The Meaning of Dust

"What profit is there in my blood if I go down to the pit? Will the dust thank You? Will it declare Your truthfulness? Hear, O Lord, and pardon me."

Concerning "dust," it is when one is under the governance of the will to receive, which is regarded as "dust." Adam HaRishon was born with this quality, but he was "dust off the earth." It is explained in the *Sulam* [Ladder commentary on *The Zohar*] that "earth" means *Bina*, which is the quality of bestowal.

When he corrupted the quality of bestowal, he fell back into being dust. It is called "dust" because the *Tzimtzum* [restriction] took place there, and no abundance of *Kedusha* [holiness] is drawn in there. This is why we taste there only the taste of dust in Torah and *Mitzvot* [commandments].

Hence, the correction is to take upon himself once more the quality of bestowal. However, it is not within man's power to do so, as it is against his nature. For this reason, we say, "Hear, O Lord, and pardon me."

"Pardoning" means as our sages said, "Although he is unworthy or deserving," which is called "And I will pardon that which I will pardon." That is, we ask the Creator to give us this power although we cannot make this power.

This is the meaning of the verse, "Lord, be my helper," as our sages said, "Were it not for the help of the Creator, he would not overcome it."

And all we can give is prayer.

209- A Groom and a Bride

The meaning of the joy of a groom and a bride is the Creator and the *Shechina* [Divinity].

It is written in *Ketubot* "enjoying being a fool," meaning that each one should pretend to be a fool, like the intellect that asserts that it is inappropriate to dance, and unbecoming to rejoice with the joy of a groom and a bride, since why should he care if the groom is marrying the bride?

However, Israel are responsible for one another, meaning that all of Israel are one quality. For this reason, each one should be happy that a part of him is gaining and enjoying now, for a part of him has received the complete correction.

210- Man's Actions

Without the body's excitement, it is impossible to make a person do something. Thus, "If he sits and does not commit a transgression, it is though he did a *Mitzva* [commandment]."

It cannot be said that this concerns a person who observes many "do not do" each day. For example, a person might say, "Today I did not commit murder, I did not rob, I did not steal" and so forth. However, all these negations do not make any excitement in the body if a person does not think about them.

Only where one thinks about them, when he has the opportunity to do, but he does not do because of the commandment of the Creator, it can be said that he observed these *Mitzvot* [commandments] not to do.

But without any movement of the body in thought or speech or action, it cannot be said that he observed the "no" without feeling it or knowing it, since everything we say about a person is only by his impressions and feelings.

But if a person is not in these places, these qualities cannot be said, for normally, the work is about conquering the inclination or about doing, or about avoidance from doing. In them there is the matter of conquering the inclination. It is about this that they said, "Do not say, 'cannot' about pork, but rather 'can,' but the Torah forbade."

Hence, there are four discernments:

1) It is hard for him to overcome the lust and he does the forbidden deed.

2) He does not do because of what people might say, for he is a person who is considered worthy, but suddenly his disgrace will become known in public.

3) He overcomes the inclination because the Torah forbade, but he is not happy that the Torah forbade and is suffering because of the prohibition in the Torah.

4) He is happy that now he is observing the King's commandment.

211- Man

The Zohar, Beresheet Bet, Item 81

1) The face of man is from the *Chazeh* and above.

2) From the *Chazeh* and below there is no face of man, but only three faces, which are ox, eagle, and lion.

3) The souls of people are from the *Chazeh* and below, yet they are called "the quality of man" because they ascend and are included in the "face of a man" from the *Chazeh* and above, as a stretched *Vav*. This is the meaning of "You are called 'man,' and not the nations of the world."

4) Before the three faces, ox, eagle, lion, ascend to be included in the face of a man, they, too, elicit offshoots into *BYA*. These are "animals," "birds," and "beasts." Afterward, they ascend and are included in the face of a man, and from all of them, the soul of *Adam HaRishon* was born.

It follows that Adam includes all of them. Subsequently, they descended to *BYA*, and since they were included in the face of a man, they are regarded as pure kinds, although they were parted and divided into many parts.

5) Both remained. The collective remains, which is the meaning of "the spirit of man, which ascends upward," and also the parts, as in "the spirit of the beast, which descends downward." They were divided into their parts as they were before the ascent.

6) After the sin of *Adam HaRishon*, called "man without merit," meaning that he does not want to ascend but to draw from above

downward, from this extend people's impure spirits, which derive from the filth of the serpent.

212- A Palace
The *Sulam* [Ladder] Commentary on *The Zohar, Pekudei*, Item 821

The first palace is "The Sapphire Brick," which is *Yesod de Malchut* (a *Heichal* [palace] is called *Malchut*).

"A woman of valor" is *Malchut* of *Atzilut*. "A harlot woman" is *Malchut* of *Tuma'a* [impurity].

At that time, Israel clung to a harlot woman and the Creator said to Hosea to take a harlot woman so as to know to what Israel clung. This is regarded as extension of *Hochma* from above downward.

The palace of the sapphire brick is the first of which it was said, "And they saw the God of Israel," for in *Malchut* there is the matter of seeing. The appointee over the palace, who stands at the door, is called Tahariel. If the soul, after one's parting from this world, is worthy, he lets her in. If the soul is unworthy, the appointee of the *Sitra Achra* lets her into the palaces of *Tuma'a* and she is sentenced for twelve months.

Also, the appointee of the *Kedusha* [holiness], if she is a "prayer of many," he lets in the prayer, where she is detained until all the prayers there become a crown on the head of the "Righteous One Who Lives Forever," called *Yesod*.

If she is a prayer of an individual, if she is "handsome," he lets her in. If not, he rejects her outside and she stands in the bottom firmament, of those firmaments below, which guide in the world. The appointee Sahadiel stands there and takes all the disqualified prayers and conceals them until a person repents.

If the person repents and prays a good prayer, the appointee takes the disqualified prayer and raises her to the good prayer, they merge together, and come before the Holy King. Sometimes, if a person is following the *Sitra Achra*, the appointee of the *Sitra Achra* takes the prayer and mentions man's iniquities before the Creator and slanders him.

Above the door of that palace is an opening that the Creator dug from judgments of the key. It opens three times a day, meaning that three lines shine there, and the door does not close.

Everyone need permission to enter, except for the gates of tears, which were not locked. When that prayer ascends, an angel called Ofan, whose name is Yerachmiel, takes the prayer, which through the prayer connects above.

213- Darkness, Fire, and Shadow

The *Sulam* [Ladder] Commentary on *The Zohar, Pekudei*

"Smoke is a mixture of fire and darkness." "Fire" is regarded as "female judgments," and darkness is "male judgments." "Darkness" is those who cling to the left line before it connects to the right. They become dark, meaning that the lights have become darkness.

"Fire" is female judgments, meaning that the quality of judgment is revealed.

"Shadow" is the judgment in their beginning, when the judgment in them is not apparent and it is considered that there is only a "shadow" of judgments there.

214- He Who Robs His Father and His Mother

"He who enjoys this world without a blessing, it was said about him, 'He who robs his father and his mother and says, 'There is no crime,' is a friend of a man who destroys'" (*Berachot* 35b). In

The Zohar, "Who is a man who destroys? It is he who blemishes the moon," since he connects to the *Sitra Achra* that prevented blessings from the world" (*Pekudei* 182).

The meaning of blessing is bestowal, regarded as "light of *Hassadim*." If the lower one does not engage in the quality of bestowal, he makes it impossible for abundance to pour down from above. Thus, he denies the world of blessings.

It can be interpreted that "world" is called *Malchut*, meaning he denies the abundance from the *Shechina* [Divinity], meaning that the abundance is extended through faith.

215- Having Guests – 1

A good guest is called "the good inclination," which comes at thirteen years. "Great is having guests," since the body does not let it in.

"I was a stranger in a foreign land," which means a foreign desire, the desire of a foreigner and not the desire of Israel.

Ysrael [Israel] is called *Yashar-El* [straight to the Creator]. Conversely, a foreign desire is a desire for a foreign God, as our sages said about the verse, "There shall be no strange God within you," and they explained, "Who is a strange God in man's body? It is the evil inclination" (*Shabbat* 105b).

Before a person feels that he has the desire of a foreigner, he has nothing to ask for to be redeemed from exile.

216- Concerning Women

"Women, how do they become worthy? ... by watching over the men" (*Berachot* 17a).

"Women" is the will to receive, which is regarded as *Lo Lishma* [not for Her sake]. What merit does one have if he is working *Lo Lishma*? The thing is, as our sages said, "A thousand walk into a room and one comes out to teach." In order for the one to come out to teach, meaning *Lishma*, a thousand *Lo Lishma* must assist.

It follows that women, those who are *Lo Lishma*, because they watch over the men, and a man means bestowing, it follows that they have a part in what they bestowed, in that through him, *Lishma* came forth.

217- Run My Beloved

First day of Passover, *Tav-Shin-Gimel*, April 20, 1943, Jerusalem

"Run my beloved, until the love of our wedlock wants."

Concerning running, that the Creator appears to us in a manner of running, it is in order to disclose the love. But why do we need the running first? It is because from the perspective of creation, all has already been completed, meaning that the love has been prepared for all in all its fullness. However, it should be revealed among the created beings, and it cannot be revealed without clothing in light of *Rachamim* [mercies], for the light of *Rachamim* qualifies the created beings to be able to receive the light of love.

The thing is that the light of love can clothe only in eternity. Hence, when a person does not feel himself as eternal, he cannot receive that light of love. Conversely, when he receives the light of mercy first, he is certain that "he will not turn back to folly." Naturally, the present and the future are the same for him.

It follows that to him, all seventy years are in one form, meaning in the form of the singular authority, and seventy years and six thousand years, which is the whole of creation, are all one, which is regarded as a complete degree. (This is as it is written, that when a person annuls his own desire and has no desire for himself, but rather for the collective, he is like a link in a chain, and the link is named after the chain while the link itself has no name in and of itself.)

It follows that he is named after the general creation, which is regarded as eternity. Hence, when he receives the light of mercy, he becomes fit to receive the love. This is the meaning of the words, "The love of our wedlock," which is a general quality and not a partial one, such as was said about Moses, "Behold, I pass all of my abundance," meaning a general form.

Receiving the light of mercy requires an awakening from below, meaning to ask for mercy. Then, when the light is revealed through the prayer, it is called "light of mercy."

How can one ask for mercy that will be in a manner of, "My soul yearns for Your salvation," meaning that he desperately needs salvation? Hence, the Creator is revealed to us in a manner of "running," and by the Creator seemingly running, meaning inverted Providence, at that time there is room to reveal the true prayer and to extend the light of mercy for eternity.

This is the meaning of "Run my beloved," so as to be "until it wants." Although from the perspective of the Creator, the love is complete, this love is not felt by the lower ones, who do not desire this love unless by receiving the light of mercy. Then the actions are fit to also want the light of love.

This is the meaning of "until it wants," meaning that there is a desire. This is so because there can be mercy in one person, whereas love pertains specifically to two. Hence, first we draw the light of mercy, which is specifically by running, and become fit to receive the light of mercy. Through the light of mercy, we become fit to receive the light of love.

This is the meaning of "You have loved us great love." Hence, when this is revealed in the lower ones, then "Great and overflowing compassion You have had for us," which is that the ability to receive the light of mercy has been prepared for us, for by this we become able to receive love.

Prayer is eternity, for the *Shechina* [Divinity] is called "prayer." Therefore, when one prays for himself, it is not eternity because while he prays and has some contact with the Creator, he has nothing to pray for, and what he extends onward is called "servitude" and not "prayer."

There is prayer only when there is a place to evoke mercy, which is as a critically ill person. But if he has some contact with the Creator, he is no longer critically ill and he can no longer pray. It follows that his prayer is not eternity.

Therefore, the Creator has prepared for us a whole world, as our sages said, "One must say, 'The world was created for me'" (Sanhedrin 37a), meaning that he should pray for the entire world. Therefore, when he comes to pray and has contact with the Creator, although he himself is not sick at the moment, he can pray for his contemporaries, meaning to extend mercies so that no one in his generation will lack abundance.

It is a great rule that the person himself is called "a creature," meaning only he alone. Other than him it is already considered the holy *Shechina*. It follows that when he prays for his contemporaries, it is considered that he is praying for the holy Shechina, who is in exile and needs all the salvations. This is the meaning of eternity, and precisely in this manner, the light of mercy can be revealed.

Another reason we should pray only for the general public is the need to disclose the light of mercy, which is the light of bestowal. It is a rule that it is impossible to receive anything without equivalence. Rather, there must always be equivalence.

Hence, when he evokes mercy on himself, it follows that he is engaged in reception for himself. And the more he prays, not only is he not preparing the *Kli* [vessel] of equivalence, but on the contrary, sparks of reception form within him.

It turns out that he is going the opposite way: While he should prepare vessels of bestowal, he is preparing vessels of reception. "Cleave unto His attributes" is specifically "As He is merciful, so you are merciful."

Hence, when he prays for the public, through this prayer he engages in bestowal. And the more he prays, to that extent he forms vessels of bestowal, by which the light of bestowal, called "merciful," can be revealed.

By receiving the light of mercy, there is an ability to later reveal the quality of "gracious." This is the meaning of "Grant us the treasure of a free gift," for grace is love, as grace is without any rhyme or reason, and so is love.

And "free" means bestowal, that He is merciful. That is, by him receiving the light of mercy, he becomes fit to receive the light of love, which is the meaning of "until it wants." At that time, the desire appears in the lower ones, as well.

218- Israel Are the Sons of Kings

Israel are called "sons of kings" because anyone who crowns His name upon himself is called "a king's son," as it is written, "And sanctify yourselves and be holy, for I the Lord am holy," for anyone who sanctifies himself is called "holy" because the Creator is called "holy."

We should understand the meaning of "holy." In the Jerusalem Talmud (82 in *Yevamot*), "Anyone who retires himself from the pudendum is called 'holy.'" In *Midrash Rabbah*, *VaYikra*, "Wherever you find a fence around the pudendum, you find *Kedusha* [holiness]," for *Kadosh* [holy] means retired [separated]. That is, one must retire oneself from enjoying.

And what is the name *Kadosh* with regard to the Creator? After all, it cannot be said that there is reception for Himself in Him, for the Creator only gives. For this reason, man, too, must only give to the Creator. "Sanctify yourselves and be holy" means that you should be only givers, "For I the Lord am holy," since the Creator is the giver. This is the meaning of *Dvekut* [adhesion].

Thus, "Wherever you find a fence around the pudendum," for the pudendum is a place where it is forbidden to enjoy, as only in a place of *Mitzva* [commandment] is it permitted to enjoy.

"God made one opposite the other": Opposite the *Shechina* [Divinity] there is a "foreign woman" called *Klipa* [shell/peel], and the *Shechina* is called "faith above reason," which is bestowal.

If a person acts with the aim to bestow contentment upon his Maker, it is considered that he unites with the *Shechina*. If he acts in order to please himself then he is uniting with the foreign woman, whose aim is only to receive for herself.

The unification of the Creator with the *Shechina* is that as the Creator only gives, so the *Shechina*, who is *Malchut*, all the desires extend from her to the lower ones by turning those desires into aiming to bestow. By this they cause the root of all the desires to be only to bestow. This is called "unification," meaning that he unites two qualities into one.

This is the meaning of "Man and woman, if they are rewarded, the *Shechina* is between them" (*Sotah* 17a). In other words, the quality of "woman" is the opposite of the quality of "giver." *Shechina* between them means that then it is evident that the *Shochen* [dweller] is present in the place of those desires. At that time, the desires are called *Shechina* because the *Shochen*, meaning the Holy One, can unite there, since there is equivalence, called *Dvekut*.

For this reason, wherever one retires from enjoying and causes unification, you find in it *Kedusha*, since the upper light can be there because the *Kelim* [vessels] can receive the light of the Creator called *Kedusha*, for the *Kedusha* is present only in a place of purity. "Purity" means purity of qualities, and then the *Kedusha* is present in a place of purity.

However, sometimes, "I the Lord, who dwells with them in the midst of their *Tuma'a* [impurity]," meaning that even when they still do not have *Kelim* that are ready to be in equivalence, in order to assist a person in achieving this, he must be aided from above. This is the meaning of *Lo Lishma*, that the light in it reforms him.

That light is called "The Lord, who dwells with them in the midst of their *Tuma'a*."

This pertains specifically to one who wants to achieve *Lishma* but cannot overcome his body. Hence, he is given that light so he can defeat the will to receive and walk in the way of the Creator, which is bestowal.

By this we will understand the verse, "And now if you surely listen to My voice and keep My covenant, you will be unto Me a *Segula* [remedy/virtue] out of all the nations, and you will be unto Me a kingdom of priests and a holy nation." These are the words that the Creator speaks to the children of Israel. These are the words, not less and not more, meaning there is no need for more than this.

219- Seek Peace and Pursue It

In the verse, "Turn away from evil and do good, seek peace and pursue it" (Psalms 34).

There are two forces in the world that give man the motivating force that will compel him to revoke his rest force. That is, the force of rest, which is in the qualities of the soul, yields to two other forces, meaning become revoked, and by this the soul takes upon itself the force of movement: 1) the rejecting force, 2) the attracting force.

The rejecting force is from something bad and loathsome that compels one to run away. The attracting force is good and nice things that one is compelled to chase. However, a single force, whether attracting or rejecting, is insufficient to revoke the force of rest.

"Turn away from evil" is called the "rejecting force," if a person feels that it is bad. "Do good" is called the "attracting force" if a person feels that this is good and he must chase it and obtain it.

"Seek peace and pursue it." The question is, What is the war that one must try to make peace, and even pursue it?

The war is the war of life, where each one is fighting with the other and by this acquires what he wants. For example, the merchant is fighting with the buyer and wants to defeat him in order to get what he wants, meaning money for no merchandise, or the worst possible merchandise. It is likewise to the contrary—the buyer with the seller—the least money for the best commodity.

The employee with the employer—the employer wants more output and more hours for a lower salary, and the employee is to the contrary, a higher salary and more rest. In other words, in the quantity of time and quality of output, we should understand who causes this whole war.

But first, we must understand what man is and how one is measured as great or small. It is said that a person has a big heart, is heavy-handed, and narrow-minded, meaning that it cannot be said that a person is the flesh and bones. Thus, what is man?

We should discern three qualities of desire: big, small, and nothing-to-it. The power of desire is measured by the suffering. A big desire means that if one does not get what he wants he will suffer terribly. A small desire means that if one does not get what he wants he will suffer very little. A nothing-to-it desire means that if he does not get what he wants he will still not suffer.

From where does the will to receive stem? From the thought of creation to do good to His creations.

We believe that "The whole earth is full of His glory," "For it is not a vain thing for you, for it is your life and the length of your days," "For they are our lives and the length of our days." Moses said all this, and the sages of Israel who established the prayers said this.

And what do we say and feel? We want to derive vitality and pleasure from other things, and the Torah takes away from us many pleasures that we could obtain if the Torah permitted us.

220- Good Taste in Small, Corporeal Things

We were given a good taste in small, corporeal things so that when we grow up, we will know how to keep spiritual, important things.

We see a small child playing with a game his parents bought for him. As long as he enjoys it, he plays with it. Afterward, the child throws it, breaks it, or deliberately or accidentally loses it." When his father yells at him, "I spent a lot of money on these toys, why do you break, or throw, or deliberately or accidentally lose them?" The child does not even understand what his father is saying.

When he grows up a little, he begins to understand but still cannot control himself and keeps things he does not need. Rather, he is compelled to break them because he is already accustomed since childhood to break anything that is not needed right away.

Then, when he grows some more, he acquires the control power to keep things in his home even when he does not find an immediate need for them. Finally, he comes to understand that even when he is no longer interested in these things, there is still no need to break them. Instead, they can be useful for small children. In other words, these things will serve people who have less knowledge than his.

Were it not for these exercises, even a grownup would do so. For example, when he does not need his jacket, he would tear it. But from experience, he knows that this jacket can be useful to a person who is less affluent than him, so he sells it or gives it for free to a poor man, but he certainly does not tear it.

From this we understand that in order for man to be able to keep the spirituality and internality that are clothed in the Torah, he must go through all of the above exercises on corporeal things. When he completes them, it will be possible to give him spirituality, as well.

This is implied in "One does not sin unless a spirit of folly has entered him," and our sages say, "Who is a fool? He who loses what he is given."

221- What Is Life?

Life means as long as there is a desire to receive pleasure, or he enjoys what he receives, or enjoys giving to others. If he loses this force, he is considered dead.

Therefore, when a person is unconscious, it is considered that he fainted, meaning that he lost the will power to receive pleasure. When a person commits suicide, it means he has come to a state where he sees according to clear evidence that he can no longer receive pleasure, or because he is indebted to many people, who will afflict him, and these afflictions will annul the little pleasure he sees that he might still receive from this world.

For this reason, he will not go to the next world because he must exert in Torah and *Mitzvot* [commandments] and derive pleasure bringing contentment to his Maker. This pleasure is so great that it can revoke the most terrible afflictions in the world.

Accordingly, we were given *Mitzvot* that are regarded as "Be killed but do not transgress," where he takes upon himself the suffering of devotion because he believes that by acting in devotion it will give Him contentment. Thus, one who commits suicide testifies about himself that he derives no delight or pleasure from observing Torah and *Mitzvot* in order to bestow contentment upon his Maker.

222- Scrutinies in the Work

"Bruria found that disciple who was learning in a whisper. She kicked him and said to him, 'Is it not written, 'ordered in all things and kept'? If it is ordered in one's 248 organs, it is kept.' That disciple who was learning in secret, Bruria kicked him and said, 'Ordered in all things; if it is ordered in one's 248 organs, it is kept in the heart'" (*Iruvin* 54a).

"Secret" means that he has still not been rewarded with "hearing," called "voice." "Kicked" means awakening. "Beruria" is the *Beruriut* [scrutinies] of the work. "One's 248 organs" are the entire level, from *Chazeh* and above, which is covered *Hassadim* [mercies], meaning bestowal. Revealed *Hassadim* are from the *Chazeh* downward, which is reception in order to bestow.

There are two discernments: 1) bestowal, 2) reception in order to bestow. "Bestowal" is when one engages in Torah and *Mitzvot* [commandments] in a manner of bestowal, and he still does not taste the taste of *Mitzvot*. Reception in order to bestow means that he already feels the flavor of Torah and *Mitzvot*, but he receives that flavor in order to bestow.

223- Entry into the Work

The entry into the work must be in *Lo Lishma* [not for Her sake], meaning that by believing in the Creator he will have a life of pleasure. This means that if he does this action called "faith," it will give him elation and superior mental forces than when he does not perform this action.

It follows that this is a *Segula* [remedy/quality/power] by which he can taste greater flavors in quantity and quality than what he tastes while he is doing other things in order to receive pleasure.

This means that there are many ways to obtain pleasure, such as eating, drinking, and sleeping, or impressive clothes, or by doing things that make people respect him. Such actions are means by which he obtains pleasure.

Yet, the pleasures that these actions yield for him are limited in quantity and quality. Conversely, the *Segula* of faith brings him greater pleasure in quantity and quality.

All this is called *Lo Lishma* because his intention is only to obtain a greater pleasure.

Only after he achieves this degree called *Lo Lishma*, he is rewarded with other phenomena, when he comes to a higher state. That is, at that time he has no consideration of himself, and all his calculations and thoughts are the truth.

In other words, his aim is only to annul himself before the true reality, where he feels that he must only serve the King because he feels the exaltedness and greatness and importance of the King. At that time, he forgets, meaning he has no need to worry about himself, as his own self is annulled as a candle before a torch before the existence of the Creator that he feels. Then he is in a state of *Lishma* [for Her sake], meaning contentment to the Creator, and his concerns and yearnings are only about how he can delight the Creator, while his own existence, meaning the will to receive, does not merit a name whatsoever. Then he is regarded as "bestowing in order to bestow."

224- The Reason for the Faith

The reason for the faith is that there is no greater pleasure than to be rewarded with the revelation of Godliness and the instilling of the *Shechina* [Divinity].

In order for one to receive all this for the purpose of bestowal, there is a correction of concealment, where he engages in Torah and *Mitzvot* [commandments] even though he feels no pleasure. This is called "not in order to receive reward." When he has this *Kli* [vessel], his eyes soon open to welcome the face of the Creator.

When a desire awakens within him, that it is worthwhile to serve the Creator for the pleasure, he soon falls into concealment. This is regarded as death, meaning that previously, he was adhered to life, and he was rewarded with it only through the power of faith. Therefore, now that he is corrected and begins to work in faith once more, he receives back his breath of life. At that time, he says, "I thank You for returning my soul with compassion."

This is precisely when he assumes once more the work in the manner of faith above reason. When he had the concealment, he says, "Great is Your faith." The faith is so great that through it, he receives the soul once more.

225- Names Are Given only According to the Lower One

Concerning names, which point to revelations of the actions of the Creator, the name relates to the instruction of the action. All the actions are revealed in the lower ones, specifically in the attaining individual. Nevertheless, the attained in itself certainly does not have the same form as that which is apparent to the one who attains, since there is a merger of two things here, which adds a third form, a form that is born out of two forces, from the qualities of male and female.

In other words, when the filling comes because of the lack, there is a new phenomenon. That is, we must discern which form the deficient one has before he receives the filling. We should discern it after he receives the filling.

We should make two discernments in the filling itself, meaning which form it has before it comes in contact with the lack, meaning the matter in itself, which is called an "abstract force, not combined with a *Kli* [vessel]." And we should also discern after it is assembled in the *Kli*. Since the root of creation is not more than

Kelim [vessels] of a lack, we therefore have no attainment in a light without a *Kli*.

Hence, when we say that the Creator is called "Mighty," it is precisely when the quality of "might" appears on us. However, calling names that we do not attain, meaning without the filling of "might," before the abundance comes into it, at that time we do not say that the Creator is called "Mighty."

It follows that he says that the Creator has the quality of might although this quality is not revealed to him. Thus, he gives forms to light without a *Kli*. This is a lie, for a light without a *Kli* has no form. This is why they did not want to say "the Mighty God," if this quality did not appear to the lower ones.

226- The Ark Carries Its Carriers

The tablets were placed inside the ark. The tablets are called Torah, and it is clothed inside the ark, meaning faith.

Faith is a big and difficult task, which is not within our power to take upon ourselves. However, one must know that "The ark carries its carriers." In other words, what one can do is only to know the fear of the Creator, how far it is from human powers to carry out this task.

This is as in "Were it not for the help of the Creator, he would not overcome it," relating to the "Who" and "What" questions. This means that one should ask for the measures of fear and see it in its true, pure, and clean form, as it is written, "If you seek her as silver and search for her as a treasure, then you will understand the fear of the Creator." Before one seeks to see her form, it is impossible to understand what is the fear of the Creator.

Then, when he sees the difficulties and the resistance of the body to it, and we see that it is utterly impossible for a person to receive it, this is the place for prayer that the Creator will help, as in "Were it not for the help of the Creator."

At that time, "And you will find the knowledge of God" comes true, for only then is the time to be rewarded with the knowledge of *Kedusha* [holiness]. This is why it is called "finding," since a person already sees that it is utterly impossible that he will be able to take upon himself the burden of faith. It follows that after all the searches, all he found was the negation, how far this quality is from him. Yet, only then is he rewarded with the revelation of His name.

It follows that this is not in a manner of cause and consequence, where the order is that today I know little and tomorrow I know more until the whole matter becomes known to him.

Here it is to the contrary: Today, I know little, and tomorrow, unless I search in a manner of purity, I find within me less and less, and the next day even less, until we arrive at the point of zero.

But only then is one fit to take upon himself the faith in wholeness. It follows that it is a find that comes absentmindedly. This is why it is written, "And you will find the knowledge of God."

This is the meaning of the ark, meaning faith, carrying its carriers. It means that the faith gives strength to the carriers, who took upon themselves the heavy task. They come to a state where they think that they cannot carry the burden of faith, and think that they are carrying the faith, meaning that they do not see that it is within human capability to carry the ark on the shoulders of faith, which is a burden, called "ark," "will be carried on the shoulder."

But we must know that faith gives man strength. It gives man vitality, regarded as "the living carries itself." This means that according to the human intellect, it is impossible to achieve such a degree that is removed from any discernment of the will to receive, whether in mind or in heart. And yet, it gives strength, as in "the living carries itself," which carries a person, as in "the ark carries its carriers."

Then, when one is rewarded with this and has this reality, he calls this "finding," and he thought that he will always remain in a state of "between heaven and earth." At that time, he sees that even in such a state it can still impart eternal life upon him.

227- In *Katnut*, *Gevurot* Appear First

In *Katnut* [smallness/infancy], *Gevurot* [judgments] appear first, and then *Hassadim* [mercies]. In *Gadlut* [greatness/adulthood], *Hassadim* appear first and then *Gevurot*.

Katnut is called "the beginning of the work." A person begins in *Gevurot*, meaning in *Hitgabrut* [overcoming], and then he is rewarded with *Hassadim*. In *Gadlut*, once he has entered the King's palace, which is called *Hassadim*, he searches for work, to have what to do, since he suffices for *Hassadim* and finds no deficiency in himself, so it is the time for *Gevurot*.

228- Moses Is the Quality of Faith

"Moses died" is the departure of faith. "Moses was born" is the appearance of faith, by which we see that there is lack of faith, which causes one to draw faith, and this is regarded as Moses being born in it.

229- She Opened Her Mouth with Wisdom

"Rabbi Elazar said, 'Why is it written, 'She opened her mouth with wisdom and the Torah [law] of mercy was on her tongue'? There is Torah of mercy and there is Torah that is not of mercy. Torah *Lishma* [for Her sake] is Torah of mercy. *Lo Lishma* [not for Her sake] is Torah that is not of mercy. That is, Torah in order to bestow is called mercy, the quality of *Hassadim* [mercies].'"

"It is said, 'Torah to teach is Torah of mercy; not to teach is Torah that is not of mercy'" (*Sukkah* 49).

We should understand why if he does not teach others, it is regarded as not being of mercy. It is possible that the meaning of "to teach" refers to its own body and not simply teaching, meaning that he teaches the body to do everything in order to bestow, and this is why it is called "Torah of mercy." This change of phrasing, each one interprets the intention of the verse differently.

230- Am I In the Place of God?

"And he said, 'Am I in the place of God, who has withheld from you the fruit of the womb?'" RASHI interpreted, "You say that I should do as father; I am not as father. Father had no sons; I have sons from you and not from him" (*VaYetze*).

We found a prayer with Isaac, as it is written, "And Isaac pleaded with the Lord on behalf of his wife, for she was barren." This is why it is written "on behalf of his wife," and not "on behalf of Rebecca," since it is not the manner of the righteous to pray that the Creator will change the ways of nature in their favor. Thus, according to the interpretation of *The Zohar*, Jacob could not pray for her.

231- Aza and Azael

It is written in *The Zohar* (p 156 [in Hebrew]): The angels Aza and Azael are from the quality of *Achoraim* of *Abba* and *Ima* in which *GAR de Hochma* illuminated in the world of *Nekudim*. Prior to the sin, they were largely corrected, and after the sin they returned to their annulment and they will not be corrected before the end of correction.

This means that since they are from the quality of GAR, and before the end of correction only VAK de Hochma illuminates, they will have no correction. The stony heart belongs to the correction of the inner Abba and Ima, to which the Mochin of the angels relate.

232- Bribing the *Sitra Achra*

We should understand the difference between Yenika [suction/nursing] to the Klipa [shell/peel] and Kedusha [holiness], which is the prohibition between the part that is given to the Sitra Achra [other side], which is permitted, such as a goat to Azazel [scapegoat], and so forth.

It is said in The Zohar that the part that is given to the Sitra Achra is so he will not slander (see "Introduction of The Book of Zohar," concerning Abraham not wanting to give to the poor one).

By a corporeal allegory, we should interpret it as a person who smokes a cigarette in order to be able to scrutinize some matter better, where by the body enjoying the smoking, he can concentrate his mind and the body does not resist him. This is regarded as giving a part to the Sitra Achra so he will not slander.

But sometimes a person wants to smoke not so that the body will not object to learning, but simply because he wants to enjoy the pleasure of smoking. This is regarded as Yenika to the Klipa.

233- Concerning *Yenika* [Suction/Nursing]

We should discern two things: In Yenika [nursing], the infant cannot suck without the consent of the one who nurses. In other words, the one who nurses must agree to carry it out. This is unlike eating, where the food is already prepared but he must obtain them. Conversely, with nursing, the lower one elicits its nourishments.

If the upper must assist the lower one to suckle, this is regarded as a deficiency in the lower one. Although the lower one must elicit its food, he certainly needs the consent of the upper one. Otherwise, against his will, this is not the case concerning *Yenika*.

But with food that has already been prepared, it is possible for the infant to receive them without the awareness of the giver, or even the consent of the giver. This is unlike nursing, where it is impossible to suck without the awareness of the giver. Rather, all his nursing is together with the giver. When his food is without the giver with it, it is no longer regarded as food.

In *Yenika*, we should discern the following:

1) The abundance always comes together with the giver. If the giver is not standing at the time of the reception of the abundance, this is not regarded as *Yenika*, for a child cannot nurse without the mother. But as for the rest of the foods, it is possible to receive them even when the owner of the food stands next to the food.

2) Although the nourishments are in the mother's milk, the eliciting comes together with the reception of the abundance. This means that if the milk comes out of the mother without the baby receiving the milk, this is no longer regarded as nursing. Rather, it is specifically when the milk is revealed outward, together with the sucking of the infant.

3) The abundance does not pour out in a stream, but drips, meaning with breaks, so each time the baby wants to suck, it must draw out once more, since the milk does not pour out from the mother in a stream but in drops. In other words, the milk is drawn out when there is a desire on the part of the infant, but the milk soon stops and the newborn must start over every time.

234- Reality and the Existence of Reality

Example: A living baby is alive. This is called "reality." On the other hand, we see that his life depends entirely on nourishment. If the baby is not given the nourishment he needs, he will die. It follows that from the perspective of the existence of reality, he must always be sustained, as in "Who renews by His goodness each day the work of creation."

Concerning *Zivugim* [couplings], meaning the soul with the body. The soul is called "good inclination," and the body is called "evil inclination." They are two opposites: One is a desire to bestow, and one wants to receive. The choice is given to man to force the evil inclination to change its quality and work in order to bestow. The Creator makes this *Zivug* [coupling], as in "Were it not for the Creator's help, he would not overcome it."

The question was that if the Creator created the world, then there are no novelties. Rather, He only sustains it. Or were new worlds created, as our sages said, "The righteous build worlds each day"? If this is so then the Creator does not create new things.

The answer to this is that even now He is making *Zivugim*, meaning that even now He creates new worlds and new souls, but this, too, depends only on us, for we were given the choice to make *Zivugim*.

Night is the time of work, and morning is regarded as "after the work," when one obtains the results from the work. At that time, there was one who was lame and one who was blind. This is as Raba said, "I beseech you, do not inherit a double Hell" because the evil inclination revokes the good inclination and the good inclination the evil inclination. Rather, this requires the help of the Creator, as in "Were it not for the Creator's help, he would not overcome it."

The question was that if He created once then there are no novelties in creation, only sustenance. The answer is that there are novelties from the perspective of the souls, and this is called a "*Zivug* to beget new souls."

235- The Forms of the Light

The light that is clothed in the soul does not have the same form as the light before it clothes in the soul. The light is called "simple," meaning one quality. But when the light is clothed in the will to receive, called a "soul," it becomes complex, meaning made of two qualities—the quality of a giver and the quality of a receiver simultaneously.

Although there is no change in the light, with respect to the receiver, it is called a "different form" because it already consists of two qualities there.

For example, when a person eats meat and tastes the meat when it touches his palate. Although the taste he feels in the meat feels concrete, since he is receiving this taste from the meat, it still does not mean that that same flavor will be in the meat itself.

Rather, through this composition, when the palate touches the meat, there is this offshoot that is born from the light, meaning the meat, and the *Kli* [vessel], meaning the desire—that he wants to enjoy the meat.

Accordingly, we can understand that there is no connection between the light in and of itself, and the light that is dressed in the *Kli*. It was said about the light, "There is no thought or perception of Him whatsoever." And yet, that same light dresses in the *Kli*.

A blind man asked Rabbi Meir. He said to him, "Is it possible that it is written about it, 'But I fill the heaven and the earth?'" He was speaking with Moses from between the two curtains of the ark.

"He said to him, 'Bring me big mirrors.' He replied, 'See Your image in them.' He saw it big. 'Bring me small mirrors.' He said to him, 'See your image in them.' He saw it small.

"He said to him, 'As you, who is flesh and blood, change yourself however you want, he who said, 'Let there be the world' is much more so. When He wants, 'I fill the heaven and the earth.' And when He wants, He speaks with Moses from between the two curtains of the ark'" (*Beresheet Rabbah*, Portion No. 1).

All the above means that all the changes are according to the *Kelim*, from the allegory of the person acquiring a different form in the *Kelim*, meaning the mirrors, while there is no change in the person himself.

236- The Whole Earth Is Full of His Glory

The expansion of the upper light is clothed in the whole of reality and is called "the sustainer of reality." It appears in all the dresses that exist in the world, meaning in every corporeal thing before us. Everything is the light of the Creator, whether in dresses of Torah, meaning the letters of the Torah, or in the letters of the prayer, or in mundane things. The only difference is in the receiver, namely those who feel.

There are people who feel that the light of the Creator is dressed only in Torah and prayer. There are people who feel the light of the Creator also in combinations of letters of mundane things, and there are those who do not feel even in combinations of letters of Torah and prayer that it is the light of the Creator in the manner of "Who fills the whole of reality."

However, since there was a *Tzimtzum* [restriction], which is concealment, they do not feel that everything is the expanding light of the Creator.

That is, the measure that the creatures can attain, meaning the light that spreads into the sensation of the created beings, and besides the Creator wanting the lower ones to attain, it is certainly called "there is no thought or perception of Him whatsoever."

However, a person must believe in the *Tzimtzum*, meaning that it is only a concealment for man's benefit, while in truth,

"The whole earth is full of His glory," and there is no reality in the world besides Godliness, and all the concealment is only in one's sensations.

Before one is fit to attain the truth, he must believe that the truth is not as he knows or feels, but that it is as it is written, "They have eyes and they will not see; they have ears and they will not hear." This is only because of the correction, in order for man to achieve his wholeness, for he feels only himself and not another reality.

Hence, if one returns his heart to trying to walk in faith above the intellect, by this he qualifies it and establishes it so as to achieve the revelation of the face, as is presented in *The Zohar*, that the *Shechina* [Divinity] said to Rabbi Shimon Bar Yochai, "There is no place to hide from you," meaning that in all the concealments that he felt, he believed that here was the light of the Creator. This qualified him until he achieved the revelation of the face of His light.

This is the meaning of the measure of the faith that pulls one out of every lowliness and concealment if a person strengthens himself in this and asks the Creator to reveal Himself.

This is the meaning of what Baal HaSulam said, "Run my Beloved until she pleases," meaning that before one is fit to reveal His light, we ask of Him, "Run my Beloved," meaning that He will not reveal Himself to the created beings because the concealment is only the correction of creation.

Hence, one must brace oneself and pray for those two:

1) To be worthy of the revelation of the light of the Creator.

2) That the Creator will give him the power to grow stronger in faith above reason, for by this, he merges *Kelim* [vessels] that are fit for the revelation of the face, as in "The Lord will light up His face for you and will give you peace," as it is written, "I will hear what God will speak, for He will speak peace unto His people and unto His followers and let them not turn back to folly."

237- Mind and Heart

The will to receive is expressed in mind and in heart. By correcting it to work in order to bestow, a person can receive the upper abundance.

Let us explain the will to receive in the heart. The heart is called "desire and yearning for pleasures." Hence, if a person can correct his actions in a manner that he can relinquish all the pleasures in the world if he sees that it will not yield any benefit to the glory of the Creator, he is rewarded with receiving real pleasures because now their reception will not be for his own benefit.

By intimation, this is implied in the verse, "And he looked this way and that, and saw there was no person, and he struck the Egyptian." RASHI interprets that he saw that nothing good would come out of his offspring, meaning that he saw that from this Egyptian, meaning from this act, there will be no benefit.

"He struck the Egyptian," not letting him satisfy his will and rejecting his request. This is called "putting to death the act and the thought of that Egyptian," who is included in his heart. Also, the pleasure of the mind is only in doing what he understands what he is doing. To the extent that he does things against his reason, when his reason demands otherwise, his suffering is measured by the measure of resistance to his mind.

When a person goes above his mind, when he is given the mind that approves of all his work, he will be able to say that he is receiving all this in order to bestow, since for his part, he can relinquish the mind.

At that time, he can be rewarded with the light of faith, for he can relinquish because his aim is not for himself. The proof of this is that he does everything even if it is against the intellect. Naturally, he is able to receive the light of faith and can be certain that his aim is to bestow.

But when he cannot work in faith, but only where the mind approves, meaning according to the will to receive, he remains inside the *Tzimtzum* [restriction]. For this reason, we need two works: mind and heart.

238- The Joy of the Groom and Bride

We have gathered here to partake in the joy of the groom. A person must delight the groom, as our sages said, "He who enjoys a groom's meal and does not delight him..." (*Berachot* 6b).

In the Seven Blessings [said at a wedding], we say, "Who delights a groom with the bride." If the Creator delights the groom and the bride, we must also partake in the joy and delight the groom and the bride. Our sages said, "He who enjoys a groom's meal and does not delight him," meaning that they decreed to delight the groom.

About the bride, we say, "How does one dance before the bride? A beautiful and graceful bride" (*Ketubot* 16b).

We should understand why specifically dancing pertains to the bride, and in general, what is a dance. We see that in a dance, there are ups and downs and turns to the four corners of the world, but in the end, we remain standing on the ground.

The groom implies the Creator, as it is written, "On the day of his espousal and on the day of the merriment of his heart," and as it is written, "And the Lord descended on the mount" which is a descent in degree.

A bride is called "the assembly of Israel." During the wedding, which is an indication of the upper root, we should know that even if all four corners of the world want to push the whole of Israel, and even after all the descents, they will remain standing in their place.

This is why we say, "A beautiful and graceful bride," since she remains in a state of beauty and not in a state of lowliness. We do not say as it is written, that now she is in exile, and we evoke the joy that will be at the end of correction.

The joy from the dance is like a sad tune that people enjoy. The tune depicts a collection of sufferings that have already passed, but now we enjoy the benefits we gained from the suffering. Likewise, the dance contains joy that after all the ups and downs they went through, they nonetheless remained standing firm in their place.

* * *

We have gathered here in order to delight the groom and the bride, as it is written in the Seven Blessings, "Blessed are You, Lord, who delights a groom and a bride." If we find that the Creator delights the groom and the bride, then we, too, must partake in this joy.

Concerning the groom, we find "He who enjoys a groom's meal and does not delight him," meaning he should delight the groom, but they did not say with what. Concerning the bride, we find, "Our sages said, 'How does one dance before the bride?'" and also to say, "A beautiful and graceful bride," like the House of Hillel, and not "A bride as she is."

The thing is that a groom is the Creator, from the words "descended in degree," as it is written, "And the Lord descended on the mount." A bride is regarded as "the whole of Israel." From the perspective of the Creator, there is no change at all, as it is written, "I the Lord do not change." All the changes come only from the receivers. Hence, a bride implies the receivers, which are the whole of Israel, where there is the matter of ascents and descents, meaning the time of exile and the time of redemption.

We should say that the guidance of the Creator is in the manner of good and doing good: "Everything that the Merciful One does, He does for the best," and "This too is for the best." It follows that during the dance, when there are changes, we should say, "A beautiful and graceful bride." This is after her end, meaning that by practicing the corporeal Mitzva [commandment], we evoke the root above, the unification of the end of correction, and in this we should delight.

239- Widows

"My anger will be kindled, and I will kill you with the sword, and your wives shall become widows and your children orphans" (Exodus 22:23).

"Rabbi Elazar said, 'From what was said, 'My anger will be kindled and I will kill you,' I know that their wives are widows and their sons orphans, so what does it mean when it says, 'And your wives will be...'? It implies that their wives wanted to marry but were not permitted to, and their sons wanted to inherit their fathers' assets but were not permitted.'"

RASHI interpreted that they would be taken captive. Thus, there will be two curses there: 1) the sword, 2) captivity. By being taken captive, they will not know if their husbands are alive or if the sons can inherit their fathers' assets (*Baba Metzia* 38b).

We should understand what it means that by veering off from the path of the Creator, a person is taken captive by the *Klipot* [shells/peels], who govern him and do not let him out of their authority. It means that at that time, a person cannot engage in Torah and *Mitzvot* [commandments] because the *Klipot* control him.

When a person walks on the path of truth, namely on the basis of faith, called "Who will find a woman of valor?" that person sustains the *Shechina* [Divinity]. It is as our sages said, "Israel sustain their Father in heaven," meaning that engagement in Torah and *Mitzvot* for the sake of the Creator is called "sustaining the Creator." This is the meaning of "My offering, My bread."

At that time, a person obtains understanding and knowledge of *Kedusha* [holiness] in Torah and *Mitzvot*, as it is written, "You grant man knowledge and teach a human being understanding." Hence, when the two are in order, a person has a wife and sons. But when one blemishes the faith, that person is "killed" and remains as merely a beast, meaning that he knows of nothing more than obtaining beastly lusts.

It follows that the "woman" is regarded as a widow, since the quality of man, who is her husband and the bestower of the faith, has been killed. However, they are not permitted to marry because he was taken captive by the *Klipot*, so it is not known if he was killed.

Hence, even though the women want to marry, they are not permitted. This means that the *Shechina* wants to reconnect to each and every one; she wants to give everyone a reflection of repentance, which is the meaning of wanting to marry, but they are not permitted. That is, the person himself does not want to reconnect to the *Kedusha* because he is captive in the hands of the *Klipot*.

If he were not taken captive, but were killed for certain, as in "The wicked in their lives are called 'dead,'" then he could introspect about his end. At that time, he would hear the reflection of repentance from the *Shechina*, which is the herald and the awakening that comes to a person from above. This is the meaning of "the wives seek to marry," but the person does not want to.

Even when he receives the awakening and feels pleasure in this, he is not awakened by it to faith. Rather, he receives the pleasure that comes along with the awakening, but he does not take the awakening so as to correct his practices, meaning that he will try to do them for the sake of the Creator.

For the same reason, the sons cannot come into their fathers' assets because the understanding and knowledge are present on the actions only while they are for the sake of the Creator. At that time, there are the secrets of Torah in this. But when they do not come in, it means that he is not learning Torah *Lishma* [for Her sake].

240- Discernments in States

A "servant" is called a "giving force." A "handmaid" is called a "receiving force." A *Zivug* [coupling] is the force that connects the receiving force with the force of giving so it will be receiving in order to bestow. An "offshoot" is that by which one is rewarded with a soul, which is a part of God above, meaning that the person feels it.

The Creator makes the *Zivug*, meaning that the Creator helps the receiving force yield to the giving force and makes it able to receive in order to bestow.

When a person makes a *Zivug*, meaning by a person, without the Creator's help, no offspring will come out of the *Zivug* because they cannot connect. Therefore, one becomes lame and one becomes blind, as Raba said, "I beseech you, do not inherit a double Hell."

"A man and a woman, if they are rewarded, the *Shechina* [Divinity] is between them." We should ask, If they are opposite, how can there be peace between them?

It is specifically when one becomes worthy, when he inverts reception into bestowal, called "receiving in order to bestow," there is peace between them. Otherwise, they are in dispute or that one yields before the other. Yielding is not regarded as love in wholeness, for the one who yields always waits for when he will regain the power of control.

241- When Wicked Are Lost, There Is Singing

"When wicked are lost, there is singing." When one is rewarded with the wicked in him being lost, he should glorify the Creator, meaning believe that the Creator helped him achieve this.

242- As He is merciful, So You Are Merciful

As there is joy above from bestowing downward, so the lower one should enjoy bestowing upward. This is called "equivalence of form." Hence, if the lower one receives because he enjoys bestowing upward, it is called "equivalence of form," where all his pleasure is that he gives. This is called "As He is merciful, so you are merciful."

243- Finding Grace

One should know that he should be rewarded with finding the grace of *Kedusha* [holiness]. Without finding grace, it is impossible to do anything not in order to receive reward, as was said, "How does one dance before the bride? The House of Shammai say, 'The bride as she is.' The House of Hillel say, 'a beautiful and graceful bride'" (*Ketubot* 16b).

244- Repentance

Repentance refers to *Adam HaRishon* prior to the sin being adhered, but became removed because of the sin. Hence, each and every one, because he is a part of the soul of *Adam HaRishon*, must approach spirituality once more.

245- The Help of the Creator

Unless the Creator helps him, he will always remain in his lowliness, and the words, "Were it not for the Creator's help, he would not overcome it," will not come true in him, as in "The Lord will finish for me." Instead, the whole world will be providing for him and he will always need people. Conversely, one who walks in the path of the Creator and not in the path of the world is rewarded with being favored by the Creator.

This is specifically one who needs the help of the Creator, as it is written, "He who comes to purify is aided" (*Shabbat* 104a). *The Zohar* interprets, "With what? With a soul," where the Creator gives him a holy soul, and with that force he can purify himself.

This is the meaning of "Rewarded more, he is given *Ruach*," meaning each time, he wants to be more cleansed, purer, and the assisting force of *Nefesh* is not enough for the purity he thinks he needs before he received the soul of *Kedusha* [holiness].

But after he receives the soul of *Kedusha*, he feels that there is more place to work in purity, and the assisting force that he received is not enough to determine to the side of purity. Therefore, he prays and asks once more for help from above.

In that state, he must be given more power than he was given before. Therefore, now he is given *Ruach*, and so forth, until he is given all the *NRNHY* in his soul.

246- Concerning *Shekalim* – 2

Understanding the meaning of *Shekalim*, which is one of the things that perplexed Moses. RASHI writes, "He showed him a sort of ring made of fire whose weight was half a *Shekel* and said to him, 'Such as this will be given.'" We need to understand why Moses was perplexed about it more than about other things. We should understand this matter that the Torah is eternal, so how is the matter of *Shekalim* relevant at this time? Also, why specifically half a *Shekel*? Half a *Shekel* is called "fissured the head." It is written in *The Zohar* (*Nasso*, Item 188), "Every *Galgalta* brings reward for the white to *Atik Yomin* when they are counted under the scepter, and opposite that, he fissured the head below when they are counted."

Baal HaSulam interpreted that *Galgalta* [head/skull] is called "beginning." "Fissured" means breaking. "White" means faith and *Dvekut* [adhesion], and this is the meaning of giving the reward for the white, which is *Dvekut* to *Atik Yomin*.

To interpret his words, that "The Torah was written black fire over white fire," black means the time of concealment and judgments that seem to a person as disrupting the work of the work of the Creator. When foreign thoughts come to a person, they prevent him from making efforts and exertions in the work, and he might fall into cessation of faith and separate from *Dvekut* with Him. That state is called "A time of blackness."

When he overcomes his state and draws upper light, this is called "brightness" and "white." It follows that by having concealments, which is called "blackness," he needs to draw the upper light. It follows that this is what causes him to be rewarded with high degrees.

Concerning half a *Shekel*: Why was not a whole *Shekel* given, but specifically a half? *The Zohar* interprets that the meaning of half is "The rich shall not give more, and the poor shall not give less than half a *Shekel*." It explains there in the *Sulam* [Ladder commentary on *The Zohar*] that every degree has "right" and "left," and *Shekel* is the balance, to weigh that there is not more *Hassadim* than *Hochma*, and not more *Hochma* than *Hassadim*.

We should also understand this in the literal meaning, that it is known that a person does not make a single move unless he weighs its benefits, whether he will gain something. At that time, he has the strength to make a move. Otherwise, he will remain at rest.

When a person wants to make a move in order to bestow, if he begins to weigh its benefits, the body objects to him because it does not see what it can gain if he acts in order to bestow.

At that time, his only counsel is prayer. This is the meaning of what our sages said, "A prayer makes half." It was said about this, "The Lord helps us," which our sages explained, "Were it not for the Creator's help, he would not overcome it." It follows that a person can only give half, which is a prayer, and the other half the Creator gives.

This is why it was said, "The rich shall not give more." One who is rich in knowledge and in attributes cannot do anything but pray, since without help from the Creator, he cannot overcome it.

The "poor" is one who does not have the intellect and knowledge and good attributes. He will not diminish the praying. In other words, in this, everyone is equal, for everyone needs the Creator's help so we can make any movement in order to bestow. For this reason, we should give only half a *Shekel*, meaning after he determined that he wants to work in order to bestow, he should give half, meaning a prayer, for "a prayer makes half."

247- He Who Is Meticulous about Turning His Gown

"Rabbi Yochanan said, 'Who is the disciple to whom a lost item is returned by casting his eye on it? He who is meticulous about turning his gown'" (*Shabbat* 114a).

We should understand why specifically for this merit is it returned to him, for it implies that even if he is versed in all the parts of the Torah and observes all the *Mitzvot* [commandments], if he does not have this quality, it is not returned to him. We also see that with this quality, people from the street are more meticulous not to turn their gowns.

We should understand this in ethics. It is known that the soul is clothed in the body, meaning that the body is the gown of the soul. The body is the will to receive, the nature with which man is created. When a wise disciple is meticulous about turning his gown, meaning turning the will to receive to work in order to bestow, he can be given back what he lost because there is nothing of which to suspect him.

Suspicion pertains to where he has a will to receive. At that time, it can be said that he is lying and wants to receive the lost item for himself. But when all he wants is to bestow, he can be given back everything because it is certain that he is not lying.

Concerning returning the lost item, it can be interpreted as our sages said, "Who is a fool? He who loses what he is given" (*Hagigah* 4). Concerning giving, it means that he is given from above some awakening and flavor in Torah and *Mitzvot*, and afterward, he loses all the awakening from above that he had.

The reason for this is that he is a fool, as our sages said, "One does not transgress unless a spirit of folly has entered him" (*Sotah* 3).

"Folly" means that one cannot adjust his practices to be in equivalence of form with the Creator, but rather wants to receive all the pleasures in the world for his own delight. By this he becomes separated from the Creator, and therefore loses the *Kedusha* [holiness] that he had. That person is called "evil eyed."

But he is given back the lost item when he casts his eye on it. "Casting the eye" comes from the words, "He who has a good eye shall be blessed," and the gauging of the good-eyed is that he is meticulous about turning his gown. This means that he inverts the body, called "will to receive," which is the gown of the soul, into a desire to bestow. At that time, he is given back his lost item, meaning he is rewarded once again with the spirit of *Kedusha*.

248- *He Who Delights the Shabbat*

"Anyone who delights the Shabbat [Sabbath] inherits unbounded inheritance." We should understand what is Shabbat, that we should delight it. That is, is the Shabbat a subject that can receive the delights that we must give?

"Six days shall you work, and on the seventh day, it will be holiness to you." What is the meaning of "Six days shall you work," which implies that after the six workdays comes Shabbat, which is holiness? If there aren't six days of work, is it impossible to have a seventh day of holiness, as in "He who did not toil on the eve of Shabbat, what will he eat on Shabbat"?

249- I Will Sin and Repent

"If one says, 'I will sin and repent,' he will not manage to repent" (*Yoma* 87). The question is, Why?

We found that it is written about the Messiah, "And smell him with the fear of the Lord." We should understand why the fear of the Creator was compared specifically to *Ruach* [spirit, spelled like *Reyach* (smell)].

We see that a person must always inhale *Ruach* [spirit/wind] or he will lose his life. This air should be going in and out. Once he has inhaled into his body, he must exhale it, and soon after inhale new air. The air he inhaled before helps him only for that moment, and if he wants to continue to exist he must promptly inhale new air.

It is the same with spiritual air, called "fear of heaven." We must draw fear of heaven every time anew, meaning the acceptance of the burden of the kingdom of heaven he took upon himself before is sufficient only for that moment.

If he wants to continue his spiritual existence, called "faith," he must take upon himself the burden of the kingdom of heaven once more, and that, too, will only do for that moment, and soon after he will have to draw once more.

He must not wait until he loses the measure of faith that he has taken upon himself, but must constantly draw upon himself faith, time and time again. While faith is still on him, he must renew and extend the fear of heaven, just as is done with breathing physical air, where one does not wait until all the air has been exhaled before he inhales new air. Rather, he renews his breathing every time, meaning replaces the air while the previous air is still in full power.

Likewise, with spiritual air, he should replace the spiritual air he has even though he feels that he can still exist with the faith he has; he must take upon himself once more. If he does not do so, he will finally lose his life, just as one loses his physical life, where if he does not inhale new air, he dies. This is the meaning of "And smell him with the fear of the Lord."

Likewise, in spirituality, if he does not take upon himself faith once again, he dies. Although he does not feel that he has died, it is like a person who, when he is dead, he does not feel it, but when he is revived he knows that previously he was dead.

So it is in spirituality, when one does not replace the faith, he is considered dead, except that in spirituality, he does not feel it. When he takes upon himself the burden of faith once again, it is considered that he has been revived, as in "the revival of the dead," a new incarnation, although the power of the body has not been revoked and left.

Accordingly, if a person can relinquish the burden of faith for just a moment, it is tantamount to relinquishing the physical life for a moment. Just as one cannot relinquish this, so he cannot relinquish spiritual life. It follows that one who sins has died, and if he repents, he is a completely different person. It is not that person, but a new creation.

This is the meaning of "If one says, 'I shall sin and repent,'" meaning that if he sins, he is considered dead. Therefore, this is regarded as "he will not manage to repent" because he died instantaneously. Rather, one who repents is regarded as a new body, meaning a new incarnation.

250- Anyone in Whom There Is Fear of Heaven – 1

"Rabbi Helbo said, 'Rabbi Huna said, 'Anyone in whom there is fear of heaven, his words are heard,' as was said, 'In the end, all is heard, fear God and observe His commandments, for this is the whole of man''" (*Berachot* 6b).

We could question this, since we have seen many great sages in Israel whose words were not heard. Also, what evidence is there from the words, "In the end"?

We should interpret his words, that the verse refers to the individual himself, that if one sees that his organs are disobeying him, and the more he engages in Torah and work, he is still standing in his previous condition and did not move one bit for the better, our sages make him understand the reason for this.

This is only because he lacks the fear of heaven. That is, when he has fear of heaven, all his organs will obey him.

This is implied in the words, "In the end," since the body is called "the end of the matter," since it is a boundary, as in, "In the end, man will die." Conversely, on the spiritual, there is no end. This is the meaning of the words, "In the end, all is heard," meaning that in the end he will be heard. That is, his organs will obey him when he has fear of heaven. This is the meaning of "Fear God," and then you will be rewarded with everything being heard.

"When Rabbi Yochanan Ben Zakkai fell ill, his disciples came to see him. They said to him, 'Our teacher, bless us.' He replied, 'May the fear of heaven be upon you as the fear of flesh and blood.' They said to him, 'Our teacher, thus far.' He said to them, 'I wish. Know that when one commits a transgression, he says, 'May no person see me''" (*Berachot* 28b).

We should ask, What was their question, which they did not understand to the point that they did not settle for the blessing he had blessed them? Also, what did they understand better through the allegory of a person who commits a transgression, so that through the allegory they agreed and understood that this blessing was sufficient and they did not need a greater blessing? Also, we should understand the meaning of the words "Know" and "thus far."

Baal HaSulam said that there are two kinds of fear: 1) fear of sin, 2) fear of heaven.

This means that there is a person who observes Torah and *Mitzvot* [commandments] because of the fear of sin, meaning that otherwise he might come to sin. Sometimes, a person is no longer afraid that he might sin because he has already cleansed his practices to make them all for the sake of the Creator, yet he observes Torah and *Mitzvot* because of "heaven," meaning because of the King's commandment, because this is His will, and this is why he observes everything.

"Fear of sin" means that he is observing everything only for his own sake, that the reason is for himself. "Fear of heaven" means that the reason is the Creator, that he observes Torah and *Mitzvot* because this is the Creator's will.

When one observes Torah and *Mitzvot* only for the sake of the Creator, it is difficult to observe the Torah and *Mitzvot* because he does not understand the necessity of the matter, as King Solomon said, "Will not do more, etc., I will do more, etc."

By this we can interpret the above words that they said to him, "Thus far." This means that they thought that he was telling them that they would have the fear of heaven such as the fear of flesh and blood, that their fear of heaven will be as the fear of flesh and blood, meaning the fear of sin, since observing Torah and *Mitzvot* is for one's own purposes, so he will not sin.

It is about this that they asked, "Thus far," meaning that it is impossible to achieve a higher degree. To this he replied to them with an allegory that if a person commits a transgression, he says, "May no person see me." He is afraid that if someone sees him, he might turn him over to the authorities, so his fear is so strong that he will not transgress if someone sees.

This is why Rabban Yochanan Ben Zakkai said to them, "Know that my intention is the inner meaning of the words, for by blessing you, 'May the fear of heaven be upon you as the fear of flesh and blood,' this is a high degree."

He said to them, "May you achieve this," and he meant that they would have the fear of heaven, that observing Torah and *Mitzvot* will be only for the sake of the Creator, and for themselves, they will have no fear that they might sin, and they will be sure of themselves that there is no possibility to sin.

And the reason you observe Torah and *Mitzvot* is only for the sake of the Creator, for such is the will of the Creator. Yet, this fear of heaven is akin to the fear of flesh and blood.

This means that as with fear of flesh and blood, we know very well that we must guard and be strict in many ways not to go one moment without fear, for you are standing guard without any allowances. Rather, you are strict in every manner that concerns the fear of flesh and blood. Likewise, with fear of heaven, you will have this fear that you will not go one moment without this fear.

This is the "May you," meaning it is a very high degree that all the fear will be because of the Creator, and yet the fear and observing will be as with the fear of flesh and blood.

251- Concerning the *Minyan* [Ten in the Synagogue]

"Rabbi Yochanan said, 'When the Creator comes to the synagogue and does not find there ten, He immediately becomes angry, as was said, 'Why have I come and there is no man, I called and no one answered?''" (*Berachot* 6b).

We should ask, 1) What should be done? Should people wait outside until ten have gathered, and then come into the synagogue? 2) Where is the proof in the verse that ten are required?

We should also understand what our sages said, "Rabbi Yehoshua Ben Levi said, 'One who walks along the way without company should engage in Torah, as was said, 'For they are a graceful accompaniment to your head'"" (*Iruvin* 54). We should understand what it means that we need company when we set out on the road, and that if one has no company, engaging in Torah will be as beneficial to him as company.

It is known that man was created with the will to receive. This separates him from *Dvekut* [adhesion] with Him, for specifically through equivalence of form, called "desire to bestow," is one rewarded with *Dvekut* with Him.

"Company" means *Dvekut*, as it is written, "One who walks along the way," meaning one who walks on the path of the Creator but has not been rewarded with *Dvekut* with the Creator, should engage in Torah, for by its *Segula* [power/remedy/virtue], he will be rewarded with *Dvekut* with the Creator, as our sages said, "One should always engage in Torah *Lo Lishma* [not for Her sake], for the light in it reforms him" (*Pesachim* 50b).

Concerning prayer, it is known that we should pray mainly about the exile of the *Shechina* [Divinity], called *Malchut*, who is the tenth *Sefira* in the ten *Sefirot*, and whose essence is faith in His guidance, that He leads the world in the manner of good and doing good.

It is impossible to see the goodness of the Creator before a person purifies his desire from receiving for himself, since there is the *Tzimtzum* [restriction] on the will to receive, which is concealment on His guidance

This is the meaning of what our sages said, "You are called 'man,' and not the nations of the world," since the sole aim is to receive for themselves. This is the meaning of "When the Creator comes to the synagogue and does not find ten men there," meaning that there will be someone there who will pray for the quality of "ten," which is the *Shechina*, so she will rise from her exile, for by engaging with the desire to bestow, one raises the *Shechina* from the dust. But when each one cares for his personal needs, the Creator is angry.

He brings evidence from the verse that said, "Why have I come and there is no man" to care for the needs that pertain to the quality of "man," and cares only to satisfy the needs that pertain to the quality of a beast? Rather, one should always answer to himself for whom he spends his time, and for whom he exerts, for he should be concerned only with the needs of the collective.

252- A Broken Heart – 1

"A broken and a stricken heart, O God, You will not despise," "He heals the brokenhearted." A broken heart means that his heart is not wholly with the Creator, as it is written in the "Introduction to The Study of the Ten Sefirot" (Item 129). If he regrets his heart not being wholly with the Creator, then he has a *Kli* [vessel], called "a lack," and then the Creator fills the lack.

253- Do Not Eat the Bread of an Evil-Eyed Man

"Rabbi Yehoshua Ben Levi said, 'Anyone who delights the selfish breaks a commandment not to do, as was said, 'Do not eat the bread of an evil-eyed man,' for as he assumes so it is, he will tell you 'Eat and drink' but his heart is not with him'" (*Sotah* 38b).

We should understand this, for it seems as though if his friend invites him for a meal, why should he care? After all, there is a rule that in several places it is said, "He is forced," and then his heart is certainly not with him, but it is said that his heart is really fine.

Therefore, here, when he invites him verbally, why is he forbidden to eat at his place, to the point that it says that he breaks a commandment not to do, and Rav Nachman Rav Yitzhak says that he breaks two commandments not to do?

But according to the rule that one must achieve the degree of receiving in order to bestow, meaning to receive all the pleasures only in order to bestow upon the Creator, one who eats at another's place and knows that this brings contentment to the host, this follows the purpose of creation that man should achieve wholeness.

But one who eats and the aim cannot be to please the host, since the host does not enjoy his eating because the host is evil-eyed, this is against the goal. Therefore, it is forbidden to eat.

254- Work Means Faith

Great is the work in which all the prophets engaged, for the *Shechina* [Divinity] was not present in Israel until they did "work" (*Midrash Gadol ve Gedola*, Chapter 14). We should interpret that "work" means faith (see the essay, "Great Is Work that Honors").

255- Words of a Dead Man

"Before the dead, only the words of the dead are said" (*Berachot* 3b). Interpretation: When the dead is lying before them, only things related to the matters of the dead man are said. RASHI interpreted that since everyone must speak of them, and the dead is still, it is to him "Mocking the poor before his Maker." Rabbi Aba Bar Kahana said, "We did not speak but only of matters of Torah, but worldly matters do not belong here." Others say, "Rabbi Aba Bar Kahana said, 'We did not speak even of matters of Torah, all the more so concerning worldly matters.'"

This is perplexing. Why is it forbidden to speak of worldly matters? After all, it is not a must that he should speak of worldly matters.

To understand this in ethics, "dead" means during the fall. At that time, he is in a state of "The wicked in their lives are called 'dead.'"

Then, when he is told words of Torah from others so he will wake up and return to work, it does not help him. It is called "Mocking the poor," since he is not impressed by others saying Torah.

However, if he is told the words of a dead man, meaning what he himself said when he was in ascent, regarded as when he was alive, and he is told, "Look what a great state you had," and that he had vitality of *Kedusha* [holiness], and "Look what words of Torah you said then," from this he can be resurrected. But if he is told words of Torah that others said, it does not impress him.

"Worldly matters do not belong here." "World [or worldly]" means faith. It is possible to speak with him about faith also from others, who encourage him and tell him, "Look, this and that person have fear of heaven, while you remain as still as dead." He might be inspired and come back to life when he hears matters of faith pertaining to others. Thus, even in worldly matters, only his own words should be said to him.

According to RASHI, this is perplexing. He says that everyone must speak words of Torah, and he is still. Therefore, it is regarded as mocking the poor. But with worldly matters, not everyone must speak, so why is it regarded as mocking the poor?

The reason it is forbidden to speak of worldly matters pertaining to faith, for faith is called "world" (as it is written in *The Zohar* in several places), since *Alma* [Aramaic: world] comes from the words *He'elem* [concealment] and *Hester* [hiding], which is faith. Therefore, they think, according to the view that some people say, that in matters of faith he will also not listen, that he will not be impressed by what others say.

But from the words of the dead, meaning from what he himself did in matters of faith during his life, it is possible that the *Reshimot* [recollections] will awaken in him and will revive him. But from others, even concerning faith, it will also not work.

Thus, when speaking to him of worldly matters that others do, he will not listen. Thus, he would be mocking the poor because all the words will be in vain. Hence, only his own *Reshimot* can awaken him. This is called "from the words of the dead himself," from when he was alive, when he was in a state of ascent.

256- The Light that Was Created on the First Day

The light that was created on the first day, Adam saw in it from the end of the world... the Creator looked at the deeds of the generation of the flood and the generation of Babylon and saw that their practices were corrupt. He stood and concealed it for the righteous in the future.

Hence, before a person corrects the generation of the flood and the generation of Babylon within him, the hidden light is concealed from him. The generation of the flood is regarded as the heart, and the generation of Babylon is called "mind." Since every person is comprised of the entire world, we attribute all the nations of the world to the evil in us.

Since the evil inclination is an angel, as our sages said, "He, Satan, is the evil inclination" (*Baba Batra* 16a), and our sages said that every angel is named only after his work, so when evil lusts awaken in a person, the evil inclination is called "the generation of the flood," which is a *Merkava* [chariot/structure] for the generation of the flood.

Also, when evil thoughts awaken in a person, the evil inclination becomes a *Merkava* for the generation of Babylon. This is why the evil inclination is named after the generation of Babylon.

When those two general attributes are corrected, the hidden light is revealed because at that time he becomes righteous. This is the meaning of "concealed it for the righteous in the future," meaning that only when there are righteous, this light is revealed and they begin to feel the delight and pleasure contained in Torah and *Mitzvot* [commandments].

257- Idol Worship

25 Shevat, Tav-Shin-Chaf-Vav, February 16, 1966

"Raba Bar Rav Yitzhak said to Rav Yehuda, 'There is idol-worship in our place, and whenever the world is in need of rain, they appear to them in a dream, telling them, 'Slay me a man and I will send rain." They slayed a man for her and she sent rain."

"He replied, 'Now if I were dead, no one would tell you the words that Rav said, why it is written 'which the Lord your God has *Halak* [divided/smoothed] to all the nations," meaning that He *Hechelik* [made smooth] their words to banish them from the world. This is as Rish Lakish said, 'Why is it written, 'If He scorns the scorners and gives grace to the humble,' he who comes to defile, it is opened to him; He who comes to purify is aided'?" (*Avoda Zarah* 55a).

To understand the above-said, we should interpret that idol-worship means one who does not serve the Creator but himself. This is regarded as performing idol-worship.

Idol-worship, meaning the idea that it is not worthwhile to work if not for one's own sake, exists in our place. This is why he says, "There is idol-worship in our place, and whenever the world is in need of rain," meaning when people need to enjoy their lives, they engage in Torah and *Mitzvot* [commandments], which causes them to abstain from several pleasures.

"They appear to them in a dream," meaning that this spirit, called "will to receive for oneself," appears to them when they are dreaming, meaning during the fall, when only a "pocket of vitality" remains of their spirituality, as it is written, "We were as dreamers." At that time, that spirit, which is idol-worship, has strength and it tells them, "Slay me a man and I will send rain."

258- Who Is Rich?

Adar Bet, Tav-Shin-Chaf-Bet, March 1962

"Who is rich? Rabbi Yossi says, 'Anyone who has a toilet next to his table'" (*Shabbat* 25b).

A "table" means a meal. When one receives pleasure, it is regarded as a meal, that he is dining.

Concerning having a toilet next to the table, the toilet is a place intended for extraction of the waste within us. That person, soon after the reception of the pleasure, sorts out the part that he receives for the sake of the Creator, and what is not for the sake of the Creator, he excretes as waste.

He receives pleasure only in order to sustain the faith, which is regarded as "the herdsmen of Abraham's cattle." Then, he remains with his wealth because he always has vitality and pleasure, since departure is precisely when one becomes a fool and receives for himself, not for the sake of the Creator. At that time, he loses what he is given. Hence, he remains poor.

But when one examines oneself and ejects the waste, he remains with his wealth, meaning pleasures, and does not lose it.

259- Building the Temple

1, Adar Bet, Tav-Shin-Chaf-Bet, March 7, 1962

"Rabbi Shimon Ben Elazar says, 'If children tell you 'Build!' and elders tell you 'Break!' heed the elders and do not heed the children, for children's building is breaking, and elder's breaking is building, and the sign of the matter is Rehoboam, son of Solomon'" (*Nedarim* 40a).

RASHI interprets that if youths tell you, "Build the Temple," and elders tell you, "Break and do not build," the sign of the matter is Rehoboam... and the Temple was ruined over that advice. But the Torah did not interpret about the Temple, and there is a Braita that interprets "Temple" differently, and see MAHARSHA.

We should interpret that the elders say that we must break all the building of *Kedusha* [holiness] that a person built in his youth, for otherwise it is impossible to build the Temple. The reason is that one must revoke everything that he has done since he was born so he can walk in the ways of *Kedusha* [holiness].

260- Great Is He Who Is Commanded and Does

"He who is commanded and does is greater than he who is not commanded and does" (*Kidushin* 31a). We should interpret that "commanded and does" means *Lishma* [for Her sake], and "not commanded and does" means *Lo Lishma* [not for Her sake].

Because he is not working for the sake of the Creator, it means that he is not performing the *Mitzva* [commandment] because he has a commander commanding him to do the *Mitzva*, since the Commander does not obligate him to do. That is, the Commander is not the cause of his performing the *Mitzva*, but rather the *Lo Lishma* is the cause. It follows that he has no commander.

Hence, one whose cause to perform the commandment is the Commander, meaning the Creator, is certainly greater because the *Lo Lishma* has merit in that it brings him to *Lishma*, but *Lishma* is certainly greater than *Lo Lishma*.

261- Hear, My Son, Your Father's Morals – 1

"Hear, my son, your father's morals and do not forsake your mother's teaching."

Musar [morals] comes from the verse, "Should one afflict [*Yiser*] his son," meaning *Yesurim* [suffering/afflictions]. There is potential suffering and there is actual suffering. When one is made to understand that it is forbidden to do something, and should he disobey the order, he will be punished, such as by being flogged for the transgression.

If a person does not know what is the punishment, meaning he does not feel the taste of the suffering before he actually receives them, he breaks the order and is punished. The punishment is so he will know that in the future, he will avoid breaking the law. In other words, the law is given for man's benefit, in particular and in general, but the person cannot keep the law because he derives pleasure breaking it.

For example, there is a law that prohibits stealing, but he loves money and there is a place where he can steal money. Since he has a craving for money, although he knows that he will suffer for the transgression, he cannot assess the level of suffering from the punishment. As a result, he assumes that the pleasure from the money is far greater than the afflictions he will suffer as a punishment.

Thus, when he is punished, meaning sentenced to be jailed for some time, he sees that the afflictions are greater than the pleasure he received from stealing. For this reason, he decides that in the future, he will keep the law.

But once he is punished and sits in jail, he is told, "Know that if you steal again you will be sentenced to a much longer jail-time than the first," since he forgets the measure of suffering he had received. Hence, when he gets a chance to steal once more, he will certainly miscalculate the levels of the suffering and pleasure.

For this reason, when he is told that he will suffer greater torments, it is possible that he will think that it is not worthwhile to steal, meaning that the suffering is greater than the pleasure.

Hence, when teaching morals, we see the importance of Torah and *Mitzvot* [commandments], meaning which level of pleasure one can have, as well as which punishment he might suffer.

In other words, the erudite make a person feel the flavor of the reward of observing the law, meaning the benefit that keeping the law brings to a person, and the punishments he will suffer for breaking the law.

By feeling this, to the extent that one feels it, he can observe the law. That is, they allow him to assume the true measure of pleasure and affliction, as our sages said, "Calculate performing a commandment against its reward, and the reward for a transgression against not doing it" (*Avot*, Chapter 2). At that time, a person can advance in the ways of the Creator more each time.

262- We Have Forgotten the Good

"A certain man once gave his slave to his friend to teach him a thousand different ways of making pap (various foods), but he taught him eight hundred. So he summoned him to a lawsuit before the rabbi. The rabbi said, 'Our fathers said, 'We have forgotten the good,''" (meaning they already saw, but now they have forgotten, "but we have never even seen the good!") (*Nedarim* 50b).

We should ask, Were our fathers so immersed in worldly lusts that Rabbi said, "We have forgotten the good, but we have never even seen it"?

We should interpret that "thousand" pertains to *Hochma* [wisdom], as in "I will teach you wisdom." "Eight hundred" means

Bina, as it is written, "The days of *Bina*, eight days," and the *Sefirot* of *Bina* are hundreds, meaning *Mochin de Neshama*.

"That man who gave his slave" means that he gave himself to be a servant of the Creator, for "his friend" means "Your friend and your father's friend," that the Creator will give him *Mochin de Hochma*. Yet, he was rewarded with only *Mochin de Neshama*, which is *Bina*, and "hundreds" implies eight.

Rabbi said about this, "Our fathers said, 'We have forgotten the good.'" That is, at the time of the Temple, there was *Mochin de Hochma*, called "the moon in its fullness." But after the ruin of the Temple, the *Mochin de Hochma* departed. This is why he said, "We did not see with our eyes," meaning vision, called *Mochin de Hochma*.

263- The Merit of the Bride

"The reward of the bride—pressure" (*Berachot* 7). A "bride" means faith, and all the benefit is that when a person feels pressure in Torah and *Mitzvot* [commandments], he has a place to accept faith above reason.

"The reward for hearing—understanding." The reward of the Torah, called "hearing," is specifically knowledge and not faith, since when one learns Torah but does not understand what is written in it, this is called *Mitzva* [commandment] and not "Torah."

"The reward for a house of mourning—silence." Where there is grief, the benefit is that one can justify Providence and say, "Silence, such was My thought."

"The reward for fasting—almsgiving." But Shmuel says that one who fasts is called "a sinner," and we should interpret that because the purpose of creation is to do good to His creations, it follows that he does the opposite of the goal. Therefore, he is called "a sinner."

However, when one gives almsgiving, it shows that now he is engaging in fear of heaven, called "faith." This is as it is written,

"And he believed in the Lord and considered for him as *Tzedakah* [righteousness/charity]." At that time, he knows about himself that this is not wholeness and he must be rewarded with the Torah, for then he receives the light concealed in the Torah, which is the purpose.

264- Ascend in Degree, Choose a Bridesmaid

"Ascend in degree, choose a bridesmaid." That is, accept a friend as greater than you. "Descend in degree, choose a wife" (*Yevamot* 63a).

In other words, one who wants to connect to the Creator, meaning "Your friend and your father's friend do not forsake," must have pride, as it is written, "His heart was high in the ways of the Lord." Afterward, he must take upon himself the burden of the kingdom of heaven, as it is written, "Who will find a woman of valor," which is precisely through submission and annulment, meaning above reason, for only then can he take upon himself the burden of the kingdom of heaven.

Rabbi Elazar said, "What does it mean that it is written, 'Should one tell you, 'What is good, and what does the Lord demand of you?' Only to do justice and to love mercy, and conceal yourself with the Lord your God.' 'To do justice' is the judgment; 'to love mercy' is almsgiving, and 'to conceal yourself with the Lord your God' is taking out the dead, and bringing in the bride" (*Sukkah* 49b).

265- Inner Keys and Outer Keys

"Raba Bar Rav Huna said, 'Anyone in whom there is Torah but no fear of heaven is like a treasurer who was given the inner keys but was not given the outer keys. Can he come in?' Rabbi Yannai declares, 'It is a shame about one who has no *Darta* [Aramaic: courtyard/house] yet makes a *Taraa* [Aramaic: gate/door] for the *Darta*'" (*Shabbat* 31).

This is a known question. This allegory implies that the Torah is the internality. From the words of Rabbi Yannai, it seems as though the Torah is the externality, and fear of heaven is the internality. We should also ask, Why does he compare fear to the outer keys if "The fear of the Lord is His treasure," and here it is implied that the fear is the internality.

We should say that there is Torah that is called "internality," and there is Torah that is called "externality," and fear of heaven is in the middle.

Accordingly, the Torah on the externality is called *Taraa*, meaning "a gate," and fear of heaven is called "internality." In other words, through the Torah, we achieve fear of heaven.

With respect to the inner Torah, fear of heaven is called "externality," meaning that through fear of heaven we come to the internality of the Torah. Hence, fear of heaven is called a "treasure" because it means that it is only internal, since we achieve it after the Torah.

The writing says, "I wish they left Me and kept My Torah; the light in it reforms them" (Jerusalem Talmud, *Hagigah*, Chapter 1). Yet, how can one observe the Torah without the Creator? How does He say, "I wish they left Me"?

However, this refers to those who want to be rewarded with "Me," meaning to have fear of heaven, to have *Dvekut* [adhesion] with the Creator.

Then they are told, "Do not stand in this work to be rewarded with *Dvekut* [adhesion] by having a desire and yearning for the Creator, since the Creator cannot connect to one who is in the quality of falsehood," as it is written, "He who speaks lies shall not be established before My eyes," or one who is proud, as our sages said, "Anyone in whom there is crassness of spirit, the Creator said, 'I and he cannot dwell in the world'" (*Sotah* 5).

It is also written that if one does not correct the evil inclination, called "serpent," then as our sages said, "Man does not dwell in the same abode with a serpent," much less the Creator. Rather, one must correct one's actions and then he can be rewarded with faith in the Creator.

This correction is found in the Torah. This is why they interpret, "And kept My Torah," for the light in it reforms them. That is, through the light, the Torah will reform them, and then they will be rewarded with the treasure of fear of heaven.

It follows that the Torah is a gate by which one can enter the treasure, and the treasure is called a "house," which is *Darta*.

Therefore, one who wants only to stand at the gate and does not notice that he can go through the gate, meaning take from the Torah the light so as to be reformed and thereby be rewarded with faith in the Creator, called "the treasure of fear of heaven," he is as one who only builds himself a gate but has no intention to build himself a house, for the main purpose of the gate is only to serve the house. But when one has no house, meaning he does not intend to achieve fear of heaven, why does he need the gate? An opening is only made to be a place of transition, meaning when we want to enter some place, we must find the door through which to enter.

Or in a place that is closed all around, he makes himself an opening in order to get in. But to make an opening and not come into the house? This means that all his work on the opening was to no avail and a waste.

Afterward, we enter the house, called "fear of heaven," which is the treasure, and then we come to the internality of the Torah. This is the meaning of learning Torah *Lishma* [for Her sake]. That is, after the Torah has brought him to *Lishma*, called "fear of heaven," the secrets of Torah are revealed to him and he becomes as a flowing stream. It follows that the heart of the work is to be rewarded with fear of heaven, called *Lishma*.

This is why Rabbi Yannai declares that if fear of heaven is the most important, and then one is rewarded with the Torah from above, then one who learns Torah and does not see that the Torah will reform him, to be rewarded with fear of heaven through the Torah, meaning that all his concern and labor will be for the house, which is the treasure of fear of heaven, while he wants only the Torah, and the whole point of the Torah is to serve as a gate for the fear of heaven, then he is as one who has no house, yet builds a gate for the house. Thus, this opening he makes is to no avail and in vain.

In this way, we should interpret the allegory about the keys that it is as a person whose concern and desire are to be rewarded with the internality of the Torah but does not see that he has the *Lishma*, which is fear of heaven. About this he says, "Can he come in?"

One who learns Torah *Lishma*, meaning for the Torah to bring him to *Lishma*—and is rewarded with fear of heaven—is rewarded with the revelation of the secrets of Torah. But before he has been rewarded with *Lishma*, it is not revealed to him. It follows that here his work to be rewarded with internality is in vain.

Hence, we must pay attention mainly to the *Lishma*, to fear of heaven, and that everything one does will focus only on this point, which is fear of heaven, since this matter is concealed and one must reveal it.

This is the meaning of "The Creator has in His treasury only a treasure of fear of heaven, as was said, 'The fear of the Lord is His treasure.'" This means that one should make an effort to find the fear of heaven.

As for the Torah, the Creator reveals it to him without any labor, as Rabbi Meir says, "Anyone who engages in Torah *Lishma*," that the only reason he engages in Torah is to achieve *Lishma*, which is fear of heaven, and in this is all of his labor. Conversely, when a person has been rewarded with fear of heaven, the secrets of Torah are revealed to him.

Regarding "concealment," it means that we should seek, for without seeking, it is impossible to find. This is the meaning of "If you labored and found," where by laboring, he is rewarded with finding, meaning when he finds what He concealed in His treasury: a treasure of fear of heaven.

But as for the Torah, Rabbi Meir says that the secrets of Torah are revealed to him and he becomes as a flowing stream and as a river that does not stop. This is the meaning of "Everything is in the hands of heaven but the fear of heaven," for he himself must find the treasure of the fear of heaven.

266- Anyone Who Is Settled in His Wine

21 *Adar Bet, Tav-Shin-Chaf-Bet*, March 28, 1962

"Rabbi Hiyya said, 'Anyone who is settled in his wine has the knowledge of seventy elders. Wine was given in seventy letters, and a secret was given in seventy letters; when wine enters, a secret exits'" (*Iruvin* 65). RASHI interpreted "settled in his wine," that "He drinks wine but his mind does not become unsound." A secret exists, since one whose secret did not come out is tantamount to a Sanhedrin of seventy.

We should ask:

1) According to this, one who wants to be tantamount to the Sanhedrin does not need to labor in Torah and work, and has the simple way of drinking wine while seeing that his mind stays clear.

2) What is the answer that his "secret did not come out"? Does one obtain the same wholeness as the Sanhedrin for not letting out his secret? And what if he did let out his secret? Does one who lets out his secret commit such a grave transgression as to say that for this he loses his value, that he is no longer regarded as the seventy Sanhedrin? And if he keeps himself from letting out, does he have the same value as the Sanhedrin?

We should understand that in ethics. The path of Torah is for one to believe in the Creator without any knowledge or attainment, but only above attainment and reason. Then, when he engages in Torah and *Mitzvot* [commandments], he is regarded as a Jew. Conversely, one who wants to be a servant of the Creator only in a manner of knowing and attainment, this is regarded as idol-worship (as explained in the *Sulam* [Ladder commentary on *The Zohar*] in several places).

Even when he is later rewarded with attainment and knowledge, he must not take this as support for the work, meaning to say that now he is delighted that he has attainment, that he has become liberated from the burden of faith, that he had work having to go above reason, that it is a great effort and now he is happy that he does not need to exert over faith and is freed from carrying that load called "as an ox to the burden and as a donkey to the load."

Rather, he must understand that being rewarded with attainment, now he is happy that he sees that the path he was on before, the path of faith, which is the view of Torah, is the real way. And the proof is that now he has been rewarded with nearing the Creator, that the Creator has given him the attainment.

Hence, now he receives strength from attainment so he can continue to walk on the path of faith. It follows that the attainment is support for faith in a way that he continues to walk on the path of faith.

This is not so. To the contrary, if he takes faith as support for attainment, meaning that faith is a means to be rewarded with attainment, so when he achieves the goal he throws away the means. Therefore, he kicks out the faith and takes to himself the way of going only where he has attainment. This is not the Jewish view.

As Baal HaSulam interpreted, there is the matter of the herdsmen of Abraham's cattle and the herdsmen of Lot's cattle. The herdsmen of Abraham's cattle are called "Abraham's possessions." This is the quality of faith, as Abraham is called "the father of faith."

"Herdsmen" means nourishments, which means that the attainment and reason that he receives are in order to strengthen the faith, that the attainment is proof that we must walk in the above-mentioned ways, meaning he takes it as proof. It follows that when we walk on the path of faith, the Creator brings him closer and gives him the light of Torah.

This is not so concerning the herdsmen of Lot's cattle. "Lot" means a curse, from the word *Latia* [Aramaic: cursed]. This means that one who receives attainment in order to be able to serve the Creator within reason, from this extends a curse, meaning that the light of Torah departs from him and he remains bare and destitute.

The reason we must walk in the ways of faith is that there is the matter of reception in mind and in heart, and reception in mind is called "knowing," thus far the gist of his words.

With all the above, we can interpret the words of Rabbi Hiyya, "Anyone who is settled in his wine." "Wine" means the wine of Torah, as it is written in *The Zohar*, meaning the light of Torah, which is considered that he is being shown the secrets of Torah. This is regarded as attainment and knowledge.

"Anyone who is settled in his wine" means that by receiving the light of Torah, his mind does not become unsound, meaning the reason that he had before he received the wine of Torah is not lost, meaning it does not disappear from him. On the contrary, the reason that he had before becomes settled within him.

By obtaining the wine of Torah, his mind becomes settled. This requires walking in the ways of faith, that he took from here a proof that the way of faith is the real way, and the evidence of this is that the Creator has brought him closer and has given him the light of Torah. It follows that through the light of Torah, the mind that he had prior to being rewarded with wine becomes settled within him.

This is the meaning of "When wine enters, a secret exits." A secret is called "faith," since something in which there is no attainment or reason is considered a secret. Hence, when wine, which is attainment, enters, a secret comes out, for the Torah is regarded as revealing, which is the opposite of the secret.

For this reason, one who has been rewarded with the light of Torah and does not let out a secret, meaning that the faith he had had before does not come out of him and he continues to walk in a manner of secret, he is tantamount to seventy Sanhedrin. By the quality of faith growing stronger in him, he becomes similar to the Sanhedrin.

Although they were regarded as "the eyes of the congregation," for they have been rewarded with the wisdom of the Torah, they still maintained themselves in the quality of faith. Hence, a person who has been rewarded with the wine of Torah and does not let out the secret, and remains with his view to continue to walk in the manner of the secret although now he has revelation and attainment, he is like the seventy Sanhedrin.

This is the meaning of "Wine was given in seventy letters, and a secret was given in seventy; when wine enters, a secret exits," since in every thing there is *Panim* [face/anterior] and *Achoraim* [back/posterior], which are regarded as light and *Kli* [vessel]. That is, the full quality of the light must be implied in the *Kli*, since the *Kli* is the instrument that will be able to draw the light within it.

This is why it is called "seventy," as in "seventy faces to the Torah," which means that when he works in the manner of "secret," which is faith, he must imagine and depict to himself that he will serve the Creator with the same vigor as though he has been rewarded with the wine of Torah, called "seventy faces of the Torah." "Eye" implies knowing, and seeing with the mind is called "the eyes of the congregation," referring to the sages of the congregation.

When he maintains himself in this manner, even when he has room to receive seeing and attainment, he is tantamount to the Sanhedrin.

This is similar to one who believes in the Creator, that He hears a prayer, although each day when he prays and does not see that the Creator hears a prayer, he still believes that the Creator hears a prayer. But when he is rewarded with the Creator answering all his requests, he no longer needs to believe that the Creator hears a prayer, since he sees with his own eyes that the Creator is giving him what he wants.

Hence, the place where he must believe is called "a secret," and the place of the revelation is called "the wine of Torah." Man must strengthen himself in faith even in a place where he can receive the revelation that the Creator hears a prayer.

267- Man Was Created in the Torah

"Man was created in the Torah, as it is written, 'And God said, 'Let us make man.'" The Creator said to the Torah, 'I wish to create man.' She said to Him, 'This man will sin and vex you. If You are not patient with him, how will he persist in the world?' He told her, 'You and I will establish him in the world, for it is with good reason that I am called, 'slow to anger''" (*The Zohar*, *Shmini*, Item 2).

We should understand what it means that the Creator asked the Torah to help Him establish man, or it would be impossible that the Creator would create, to the point that they explained about the verse, "Let us make," in plural form, that it refers to the Creator together with the Torah.

The thing is that it is known that the purpose of creation is to do good to His creations. For this reason, a nature has been imprinted in man that he will want to receive pleasure for his own delight. This is called the "evil inclination" (as explained in the introduction to the *Sulam* [Ladder commentary on *The Zohar*]), as it is written, "For the inclination of man's heart is evil from his youth."

It is called the "evil inclination" because by wanting to receive pleasure, a person becomes removed from the real pleasure because he has no equivalence of form. However, through the Torah, he will have a correction where through the Torah, it will be possible for him to receive the real pleasures, as our sages said, "I have created the evil inclination; I have created the Torah as a spice" (*Baba Batra* 16).

The spice is as our sages said, "I wish they left Me and kept My Torah [law], for the light in it reforms them" (Jerusalem Talmud, *Hagigah*, Chapter 1, Rule 7). It therefore follows that the Torah has the power to reform a person, referring to the evil within man, meaning the will to receive, that it will work in order to bestow.

In this manner, he will have *Dvekut* [adhesion] and will be able to receive the real pleasures and will not be considered a receiver. Thus, through the Torah, it will be possible to sustain man in this world, for the Torah will reform him.

This is the meaning of "Let us make man," which they explained, "I and you will establish him in the world." That is, from the Creator comes the will to receive and from the Torah comes the desire to bestow, and from those two, man will be able to exist in the world. That is, through those two, he will be able to receive abundance yet remain in *Dvekut*.

268- One Learns Only Where One's Heart Desires

"One learns only where one's heart desires" (*Avoda Zarah* 19).

We should understand why one learns specifically where one's heart desires. According to this rule, that one learns specifically where he wants, it follows that it is impossible to teach a person ethics if he does not want this. Since a person does not want to hear words of admonition, how can one admonish one's friend?

We also need to understand what our sages said, "One does not see one's own faults" (*Shabbat* 119). Accordingly, how can one correct his practices if he never sees that they are corrupt and require correction? According to this, a person should always remain corrupted.

The thing is that it is known that man was created with a nature that he wants to delight only himself. Hence, everything he learns, he wants to learn from this how he can enjoy. For this reason, if a person wants to enjoy, he will not learn other things that his heart desires because this is his nature.

Therefore, one who wants to come closer to the Creator and be able to learn things that show ways by which to bestow upon the Creator must pray to the Creator to give him a different heart, as it is written, "A pure heart, create for me, O God."

In other words, when there is another heart, and the desire in the heart is a desire to bestow, everything he learns will show ways of things that show only bestowal upon the Creator. However, he will never see against the heart, as was said about it, "And I will remove the stony heart from within you, and I will give you a heart of flesh."

Also, one cannot see one's own faults because he learns where his heart desires. And since the heart wants to enjoy, and a person does not enjoy faults, the person does not enjoy and will therefore never see his own faults.

The only advice is to pray to the Creator to give him a different heart, meaning to understand that there is nothing better than to give contentment to the Creator.

At that time, he will be able to see his faults, for specifically by understanding that if he sees the fault, he will gain merit for himself because he will be able to correct, for otherwise he will remain with all the faults.

It follows that the debt is his privilege. At that time, it will be possible to examine the fault, unlike one who does not work in correction, and who will never see the faults.

269- One Does Not Toil Over a Meal and Misses It

"Be certain, one does not toil over a meal and misses it" (*Ketubot* 10).

We should interpret that since one can only work *Lo Lishma* [not for Her sake], since his nature is the will to receive for himself, if one dedicates much time and effort over the intention *Lo Lishma*, in the end he will wonder what will he get out of all the work that he had done throughout his life. If the intention is not *Lishma* [for Her sake], then it will all go to waste, since *Lo Lishma* is a lie, and a lie can exist only in this world. Conversely, in the world of truth there is no room for lies.

It follows that all the efforts he has given throughout his life for Torah and work, who will take it, since there is no room for this in the world of truth, and there is a rule that one does not toil over a meal and misses it.

According to the above, it follows that he will lose at once all the efforts he had made in this world, for the moment one must go to the world of truth, he leaves all his toil in this world. It follows that this calculation causes him to repent in order to correct all his work so it is *Lishma*, since he does not want his work in this world to be in vain.

Therefore, the advice is that if a person sees that he still cannot work *Lishma*, he should increase his actions in *Lo Lishma*, since when he sees that he has done many actions in *Lo Lishma*, he will have no other choice but to repent and work *Lishma*, or his entire work will be in vain.

The rule is that a person does not toil over a meal and misses it. Hence, if one has done many actions in *Lo Lishma*, he will not want to lose all his trouble, so he will need to correct all his work so it enters the *Kedusha*.

But one who works *Lo Lishma* and did not do many works, meaning he did not dedicate much time to the Torah and work in

Lo Lishma, he will not have such a need to repent, since he will not have that many actions to lose. For this reason, we must try to do many good deeds even in *Lo Lishma* because this is the reason he will have a need to repent and work *Lishma*.

270- Anyone with Whom the Spirit of the People Is Pleased - 2

"All with whom the spirit of the people is content, the spirit of the Creator is content with him." We need to understand, since there are many righteous people in the world with whom the spirit of the people is not content, but on the contrary—they hate them. Also, it is known that uneducated people hate disciples of the wise.

Our sages said, "That disciple of the wise whom the people of the town love because he did not admonish them on matters of Above." But there is the imperative to admonish your neighbor, which means that they hate the disciple of the wise. So why did they say, "Anyone with whom the spirit of people"? And even more confusing is that they gave it as a sign for fear of Heaven, because he said that only those with whom the spirit of the people is content, the spirit of the Creator is content with him.

We should interpret that it is known that it is impossible to achieve love of the Creator before a person is rewarded with love of people through "love your neighbor as yourself," which Rabbi Akiva said is a great rule in the Torah. That is, by this a person accustoms himself to love people, which is love of others, and then he can achieve the degree of loving the Creator.

By this we should interpret the above-said, "Anyone with whom the spirit of the people is content," meaning that the spirit of the people is content with him, for he always engages in love of people, and always watches out for love of others. Then the spirit of the Creator is also pleased with him, meaning he enjoys making the spirit of the Creator, meaning bestowing upon the Creator. But it is not so with one who engages in love of self; then it is certain that the spirit of the Creator is also not pleased with him.

271- Any Person Who Is Favored

Any person who is favored, it is known that he has fear of heaven, as was said, "And the mercy of the Lord from the world onto the world is upon those who fear Him" (*Sukkah* 49). We should ask, for we see that there are many righteous ones who people hate. And vise-versa, there are many secular people and transgressors who are liked.

We can interpret this through ethics. Our sages teach a person how to measure so he will know if he has fear of heaven or not, as it is written, "One should know in one's soul whether or not he is a complete righteous" (*Berachot* 61b).

Therefore, he was given a sign: If the Creator favors him, it is certain that he, too, favors the Creator. It is as Baal HaSulam said about what Moses said, "If I am favored in Your eyes." He asked how Moses knew that the Creator favored him, and he replied that since Moses saw that he favored the Creator, it must be that the Creator favored Moses.

There is a rule from the Baal Shem Tov, "The Lord is your shade," meaning however a person walks with the Creator, so the Creator walks with man. This is the meaning of "The mercy of the Lord is upon those who fear Him."

272- Anyone Who Associates the Aim for the Creator with Another Thing

"Anyone who associates the aim for the Creator with another thing is uprooted from the world, as was said, 'to the Lord alone'" (*Sukkah* 45).

We should understand what it means that one associates another thing. Why is he uprooted from the world? He is committing idol-worship, meaning serves the Creator, as well as that other thing, so his sentence should have been the same as that of an idol-worshipper, so why specifically he is uprooted from the world?

We should interpret that the words "to the Lord alone" do not mean that he is also committing idol-worship. Rather, it means that since one must observe Torah and *Mitzvot* [commandments] because of the fear of heaven and not for his own delight, when he works for the Creator and also wants to benefit from his work, meaning for his own delight, as well, this is called "associating the aim for the Creator with another thing," namely himself.

Our sages said about him that he is uprooted from the world because man was created in the world for the purpose of fear of heaven, as our sages said, "The whole world was created only for this, to command this" (*Berachot* 6b). Thus, one who associates his own delight, as well, is uprooted from the world because his intention is not solely for the Creator. This is the meaning of the verse, "to the Lord alone," and not for his own delight, as well.

273- The Mightiest of the Mighty

"Who is the mightiest of the mighty? He who makes his foe his friend" (*Avot de Rabbi Natan*, Chapter 23).

In ethics, we should interpret that "mighty" is "one who conquers his inclination" (*Avot*, Chapter 4). That is, he works with the good inclination and subdues the evil inclination.

The mightiest of the mighty is one who works also with the evil inclination, as our sages said, "With all your heart—with both your inclinations" (*Berachot* 54), where the evil inclination, too, serves the Creator. It follows that he makes his foe, the evil inclination, his friend. And since the evil inclination is also serving the Creator, it follows that here he has more work, for which he is called "the mightiest of the mighty."

274- Specifically through a Man and a Woman

A newborn is born specifically through a man and a woman. From a male alone or from a female alone, there cannot be offspring. In ethics, the male is considered "the power of bestowal," and the female is "the power of reception." Offspring are good deeds, in which there is the breath of life.

Hence, when one has only the power of bestowal, he does not have the labor, and there is a rule that the reward is according to the labor. Since he has only the power of bestowal, he is devoid of labor, and without labor, it is impossible to be rewarded with the light of the Creator, as our sages said, "If you did not labor and did not find, do not believe" (*Megillah* 6b).

Also, if one has only the power of reception without sparks of bestowal, he can no longer make a choice to reject the bad and choose the good, since then he does not have the strength to decide to the side of merit.

Hence, specifically when the two forces are equal—the power of reception and the power of bestowal—he has room for work and labor to be able to prevail through the labor and determine to the side of merit. At that time, this deed that he has decided to the side of merit is called "newborn," meaning that the Creator places the spirit of life in this action. This is called "Wherever I mention My name, I will come to you and bless you."

275- I Wish They Left Me and Kept My Law

"I wish they left Me and kept My Torah [law]" (Jerusalem Talmud, Hagigah, 6b). One should not think that if he sees tokens and signs from the Creator, he will be able to engage in Torah and Mitzvot [commandments]. Rather, "and kept My Torah," meaning that only through the Torah does one acquire the strength to engage in Torah and Mitzvot for the sake of the Creator.

The proof of this is the tearing of the Red Sea, where after all the miracles and wonders, Amalek still had the power to come and fight against Israel.

276- If a Human Being Has on the Skin of His Flesh

"If a human being has on the skin of his flesh a swelling or a scab or a bright spot, and it becomes an infection of leprosy, he shall be brought to Aaron the priest."

The interpreters asked why it is written "a human being" and not "a man," perhaps as was said, "You are called 'man'" (*Yevamot* 61). This is a proof that the idol-worshippers do not defile with afflictions.

They said, "If a human being has on the skin of his flesh," meaning that the *Tuma'a* [impurity] of leprosy is not on the Israeli man, but on the skin of his flesh and not inside, for in idol-worshippers, their very selves and soul was leprosy and its kind. But when they afflict the Israeli soul, it is next to the sin that he will sin, and as the appearance of leprosy in the skin of his flesh and specifically on his skin and not in his flesh, much less in his interior (*Light of Life*).

We should ask, 1) Why specifically "You are called 'man.'" 2) Why next to his being called "man," in his interior, he is pure.

We should explain according to what our sages said about the verse, "In the end, all is heard, fear God and observe His commandments for this is the whole of man." He said, "What is 'for this is the whole of man'?" The whole world was created only for this man; he is equal to the whole world; the whole world was created only to command this (*Berachot* 6).

This means that the meaning of "man" is fear of heaven. Hence, "You are called 'man'" refers to fear of heaven, for one who has fear of heaven is called "man." It therefore follows that sometimes he commits a sin by chance, which is called "his externality," implied by the skin, for skin is externality, as is explained that there are discernments of *Mocha* [marrow], *Atzamot* [bones], *Gidin* [tendons], *Bassar* [flesh], and *Or* [skin].

It is explained that one who is called Adam [man] is internally pure and the *Tuma'a* that sometimes appears in him through a sin is only on the outside. Hence, idol-worshippers, namely those who have no fear of heaven, are without leprosy; they are impure from within.

"Sin" pertains only to one who has fear of heaven, who is called "man." The sin manifests in him in the form of leprosy, attached to the person.

But one who has no fear of heaven is full of sins and his interior is also inappropriate. Hence, a sin cannot be regarded as his exterior; rather, he is impure also within.

And to achieve fear of heaven is through the Torah, as our sages said, "The light in it reforms him."

277- When One of the Members of the Group Dies

"When one of the members of the group dies, all the members of the group should be concerned" (*Shabbat* 106).

When a person makes a daily schedule and divides the day into several parts, he connects himself to these arrangements. At that time, each part in itself is regarded as "one of the members of the group," since all the parts connect into one order.

If one of the arrangements is cancelled by coercion, or a mistake, or on purpose, the rest of the group should be concerned. He should be concerned about all the other arrangements of the day, that they will not be cancelled, since the arrangement that was cancelled is regarded as dead, and then he should be afraid that all the other arrangements might be cancelled.

278- The Light that Was Created on the First Day

The light that was created on the first day, *Adam HaRishon* was observing in it from the end of the world to its end. We should understand why he says, "from its end to its end," and not "from the beginning of the world to its end."

It can be said that when the light shines brightly, the whole world is in equivalence, and there is no beginning or end, but rather the end shines as the beginning. This is similar to saying that he saw the city from afar from the first end to the last end. This is called "from end to end." But when there is a difference of degrees, we say "beginning and end."

279- Why Israel Are Compared to an Olive Tree

"Rabbi Yochanan said, 'Why are Israel compared to an olive tree? It is to tell you that as the olive oozes its oil only by grinding, so Israel are reformed only by suffering'" (*Minchot* 53b).

Concerning the suffering that reforms a person, first one must know the meaning of being reformed. It is known that "The inclination of a man's heart is evil from his youth." This means that by nature, man cares only for his own sake. Naturally, it is impossible that he will be able to observe Torah and *Mitzvot* [commandments] for the sake of the Creator and not for his own sake.

However, through suffering, when he does not feel a good taste in corporeal things, meaning when they do not give him satisfaction in his life, since man was created with the aim to do good to His creations, he does not receive sufficient pleasure that will make it worthwhile to live in the world and tolerate everything in order to obtain the little pleasure that corporeality gives him.

To the extent that one feels torments in his life, when he has nothing from which to receive vitality, he is necessarily cancelled into working in the manner of bestowal. In other words, when he sees that he will not obtain vitality through acts of reception, he begins to perform acts of bestowal so that the acts of bestowal will give him pleasure.

It follows that the suffering reforms him, meaning the suffering he feels when he has nothing from which to derive pleasure makes him become reformed, meaning perform acts of bestowal, since "being reformed" means bestowal, as it is written, "My heart overflows with a good thing, I say, 'My work is for the King,'" meaning to bestow.

It follows that through the suffering he suffers from having no vitality, he chooses for himself a new way and begins to engage in bestowal.

Although this, too, is with the aim to receive, it is called *Lo Lishma* [not for Her sake] that is close to *Lishma* [for Her sake]. This is the meaning of "From *Lo Lishma* we come to *Lishma*," since "the light in it reforms him." Since he acts in order to bestow, by this he begins to feel light in the acts of bestowal, and that light can then make him bestow.

280- *This World and the Next World – 1*

"Her price is far above pearls," etc., and "who are nicer than gold, than much fine gold." It was said about this, "This world," meaning the path of preparation, is only a transition where there is a life of sorrow.

But the next world is like the living room, since in the living room there are all kinds of pleasures. Also, in the next world, called "Torah itself," there are all kinds of pleasures, as it is written, "nicer than gold." It is called "the next world" because it comes after one goes through the path of Torah, called "a sorrowful life," since there is labor in it.

It follows that this world is regarded as the state in which one is while he begins to enter the path of Torah, and this is the situation he is in now, in his beginning. This is why it is called "this world," and it is only a corridor.

Afterward, when he comes to the life of Torah itself, it is called "the next world," which is regarded as the next state, after he successfully went through the path of Torah, called "a corridor," when one feels the state of "you shall have a sorrowful life." In ethics, this is regarded as "this world" and "the next world."

"Why are Israel compared to an olive tree? It is to tell you that as the leaves of an olive tree do not fall during the summer or during the rains, so Israel have no rest, neither in this world nor in the next world" (*Minchot* 53b).

We see that there are three discernments concerning the olive tree: leaves, fruits, and oil. Leaves are fit as food for beasts. Fruits are fit as food for man. But the main purpose of the olive is not the fruit but the oil.

Man is like the tree of the field, as it is written, "for man is the tree of the field." The beginning of the blossoming is the leaves, since as soon as one begins one's work on the path of truth, he begins to feel a shadow, which is the concealment, for we see in corporeality that the leaves cast a shadow on the person. Hence, the shade, which is concealment, is called "leaves."

Afterward, when one takes upon oneself all the concealments and prevails over them, this yields fruits. In other words, the leaves are the reason for the bearing of the fruit, since after the acceptance of the burden above reason, it becomes food that is fit for human consumption.

In other words, during the time of the leaves, which is concealments, it is called "animal food," and it is called "faith" for human consumption. When he takes upon himself all these concealments, he turns them into food for humans. But the taste of olives is bitter, since when he made food out of the leaves, it is bitter. However, by grinding, he extracts its oil, which is the Torah, called "Your oils have a pleasing fragrance."

281- Be Mindful with a Minor Commandment as with a Major One – 1

"Be mindful with a minor *Mitzva* [commandment] as with a major one, for you do not know the reward given for them."

During the descent, when the Torah and *Mitzvot* [commandments] are minor in his eyes and he does not feel any importance or preciousness about them, he thinks he has no reason to engage in Torah and *Mitzvot* because his work is in vain and that his work is worthless, since he does not find any rhyme or reason in it. Therefore, what point is there in exerting uselessly?

Our sages said about this that one should be mindful with observing them the same as with a major one, as though the Torah and *Mitzvot* are a grave matter to him now, meaning in their full importance, for then he could make efforts because he knew how to appreciate them.

They said about this, "You do not know the reward given for the *Mitzvot*." That is, a person does not know the reward for *Mitzvot*, if he engages in Torah and *Mitzvot* that he regards as important, or even if he does not regard as important, and yet he overcomes and does them.

Perhaps there is more benefit in this overcoming that he does during the descent than during the ascent, since one cannot know which state brings more contentment above.

This is why they said, "Be mindful with a minor *Mitzva*, from the words [in Hebrew], "trifling and contemptible." A "major" one means that he feels the importance of Torah and *Mitzvot*, for then is the time when he can engage above reason, for the reason of the descent always mandates the opposite of the truth. In other words, it should be said that he can gain more from the lowly state if at that time he overcomes.

282- Be Mindful with a Minor Commandment as with a Major One – 2

19, Kislev, Tav-Shin-Lamed-Gimel, November 25, 1972

"Be mindful with a minor *Mitzva* [commandment] as with a major one, for you do not know the reward given for *Mitzvot* [commandments]" (*Avot*, Chapter 2). It is also written, "And it shall come to pass that if you surely listen."

We should understand this, since they said, "Be as slaves serving the teacher not in order to receive reward" (*Avot*, Chapter 1).

Yet, "reward" is regarded as "money," for anyone who works, it is only for a reward, and each one is rewarded according to his labor. Concerning the money that is paid for the labor, with money, one can buy all the pleasures that he wants, as it is said, that with money one can enter the King's innermost quarters.

This means that the reward is a general thing with which we can obtain all the pleasures. In spirituality, it is known what is written in *The Zohar* and in the words of the ARI, that all the pleasures that we find in corporeality are but a tiny light extending from spirituality, but the bulk of the pleasure is revealed in Torah and *Mitzvot*.

And the reason we feel concealment in Torah and *Mitzvot* is due to the power of the *Tzimtzum* [restriction], which is to correct the bread of shame, which is equivalence of form, as in "As He is merciful, so you are merciful."

Hence, when one is rewarded and comes to a degree where all his actions are for the sake of the Creator, to the extent that he can receive in order to bestow, to that extent he emerges from the *Tzimtzum* and achieves revelation, as in "He stood and concealed it for the righteous in the future."

It follows that all the darkness that we feel in spirituality extends from the evil within us, which is to receive in order to receive. Our sages said about this, "I have created the evil inclination; I have created the Torah as a spice" (*Kidushin* 30b), meaning that through the Torah we obtain the power to subdue the receiver in us so he can work in order to bestow.

In other words, all we want to receive from the Torah and *Mitzvot* is the power to subdue the evil. This is the only reward that we hope to receive from Torah and *Mitzvot*, since once we obtain the power to bestow, we will be able to obtain all the delight and pleasure that the Creator has prepared for us.

It therefore follows that they said, "Be mindful with a minor *Mitzva* as with a major one, for you do not know the reward given for *Mitzvot*, meaning which *Mitzva* is more effective for obtaining the power to bestow, which is called in the wisdom of Kabbalah by the name *Ohr Hozer* [reflected light].

This is why the verse says, "And it shall come to pass that if you surely listen," meaning that by observing the Torah we will be able to obtain the power to bestow contentment upon the Creator. At that time, we will have abundance, since more than the calf wants to suckle, the cow wants to nurse, and all that we are missing is the aim to bestow, since there was a restriction on receiving in order to receive.

Hence, the main reward that one should receive for observing Torah and *Mitzvot* is only to emerge from the bad called "receiver" and enter a state of where he only gives contentment to the Creator.

283- Be Mindful with a Minor Commandment as with a Major One – 3

Adar Aleph, Tav-Shin-Chaf-Bet, February 1962

Be mindful with a minor *Mitzva* [commandment] as with a major commandment.

"A minor *Mitzva*" means that it seems to a person that this is something not very important, which is faith, since it is something that is above reason, and faith does not require much knowledge because it is only acceptance in the heart and not attainment in the mind.

"A major *Mitzva*" means that which a person knows is important because he knows that not every person is rewarded with attainment.

Therefore, with matters pertaining to attainment, a person walks carefully, lest he will not acquire the attainment. Or, only in matters by which one can achieve knowledge can one exert because it is worthwhile for him, but things that pertain to faith are trivial in his eyes and he cannot overcome his laziness, to make it worth his while to exert for something not very important.

This is why they said, "Be mindful with a minor *Mitzva* [commandment] as with a major one, for you do not know the reward given for *Mitzvot* [commandments]."

A person thinks that receiving the reward is from something that gives contentment above. Hence, when he learns and finds success in his learning, meaning that he has vitality and can present innovations in the Torah, or feels while he prays that he has love and fear and *Dvekut* [adhesion] and excitement during the prayer, at that time he is mindful about the matter and wants to continue his work.

Although he sees that he has no time and he is preoccupied, he still has the strength to give even to the point of devotion so as not to rest from Torah and from prayer, since he feels in this knowledge, meaning he knows and feels on himself that these Torah and prayer give contentment above. Hence, at such a time he is mindful to do his work however he can.

This is not so with a minor *Mitzva*, which is only by acceptance of the burden of the kingdom of heaven, where he does not feel a flavor in the Torah, and where he has no vitality in the prayer. At such a time, it is regarded as "minor."

When he has no importance for such work, he does not want to be mindful and overcome the disturbances he has because he says that in any case, the engagement in Torah and *Mitzvot* is not so important above when he has no vitality. He wants to stop over a small disturbance because above it is also unimportant and he will not receive a great reward.

Therefore, they said, "You do not know the reward given for *Mitzvot*." In other words, the Creator derives contentment from his state of *Katnut* [smallness/infancy], which is only by acceptance of the burden of the kingdom of heaven without any knowledge, intellect, or other feeling from the time of *Gadlut* [greatness/adulthood], as his importance above is mainly the work during the *Katnut*, and not the *Gadlut*.

Because a person does not know which state gives more contentment above, "Be mindful with a minor *Mitzva*," meaning in the state of *Katnut*, "as with a major one," namely in the state of *Gadlut*.

284- I Have a Minor *Mitzva* [Commandment], Whose Name Is *Sukkah*

Tamuz, Tav-Shin-Chaf-Bet, July 1962, Antwerp

"I have a minor *Mitzva*, whose name is *Sukkah* [a *Sukkot* hut]" (*Avoda Zarah* 3). Why is it called "a minor *Sukkah*"? It is because there is no shortage of money in it.

We should understand why specifically *Sukkah* is regarded as having no shortage of money in it, since a *Sukkah* certainly costs more than other *Mitzvot* [pl. of *Mitzva*], such as a *Mezuzah* [a case affixed on the doorpost containing excerpts from the Torah], for example. According to what is explained in *The Zohar*, a *Sukkah* is called "a shadow of faith." Baal HaSulam interpreted that the word *Sukkah* comes from the word *Sechach* [thatch], which covers the mind, since faith is considered specifically above reason.

Hence, in the future, when everyone seeks reward, we should interpret that it pertains to people who are from the descendants of Israel. If they did not engage in Torah and *Mitzvot* [commandments] for the sake of the Creator, they can ask for reward for their actions, what they intended while they engaged in Torah and *Mitzvot*, but the Creator pays only those who work for Him (as in the story that was written in the books, about someone who was learning for a cat).

At that time, the Creator tells them, "Observe a minor *Mitzva*," namely faith, meaning when you perform *Mitzvot*, your intention should be *Lishma* [for Her sake].

In this there is no shortage of money, meaning they do not need to do other works or *Mitzvot* for the sake of the Creator, but through that same *Mitzva* that he does and for which he spends money, for the *Lo Lishma* [not for Her sake]. Because when working for the sake of the Creator, all he needs while doing it is the thought, and thinking does not cost him money, for in any case, he is performing the *Mitzva*.

However, his intention is for the sake of others. Hence, when he aims for the sake of the Creator, meaning with faith in the Creator, called *Sukkah*, he has no shortage of money. At that time, through faith in the Creator, it turns out that he works for the sake of the Creator, and then the Creator pays his reward, to all those who work for Him.

285- A Person Builds a Building

Adar, Tav-Shin-Chaf-Bet, 1962

In this world, a man builds a building and then ruins it. But in the future, he will not build and then dwell.

This world is called *Lo Lishma* [not for Her sake], and the future is called *Lishma* [for Her sake], since from *Lo Lishma*, we come to *Lishma*. The place of the present, which is in *Lo Lishma*, is called "this world," where one is now. "In the future" means later, when he comes to Lishma.

A building means that a person engages in Torah for the sake of others, not for the sake of the Creator. It is considered that he builds a building (as in "Do not pronounce it *Baneicha* [your sons], but *Boneycha* [those who build you]) but for others, since his aim is not for his own benefit, meaning that with the Torah and Mitzvot [commandments], he thereby brings contentment to the Creator, for by this he himself will approach the Creator and the words, "The Creator yearned to dwell in the lower ones" will come true in him. Instead, he works for others.

But in the future, when he engages Lishma, he will build for himself so that he himself will benefit from his work.

We should also interpret "this world." When one engages in Torah and Mitzvot for his own sake, when the aim is to receive, he cannot benefit from the building he is building.

An hour of Torah and an hour of prayer is similar to a brick over a brick. By this, a large building is made, according to the value of one's work in Torah and Mitzvot. Those Kelim [vessels] that can be filled with the concealed light, as in "In every place where I mention My name," as in "until He who knows the mysteries will testify that he will not return to folly," at that time, "I will come to you and bless you," and in all the Kelim that a person has prepared, there will be the blessing of the Creator.

This is called "the building of the Temple," but this is only if his work is for the sake of the Creator. At that time, a person can benefit from the blessing of the Creator. It follows that he dwells in the building he had built. Yet, this is only for the next world. One who works for the spirituality of Lishma, as this world is called "present," the place where one is now, this is as in "one should always learn Torah and Mitzvot Lo Lishma."

Afterward is called "future," meaning a world that approaches and comes, as it is written in The Zohar, and which the sages call "coming to Lishma." At that time, they will not build but engage in

Torah and *Mitzvot*, and then sit, but he himself, for because his aim is *Lishma*, the secrets of Torah are revealed to him and he becomes as a flowing stream.

But in *Lo Lishma*, what our sages said can be said about him: "One comes out to teach," meaning that he has the privilege that through him, one will come out to teach. It follows that he exerts in Torah and *Mitzvot* and others benefit from this—those who come out to teach. This is the meaning of "If he is rewarded, he takes his share and his friend's share in the Garden of Eden."

286- *Truth and Peace Loved*

Elul, Tav-Shin-Chaf-Bet, September 1962, Bnei Brak

"Truth and peace loved." We should understand what it means that particularly in matters where there is hatred between them we can speak of something new, meaning that they love each other. Yet, what hatred can be said between truth and peace?

287- *Turning His Ear from Hearing Torah*

8 *Tishrey, Tav-Shin-Chaf-Gimel*, October 6, 1962, Bnei Brak

"Rabbi Hanina Bar Papa said, 'Anyone who turns his ear from hearing Torah, his prayer becomes loathsome, as was said, 'He who turns his ear from hearing Torah, his prayer, too, is abomination''" (*Midrash Rabbah, Haazinu*).

We should ask, 1) What is the meaning of "turning his ear"? Why did he not simply say that he did not listen to the Torah, since the word "turning" implies that all we need is to listen, and we do not need to learn Torah, for by listening alone, we do our duty. 2) Why would his prayer become abomination? Can the whole world be learning Torah, and one who is not among the learners of Torah, his prayer will be abomination? 3) It is known that there is the issue of necessity and luxury. A prayer is regarded as necessity, and Torah is regarded as luxury. Therefore, the Torah is called "a gift," since a gift pertains only to luxuries. Accordingly, we should understand why if he turns his ear from hearing luxuries, the necessity becomes abomination, too.

We should interpret that it is known that the purpose of creation is to do good to His creations. To be able to receive the Creator's gift abundantly and for the gift to be complete, without any feeling of unpleasantness, He has given us the work of choice and that our aim will be for the sake of the Creator. Otherwise, a person is placed under the governance of the *Tzimtzum* [restriction], meaning he does not feel that there is pleasure in the work of the Creator.

All this was so that by this, man will come to a state where he can receive all the King's gifts and there will not be the quality of "bread of shame" in it, but only the completeness of the purpose.

It follows that the whole matter of work and prayer is that he can receive the luxuries that the Creator has for man. This is called Torah, which is a gift, regarded as luxuries. Hence, one who turns his ear, it means that he does not prepare himself to hear the Torah, since the Torah is a gift he should receive from the King.

This is the meaning of "We will do and we will hear." "We will do" alone is not enough, for "We will hear" is also required. That is, through "We will do," he will be rewarded with the quality of "We will hear," for the purpose of creation was on the quality of "We will hear." Hence, one who turns his ear from hearing Torah, his purpose is not needed; this is why it is loathsome, since anything that is unneeded becomes loathsome.

288- With Me, from Lebanon, Bride

"'With Me, from Lebanon, bride.' Rabbi Levi said, 'The conduct is to adorn the bride and perfume her, and then bring her to the *Huppah* [wedding canopy].' But the Creator did not do so. Rather, He said to the assembly of Israel, 'With Me, from Lebanon, bride. From silt and bricks I took you and made you a bride'" (*Midrash Rabbah, BeShalach,* Chapter 23).

Interpretation: The Creator brings a person closer not because of one's good qualities, but due to lowliness, when one feels that he is submerged in sludge and bricks, meaning he wants to make himself white but he cannot. At that time, he is in lowliness, and from this discernment, he is rewarded with nearing the Creator.

289- The Creator Is Meticulous with the Righteous

9 Sivan, Tav-Shin-Chaf-Bet, June 11, 1962, Antwerp

"The Creator is meticulous with the righteous as a hairsbreadth" (*Yevamot* 121b).

When a person is in a state of "righteous," when he is in ascent, He is meticulous with him that his aim will be for the sake of the Creator, meaning not to take this ascent as support and say, "Now I see that it is worthwhile to serve the Creator," since now he feels pleasure in his work. It follows that this is not for the sake of the Creator because it is not the faith in the Creator that makes him be a servant of the Creator, but rather the pleasure is the cause.

So what does the Creator do? He drops him from his high state into a state of lowliness. It follows that he is punished on the spot. This is the meaning of the words, "It is very stormy around Him," meaning that the Creator is meticulous with the time of righteousness.

But when a person is in a state of lowliness, when he does not feel a good taste in the work, it is pointless to be meticulous with him because he is in lowliness anyhow, and he has work to approach the Creator. Hence, it cannot be said that He will deny him the flavor of the work because now he feels no flavor.

The blow that one receives from the Creator, when He takes from him the flavor of the work, by this itself He heals him because then he has no other way to serve the Creator but with faith above reason. It follows that the blow that he received from the Creator, from this itself he can be healed, for otherwise, he will remain in separation.

By this we understand what our sages said, that by the blows of the Creator, He heals (*Mechilta BeShalach*). In other words, this is the healing—that He gives him room to work with faith without any support.

Also, we should understand what our sages said, "The Creator makes a decree and a righteous revokes it" (*Moed Katan*, 16). This means that the Creator makes a decree, taking from him the pleasure of the work, and there is no harsher decree than taking from someone the vitality in the work.

But the righteous revokes it. That is, if a person says he wants to work without any reward of vitality and pleasure, then the decree is revoked in any case. Moreover, now he rises to a higher degree, for now he is in a state of pure faith and is regarded as having no self-interest.

290- A Righteous Shall Live by His Faith

3 *Tamuz*, *Tav-Shin-Chaf-Bet*, July 5, 1962, Antwerp

"Habakuk came and based them all on one, 'A righteous shall live by his faith'" (*Makkot* 24a).

We should interpret "based them all on one," meaning that the whole Torah is interpreted on one matter, which is faith. Once he has the basis, the Torah for the sake of Torah begins. But before the Torah, it is for the sake of "one," meaning that through the Torah he will come to the *Mitzva* [commandment] that is called "one."

It follows that we should learn Torah and see how the Torah speaks only of matters of faith. And besides learning the revealed in the Torah, we should also learn it in the manner of intimation, which speaks of matters of faith.

291- Man and His Role

Before we begin to speak of some matter, we must know who is speaking and to whom. In this, we have no doubt that we are called "created beings," meaning that we are living in a world that was created existence from absence. Baal HaSulam established in great detail in his books that the thing that is innovated existence from absence is only the will to receive within us, for as long as we exist in our world, we want only to acquire possessions of pleasure.

We see that concerning pleasure, there is no difference among people, and everyone wants to have pleasures. From a day-old child to one's final day, we want only to enjoy.

The only difference is the clothing with which the light of pleasure is dressed in him, since pleasure is something spiritual and cannot be attained or grasped without clothing. In the books of Kabbalah, this is considered that there is no light without a *Kli* [vessel]. Hence, only in the *Kelim* [vessels] is it possible to distinguish one from the other. Some can receive pleasure only from a clothing of falsehood but are still unable to receive pleasure from a clothing of truth.

We see this with a baby who is playing with a doll that the boy or the girl made from rags. It is a false child, yet they like it and it gives them pleasure.

Conversely, a real child, meaning if there is a six-month-old baby in the house who is crying, and the mother asks her six-year-old daughter, "Why do you need to play with a false child? Play with the real one, so all three of us will benefit from this," meaning the mother, who cannot stand the child's crying, the child, who will enjoy your playing with him, and you will enjoy just as much as when you enjoy playing with a doll.

To this, the girl replies, "This is all very nice, but I find no taste or pleasure in this real child." Should the mother say to the girl, "But you see that when I have time, I play with the real child and not with the doll," the girl will answer, "I see that you don't want to enjoy in this world; this is why you are playing with the real child. I want to enjoy, so I play with the doll."

That is, one does not understand the other, since she still cannot derive pleasure from something real, but from something false.

In this we should discern between one and the other, meaning only in the clothing. But with regard to pleasure, everyone is the same and where there is no pleasure, one cannot enjoy. When he engages in something that is not enjoyable, this is only if he knows that in return for the labor he will receive pleasure later on.

We must understand where it comes from and what is the reason that we must receive pleasure and cannot live without it. This stems from the thought of creation to do good to His creations, as it is written in the *Midrash*, an allegory about a king who has a tower filled abundantly, and for this purpose, the desire to want only pleasure has been imprinted in us, like the meal, where if there is no appetite, we say that the meal is not good.

292- One Who Restrains Himself in Strife

Tevet, Tav-Shin-Lamed-Bet, January 1972

"Rabbi Ila'a said, 'The world exists only on account of him who restrains himself in strife, as it is said, 'The earth hangs on nothing''" (*Hulin* 89a).

Understanding that the existence of the world depends on this—that if two people who are quarreling with one another, the world cannot exist. Only if one keeps silent, meaning avoids answering, then the world can exist.

We should understand this in ethics. It is known that man has the evil inclination as soon as he is born. When one wants to engage in Torah and *Mitzvot* [commandments], the evil inclination asks him, "What will you get out of it?"

There are four answers to this:

1) He replies to the evil inclination that he intends to avenge, meaning to make the other party feel bad. Our sages call this answer *Lo Lishma* [not for Her sake], "and it would be best if he had died at birth" (*Berachot* 17a).

2) In order to be called "Rabbi" [title of honor]. That is, he answers to the evil inclination that he is learning so that people will reward him. If he is unmarried, he will find a good wife. And if he is married, people will respect him for his Torah and work. This, too, is called *Lo Lishma*, but from *Lo Lishma* we come to *Lishma* [for Her sake].

3) He replies that he is learning *Lishma* in concealment, so no one will see his work in Torah and *Mitzvot* [commandments], so that people will not respect him for his Torah and *Mitzvot*.

This is regarded as *Lishma* because *Lishma* means that he engages in Torah and *Mitzvot* so the Creator will pay his reward. This is similar to one who works for a certain company. He will certainly not ask for his salary from another company.

Also, one whose aim is that people will respect him for the Torah and *Mitzvot* is regarded as working not for the sake of the Creator, but for the sake of the created beings, that people will reward him.

But one who works in concealment intends for the Creator to pay his reward. This is regarded as working for the sake of the Creator, that his aim is that only the Creator will pay his reward.

4) Not in order to receive reward, meaning he serves the Creator but without any reward. At that time, the evil inclination asks, "What is this work that you are doing without any reward?" Then there is nothing to reply to the evil inclination, as it is written in the Passover Haggadah [narrative], "Blunt its teeth," and then he can accept the work only above rhyme and reason.

By this, one is rewarded with complete faith, for through the faith he is rewarded with the real wholeness, as for this, man was created. Therefore, at that time, the verse, "If he is rewarded, he sentences himself and the entire world to the side of merit" comes true.

This is the meaning of restraining himself in strife with his evil inclination, meaning that when the fight is over the work in the manner of not in order to bestow, at that time he has nothing to answer. This is called "hangs the earth on nothing," meaning he has no basis, which is called "nothing," but only above rhyme and reason.

293- Anyone Who Observes the Shabbat [Sabbath] Properly, Desecrates It

On the matter of observing Shabbat in the work, since there are six days of action, which are weekdays, and there is Shabbat, when it is forbidden to work, "weekday" means when a person feels that he is far from *Kedusha* [holiness]. At that time, he has the work of correcting his practices so as to bring himself closer to *Kedusha*. *Kedusha* means that he has equivalence of form. Then, to the extent that he draws closer, he feels the abundance of *Kedusha*.

Naturally, when he comes to feel the *Kedusha*, he has no work in correcting the evil. This is why at that time it is called Shabbat, since he *Shavat* [ceased/rested] from all his work. This means that only when one is in the weekdays, when he does not feel the *Kedusha*, there is work in correcting the evil.

Hence, the work of the weekdays is called an "awakening from below," and on this comes an awakening from above called Shabbat, when the *Kedusha* is poured upon him by the Creator. At that time, one should observe the Shabbat, meaning that all his work is to observe the Shabbat—not to distract his mind from the *Kedusha* of the Shabbat.

In the matter of observing, its importance becomes clear. There is a rule in nature that the more something is important, the better guard it needs. Likewise, the less something is important, its keeping is also not as much. Hence, the work of observing Shabbat is expressed in the greatness and importance of the *Kedusha* of the Shabbat.

This brings up the question, How can one come to feel the importance of *Kedusha*? The answer is that it comes from the work during the weekdays. To the extent that he regrets during the weekdays that they are regular days and not holy days, to that extent he values the Shabbat, as it is written, "Anyone who observes the Shabbat properly, desecrates it." That is, the fact that he can observe the Shabbat properly depends on his secularity, namely on his work during the weekdays.

294- We Will Do and We Will Hear – 1

11 *Shevat, Tav-Shin-Chaf-Vav*, January 22, 1967, Bnei Brak

"We will do and we will hear." We must understand why it should be "We will do" and subsequently, "We will hear." We see that a person is biased where he himself is concerned. Hence, even if he is made to understand that he is behaving inappropriately, he cannot agree because of the bribe he is receiving from himself, as it is written, "Bribe blinds."

Naturally, he cannot act other than his own view, since he is confident that he is following the path of truth according to how the intellect obligates him.

According to the above, when one takes upon himself an action, he is not involved in this matter because he takes upon himself what he is told to do. At that time, he does not have the bribe to blind him.

Hence, he can come to a state of hearing, meaning that he will hear that the Commander is correct. This is called "We will hear," meaning that he understands Him. Hearing means understanding in the mind and in the heart, for precisely once he has no self-interest, he can understand that what the Commander is commanding him to do is right.

But before he takes upon himself the action, he is still receiving bribe, and therefore thinks that the Commander is not making sense. This is "We will do," and later "We will hear."

295- Anyone Who Sanctifies the Seventh – 1

16 *Kislev, Tav-Shin-Lamed-Bet*, December 4, 1971

It is written in the poem "Anyone Who Sanctifies," "His reward is great, according to his work." There is a famous question about saying, "His reward is great," and then contradicting himself saying "according to his work," meaning specifically according to his work and not more.

To understand the above, we must first know what is the reward. It is known that our sages said, "Be as slaves serving the rav not in order to receive reward." Rather, we must work *Lishma* [for Her sake].

Concerning reward, we say that a reward comes after labor, when one exerts oneself to find something that cannot be found without labor. But with things that are already present, we cannot speak of labor.

Likewise, it is impossible to say that a person is laboring to find a tiny stone the size of one centimeter by one centimeter, since for this he can walk into any construction site and find gravel stones that are larger than one centimeter by one centimeter. Therefore, it cannot be said that he received the reward of several gravel stones, since there is no labor for something that is abundant. Hence, when we obtain it, it cannot be considered a reward for something that is prevalent.

However, in order to obtain a one centimeter by one centimeter diamond, which is very hard to find, for this a person must make great efforts to obtain the diamond. When he obtains it, it is regarded as having received his reward for the effort.

Now, we must believe that "The whole earth is full of His glory," as it is written, "I fill the heaven and the earth," and as it is written in *The Zohar* and the writings of the ARI that all the pleasure we feel in corporeal pleasures are but a tiny light of the light of the Creator.

Naturally, where the light of the Creator is revealed, there is no end to the pleasure. It follows that when we believe that the whole earth is full of His glory, the pleasure fills the entire world.

In something that fills the whole world, it means that we do not need to look for the pleasure, since there is no place in the world that is not filled with pleasure. Clearly, it is irrelevant to speak of laboring for the pleasure, and it is irrelevant to say when we receive the pleasure that we received a reward, since receiving something for which there is no labor cannot be regarded as reward.

Hence, the question is, What is the reward that we receive in return for our labor?

Regarding what we said, that the world is filled with pleasures, as in "The whole earth is full of His glory," the question is why we do not feel the light of the Creator filling the world. The answer to this is that the Creator made a *Tzimtzum* [restriction] and concealment not to feel the light of the Creator so there will not be bread of shame (as it is written in "Preface to the Wisdom of Kabbalah," 4,1).

But when one comes to a degree where he wants to bestow upon the Creator, meaning give contentment to his Maker, he begins to contemplate what the Creator needs so he can give it to Him, since all his concerns are to please the Creator. At that time, he realizes that the only reason He created the world was to receive pleasures from Him, and that more than this, the Creator does not need. Hence, he follows the Creator's will and receives the pleasures.

At that time, there is no issue of bread of shame because he is not receiving the pleasures because he wants to enjoy, but because he wants to bestow upon the Creator, for when one achieves the degree of wanting only to bestow upon the Creator, the *Tzimtzum* is lifted from him and he sees the world as full of His glory.

Then he sees that all this was revealed to him so he would enjoy it. Hence, once he has obtained the degree of bestowal, meaning obtained the degree where all he wants is only to bestow contentment upon the Creator, he fills himself with all the pleasures that his eyes see, as in the explanation, "The whole earth is full of His glory."

It follows that all that one needs to obtain that he can define as a reward after he has toiled several years is only one thing: the desire to bestow, meaning the degree of wanting to serve the rav not in order to receive reward.

All the labor where one needs to exert himself in Torah and *Mitzvot* [commandments] is only to obtain this. This is called "fear of heaven," as it is written, "What does the Lord your God ask of you? Only to fear Me."

This is so because fear is expressed as our sages said, "In return for 'and Moses hid his face for he was afraid to look,' he was rewarded with 'The image of the Lord does he behold'" (*Berachot* 7a).

The matter of fear is clarified in that since man has to approach the Creator, meaning adhere to him, as it is written, "And to cling unto Him," and as our sages explained, "Cling unto His attributes, as He is merciful, so you are merciful" (*Sotah* 14a), meaning equivalence of form, and one must be afraid that he will be far from the Creator in that he cannot emerge from self-love, which is reception, called "will to receive," for this reason, the only reward that one should hope for is to obtain the power of bestowal.

This is the meaning of "His reward is great, according to his work." If one exerts oneself in Torah and *Mitzvot*, he will get his reward, which is the power of bestowal. At that time, the power of bestowal, called "His reward is great," that reward will increase the "very," as it is written in *The Zohar*, "Good" is the angel of life, "very" is the angel of death, for he is an excess (*Trumah*, Item 433).

In other words, this is the abundance that pertains to the original will to receive, which is *Behina Dalet* [Fourth Phase], on which there was the *Tzimtzum*, and one who goes into the will to receive dies because the light of life departs from him.

However, by obtaining the *Kli* [vessel] for bestowal, we receive parts of the pleasure that pertains to *Behina Dalet* until the final correction, when he receives all the pleasure attributed to *Behina Dalet* in order to bestow, and this will be called "the end of correction."

296- The Core of Creation and the Correction of Creation

29 *Tamuz, Tav-Shin-Chaf-Dalet*, July 9, 1964

The core of creation and the correction of creation. It is known that the purpose of creation is to do good to His creations, meaning that the Creator wants to bestow abundance upon the lower ones. As long as one has not received all the pleasures and still feels some deficiency, it is a sign that he has not achieved the goal in full.

However, achieving the completion of creation must be a correction, as it is the correction of creation, which is upon the created beings to do. This is the meaning of "which God has created to do."

This correction is the desire to bestow, as explained in the books of Baal HaSulam, that before a person corrects his intention that all his actions will be for the sake of the Creator, it is impossible to receive the upper pleasures, a discernment called "receiving in order to bestow."

This work of bestowal is all the work that we should do, since it is against the nature imprinted in us, called "will to receive." We must do the opposite, to crave only to bestow and not receive for ourselves.

We can understand this through an allegory. If a person wants to build a house, having the house is regarded as the goal, and the completion of his desire is to have the house. However, in order to be given the house, he must make a correction, and before he makes the correction, he will not have the house.

It follows that he must do two things: 1) He engages in achieving the goal, which is having the house, meaning to come into the house and put his belongings in there, and so forth. 2) He engages in correction, meaning how to have the correction by which he will have the house. The correction in order to have the house is called "money," meaning that by giving money to the owner, the owner will give him the apartment.

However, having money requires labor. After he labors, he will be paid a reward for the labor, and when he has the money, he will receive the house from the owner of the house. Before he gives him the money, he will not have the house. It follows that the correction and qualification to deserve receiving the house is the money.

It therefore follows that when one exerts in order to obtain money, it is considered that he engages in corrections. That is, all the work that a person does and in which he should have success was said only about obtaining the correction, which is the money. This is not so with the work on receiving the house; at that time, he has no work.

The size and importance of the house depend only on the corrections, on how much money he has.

From this we understand that in spirituality, too, it is impossible to achieve the goal, meaning pleasures, before a person makes the correction, and the correction is the desire to bestow, meaning *Lishma* [for Her sake]. If one works *Lishma*, then as our sages said, "the secrets of Torah are revealed to him and he becomes like a flowing stream, and all the world becomes worthwhile for him." But if he does not have the desire *Lishma*, he will not be given any of the spiritual things.

It follows that the desire *Lishma* is like money in corporeality, where measuring the attainment of the goal depends on the intensity of the desire *Lishma*. As it is impossible to obtain money without work, but only after the work does he receive money, so it is impossible to receive the desire *Lishma* without labor.

In other words, by exerting in Torah and *Mitzvot* [commandments], one is rewarded with the desire *Lishma*. A person must see that all the reward that he hopes to be given from Torah and *Mitzvot* is the desire *Lishma*. When he has this desire, he will be able to receive the goal and the completeness. Hence, there is work on corrections, on engagement in achieving the correction, and there is work on receiving the goal.

297- He Raises the Poor from the Dust, Lifts the Indigent from the Trash

1 *Kislev, Tav-Shin-Lamed-Gimel*, November 19, 1971

The difference between dust and trash is that dust is something natural that was made this way while trash is waste. Our sages said, "None are poorer than a dog and none richer than a swine" (*Shabbat* 155b), since a swine finds its nourishment everywhere, for waste, too, is food for a swine.

We should interpret that as long as one has not corrected the sin of the primordial serpent, all of one's flavor in Torah and *Mitzvot* [commandments] is only as dust. This is called "*Shechina* [Divinity] in the dust." One's aim in Torah and *Mitzvot* should be that through our work we can raise the *Shechina* from the dust.

This extends from the creation of the worlds, which was with the intention that we would be able to make the correction of equivalence of form, as our sages said, "As He is merciful, so you are merciful" (*Sotah* 14a). Hence, *Tzimtzum* [restriction] and concealment were placed on the vessels of reception so as to be a vacant space devoid of *Kedusha* [holiness]. This is why by creation, there is the taste of dust.

This is why the verse says "He Raises the Poor from the Dust," meaning that the *Shechina* is called poor and meager because everyone sees that she has nothing to give in return for engaging in Torah and *Mitzvot*.

It follows that all of people's pleasures are only from waste of *Kedusha* that extends into the corporeal pleasures. It is called "tiny light," and it sustains the *Klipot* [shells/peels], and this is called "trash."

Hence, He raises from the trash, meaning He has to lift man so he will not be taken after the ignoble pleasures called "trash." When he refrains from trash, he is rewarded with raising the *Shechina* from the dust, since one depends on the other.

298- Associating the Quality of Mercy with Judgment

Av, Tav-Shin-Lamed-Gimel, August 1973, Bnei Brak

Since man is born out of *Behina Dalet* [Fourth Phase], which is from the vacant space, and her aim is to receive in order to receive, if he remained this way, only from this root, it would be utterly impossible to turn her into working in order to bestow. Hence, when the quality of bestowal merges with him, namely the quality of mercy, by this he has the remedy of Torah and *Mitzvot* [commandments] in order to bestow, which can invert him.

We should understand this, since we see that it is human nature that he is immersed in worldly lusts. Sometimes, he has an awakening and desires to achieve *Dvekut* [adhesion] with the Creator. At that time, we see that during the awakening we have no work to emerge from corporeality and all our thoughts and desires are about spirituality. When we descend from our degree and return to our bad ways of thinking only about corporeal matters, it can be said that when the *Behina Dalet* is revealed in him, namely when he craves something, he cannot overcome his inherent will to receive. But when the quality of mercy awakens in him, which is the power of bestowal, then, too, he has no freedom of choice but to aspire for spirituality. Then, when *Behina Dalet* awakens in him, he turns astray again.

Therefore, we see that when a person has fallen and is under the control of the will to receive, he has no freedom of choice. And when the desire to bestow works within him, he does not need choice. It therefore follows that the choice that he has is only over who will be in control—the quality of judgment in him or the quality of mercy.

But with arguments, conjectures, and reasoning, it is impossible to win when the quality of judgment rules within him.

Thus, the only thing that one can do is connect to books and authors that deal with the desire to bestow. Then the quality of mercy awakens in him, and he will yearn for spirituality without any effort. That is, the work can be primarily when neither is in control. At that time, he has the choice of who will be in charge.

299- Having a Clean Mind

1 *Sivan, Tav-Shin-Lamed-Gimel,* June 1, 1973

"Thus would the clean-minded in Jerusalem do: They would not come into a meal unless they knew who was dining with them" (Sanhedrin 23a).

"Clean-minded" means people who are cleansed from reason, as our sages said, "So and so was cleansed of his possessions." This means that they are people who go above reason, which in plural form [in Hebrew], it is called "clean-minded." These people should be careful not to come in contact with people who can only work within reason, since the view of landlords is opposite from the view of Torah.

"The view of landlords" means within reason, when one understands what he is doing and always thinks whether it is worth his while to do or not to do, meaning what benefit the act he is doing will yield for him.

Conversely, "the view of Torah" is as our sages said, "The Torah exists only in one who puts himself to death over it" (*Berachot* 63b). This means that he should annul his self, meaning annul all of his existence. Thus, there is no reason here with which to think what observing Torah and *Mitzvot* will give him.

A landlord always thinks about property. Hence, with everything he does, he thinks what this can add to his property. But the path of Torah is annulment of property. Thus, those who study Torah and go within reason, meaning with the view of landlords, have a different way than the students of Torah who are going above reason, which is called "clean-minded," for they are cleaned from reason because they want the cancellation of reality.

Thus, which view can be said that obligates him to completely annul himself? This discernment is called "not in order to receive reward." Therefore, they need great care so they will not be taken after the students of Torah who are going within reason.

300- A Land Where You Will Eat Bread Without Scarcity

15 *Shevat*, *Tav-Shin-Lamed-Gimel*, January 18, 1973

"A land where you will eat bread without scarcity." Eating bread refers to the upper abundance, as our sages said about *Adam HaRishon*, "By the sweat of your brow shall you eat bread" (*Pesachim* 111). Scarcity is when a person is needy of people. At that time, he is considered "poor." But when he is happy with his lot, he is considered "rich." *Eretz* [land] comes from the word *Ratzon* [desire], as it is written in the *Midrash*, "Why was she called *Eretz*? Because she *Ratzta* [wanted] to do her Maker's will."

When a person is poor, meaning deficient, it means that his observance of Torah and *Mitzvot* [commandments] is inappropriate in both mind and heart. At that time, he comes to the point of truth called "recognition of evil," when he sees his true state. By this, he can be rewarded with the filling of the lack. However, if he has no lack, meaning a *Kli* [vessel], how can abundance be poured into it?

We can interpret this as in "Poverty befits Israel like a red trapping a white horse" (*Hagigah* 9b), for each time he has a lack, he can receive for it, and by this he moves from degree to degree. Otherwise, he remains as though standing still and not as one who walks.

However, along with having a *Kli* [vessel] called "poverty," he should also be happy with his lot, regarded as being rich, meaning to agree that if the Creator wants him to remain in the state of deficiencies that he is in, he is also content.

This is as our sages said, "As one blesses for the good, so one blesses for the bad" (*Berachot* 54a). In other words, a person should depict to himself how he would praise the Creator if the Creator bestowed upon him the satisfaction of the lacks, and this is how he blesses for the bad that he is in, so that with all the recognition of evil that he feels about himself, he is still happy with his lot, and then the Creator bestows upon him bread.

This is the meaning of *Eretz* [land] being *Ratzon* [desire] "without scarcity," meaning that with a lack alone, he cannot be rewarded with bread from above. Rather, he also needs wealth, which is called "without scarcity." At that time, "you will eat bread" there, meaning upper abundance.

Baal HaSulam said that because "The cursed does not cling to the Blessed," "The *Shechina* [Divinity] is present only out of joy," since he agrees to remain with all the bad if the Creator wants it this way, and in this way he engages in Torah and *Mitzvot* [commandments].

This is called "happy with his lot," and at that time, he is rich. This is the meaning of "As one blesses for the good, so one blesses for the bad." It means that if he were to be rewarded with the good that is concealed in Torah and *Mitzvot*, he would certainly work with joy and excitement and peace of mind. Likewise, now that he is deficient, he should also make his work be with joy and peace, and then he will be rewarded with food for humans, called "bread."

This is what it means that one must engage in Torah day and night, that the night and the day should be equal for him, as written in *The Zohar* (*BeShalach*). In other words, the state of completeness called "day," and the state of incompleteness called "night," should be equal. That is, if his aim is for the sake of the Creator then he agrees that he wants to bring contentment to his Maker, and if the Creator wants him to remain in the state of incompleteness, he agrees to this, as well. The consent is expressed by doing his work as if he were rewarded with wholeness. This is regarded as "agreeing," when the day and the night are equal to him.

But if there is a difference, to the extent of the difference, there is separation, and on that separation there is a grip to the outer ones. Hence, if a person feels that to him there is a difference, he must pray to the Creator to help him so there will not be a difference for him, and then he will be rewarded with completeness.

301- The General Public and the Chosen Few

16 *Tevet*, *Tav-Shin-Lamed-Gimel*, December 21, 1972

There is the general public, and there are the chosen few. Also, there is upbringing, and there are customs. And also, there is the fear of heaven.

The general public is regarded as "upbringing." That is, what obligates them to observe Torah and *Mitzvot* [commandments] is that they were raised this way. This means that if the body asks the person why he is doing these things, he answers to himself that it is because he was brought up this way and this is the custom in the environment where I was born.

Hence, this is a strong basis for a person not to fall from his state because habit becomes nature. Therefore, all the things and actions by which a person was brought up are not difficult for the body to do because he has a strong obligator called "upbringing" or "custom."

For this reason, if a person does not blemish the customs of Israel and his upbringing, he can continue with his habits. For example, a person does not face a temptation to drive a car on Shabbat [Sabbath] because he was brought up this way.

But if a person wants to do things for which he was not brought up, then even for the smallest action, the body asks, "Who are you doing this for?" meaning who is the obligor.

At that time, a person faces a test and a choice, since he still does not have an obligation to do this, since the environment he is in does not do such things, so he has no one to look at and say that many people do, or say, or think similar to what he wants to do now.

It follows that he has no one on whom to rely because he has no basis from his upbringing or environment. Instead, he must say that the fear of heaven obligates him to do this or that. Hence, the only one he can rely on is the Unique One.

For this reason, this person is among the "chosen few" and not one of the general public among whom he was born and from whom he received his upbringing. Therefore, at that time he needs the Creator's help. This is the meaning of "He who comes to purify is aided" from above, since he cannot receive help from the general public and therefore needs mercy from above and must receive the Torah from above.

However, the Torah that is prevalent in the general public cannot help him because they will not give him the strength to work more than what they have.

302- *For the Lord Chose Jacob for Himself*

Hanukkah, 23 *Kislev*, *Tav-Shin-Lamed-Gimel*, December 4, 1972

"For the Lord chose Jacob for Himself." Our sages asked, "Who chose whom? Did the Creator choose Jacob or did Jacob choose the Creator?"

The thing is that on one hand, one must believe that the Creator chose him, and this is called "private Providence," and a person must praise the Creator for giving him the possibility to serve Him with the work in Torah and *Mitzvot* [commandments].

Although one still does not feel the importance of the matter, since he is used to engaging in Torah and *Mitzvot* since childhood, when he was still unable to feel the importance in Torah and *Mitzvot*, and afterward, when he grew up, the habit stayed with him and his heart became insensitive while engaging in Torah and *Mitzvot*, so he did not feel any deficiency about feeling the importance of the matter. At that time, one must overcome the habits and always look into who and what he is engaged in now. Also, he should consider that he is among those who were invited to come to the King's palace.

This means that Providence has made it that he was not born among the nations or among secular Jews, but specifically to Jewish orthodox parents and he is always in an environment that obligates him to engage in Torah and *Mitzvot*, and this is considered that the Creator chose Jacob for Himself, meaning that the Creator has chosen him.

Afterward, one must engage in the intention in Torah and *Mitzvot*, meaning to what goal the Torah and *Mitzvot* should bring him. This requires much attention, meaning that the Torah and *Mitzvot* can bring him to choose the path of the Creator, where all his actions and thoughts will be only to bestow contentment upon his Maker. This falls into the category of reward and punishment, meaning that the work comes from man's choice.

This is regarded as Jacob choosing the Creator, meaning that he chose that all his actions will be for the Creator. This is regarded as "intention." As for actions, any person belongs to this, meaning that in any state that one is in, he should praise the Creator for awarding him the opportunity to engage in Torah and *Mitzvot*, in the practical part of Torah and *Mitzvot*. This falls into the category of "private Providence."

On the intention, there is prayer. One should pray that his actions will be for the sake of the Creator. This choice pertains specifically to those who want to walk in the ways of the Torah, in the view of Torah. Conversely, those who belong only to the view of landlords belong only to the first discernment, meaning to the part of actions without intentions, since the prime intention is only to achieve the power of bestowal.

Also, the matter of reception and bestowal applies to all the degrees, since before the correction of the *Masach* [screen], it is called "reception," meaning *Lo Lishma* [not for Her sake], and the correction of the *Masach* is the meaning of *Lishma* [for Her sake], meaning bestowal.

303- Delight Them with a Complete Building – 2

13 *Heshvan, Tav-Shin-Lamed-Gimel*, October 21, 1972, after Shabbat

"Delight them with a complete building; brighten them up with the light of Your face" (Shabbat [Sabbath] songs).

We need to understand what is a "complete building" and what is an "incomplete building." The thing is that in everything that one does, he wants that through his work he will have a complete building in which to live.

There is a building where the person himself will live, and this is called an "incomplete building" because a person is regarded as deficient. Therefore, the building is named after the person, and naturally, it is regarded as an incomplete building.

But if a person wants his work to yield a building for the Creator, that the Creator will live there, this is called a "complete building," since the Creator is complete. Hence, the building is named after Him, and is therefore called a "complete building," as it is written, "And let them make Me a Temple and I will dwell in the midst of them."

"Delight them" means that when a person decides that it is not worthwhile to work for himself, meaning to build a construction for himself, and begins to build for the sake of the Creator, it is considered that "He has left the general public, but has not yet arrived."

This is so because when he wants to work *Lishma* [for Her sake], the body comes and asks, "What is this work for you?" At that time, he has no joy because the body objects to him and tells him that he should not exclude himself from the public, since all of the public engages only in their own buildings, meaning that man will have a reward for his work.

Hence, we say, "Delight them" when they engage in a "complete building," where by the Creator imparts upon them joy, which is a joy of *Mitzva* [commandment], which is the light of faith, called "Brighten them up with the light of Your face," they will be able to complete their work.

304- Fear and Love
13 Heshvan, Tav-Shin-Lamed-Gimel, October 21, 1972, after Shabbat

Concerning love and fear, it is known that fear precedes love. The reason for this is in order for one to be able to observe Torah and *Mitzvot* [commandments] out of love, meaning that he will feel the taste of pleasure in Torah and *Mitzvot*, which will cause him to love the Torah and *Mitzvot*.

But one who observes Torah and *Mitzvot* because of fear, at that time he still does not feel the pleasure of Torah and *Mitzvot*, but observes because of the fear of the Creator. That is, he is afraid that the Creator might punish him if he does not observe Torah and *Mitzvot*.

It follows that then, all his work is because of fear of the Creator, meaning that the body gives him thoughts of doubts about the fear.

Hence, each time, he must grow stronger in faith in the Creator until he is rewarded with permanent faith.

Afterward, he is rewarded with observing Torah and *Mitzvot* because of love, meaning to feel the flavor of pleasure in Torah and *Mitzvot*.

Conversely, if the Creator were to let him serve Him with love from the beginning, by feeling pleasure in Torah and *Mitzvot*, he would not need faith in the Creator, like those whose vitality comes only from corporeal pleasures and they observe all the manners of nature such as eating and drinking. They do not need faith in the Creator and observe all of nature's commandments because of the feeling of pleasure.

Likewise, if they felt pleasure in Torah and *Mitzvot*, everyone would be observing the Torah and *Mitzvot* because of pleasure and not because it is the commandment of the Creator. In other words, they would not need to believe in the Creator and would be able to receive the pleasure of Torah and *Mitzvot* without union with the Creator. Hence, a concealment was placed on Torah and *Mitzvot* not to reveal the pleasure of Torah and *Mitzvot* until after one is awarded through fear with permanent faith in the Creator.

305- *The Meaning of Evil*

Isru-Chag [the day after] Passover, *Tav-Shin-Lamed-Bet*, 1972

The evil in a person is regarded as evil only when one feels that it is evil. That is, the extent that the evil prevents him from receiving abundance determines the measure of the evil.

Normally, if one loses a penny to one's friend, he does not hate him for this, since a penny is not important enough to fight with the other over it. But to the extent that his friend causes him losses, the level of hatred forms in him until he cannot stand him.

It follows that to the extent that a person has importance of Torah and *Mitzvot* [commandments], to that extent he can determine the measure of hatred for the evil, which interferes with his engagement in Torah and *Mitzvot*. For this reason, if a person wants to come to hate the evil, he must increase the importance of spirituality.

At that time, he will receive such a measure of hatred that will remove him from befriending his evil, as it is written, "You who love the Lord hate evil." That is, to the extent that a person loves the Creator, so he hates those who interfere with loving the Creator.

306- If the Rav Is Similar to an Angel of the Lord

1 *Adar Tav-Shin-Lamed-Bet*, February 15, 1972

"If the rav is similar to an angel of the Lord, let them seek Torah from his mouth." An "angel" means he has no evil inclination, as our sages said, "When Moses rose to heaven, the angels said, 'Place your glory over the heaven.' The Creator said [to Moses], 'Give them a convincing answer.' He [Moses] said to them, 'Do you have evil inclination?'" (*Shabbat* [Sabbath] 88b). That is, an angel has no evil inclination.

For this reason, we should interpret "If the rav," meaning that the rav says that each one will be similar to an angel, meaning that the disciples will have equivalence of form like an angel, who has no evil inclination, they should seek Torah from his mouth.

That is, they should seek Torah from the rav concerning how to achieve equivalence with an angel, since it is impossible to subdue the evil unless through the Torah, as our sages said, "I have created the evil inclination; I have created the Torah as a spice."

And if not, meaning if the rav does not teach them how to be like an angel, "let them not seek Torah from his mouth," since his Torah is not going in the true direction.

307- You Have Not a Blade of Grass Below

At a beginning-of-the-month festive meal, 1 *Adar*, *Tav-Shin-Lamed-Bet*, February 15, 1972

"You have not a blade of grass below that does not have an angel that strikes and tells it, 'Grow!'"

We should ask why it needs to strike it or it does not want to grow. After all, we see that in nature, each and every one wants to grow and not be small.

To understand this, we need to interpret this in the work. By nature, as long as one is immersed in the earth, he relinquishes any kind of *Gadlut* [greatness/adulthood] and wants to remain in earthliness. However, there is a force from above called an "angel," and an angel is a force that bestows and strikes him and tells him, "Grow!" In other words, it strikes him with its power of bestowal and tells him, "Grow! Come out of your earthliness," although one is born with a desire to receive called "earthliness."

As far as the will to receive is concerned, a person would remain in the earth and would never be able to emerge from earthliness. But the power of bestowal that exists in the world, called "angel," afflicts him by not satisfying the will to receive. Thus, the afflictions he feels push him out of earthliness.

This is as it is written, "Happy is the man whom You afflict, Lord," for by the Creator sending afflictions into the earthliness, he has no satisfaction with earthliness, which pushes him to grow and emerge from the earth.

It therefore follows that to the extent that one feels the beating, so he begins to grow and emerge from the earth. Otherwise, he would remain submerged in the earth.

308- You Have Chosen Us – 2

27 Shevat, Tav-Shin-Lamed-Bet, February 12, 1972

Concerning "You have chosen us," there is an explanation to the question: Our sages said that the Creator wooed all the nations of the world but they would not receive it. Only the people of Israel said, "We will do and we will hear." Thus, why do we say, "You have chosen us"?

We should interpret this in the work. It is known that man is a small world. For this reason, he himself consists of the children of Seir and the children of Paran. But only the qualities in man that say, "We will do and we will hear," only to them the Creator chose to give the Torah, while to the rest of the desires in man, to them the Torah was not given.

This is the meaning of the prohibition to teach Torah to idol-worshippers, referring to the nations of the world within the person himself; they are forbidden to learn.

Baal HaSulam explained that wherever our sages said "forbidden," it means "impossible." That is, because "the Torah exists only in one who puts himself to death over it," meaning cancels his self and wants to annul before the Creator, then the Creator gives him the Torah as a gift.

Hence, one should know that the Creator chose only the quality of Israel within man. It was only about this quality that it was said, "You have loved us and wanted us." Therefore, when one says, "You have chosen us," he must respect and appreciate the quality of Israel in him, and annul the rest of the desires of the nations of the world of which he is comprised.

309- Concerning Walking in Secrecy

27 *Shevat*, *Tav-Shin-Lamed-Bet*, February 12, 1972

"He has told you, 'O man, what is good, and what does the Lord require of you but to do justice, to love mercy, and to walk in secrecy with the Lord your God'" (Micah 6).

"Walking in secrecy" means something that is secret, that is not visible. Something that is visible is called "revealed," meaning actions that anyone can see what his friend is doing, but not what his friend is thinking. Even when his friend tells him his thoughts, it is still not certain that this is his real thought.

For example, a person who has made a fortune and then donated it to a religious institution and says he wants to give them this large sum provided they advertise it in the papers. He says that it is worthwhile for him to donate the large sum in order to get the publicity and great respect.

However, even if he says explicitly that his intention is respect, it can be otherwise. That is, he might want to do this so as not to be respected for doing a righteous deed, giving such a large sum although he is not that wealthy, and still because the commandment to support students of Torah is important in his eyes, he donates the money. But in order for people not to say that he is working for the sake of the Creator and respect him for doing a righteous deed, he says that his intention is respect. Therefore, he will not be respected. It follows that a thought cannot be revealed. Rather, something that is revealed is only actions. For this reason, the verse says, "walk in secrecy," meaning the intention, so it will be "with the Lord your God," meaning that he should see that the intention is for the sake of the Creator.

310- The Righteous Perishes and No One Notices

"The righteous perishes and no one notices ... for because of the evil, the righteous perishes" (Isaiah 57). *The Zohar* interprets that "When the Creator looks at the world, and the world is not worthy of existing, and judgment is in the world, He takes the righteous one who lives among them."

We can interpret that if a person should be given a descent, the righteous is taken away from him, meaning that beforehand, he loses the faith in the righteous, for otherwise he might receive strengthening from the righteous. This is the meaning of "The righteous perishes and no one notices," for because of the evil, he lost the faith in the righteous (*VaYeshev*, 4,4).

311- The Tree from which Adam HaRishon Ate Was Wheat

15 *Shevat*, *Tav-Shin-Lamed-Bet*, January 31, 1972

"Rabbi Yehuda said, 'The tree from which *Adam HaRishon* ate was wheat, for the infant does not call out 'Father and Mother' before it tastes the taste of grain" (Sanhedrin 70b).

We should ask, 1) Since there are five kinds of grain, where is the proof that it is wheat? 2) If you say that we know that it is grain, meaning wheat, since precisely when the infant tastes the taste of wheat, it can call out "Father and Mother," we must understand why specifically when it tastes the taste of wheat it knows, and when it tastes another kind, it does not know how to call out "Father and Mother."

"Rabbi Yehuda said in the name of Rabbi Akiva, 'Why did the Torah say, 'Bring *Omer* [sheaf of wheat] on Passover? So that the crop in the fields will be blessed for you. And why did the Torah say 'Bring two loaves of bread' on *Shavuot* [Feast of Weeks]? It is because *Shavuot* is the time of the fruits of the tree.' The Creator said, 'Bring two loaves of bread before Me on *Shavuot* so that the fruits of the tree will be blessed for you'" (*Rosh Hashanah* 16).

It is known that there are two degrees: There is a "field" that is "a field that the Lord has blessed," and there is "a tree of the field." Man is called "a tree of the field," as it is written, "For man is a tree of the field."

A "field" is called *Malchut*, a beast, *Gematria* BON, for the number of the name BON implies animal food. Hence, we offer a harvest of barley, which is animal food, for then Israel came out of Egypt, as it is said in *The Zohar*, that they came out from the authority of the *Sitra Achra* [other side] into the authority of *Kedusha* [holiness].

This is regarded as "I and not a messenger." However, this is called "faith above reason," when they still have not been rewarded with Torah, which is called "the quality of man," regarded as "the view of Torah."

This is what they were awarded on *Shavuot* at the time of the giving of the Torah, at which time man is called "a tree of the field." Hence, at that time, wheat, which is man's food, pertains to the sin of the tree of knowledge, which means that an infant does not call out "Father and Mother" before it tastes the taste of wheat.

The issue of "Father and Mother" pertains to the *Mochin* of *Abba* and *Ima*, which is the quality of *Hochma* and *Bina*, meaning *Bina* that returns to being *Hochma*.

312- If You Go to War – 1

"If you go to war against your enemy." RASHI interprets that this means optional war.

We should understand that this implies that there are two types of war: 1) over actions, meaning doing *Mitzvot* [commandments] or transgressions, 2) over permission, meaning that all the observing of Torah and *Mitzvot* is in order to expand man's authority, to have more possessions each time, or over annulling of authority, when he wants to achieve the annulment of his own authority by means of observing Torah and *Mitzvot*, and that the authority of the Creator will expand instead so there will not be multiple authorities, but a singular authority.

"Multiple authorities" means that he extracts from the authority of the Creator into his own authority, and "singular authority" means that he annuls his own authority and wants only the authority of the Creator to exist. This is regarded as achieving a degree where all his desires are in order to bestow.

313- When the Lord Rejoices Over You

"And it came to pass when the Lord rejoiced over you to do you good, ...so the Lord will delight over you to make you perish" (Deuteronomy 28).

There is joy when a person achieves a goal or sees that he is approaching the goal.

In the world in general, the whole basis was built upon receiving reward in this world and in the next world, and there is no such matter of revoking the doing of *Mitzvot* [commandments]. Rather, at times a person does more, and at times less. But one does not become a wicked man by subtracting or by adding, since his faith is constant, and on the actions that he cannot do so much, he has excuses why it is justified.

But on the individual level, although he observes, still, because on the individual level, the main thing is the intention, which is in order to bestow without any reward, the body does not agree to this. This causes him alien thoughts, and then he sees that he is wicked, although in terms of actions, he is acting as always. But on the intention, he cannot justify himself, so he must say about himself that he is wicked.

We should ask why this is so. Why did the foreign thought come to him? It is so because the Creator wants the person to walk on the path of truth. And in order not to remain in a state of *Lo Lishma* [not for Her sake], he is not permitted to observe the Torah and *Mitzvot* in *Lo Lishma* and is sent a foreign thought so that if he wants to engage in Torah and *Mitzvot*, his only way is in *Lishma* [for Her sake].

It therefore follows that "when the Lord delights to do good," it means when one engages in Torah and *Mitzvot*. And "so the Lord will delight over you to make you perish" means He does not let one remain in the state that he is in and observe Torah and *Mitzvot* like the general public. Why? It is because by this he will have to have the matter of *Lishma* [for Her sake], for otherwise, the general public will be able to observe Torah and *Mitzvot* and he will not. It follows that he is even worse than the general public.

314- Smallness and Greatness

"And I will give the reward of the light of seeing to *Atik Yomin*." He interprets in the *Sulam* [Ladder commentary on *The Zohar*] that when raising MAN to receive *Katnut* [smallness/infancy] of *Bina*, called VAK, this is the reward of *Atik Yomin* (*The Zohar, Idra Raba*, Item 188).

We should understand why *Katnut* of *Bina* is regarded as reward for *Atik Yomin*. We can interpret that because he agrees to receive *Katnut*, which is *Hassadim*, regarded as above reason, by this he can give him *Gadlut* [greatness/adulthood].

It is as though someone received a salary and by this he bestows upon him in return for the salary that he received. It is likewise here: By taking upon himself the sweetening of *Bina*, which is covered *Hassadim*, he can later receive revealed *Hassadim*. For this reason, this is regarded as "reward," which is also called "fissured the *Galgalta*."

315- Three Souls

"Thus shall you say to the house Jacob, and tell the children of Israel." In the *Midrash*, "'Thus shall you say' are the women, tell them the abstract [summary]. 'And tell the children of Israel,' tell them the details of the matter, since they can hear. And why to the women? It is because they hurry with the *Mitzvot* [commandments].

"Another interpretation: They lead their sons to learn the Torah. Rabbi Tachlifa deKeisarin said, 'When I created the world, I commanded only *Adam HaRishon*. Afterward, Eve was commanded, and she transgressed and corrupted the world. Now, if I do not call the women first, they will cancel the Torah. This is why it was said, 'Thus you shall say to the house of Jacob.'" And Rabbi Yochanan said, "The house of Jacob' are the Sanhedrin, as was said, 'House of Jacob, let us walk.'"

We should interpret the above-said in the work. It is known that man consists of a quality of reception, called "woman," and a quality of bestowal, called "man."

When *Adam HaRishon* was created, the order of his creation was from above downward, meaning from *Zach* [fine] to *Av* [coarse], where first there was the quality of bestowal and then emerged the quality of reception in him. As is explained in *The Zohar*, *Adam HaRishon* did not have anything from this world, meaning that before the sin, he did not have the complete desire to receive.

Man has three souls, as is explained in the words of the ARI: 1) a *Nefesh* [soul] of *Kedusha* [holiness], which is a *Kli* [vessel] of holiness,

2) a *Nefesh* from the *Kli* of *Noga*, which is half and half, 3) a *Nefesh* of the three impure *Klipot* [shells/peels].

"Half and half" means that if a person performs a *Mitzva* [commandment], the second *Nefesh* connects to *Kedusha*. If he performs a transgression, she connects to the third *Nefesh*. *Adam HaRishon* was born circumcised, meaning he did not have the third *Nefesh*, and only by the sin was his foreskin pulled, meaning he extended upon himself the third *Nefesh*, called "this world."

Hence, when the world was created, *Adam HaRishon* was commanded first because the order is from *Zach* to *Av*. But at the time of the giving of the Torah, when they already had the foreskin, which is filth extended from the serpent, one must begin from below upward, meaning from *Av* to *Zach*.

We should interpret *Av* in relation to the time of *Katnut* [smallness/infancy], for during the *Katnut*, which is the quality of *Nukva* [female], the will to receive has the governance. At that time, we must say that acceptance of Torah and *Mitzvot* [commandments] is regarded as a "soft saying."

316- Adam HaRishon – 2

The root of *Adam HaRishon* is dust that is unfit for sowing, as it is written, "And the Lord God formed the man from dust of the earth." This means that were it not for the correction of the *Adama* [earth], which is *Bina*, *Adom* [red], it would be unfit to receive the abundance.

This is considered that *Adam HaRishon* was born circumcised. Because of the sin of the tree of knowledge, he was pulled at his foreskin, as it is written, "From dust you are and unto dust you shall return." By retrieving the foreskin to himself, which is the vessels of reception for himself, the will to receive became rooted in the generations following him.

This is why Abraham went on the right, the correction of the quality of *Hesed* [mercy], meaning that he wants *Hassadim* [pl. of *Hesed*]. For this reason, from the quality of *Hassadim*, he extends *Dvekut* [adhesion] with the Life of Lives.

However, Isaac went on the left line, called *Gevura*, to work in *Hitgabrut* [overcoming] the vessels of reception so as to work in order to bestow.

And because he was working on the left, to see his situation within reason, he sees the faults and the state of separation, since in the state of the left, a person is in a state of deficiency while the Creator is called "whole," and "The cursed does not cling to the Blessed."

For this reason, Isaac had to be included with Abraham. This is why it was written, "Abraham begot Isaac." Although everyone knows this, but it teaches us that in the quality of Isaac, who is "left," there is also the quality of "right," which is *Hesed*, and from there it receives life. Jacob is the middle line, so he certainly contains *Hassadim*.

However, David, whose quality is *Malchut*, Messiah—on which there were the *Tzimtzum* [restriction] and concealment—cannot receive any light on her own quality. Instead, she must receive from *Zeir Anpin*, her husband, which means that she was built from *Malchut* of *Zeir Anpin*, regarded as "the vacant space." Hence, she received from them, meaning from Abraham, Jacob, and Joseph, who are above *Malchut*. Therefore, she received illumination from them.

317- Faith – 1

Tav-Shin-Dalet, 1943-1944

Faith is called "above reason," and it is called *Nukva* [female] and "law." Torah is called "within reason," and it is called "sentence." This is the meaning of saying in the *Asher Yatzar* [Who Formed] prayer, "and created in him holes over holes, hollows over hollows."

He interpreted that "holes" means that it is *Nukva* and a lack that is going to be filled. This is regarded as Torah. "Hollows" means that he must remain hollow, and this is the quality of faith above reason.

318- Seeing and Hearing

"Hearing" is called "faith," that we must believe what we are hearing that we are being told—that it is true. "Seeing" is called "knowing," when he does not have to believe if he sees for himself.

319- Anyone Who Is Proud, It Is as though He Commits Idol-Worship

Av, Tav-Shin-Lamed-Het, August 1978, Jerusalem

"Anyone who is proud, it is as though he commits idol-worship." Pride means that a person does not feel his lowliness, meaning that it is of great importance to a person that he is serving the Creator and not himself, since man is a lowly creature that is not worth caring for, and to spend all the years of his life with the sole purpose of serving and delighting himself, which is called "to serve man."

However, he cannot serve his Creator, meaning feel the benefit in serving and delighting the Creator, and spend all his energy and thought on this, since he does not feel himself as lowly.

Rather, a person feels that it is more important to serve himself than to serve the Creator. This is regarded as a person being proud, and this is called "doing foreign work" [idol-worshipping], since he cannot serve the Creator, but rather serve himself, meaning work that is foreign to us.

320- It Is Not the Shy Who Learns

Av, Tav-Shin-Lamed-Het, August 1978, Jerusalem

"It is not the shy who learns," and "Be careful with the honor of the Torah."

Why? It is because man must degrade himself and go study. If a person is careful with the honor of the Torah, meaning accustomed himself that his body will respect the Torah, that the Torah is something important to him, he can degrade himself for the Torah.

This is so because shame comes primarily when one thinks he might be despised. However, for something important and respectable, it is worthwhile to suffer. Therefore, one who is not careful with the honor of the Torah will find it difficult to degrade himself over words of Torah.

321- Eating from the Waste

On Shabbat [Sabbath], it is forbidden to sort out the waste from the food, but only the food from the waste. The body contains both, and on Shabbat we sort out only the food, only good deeds. On weekdays, we should sort out the waste, meaning to correct the qualities.

322- Concerning Choice

Tav-Shin-Lamed-Het 1977-78

How is it possible to speak of choice, since courthouses punish for transgressions "not to do," and there are the "four deaths of the courthouse," and whipping and flogging. Conversely, on choice there is a reward, meaning what reward he wants for the labor in Torah and *Mitzvot* [commandments]. At that time, a person chooses whether he wants the reward for the labor to be for his own sake or for the sake of the Creator, meaning to the not-in-order-to-receive-reward.

323- Discernments in a Spiritual Kli [Vessel]

End of *Rosh Hashanah*, 2 *Tishrey*, *Tav-Shin-Mem-Bet*, September 30, 1981

Malchut of the upper one becomes a *Keter* to the lower one.

The still, in itself, has wholeness.

The vegetative must have a place in which to annul inside the still.

Afterward, it can grow in the *Masach* [screen] that comprises love and fear.

"Love" and "fear" are regarded as two angels serving a person in order to achieve the goal.

Returning the *AHP* into ten *Sefirot* is called "ten days of repentance" [Ten Penitential Days].

There is still that has a vital force, but all are unable to make any individual movement. Rather, they have a general movement. Those who want to be in the quality of "vegetative" must put an end on the "still," meaning they do not want to accept the reason that vitalizes the "still of *Kedusha* [holiness]," which is the quality of going by rote.

This means that the only thing that obligates a person to walk in the path of the Creator is the environment, that the environment brought him up to behave in this manner, namely as it obligates him. But for themselves, they have wholeness, called "the whole of Israel," and a surrounding [light] shines in them, called "illumination from afar." That is, although they are remote due to disparity of form, a general illumination nonetheless shines in them.

But one who puts a stop on it and does not want to follow the collective, but wants to be a "vegetative," to have his own movement and not be dependent on the general public, when he is a *Sof* [end], called "*Malchut* of the upper one," regarded as the previous state becoming *Keter* to the lower one, this end that he puts on the "still" is the root to entering the next degree, called "vegetative."

As there cannot be any growth until the seed rots and disappears in the still, so he should be lost in the "still," meaning not to feel his own existence, namely not to feel any vitality in the "still." One who sets a place for his prayer, at that time, individual movement begins to grow in him, called "vegetative." However, in order for a plant to bud, there must be plowing and other works.

The *Masach* at the *Rosh* [head] contains love and fear. This means that by having a *Masach* and raising *Ohr Hozer* [reflected light], he calculates that however much he can receive in order to bestow he will receive, and the amount of abundance that if he receives it, he will not be able to aim to bestow, he will not receive it.

We must know the meaning of *Ohr Hozer*. According to what is explained in *The Study of the Ten Sefirot*, since he feels great pleasure in wanting to bestow upon the Creator, and at that time he sees what can be said, that with this action that he will do, he will be able to delight the Creator, he sees that since the purpose of creation is to do good to His creations, therefore, when he receives the pleasures of the Creator, he thereby delights Him.

This is called "receiving delight and pleasure in order to bring contentment to his Maker," and this is called "love." Out of the love of the Creator, he receives the pleasure, and the part that the *Masach* said not to receive—since he does not want to be far from the Creator due to disparity of form—is called "fear," as explained in the *Sulam* [Ladder commentary on *The Zohar*].

By this we understand what is written in *The Zohar*, "My name with *Yod-Hey* is 'Do not do.'" He is afraid to receive, so as not to become separated from the Creator because of disparity of form. This is the large part that the *Masach* cannot receive in order to bestow.

This is why *Yod-Hey* is considered GAR, and that light is called *Ohr Makif* [surrounding light]. The small part that he does receive is called *Ohr Pnimi* [inner light], and this is why it is called "This is My memory, with *Vav-Hey*, it is the 248 'to do,'" which is what we should receive. This is called "love." However, on the part that he cannot aim in order to bestow, there should be fear that he might not be able to aim in order to bestow and might come into disparity of form.

324- The Preparation Period
14 Av, Tav-Shin-Tet-Zayin, July 22, 1956, Jerusalem

During the preparation period, a person can qualify himself in all the matters, meaning both on the right and on the left. In other words, he has ways by which to achieve the goal, and he has ways by which he already achieved the goal.

The final wholeness is for one to receive all the pleasures of the King because such was the King's will. That is, the only reason he enjoys in this world is because of the King's commandment. This is called "receiving in order to bestow."

The material for work on becoming accustomed is the Torah and *Mitzvot* [commandments] and the pleasure of Shabbat [Sabbath] and so forth. Also, all the blessings for pleasures is precisely in this way, meaning reception in order to bestow.

There are many discernments about this: There are people who enjoy plentifully in order to be able to bless and thank the Creator for giving us the pleasures, as from the perspective of the Giver, it is certainly good and mercy. But if the receiver does not derive benefit from the pleasures he receives... but it cannot be said that He is giving him money and he is not buying with the money things that are harmful to him—for then there should not be gratitude for the gift—since the intention of the Giver was certainly to benefit him.

Therefore, this is similar to a person whose father died and left him an inheritance. For the death he says, "true judge," and for the inheritance he says, "good and does good."

Likewise, about the lower one becoming materialized, he should say, "true judge," since before one repents, reception of pleasures separates him from the Life of Lives, so in regard to death we say "true judge." But over the Giver of the gift, meaning over the pleasures that the Creator has given him, he should say "good and does good."

But since it is forbidden to sort on Shabbat, on Shabbat there is no work on the purification of the body. Rather, the work is mainly on The Good Who Does Good. The Good Who Does Good is measured by the size of the inheritance, meaning by the measure of delight.

Conversely, on weekdays, the time of the work of sorting, we must remember that we should say "true judge." Hence, many people are not looking forward to the inheritance of their fathers because it is hard for them to tolerate the death of the body. For this reason, they choose the least bad and are not enjoying this world, but only as much as is necessary, and necessity is neither praised nor condemned.

But according to Baal HaSulam, diminishing the pleasures of the body does not yield any crops, since "Revenue comes by the strength of the ox," meaning that specifically by regretting that he has become separated from the Creator and wanting to be adhered, precisely this way yields the desired wholeness.

In the end, we mainly give the praises and gratitude to the King and not the weeping, for it is written, "Strength and joy are in His place." In other words, one who works in the way of truth and stands in the place of the Creator feels only strength and joy.

325- The Light of *Hassadim* on which There Was No *Tzimtzum*

The light of *Hochma* [wisdom] is called "attainment of the Torah and clear knowledge." This is received in a *Kli* [vessel] of a desire to receive. Hence, if a person is not qualified to receive not for himself, for then he will fall into separation, the light does not spread in him.

This is not so with the light of *Hassadim* [mercies], regarded as the *Kli* being a desire to bestow, meaning annulment before the Creator, and not wanting any right for its own existence. On this there was no *Tzimtzum* [restriction]. That is, even if a person is in a lowly state, he can still receive a thought about repentance, meaning that he has the ability to take upon himself devotion to the Creator.

This is as our sages said, "He who betroths a woman even if he is completely righteous, she is betrothed, for he may have meditated repentance in his heart" (*Kidushin* 49b). In other words, there was no *Tzimtzum* on this quality, and he can always receive the light of *Hassadim*, meaning extend powers from above so he can dedicate his soul and spirit to the Creator.

There are no tests on this, whether his intention has always been solely for the sake of the Creator. Rather, he can repent every single moment. Conversely, in order to obtain the light of *Hochma*, meaning to obtain upper degrees in the manner of the secrets of the Torah, his intentions must always be only for the Creator.

326- Man's Work

Man's nature is that he can relinquish a small pleasure in return for receiving a greater one. Hence, there is no matter of choice about this. This is not so with one who works in order to bestow, only because of the truth, meaning that the real way is only in work in order to bestow. In this, there is choice because he chooses to work on the path of truth although he will not have any pleasure, and although on this path, there is suffering. And all this is only because he wants to choose the truth (as in "Let my nourishment be as bitter as olive from the hands of the Creator").

We should understand that if one engages in Torah and *Mitzvot* [commandments] for the purpose of reward and punishment and not in order to bestow, he is satisfied with the faith that he has, since it is the nature of the body to fear suffering and pursue pleasure. For this reason, he has no necessity to be rewarded with the greatness of the Creator, since why does he need to know the greatness of the Creator?

In other words, he has no need to know the greatness of the Creator if he is serving the Creator with faith in reward and punishment, since the greatness of the King is not a reason that will obligate him to increase the work in Torah and *Mitzvot*, since there is no connection between them. Rather, the reason for the work depends on the measure of faith in reward and punishment.

Conversely, one who works in order to bestow, meaning that it is in the nature of his body that he can submit himself under one who is greater than him, and he has the strength to serve the one who is greater than him, then only the measure of greatness of the Creator obligates him to work. To the extent that he believes in the greatness of the Creator, to that extent he has the strength to work.

And since the Creator's will is for the lower ones to be rewarded with seeing the greatness and exaltedness of the Creator, for this reason, the lower one must work only in order to bestow, meaning not because of the King's gift, called "conditional love," but because of the King Himself. Because he believes in the greatness of the King, he has the power to bestow and serve the King.

It follows that all his work is to observe His greatness and exaltedness. To the extent that he recognizes His greatness, to that extent he increases the work. Hence, there is great merit in the work in order to bestow contentment upon one's Maker.

327- *The Merit of Having Guests*

"Having guests is greater than welcoming the face of the *Shechina* [Divinity]" (*Shabbat* [Sabbath] 127a).

The *Shechina* is regarded as *Malchut*, meaning *Hochma* [wisdom]. But having guests, which is *Hassadim* [mercies], is greater. In other words, once he has *Hochma*, he should look for *Hassadim* or the *Hochma* will not persist, since *Hochma* must clothe in a clothing of *Hassadim*. In corporeality, He gives the *Mitzva* [commandment] according to the value of the root, since in corporeality, the matters are not as they seem.

It is known that "The whole earth is full of His glory," but how does saying that he left the *Shechina* and went outside to welcome guests belong here? Also, it cannot be said that one who has been rewarded with installing the *Shechina* is exempted from the rest of the *Mitzvot* [commandments] in the Torah. On the contrary, once he has been rewarded with installing the *Shechina*, he observes the Torah and *Mitzvot* in truth, where the whole Torah is the names of the Creator, and according to the above-said, this is simple.

328- Their Idols Are Silver and Gold, the Work of Man's Hands

There is spirituality that a person makes for himself, meaning that he depicts to himself for what he is working, namely that it is worthwhile to work for this spirituality. This is called "the work of man's hands." That which a person can depict as being called "spirituality," to this he prays.

But when a person repents and is rewarded with opening the eyes in the Torah, in the manner that He who knows the mysteries testifies about him, only then is it considered that the spirituality he has attained is not the work of his own hands, for then the light is revealed to him according to the depiction he is given from above and not according to the depiction that the lower one made for himself. Hence, the work of man's hands is according to man's depiction.

329- Prayer

Concerning the prayer, it should be in the manner of "One should always establish the praise of the Creator and then pray."

We should ask, If a person establishes the praise of the Creator, that He is good and does good to the bad and to the good, and His mercy are on all His works, then it is certain that the Creator also gave him abundance and satisfied all his deficiencies, so for what else should he pray? Also, to the extent that he is happy with his lot, to that extent he can praise Him, so what else should he add?

In "Master of All the Worlds" that we say on the eve of Shabbat [Sabbath] after "Peace Be Upon You," it is written, "I thank You... for all the mercy that You have done with me and that You are destined to do with me."

This means that in everything, there must be an awakening from below. Hence, for the past we must say, "I thank," meaning gratitude, and to the extent that he feels more completeness in himself, the truer is the gratitude. Hence, when he is happy with his lot, the gratitude he gives to the Creator is truer. However, for the future, he must offer prayer and awakening.

This is the meaning of "One should always establish the praise of the Creator and then pray" for the future. Baal HaSulam said that when a person feels deficient, he is regarded as "cursed," and "The cursed does not adhere to the Blessed." Hence, when he establishes the praise of the Creator and is happy with his lot, at that time he is called "blessed," and then he can adhere to the Blessed. This is why all the prayers are for the future.

Concerning being happy with one's lot, a person can be happy that he was rewarded with entering the synagogue although he has no desire to pray or learn, but at that time, one should say that simply coming to the synagogue is a great privilege that is not awarded to anyone. This is regarded as "Walks but does not do, the reward for walking is in his hand."

But if a person can consider that he has come to the synagogue, which is a place where each and every one can unite with the King of all Kings, and think to whom he prays, this in itself is enough for a person to be happy. This falls into the category of "One should always establish the praise of the Creator and then pray."

However, concerning being happy with one's lot, we should know that it is a matter of being content with little. Being content with little refers primarily to spirituality and pertains to the "little" reward. That is, it is when he can do the most work although he sees very little profit and settles for that little profit.

Settling for little does not mean that someone who needs to eat 200 grams of bread a day eats 200 grams. Although this is little, this is all he consumes and he does not need more, meaning he has no *Kelim* [vessels] in which to receive more. Rather, settling for little means that one needs 1,000 grams a day but has not more than 200 grams, and he happily settles for this. This is called "happy with his lot."

Hence, those who should understand more and have more sensation of spirituality, still, although they have not been rewarded with feeling or understanding, they settle for this and are happy with their lot. It follows that although they are happy with their lot, their *Kelim* still remain unfilled with wholeness, for according to their spirit, they have no satisfaction. Therefore, by being happy with their lot, they are in a state of "blessed." And then, "The blessed adheres to the Blessed," and then they can be rewarded with the Creator illuminating their eyes and hearts in the law [Torah] of the Creator and with having a feeling and understanding.

330- Lowliness

One should see one's own lowliness, since there are many flavors in it. Lowliness is mainly to see the truth that his own benefit is more important to him than the benefit of the Creator. In other words, a person cannot see that which is outside his own benefit.

Hence, when he does something and does not see how he will derive self-benefit from this act, he cannot do it. Thus, there is no greater lowliness than this. This is "They are as beasts." This is the whole matter of the recognition of evil. However, there are two matters about it, in mind and in heart.

331- The Voice Is Good for Perfumes

"Rabbi Natan says, 'When he laughs he says, 'Tighten well, tighten well, for the voice is good for perfumes.'"

"Perfumes" means a scent that ascends from below upward. This is the quality of *Hochma* [wisdom] that is received in *Atzilut* specifically in this order. But when receiving *Hochma* from above downward, it is regarded as GAR, and there is no room for *Hassadim* [mercies] there, and *Hochma* without *Hassadim* does not shine. It follows that "perfumes" are regarded as *Hochma*.

See in *The Zohar* and in the *Sulam* [Ladder commentary on *The Zohar*] that "voice" is called *Hassadim*. This is the meaning of saying that when he had to extend *Hochma* when it is included in *Hassadim*, he says "Tighten well, tighten well," meaning not to receive the *Hochma* only in narrowness, which is VAK, illumination from below upward, so there will be room to extend *Hassadim*, which is called "voice."

This is so because "The voice is good for perfumes," meaning that *Hassadim* is good for *Hochma* because *Hochma* without *Hassadim* cannot shine.

332- Concerning Equivalence of Form

Av, Tav-Shin-Lamed-Tet, August 1979

Concerning equivalence of form, which is a correction to avoid the bread of shame, we can interpret in a literal manner, that since what is permitted about Him—the discernment of by-Your-actions-we-know-You—that He has contentment when He bestows upon the created beings, called "His desire to do good to His creations." For this reason, the lower ones should also achieve this quality of having pleasure when they are bestowed upon. In the words of our sages, this is called "cleave unto His attributes, as He is merciful, so you are merciful."

But since the creatures were born in the opposite state, since the upper desire, called "to do good to the created beings," created in the created beings a desire to receive and not to bestow, and we desire to bestow only if we can thereby obtain a greater pleasure and we will receive some reward in return for our bestowal, but without pleasure, one cannot bestow anything, it follows that we are opposite in form from the Creator, and in spirituality, oppositeness of form is regarded as separation.

When one is separated from the Creator, how can he connect? Indeed, this is all the bad that there is in the creatures, which they must correct, and this is called "recognition of evil," that one should come to recognize that nothing in the world hinders him from obtaining delight and pleasure, except for the will to receive. But our sages said, "I have created the evil inclination; I have created the Torah as a spice" (*Kidushin* 30b). This is thoroughly explained in the "Introduction to The Study of the Ten Sefirot."

It therefore follows that when one engages in Torah and *Mitzvot* [commandments], the reason for his engagement should be to come to a state where the Creator gives him a reward for his work in Torah and *Mitzvot*, and his reward should be that he will be rid of the bad and achieve the good, meaning to be able to adhere to the Creator, who is called "Good."

One should always have the reason before his eyes—that he wants to achieve the degree where he enjoys acts of bestowal, like the Creator, who enjoys being a Giver and does not need the creatures to give Him anything.

Likewise, man should ask the Creator to give him reward for his work, and the reward is that he will be able to work not in order to receive reward, that he will not need any reward for his work but will receive delight and pleasure during his acts of bestowal.

It follows that a person overcomes himself and performs acts of bestowal because he needs overcoming and coercion. It follows that on one hand, he has equivalence that he is not receiving but only bestows, yet he does not have delight and pleasure while bestowing without a reward. Thus, he has no equivalence of form with the Creator.

This means that one's main work should be to enjoy while performing acts of bestowal. This is the meaning of what is written, "Serve the Lord with gladness" in order to have equivalence of form. Just as He enjoys when He bestows, as our sages said, "His desire to do good to His creations," so man should achieve this degree.

This should be man's entire reward, and this is called "bestowing in order to bestow" without any reward because he has no greater pleasure than this.

But once he is rewarded with this degree where all his pleasure is in bestowing upon the Creator, he sees and feels that he cannot give anything to the Creator that will please Him, other than to receive from Him the pleasures that He has prepared for His creations, which was the purpose of creation.

Hence, at that time, he is at a degree where he says to the Creator, "Give me greater pleasures because I want to give You contentment." And since the Creator does not lack a thing, and the only discernment of a lack that we can speak of is for creation to achieve its goal, which is to delight His creations, it follows that not in order to receive reward means that a person has achieved a degree—which he was given as a gift from heaven—that his only pleasure is that he bestows upon the Creator. However, if he bestows and derives no pleasure, then he has no equivalence of form because he has no pleasure while bestowing and only yearns to be given something for his work in bestowal.

Conversely, when a person engages in matters of reception, he does not ask the Creator for anything in return or as a reward for his work in matters of reception. For this reason, the goal must always be in front of him, what he is asking in return for his work in Torah and *Mitzvot*, which is only that the Creator will grant him equivalence of form, which means that he will derive pleasure from engaging in bestowal.

333- He Who Begins a *Mitzva* [Commandment]

Sivan, Tav-Shin-Mem-Aleph, May-June 1982

"He who begins a *Mitzva* is told, 'Finish it,'" as in "He who comes to purify is aided." For this reason, he who begins a *Mitzva*, meaning comes to purify, is told from above, "Finish it," meaning he is given power from above. This is the meaning of "All beginnings are hard," since he must begin, but afterward he receives assistance from above.

334- The Difference between Charity and a Gift

Charity should be in concealment, as it is written, "A gift in secret subdues anger," meaning that he does not know to whom he gives. A gift is to the contrary, as our sages said, "He who gives a gift to his friend must let him know," as our sages said, "I have a good gift in My treasury, whose name is Shabbat [Sabbath]; go and notify them" (*Shabbat* 10b).

The thing is that charity is regarded as faith, as it is written, "And he believed in the Lord and considered for him as *Tzedakah* [righteousness/charity]." When he believes above reason, it is called "giving in secret," meaning that he does not know to whom he gives or if what he gives has been received.

This is a preparation for the reception of the Torah, since the Torah was given only to Israel, as it is written, "Says His words to Jacob," as our sages said, "Wisdom in the nations, believe; Torah in the nations, do not believe."

Hence, afterward, when they are rewarded with the Torah, the Torah is called "a gift," as our sages said about the verse, "From Matanah [Hebrew: gift] to Nahliel" (*Iruvin* 54a). Torah means specifically that he has been rewarded with the Giver of the Torah. Hence, the Creator lets him know that He is the one who gives him the gift, as was said, "Shabbat, when he feels the light of Shabbat," at that time it is called "a gift," which is knowing.

Before he is rewarded with knowing, it is called "faith," which is charity.

335- A Messenger of the Public

3 Tishrey, Tav-Shin-Mem-Tet, September 14, 1988

It is good for a cantor to have a nice and big congregation. At that time, he is a messenger of the public for a large and respectable crowd. Thus, the greatness of the cantor is measured by the size of the crowd, meaning in quantity and quality. "Quantity" means a large audience and many people. "Quality" means that everyone is listening to what the cantor lets out of his mouth, and not that part of the audience is busy with other matters and have no interest in hearing what the cantor says.

Likewise, when speaking of individuals, every person is a small world that consists of many thoughts and desires. When one comes to pray, he takes his mouth to be the cantor. When the mouth asks his organs and desires what he should pray for on their behalf, the heart replies in the name of all the desires, "You have the phrasing of the prayer that the members of the great assembly established; say this for us."

When the mouth, which is the cantor, says what is written in the prayer book, sometimes his organs listen to what he says, meaning that throughout the prayer they do not get distracted and they pay attention to what the mouth says. But sometimes he does not hear with all the organs, meaning he hears and does not hear. That is, in the middle of the prayer, he has other thoughts. And sometimes, he does not hear at all what he is saying, and the mouth can say whatever it wants while he can hear what his friends are saying during the prayer.

Even when he hears but does not know the meaning of the words, meaning how he is connected to the words that are written in the prayer, meaning what benefit the things he says with his mouth will bring him, and at times he does... the connection between what he says and his body, but the body disagrees with what he says. And sometimes, the body does agree with what the mouth is saying.

Thus, a nice and big congregation is when the mouth, which is his cantor, prays that the heart will hear what he is uttering with his mouth, in quantity and quality. If he sees that the organs disagree with what he says, this is the real place for prayer, for then he must pray for the exile of the *Shechina* [Divinity], which is called "*Shechina* in the dust."

This means that he has no place in any organ in his body that will agree to walk on the path of truth. When he prays for this, it is considered that he is praying for the exile of the *Shechina*, meaning that she will emerge from exile to redemption.

This is the meaning of the cantor needing to please the audience, meaning that his servants will agree to what the mouth says. Then he is called "a messenger of the public," meaning that his organs send him to ask the Creator for what they need.

However, if the public does not agree with what the cantor says, that audience is one thing and the cantor is another thing. Thus, on whose behalf does the cantor, meaning the mouth, pray and ask requests? For this reason, the first *Hassidim* would wait one hour in order to have a good and large crowd, meaning that the organs will listen to what the cantor says and will agree with what he is praying so that his prayer will be accepted.

336- He Who Cries over a Fitting Person

"Anyone who cries over a *Kosher* [fitting/worthy] person, all his iniquities are pardoned. Anyone who sheds tears over a fitting person, the Creator counts them and places them in His treasury" (*Shabbat* [Sabbath] 105b).

We should understand why all his iniquities are pardoned if he sheds tears over a fitting person. What is the reason for which all his iniquities will be pardoned? We should also understand why the Creator counts them, what is the number that one should reach, and why He places them in His treasury, why He needs them.

It is known that a person is regarded as walking and not standing. That is, as long as a person is poor in knowledge, there is the matter of "ascending and descending offering" in relation to him. This means that his nearness to *Kedusha* [holiness] changes—at times he ascends in degree, when an awakening from above comes to him, and at times he descends, when he comes to a state of decline in spirituality. When he is in a state of ascent, he is called a *"Kosher* [fitting/worthy] man."

337- Happy Is the Man

"Happy is the man whom the Lord afflicts." We should ask, but is the purpose of creation not to do good to His creations? Thus, this is the opposite of the goal.

We can interpret that it is known that every branch wants to resemble its root, as it is written in the "Introduction to The Book of Zohar," that the whole world loves rest. However, this is like a person holding a stick in his hand and beating everyone to make them work. Hence, each one must relinquish his rest in order to be saved from the afflictions of being beaten with a stick.

The stick is the afflictions when a person feels that he is lacking something. Therefore, when a person has a deficiency of having nothing to eat, he must labor in order to quiet the suffering of hunger. The bigger the lack, the more he must exert until he is compelled to obtain the object of his yearning.

Hence, if the Creator afflicts when he has no spirituality, the suffering compels a person to make great efforts until he must obtain the spirituality that he feels he lacks. Then, through the suffering, he will try to achieve spirituality, where he will receive the purpose of creation, which is to do good to His creations.

At that time, he will see what spirituality means, since prior to that, he is suffering only from not having, but he still does not know what is spirituality. But once he obtains it, he sees the purpose of creation.

This is as Baal HaSulam said about the difference between corporeality and spirituality. Corporeality is that when he does not have, he suffers, and when he has all the corporeal things, he still does not feel satisfied with corporeality. But in spirituality, a person does not suffer when he does not have, and when he does have, he has satisfaction in life. Hence, when he feels suffering from not having spirituality, this is the reason that he wants spirituality.

338- A Cure before the Blow

Rosh Hashanah, 18 Tishrey, Tav-Shin-Mem-Gimel, September 1982

The Creator sends a cure before the blow. We should ask, If there is no blow, how can we speak of a cure?

We should understand that we find with our sages that the Torah is called *Tushia* because it *Mateshet* [exhausts] a person's strength (Sanhedrin 26b). Our sages said, "If one's head aches, let him engage in Torah" (*Iruvin* 54a). Baal HaSulam interpreted that first we need Torah, to see that man's strength is not as it should be, meaning that "one's head aches" implies that he has foreign thoughts. "His stomach aches," meaning that all he wants is to receive into his own stomach.

In medicine, one who receives a medicine but is not sick, the medicine harms him. Hence, first he needs to learn Torah, since through the Torah he will see that he is sick, and then he will receive the Torah and will be healed from his illnesses.

It follows that we grasp the Torah in two manners: 1) that he is sick, for which the Torah is called *Tushia*, for it *Mateshet* [exhausts] man's strength, and all his power and vitality are only from the quality of a beast. In order to correct this, there is Torah in manner number 2) when it heals him from all the illnesses.

By this we should interpret that the Creator sends the cure before the blow, meaning the Torah, which is called "cure," precedes the blow, for the Torah brings him the recognition of evil.

Afterward, when he suffers the blow, meaning the measure of the evil in him, "he fixes a bandage from the blow itself," meaning from the Torah, which makes him see that he is stricken in his qualities. Subsequently, the Torah heals him.

It therefore follows that if he has no recognition of evil, how can he be rewarded with the good? This is why we need both discernments in the Torah.

339- Let the Earth Put Forth Grass

Shabbat [Sabbath], 24 *Tishrey*, *Tav-Shin-Yod-Het*, October 19, 1957, Manchester

"And God said, 'Let the earth put forth grass... a fruit-tree.'" RASHI interpreted that the taste of the tree will be as the taste of the fruit. Yet, she did not do so, but rather, "And the earth put forth... and a fruit-bearing tree," and not the "fruit-tree."

For this reason, when Adam was cursed for his iniquity, she, too, was included for her iniquity and was cursed, as it is written, "The ground is cursed because of you."

The interpreters asked how it can be said that the earth did not obey the Creator. Does the earth have free choice? They also asked why the earth was not punished right away but rather together with *Adam HaRishon*.

We should understand this in the work. The earth implies man, as it is written in *The Zohar*, "The heart of the earth is people" (*Beresheet* 4, 61). The purpose of man's creation was for man to engage in Torah and *Mitzvot* [commandments] *Lishma* [for Her sake], as it is written, "Anyone who is called by My name, I have created for My glory."

The Zohar interprets "My name" as "man," as it says, "Anyone who is called by My name is man, for the Creator created him with His name, as it is written, 'And God created the man in His image.' He called him by His name when He brings out truth and judgment in the world, and He is called *Elokim* [God], as it is written, 'You shall not curse God'" (*VaYikra* 104).

Lishma should be in two manners—in action and in intention. This is called "His mouth and his heart are equal."

Sometimes, a person does something *Lishma*, and it is called *Lishma* because in the action, there is nothing to add, since even the greatest of the greatest cannot add to the action. That is, it cannot be said that one should put *Tefillin* also on the right hand, and so forth, as it is written, "Do not add and do not subtract."

The main dispute among people is only on the intention, since one should try to make the intention the same as the action, and then it is called *Lishma*.

The *Etz* [tree] is man's *Atzmut* [self/core], meaning the intention, and the "fruit" is the action. The Creator wanted the earth to elicit fruit trees, meaning that the flavors of the tree and the fruit will be the same.

But the earth implied (and *Eretz* [earth] implies mainly man) that the man who will be created will not have equal intentions and actions. It is still tolerable that the earth did not want to obey the Creator, but she elicited like the man who will be later.

It is understandable why she was not punished right away, since the man did not sin so there was nothing for which to punish her, since the punishment that the earth received also implies man, meaning man's punishment.

Therefore, specifically after *Adam HaRishon* was punished, it is pertinent to punish the earth, meaning that man's punishment will be apparent on the earth. This is why it was said, "The ground is cursed because of you," and RASHI interpreted, emitting cursed things for you like flies, fleas, and ants, like those who go astray and people curse the breasts that nursed him.

Also, we should know that the curse is also a correction, as it is written, "The harms will not come from Him," but it is a correction, for were it not for the curse, the man would find flavor in the fruit even though the aim is not *Lishma*. And had the man found sweetness even in the *Lo Lishma*, there would have been no need for man to exert in *Lishma*, since the *Lo Lishma* [not for Her sake] would completely satisfy him.

Conversely, after the curse, when man finds no sweetness that satisfies him in the actions, and feels as in the above-mentioned allegory, that demons are nursing off of his actions, and as it is written, "Thorn and thistle you will grow for yourself," where one finds no flavor in the *Lo Lishma*, but rather "Thorn and thistle," "And you will eat the grass of the field," feeling the taste of grass, then there is room for man to see and exert that the actions will be *Lishma*, meaning that his fruit and tree will be equal.

This is the meaning of what our sages said, "Rabbi Yehoshua Ben Levi said that when the Creator said to the man 'Thorn and thistle you will grow for yourself,' His eyes teared. He said to Him, 'Master of the world, will I and the donkey eat from the same manger?'" (*Pesachim* 118).

That is, man will feel the same taste in Torah and *Mitzvot* as a donkey, who enjoys only corporeality. "Eating" means foods from which man enjoys in which he finds flavor. As the donkey enjoys and finds flavor only in corporeal things, so man will find no flavor in Torah and *Mitzvot*, but only in corporeality.

He was not at ease until the Creator said to him, "By the sweat of your brow you shall eat bread," meaning that through man's labor, he will be rewarded with *Lishma*, and then he will feel the taste of bread and not of thistle and thorn.

Before the sin, *Adam HaRishon* found the same flavor in his tree and his fruit, as our sages said that the taste and the fruit of the tree of knowledge were the same. In other words, even while eating the tree of knowledge, the action and intention were *Lishma*, since the sin was not in the first eating, but rather afterward, as our sages said about the verse, "I ate, and I will eat more" (see "Introduction to Panim Meirot uMasbirot").

Only after the sin was the act not as the aim. But through the labor in Torah and *Mitzvot*, man will be rewarded with *Lishma* and will be rewarded with "bread." It follows that it was not a curse, but a correction, for by this, man will achieve the desired wholeness.

340- In the Beginning [God] Created

Tishrey, Tav-Shin-Lamed-Het, October 1977

"In the beginning." RASHI interpreted, "Rabbi Yehuda said, 'The Torah should have started from 'This month is to you,' which is the first *Mitzva* [commandment] that Israel were commanded. What is the reason it begins with 'In the beginning'? Because He said to His people the power of His deeds, to give them the inheritance of the nations, for should the nations of the world say to Israel, 'You are robbers, for you conquered the lands of seven nations,' they would tell them, 'The whole earth belongs to the Creator. He created it and gave it to whom He pleases. Upon His will, he gave it to them, and upon His will, He took it from them and gave it to us.'"

We should understand why He gave it to them to begin with, since He could have given them other lands, since the world is big, so why did He give them the land of Canaan?

This is an intimation of branch and root. In the root, He gave the land, which is the will to receive as it is. This is called "the evil inclination," which has seven names, implying the seven nations, meaning that the will to receive is enslaved to them.

Afterward, he must correct the land to work in order to bestow, for it is impossible to correct something before the thing itself is revealed and it is evident that a correction is required. To this comes the intimation that He placed the body under the governance of seven nations.

Afterward, in order to correct the matter of the bread of shame, there is a need to use the desire to bestow, called *Ysrael* [Israel], meaning *Yashar-El* [straight to the Creator]. Hence, when one wants to elicit the body from the governance of seven nations, they say "You are robbers," meaning "We were given the will to receive to be under our control, and you cannot bring out the body, so you are wasting your efforts."

At that time, they say, "He said to His people the power of His deeds," that the people of Israel will tell them that this act of the body being under their control is the power of the Creator; otherwise, you would not have any control. Hence, upon His will, He took it from them and gave it to us. We believe that "He who comes to purify is aided," meaning that He took from them the power He had given them and has given it to us.

341- And the Lord Saw

Tishrey-Heshvan, Tav-Shin-Lamed-Het, October 1977

"And the Lord saw… I will curse no more the earth because of man, for the inclination of a man's heart is evil from his youth, and I will strike no more every living thing, as I have done."

We should understand how it can be said that only after the flood, the Creator saw that the inclination of a man's heart is evil. Can it be said that beforehand He did not know about it?

We should interpret this as having two types of people. There are those who belong to the general public. They are regarded as "The whole world tells you that you are righteous." And there is also the quality of "Be as a wicked in your eyes."

In order for one to achieve the final goal, he must walk on the path of truth, which is *Lishma* [for Her sake], meaning that the whole intention of engaging in Torah and *Mitzvot* [commandments] is to achieve *Lishma*. However, we begin in *Lo Lishma*, meaning that we think that there is nothing more to the work of the Creator than observing in practice.

In this manner, they can engage in Torah and *Mitzvot*. However, working in order to achieve the goal for which the Torah and *Mitzvot* were given, which is regarded as "I have created the evil inclination; I have created the Torah as a spice," they do not think about this. They excel only in quantity, meaning in being stricter and imposing more limitations and so forth.

By this we will understand what our sages said, "Why is her name called 'empty'? Even the empty ones in her are filled with *Mitzvot* like a pomegranate." We should understand why then are they called "empty." However, they are devoid of content, meaning they lack the real reason for which to observe the *Mitzvot*, since they do not mind the intention.

It follows that after the flood, when man saw that those who do not walk on the path of truth die in the waters of the flood, called "evil water," as in "Who is the Lord that I should obey His voice?" which is Pharaoh's question, and the question of the wicked one, "What is this work for you?" then we see that there is an evil inclination. But before we see that we can die in the flood, we do not see any evil.

It follows that we say that what the Creator says pertains to man, that now he sees that the Creator is looking at him. Thus, among people who want to walk on the path of truth, this is not called "strike every living thing." Rather, this is regarded as being shown the truth. Hence, a person attains that this is not regarded as a curse, but the opposite.

342- Noah Was a Righteous Man

Heshvan, Tav-Shin-Mem, October 1979

"Noah was a righteous man." Even Ezra interprets "righteous" in good deeds, "whole" in his heart, "in his generations," some condemn and some praise. In generations of wicked ones, when the thoughts of the generation are that it is not worthwhile to work in order to bestow, the body sometimes praises, meaning that his view is with his contemporaries. And sometimes, it condemns what his contemporaries say.

At that time, he has the choice to do good deeds, meaning that he can overcome through actions. However, man has no control over his heart, to be able to change the feeling in the heart, if the heart feels what his contemporaries tell it, and the heart takes after the majority.

For this reason, there is no other choice but to overcome through actions, perform acts of bestowal, and ask the Creator to give him another heart, as it is written, "Purify our hearts." However, in the argument, he cannot succeed. When he becomes righteous in terms of the practice, he is rewarded and becomes whole in his heart, as Even Ezra said.

Afterward, he comes to a state of "Noah walked with God," meaning that when the Creator is revealed to a person, when he begins to feel the existence of the Creator, he has no choice but to annul as a candle before a torch. At that time, he is unimpressed by what he hears from his contemporaries because they all annul before the light of the Creator.

According to the above, it follows that "whole" comes after he overcomes in practice. At that time, his wholeness comes to complement all the flaws he had before. This is as Baal HaSulam said, "*Tamim* [whole] has the letters of *Tav-Mayim* [*Tav*-water], which is only on one who knows how to deceive himself and sees the truth as his eyes see it, yet still accepts everything in wholeness." This is called "faith above reason."

343- Gopher Wood
Tishrey-Heshvan, Tav-Shin-Mem-Bet, October 1981

"Make for yourself an ark of gopher wood, and cover with pitch inside and out."

The flood means "evil water." When the "Who" question comes to a person, which is Pharaoh's question, "Who is the Lord that I should obey His voice?" and also the wicked one's question, "What is this work for you?" The *Mayim* [water], which is the flood, is made of those two—the *Mi* [Who] and the *Ma* [What]. By this, the whole world that a person has in *Kedusha* [holiness] was obliterated.

The advice for this is to go into the ark, for the *Teiva* [ark] has the letters of *Bait* [home] (as it is written in the *Sulam* [Ladder] commentary on *The Zohar*]), since "home" means wisdom, as it is written, "In wisdom shall a house be built." The opposite of "home" is an "ark," which is *Hassadim* [mercies], which is faith above reason, as in "for he desires mercy."

This is the meaning of "Cover with pitch inside and out," since there must be the light of faith there. Hence, it must be covered with pitch from inside and out, and then it is a place in which to install the light of faith, since then he needs the light of faith. When one is on the path of faith, there is no room for the "Who" and "What" questions. Hence, precisely through the ark we are saved from the waters of the flood.

344- Go Forth
Tav-Shin-Mem, 1979-1980

"Go forth from your land, from your kindred, and from your father's house, to the land that I will show you." It is written in the *Midrash*, "Hear, daughter, and see and lend your ear, and forget your people and your father's house, and the king will desire your beauty."

To understand the proximity of the verses, when beginning to guide a person to walk in the ways of the Creator, the beginning is through education. One is brought up to observe the Torah and *Mitzvot* [commandments] in a manner of *Lo Lishma* [not for Her sake], as Maimonides said in *Hilchot Teshuva*.

Afterward, when he wants to walk on the path of truth, he is told "Go forth from your land." *Eretz* [land] comes from the word *Ratzon* [desire] (as it is written in *Midrash Rabbah*, "Why was she called *Eretz*? Because she *Ratzta* [wanted] to do her Maker's will). In other words, a person must walk away from the previous desire, which was only to satisfy the will to receive, called *Lo Lishma*.

"From your kindred, and from your father's house." This pertains to one's prior upbringing, which is called "going by rote." This is regarded as "your kindred." "To the land that I will show you" is the desire to bestow.

However, he cannot obtain this desire because it is against nature. This is why it was said, "that I will show you," that the Creator shows the person this land, meaning the desire to bestow. A person can assist the Creator in showing him the desire to bestow only with the desire, when he wants to be rewarded with such a desire. However, by himself, a person cannot emerge from his customs.

It is to this that the verse intends by "Hear, daughter," meaning man's internality, the dwelling place of the soul, which can hear that there is such a thing called "bestowal," but it is not within man's hands to see this, meaning to attain it.

This is why it was said that only if you have hearing, meaning that the person will consider this quality a privilege, then the verse promises a person, "and see," meaning that he will also be rewarded with seeing. "Lend your ear" to hear that there is such a thing in reality that a person can work only to bestow and not for his own sake. Then you will be rewarded with "forget your people and your father's house," and then "the Creator will desire your beauty," meaning the new qualities, which are to bestow and not to receive.

This is called "to the land that I will show you," that the Creator will show him this quality, that He will give him the power to be able to work in order to bestow. This is called "Cursed is the man who trusts man," who thinks that there will ever be a time when the body will permit him to work in order to bestow. Rather, this is a gift from heaven. This is the meaning of "Blessed is the man who trusts in the Lord."

By this we will understand the *Midrash* (2, Chapter 39), "Rabbi Levi said, 'When Abraham the patriarch walked to Aram-Naharaim [Mesopotamia] and saw them scurrying, eating and drinking, he said, 'I wish to have no part in this land.' When he came to Sulam Tzor and saw them engaged in weeding at the time of weeding, and in hoeing at the time of hoeing, he said, 'I wish I had a part in this land.' The Creator told him, 'Unto your seed will I give this land.'"

"Aram-Naharaim," when he saw them scurrying to receive reward, for eating and drinking implies the reward he receives for the work, meaning that he is working for his own benefit. At that time, he said that he will not have a part in this land, meaning in this desire that is for his own benefit.

"When he came to Sulam [Tzor]," as in a "*Sulam* [ladder] that is set on the earth and its top reaches the heaven," for Tzor implies *Tzur Israel* [the rock of Israel], and saw them weeding, meaning uprooting the bad qualities within them, since it was time to do so, and not because of a reward, and also hoeing because it was time to do so, which is called "at the time of hoeing," and not because of his own benefit, he said about such a desire, "My lot will be in this land."

Then, the Creator promised, "Unto your seed will I give this land," meaning He will give them the desire to bestow.

345- Anyone with Whom the Spirit of the Creator Is Pleased

Heshvan, Tav-Shin-Mem-Bet, November 1981

"Anyone with whom the spirit of the Creator is pleased, the spirit of the people is pleased with him. And anyone with whom the spirit of the people is displeased, the spirit of the Creator is displeased with him."

It is known that there are righteous in the world with whom the world is displeased and they are disputed. Also, our sages said, "That disciple of the wise whom the people of the town love because he did not admonish them on matters of Above." Thus, the spirit of the people is displeased with him if he admonishes them on matters of above.

We should understand that in the work, this means that before one wants to do everything for the sake of the Creator, the people of the town, meaning his desires and thoughts, do not resist his actions. But when he admonishes them on matters of above and says that we must work for the sake of the Creator, all his organs oppose him until he tries to make the Creator help him be able to work for the sake of the Creator.

This cannot be done without the light of Torah, as our sages said, "The light in it reforms him." It is as Baal HaSulam interpreted, "Until He who knows the mysteries will testify that he will not return to folly." By the Creator giving him the light of Torah, it is a sign that the Creator testifies to him, and this is considered that the spirit of the Creator is pleased with him.

At that time, the spirit of the people, meaning all his organs, desires, and thoughts, are pleased with him, as was said, "When the Lord is pleased with man's ways, his enemies, too, will make peace with him." This is the meaning of "with all your heart—with both your inclinations."

346- Mind and Heart

Heshvan, Tav-Shin-Mem-Gimel, October 1982

Mind and heart. That is, a person enjoys and delights in the fact that the Creator has given him a place for faith. Also, he is happy that the Creator has given him a place of work in the heart.

"When a man regrets, what does the *Shechina* [Divinity] say? 'It is lighter than my head and than my arm.'" This means that a person regrets the fact that the Creator wants people to serve Him in a manner of faith and would be happy if we could work in the manner of knowing. Also, a person is sorry that we were forbidden to use the will to receive.

The answer to this is "It is lighter than my head," meaning that the work I gave you in the mind, I could certainly give you work in a manner of knowing but I chose the path of faith, for by this they will be able to achieve the goal, which is to do good to His creations.

It is likewise with work in the heart that a person is commanded to do, as it is written in placing the head-*Tefillin* next to the brain, and on the arm, the stretched out arm, which is next to the heart. "Lighter than my head" means that they think that the way I gave them is a way of ignominy. However, we must believe that this is the best way that the Creator has given us, and we must be happy about it.

347- Passed By Your Servant

Heshvan, Tav-Shin-Yod-Het, November 1957

In the verse, "for you have passed by your servant," RASHI interpreted, "for this I ask of you, since you passed by me, to honor me." We should understand the words "to honor me." Abraham said, "And I am dust and ashes," and he said, "since you passed by me, to honor me."

We should understand that since he feared that they would not want to eat at his place because of shame, he said, "to honor me," meaning by this you will honor me, namely that they would be the givers and not the receivers. By this, he removed from them the shame, called "bread of shame."

348- When the Creator Loves a Person

Heshvan, Tav-Shin-Mem, November 1979

It is written in *The Zohar* (*VaYera*, Item 167): "When the Creator loves a person, He sends him a gift. And what is the gift? A poor person, by whom to be rewarded. And when he is rewarded by Him, the Creator draws upon him a thread of grace that extends from the right side, spreads over his head, and registers him so that when judgment comes to the world, the saboteur will be careful not to harm him. He looks in that list and then retreats from him and is careful with him. For this reason, the Creator first gives him something to be rewarded with."

We should understand why his gift is called "a poor person." According to the rule, there is none who is poor except in knowledge. Therefore, when one feels that he is poor in knowledge and believes that the Creator has sent him this awareness, to feel that he is poor, what makes this thought a gift from the Creator?

The thing is that it is known that one does not ascend in degree unless he has a need. At that time, he can receive the filling from the Creator because there is no light without a *Kli* [vessel], meaning that there is nothing if there is no desire, for the desire for something is called the *Kli* in the filling.

Hence, when one thinks that he does not have a real lack, meaning he sees that he is worse than the rest of the people, it is said about him, "I dwell among my own people."

But when he feels that he is worse than the rest of the people, that he is poor in knowledge and has no attainment in Torah and *Mitzvot* [commandments], although many people have no attainment whatsoever, but since they have no need for attainment in Torah and *Mitzvot*, they do not feel any suffering because of it.

In spirituality, it is said "according to the sorrow is the reward," since the sorrow and affliction from what he lacks, and to the extent of the need, so is the measure of the reward when his lack is satisfied. Hence, when the Creator sends him the gift of feeling poor, by this he can receive the filling.

This is the meaning of what he says, "How can one be rewarded with the quality of judgment and *Tzimtzum* [restriction] not governing him?" At that time comes the answer that he is rewarded by this with the Creator sending him a gift. It follows that the gift is the lack, which is the *Kli*.

When he has the *Kli* and receives the *Kli* in the right place, the Creator draws upon him a thread of grace. That is, He gives him the power to be able to engage in Torah and *Mitzvot* in order to bestow, which is called *Hesed* [grace/mercy]. At that time, the judgment and *Tzimtzum*, which cause the concealment, cannot rule over him.

349- The Tree of Knowledge of Good and Evil

January 15, 1972

It is written in *The Zohar*, "The tree of knowledge of good and evil, if they are rewarded—good, if they are not rewarded—bad."

It is explained in the *Sulam* [Ladder commentary on *The Zohar*] that if he is rewarded, quality of judgment—the unmitigated *Behina Dalet*—is concealed, and quality of mercy is revealed; that is, *Malchut* that is mitigated in quality of mercy is revealed. But if he is not rewarded, it is to the contrary.

We should understand the meaning of "disclosure" and "concealment." It is known that man consists of virtues and good qualities, as well as of bad qualities. This is because "There is not a righteous man on earth who will do good and will not sin."

In other words, there is always a deficiency in a person, something more to correct; otherwise, there is nothing more for him to do in the world.

It is as two people who unite with each other and there is friendship between them, and suddenly one of them hears that the other did something bad to him. He immediately moves away from him and cannot look at him or stand near his friend. But afterwards they make up.

Our sages cautioned, "Do not appease your friend while he is angry." The question is "Why?" During his anger, he sees his friend's fault and cannot forgive him anyway, since his friend's fault is disclosed and his friend's good qualities—for which he chose him as a friend—are now covered and only his friend's fault is revealed. Thus, how can he speak to someone who is bad?

But later, after some time, when he forgets the harm that his friend caused him, he can rediscover his friend's good qualities and conceal his friend's bad qualities, meaning revive the sensation of his friend's good qualities.

Naturally, when not giving power and sustenance to his friend's bad qualities, they are pushed aside and concealed. This is because when speaking of something, the speech gives strength and livelihood to the thing being discussed. Hence, when the anger is forgotten, meaning when the sorrow that his friend caused him loses its sting, it is possible to begin to speak of the pleasure that he received from his friend's good qualities.

This depiction is better sensed between a husband and his wife. At times, they are in such disagreement that they wish to part from one another. But afterwards they make up. The question is, "What about the bad things that happened between them while they were quarrelling? Have they passed away from the world?"

Indeed, we must say that they concealed the reasons, meaning the bad qualities that each saw in the other, and now, during peace, each of them remembers only the good qualities between them, the virtues for which the match between them was made.

But even then, if someone from the family came and began to speak to the man or to the woman and showed the other's faults, he would give power and vitality to things that they suppress and conceal, and he would expose them. In that state, one can cause separation between them.

Similarly, between two friends, if a third person comes and begins to show one of the friends the faults and drawbacks of his friend by speaking of things that are concealed in them, he would give them power and vitality, and that third person would cause separation between them.

And perhaps this is the reason why slander is forbidden even when it is true, since it discloses things that were previously hidden. This causes the opposite—conceals the virtues and discloses his friend's faults—thus causing separation and hatred between them. And although everything he says is true, the reason is as was said above—that it all depends on what is revealed and what is concealed.

It is the same between man and the Creator. While man's evil is covered and a person considers himself virtuous, he feels qualified for engagement in Torah and *Mitzvot* [commandments], since he is worthy of ascending in degree. But when it is to the contrary, and his virtues are covered and only his drawbacks are disclosed, he cannot engage in Torah and *Mitzvot* because he feels that he is unfit for anything.

Thus, he will at least enjoy this world like a beast, since he cannot be a human being. Baal HaSulam said about this that usually, as long as one engages in Torah and *Mitzvot*, he feels his baseness, and when he engages in corporeal matters, he doesn't feel any lowliness.

But it should have been to the contrary—while engaging in corporeal matters, he should feel his lowliness and naturally do everything without any liveliness, and while engaging in Torah and *Mitzvot*, he will regard himself as whole. Indeed, it is the same issue as we mentioned above.

Assorted Notes

350- The Lord Appeared to Him by the Oaks of Mamre

Heshvan, Tav-Shin-Mem-Gimel, November 1982

The *Zohar* asks about the verse, "The Lord Appeared to Him by the Oaks of Mamre," why Mamre and not elsewhere? It is because he advised him about the circumcision.

When the Creator told Abraham to circumcise himself, he consulted his friends. Aner told him, "You are more than ninety years old and you will torment yourself." Mamre told him, "Remember the day when the Chaldeans threw you in the furnace, and that famine that the world went through, etc., and they went down to Egypt, and those kings whom your men chased and whom you struck, and the Creator saved you from them all, and no one could harm you. Arise, do as your Master commands."

The Creator said to Mamre, "You advised about the circumcision, be sure that I will be revealed only in your hall." This is why it is written, "by the Oaks of Mamre."

There is a famous question that when the Creator told Abraham to circumcise himself, he went and asked his friend. It seems as though he doubted whether he should heed the Creator.

We should also understand what this comes to teach us that the Creator said to him that He will be revealed to Abraham only in his hall. It would have been clearer had the Creator been revealed to Mamre himself than His revealing to Abraham only in the hall of Mamre.

According to the rule that the Torah is studied in a singular authority, it follows that his three friends, Aner, Eshkol, and Mamre were within him.

After he heard the Creator's commandment, he went to his body so they would observe the Creator's commandment. At that time, there were three views in his body: 1) Aner, which is 320 in *Gematria*, implying the 320 sparks in the body. In the 320, there is still the stony heart, which says, "I can do everything required of me, but I need to understand what I must do."

The second one, Eshkol, comes from the word *Eshkol* [I will weigh/decide], meaning he weighs the matter. Once Aner said that he is a boy who does not understand what is required of him, Eshkol comes and weighs the benefits, meaning what the will to receive gains from this.

Sometimes, he also has the quality of Mamre, who counters the old man of Mamre, for "old man" is called "an old and foolish king." Here Mamre speaks against Aner and Eshkol, arguing that he wants to go against reason, which is the quality of Aner, and against the will to receive, which is Eshkol.

This is the meaning of the advice he gave him about the circumcision, that specifically in the hall of Aner, meaning precisely in the place called "above reason." Above reason because it is regarded as the *Ruach* of the will to receive, precisely in this place the Creator appeared to him, for precisely in this place there is the delight and pleasure. At that time, it is called "And you shall love the Lord your God with all your heart—with both your inclinations."

It therefore follows that the three friends he went to ask refer to his own body, and they themselves must agree. If they do not agree then we must go by force. First, we must try in peace, but if it does not work in peace, then we must fight against the body.

351- *How to Draw Near Him*

Heshvan, Tav-Shin-Mem-Gimel, November 1982

Question: If there is no equivalence of form between two people, we can see that each one moves away from the other. Therefore, before a person corrects himself so that all his actions are for the sake of the Creator, meaning in order to bestow, there is disparity of form between the Creator and the created beings. Thus, how is it possible to draw near Him? If this is so then how do we pray to the Creator, since He is far away from us and we from Him?

Answer: There is action and there is intention. Our sages said, "From *Lo Lishma* [not for Her sake], we come to *Lishma* [for Her sake]." We should understand the connection whereby *Lo Lishma* leads to *Lishma*.

It is written that the people of Israel said, "We will do and we will hear," meaning that along with the action we will be rewarded with hearing, since there is an intermediary, and this intermediary will yield equivalence of form because we are performing acts of bestowal. Hence, in the actions, there is equivalence of form. Although the intention is still not to bestow, we say that the act will induce the thought.

It follows that although the act is *Lo Lishma*, it will later cause us to achieve *Lishma*, called in order to bestow. It follows that this is why we were given the work in Torah and *Mitzvot*, for it brings us equivalence with the action, and this causes us some nearing. This is regarded as an intermediary between receiving and bestowing.

352- Before I Was Circumcised – 1
Heshvan

It is written in the *Midrash*, "Before I was circumcised, passersby would come to me. Now that I am circumcised, they do not come to me." The Creator said to him, "Before you were circumcised, the uncircumcised would come to you. Now, I and My entourage come to you."

We should understand what the Creator replied to him, that He and His entourage come to him, since Abraham's wish was to observe the commandment to have guests.

We should interpret that in ethics, "circumcision" means acceptance of the kingdom of heaven, and its purpose is to detach him from the *Klipa* [shell/peel]. This is called "severing and circumcising from the *Klipot* [pl. of *Klipa*]."

A person sees that before this, before he takes upon himself to work only for the sake of the Creator, the guests would come to him in a manner of "coming and going." A "guest" means the good inclination, since it comes after the evil inclination has already been residing with him for thirteen years. The custom was that the good inclination would advise him to engage in Torah and *Mitzvot* [commandments] in a manner of ups and downs.

This is called "having guests," that many times a day he had states of ascent, admitting the guest many times. This is why it is referred to in plural from, "having guests."

He said, "Before I was circumcised, passersby would come to me," meaning they were always in a state of coming and going. Now that he has been circumcised, he waits for the guests to come but they do not come. To this the Creator replied, "Now, I and My entourage come to you."

That is, when we work *Lo Lishma* [not for Her sake], we do not need so much preparation in order to obtain ascents. With a small effort, we can observe Torah and *Mitzvot*, since the *Lo Lishma* is regarded as working along with the will to receive, and this work is natural, meaning it is human nature to work for himself.

But when he comes to work in a manner of bestowal, since this work is against nature, the work that he was used to doing before is no longer enough for him, and he needs reinforcement. As long as he does not add in the work, he sees himself as worse than in his previous state. Therefore, he cries out, "Why have You done harm to this people?" since now he has no guests.

And the Creator replied to him, "Now," when he begins to work in bestowal, called "for My sake," "I am calling on you the verse, 'Wherever I mention My name, I will come to you and bless you.'" Blessing means that he will be rewarded with the installing of the *Shechina* [Divinity]. This is called "I and My entourage come to you."

For this reason, you should know that you are now at a higher degree, so you need to make greater efforts in order to be worthy of having Me and My entourage, since "According to the sorrow, so is the reward," for when we should receive a higher degree, we must make more efforts.

However, it is not as you think, that you are in a worse state when you took upon yourself to work in bestowal, called work *Lishma* [for Her sake].

353- Abraham Arose

Heshvan, Tav-Shin-Mem, November 1979

"Abraham arose from before his dead, and spoke to the sons of Het, saying."

Baal HaTurim writes, "Ten times 'sons of Het' in the portion since one who scrutinizes the value of a wise disciple, it is as though he observed the Ten Commandments, in which there is the letter *Het* ten times." We need to understand why one who scrutinizes the value of a wise disciple is as though he observed the Ten Commandments, and also, where is the proof in the verse?

The Zohar interprets that Abraham means the soul, and Sarah means the body. The soul is regarded as the light that dresses in the *Kli* [vessel], which is called "body," and is the will to receive. We must distinguish a portion for the will to receive that is called "body," meaning give a place in the earth. The will to receive called "body" was sorted out of the 320 sparks that fell to *BYA*, and the *Klipot* [shells/peels] grip the sparks of *Kedusha* [holiness] that fell into *BYA*.

When we want to sort out for *Kedusha*, when we scrutinize the body to make it a *Kli* [vessel] that is fit to receive the soul, at that time the body is called "wise disciple." It is as Baal HaSulam said, that the Creator is called "wise," and if a person learns from the Wise then he is called "a wise disciple."

Hence, if the body, called "will to receive," learns the quality of the Wise, meaning to be a giver, the body is called "a wise disciple."

Yet, this is impossible before we observe the Ten Commandments, as our sages said, "I have created the evil inclination; I have created the Torah as a spice" (*Kidushin* 30b), meaning that through the Torah we can defeat the evil inclination.

This is the meaning of "One who scrutinizes the value of a wise disciple, it is as though he observed the Ten Commandments."

"Grave" is the resting place of the body. Hence, there are graves of idol-worshippers, and there is the Cave of Machpelah. As was asked in *The Zohar*, sometimes it is written, "the Cave of Machpelah," and sometimes it is written "the Field of Machpelah." He interprets in the *Sulam* [Ladder commentary on *The Zohar*] that the duality is the association of the quality of mercy with judgment, that *Malchut* rose to *Bina*. There is *Malchut* of *Bina* and there is *Bina* of *Bina*, and there is *Bina* of *Malchut* and there is *Malchut* of *Malchut*. The meaning is that the body should receive a correction of the quality of mercy with judgment.

Hence, the scrutiny should be for the will to receive, which is the quality of judgment, to be included in the quality of mercy, and by this the body will become a *Kli* that is fit to receive the light of the soul. He needed to receive the consent of the sons of Het, meaning he had to give them something so they would not slander the body. This is similar to giving a portion to the *Sitra Achra* [other side] in order to remove it and be saved from it.

At that time, the soul, which is the quality of Abraham, can reside in the body. This is called "the revival of the dead," meaning that the body is revived from the state of the breaking of the vessels and the sin of the tree of knowledge, which is the meaning of the "shedding of organs." By the corrections of the quality of mercy with judgment, the body is corrected and is called a *Kli* in which the light of the Creator, regarded as a soul, can reside.

354- Abraham Gave All that He Had

Heshvan

A good lesson in the *Midrash*, in the portion "The Life of Sarah," about the verse, "And Abraham gave all that he had to Isaac." Rabbi Yehuda said, "This is *Gevura* [strength/judgment]." Rabbi Nehemiah says, "This is a blessing."

We should understand the following:

1) How can it be said that one gives *Gevura* to another? This is not something that can be passed on from hand to hand.

2) What is the dispute that one says specifically *Gevura* and the other says "blessing"? In what are they disputed?

We should interpret that both meant the same thing, and both are the words of the living God. That is, he passed on to him that he will walk in the way of *Gevura*, as it is written, "And he swore by the fear of Isaac his father." That is, through the quality of *Gevura*, this is the meaning of "all that he had," that Abraham gave him the way by which to walk. And that which he had to complete, by this he was rewarded with the blessing, meaning "and the Lord blessed him."

In other words, through reinforcement in Torah and work, he was rewarded with repentance from love, when sins became as merits. It follows that his work created a full fruit.

Accordingly, we can understand what our sages said, "Rabbi Shmuel Bar Nachmani said, 'Rabbi Yonatan said, 'Why is it written, 'For You are our father, for Abraham did not know us and Israel did not recognize us. You, Lord, are our Father, our Redeemer.'''"

In the future, the Creator will say to Abraham, "Your children sinned against Me." He said to Him, "Master of the world, let them be abolished over the sanctity of Your name."

He said to Jacob, "It is painful to raise children, can I ask for mercy on them?" He said to him, "Your sons have sinned." He said to Him, "Master of the world, let them be abolished over the sanctity of Your name." He said, "There is no reasoning in the elderly, and no counsel in youths."

He said to Isaac, "Your sons have sinned." He said to Him, "Master of the world, my sons and not Your sons? When they gave precedence to 'We will do' over 'We will hear,' You called them 'My son, My firstborn,' now they are my sons and not Yours?' And also, how much did they sin? How many are man's years, 70 years? Take off twenty for which You do not punish, and they are left with fifty. Subtract twenty-five, which comprise the nights, and they are left with twenty-five. Subtract twelve and a half of prayer, eating, and the toilet, and there remain twelve and a half. If You bear them all, very well. But if not, half is on me and half is on You. And if You wish to say that they are all on me, then I offered my soul before You." They started and said, "For you are our father" (*Shabbat* [Sabbath] 89b).

The meaning of "abolishing" is the transgressions. Therefore, it will not be to the full extent, since a time of transgressions still remains. Yet, through the quality of *Gevura* he will have the strength to extend this force onto Israel so the sins will become merits.

It follows that all the blessings come through reinforcement in the Torah. Therefore, if we hold on to the learners of the Torah and become strengthened by them, so they can draw the power of *Gevura*, we will have the full measure of the blessings and we will be able to extend blessings on the whole of Israel, Amen.

* * *

We see that all that Isaac took upon himself was the Torah, as it is written, "twelve and a half of prayer, eating, and the toilet," but not the prayer. The rule is that if there are no learners of the Torah, there will not even be anyone who will pray.

It is as the allegory about the king who lowered all the princesses by one rank until common soldiers were left with no rank at all. Hence, if we want them to be in the next world and for our sons to pray over us, we must keep the learners of Torah.

355- He Who Has No Sons

The holy books write about "A son makes the father worthy," meaning that what the father could not complete, the son makes him worthy by complementing his father's part, and thereby completes it.

For this reason, Abraham did not have sons, for both were complete, and by adding the *Hey* to Abraham, he found a place of lack on which he could pray for sons. Likewise, Isaac did not find a place of lack, and through the prayer, the Creator provided him with a place of lack on which he could pray.

Also, Righteous Rachel was handsome and of good looks, not having a place of lack. For this reason, Rachel said, "Bring me sons, for if not, I will die."

One who has no sons is regarded as dead, meaning that he has no place of lack on which to need to extend new life. For this reason, he gave him the *Gevura*, where by always overcoming in the Torah and *Mitzvot* [commandments], he will extend the complete wholeness, for man's ways is that he corrects his actions through repentance.

There is repentance from love, and there is repentance from fear, and there are all inclusive righteous, who have been rewarded with repentance from love even with respect to their own selves. However, for the sake of the general public, they did not correct the repentance from love.

This was the quality of Isaac, as it is written, "And Isaac sowed in that land and found in that year one hundred gates," meaning the full and complete measure.

By this we will understand the words of our sages, "Rabbi Shmuel Bar Nachmani said, 'Why is it written, 'For you are our father,'" etc. (*Shabbat* [Sabbath] 89b).

356- A Son Makes the Father Worthy

We need to understand what our sages said, "A son makes the father worthy, but the father does not make the son worthy." King Ahaz, who was a complete wicked, has the next world thanks to his son, Hezekiah, who was righteous, but Menashe [Manasseh] son of Hezekiah does not have a part in the next world although his father Hezekiah was righteous (Sanhedrin 104).

I heard from Baal HaSulam that the sons come to correct what the parents did not manage to complete. Therefore, when Abraham completed only the quality of *Hesed* [mercy/grace], afterward Isaac was born in order to complete what was missing. Then, when Isaac completed only the quality of *Gevura*, Jacob was born, who is the quality of *Tifferet*, and completed the middle line.

So it is in all the generations—they complete what the previous generations did not manage to complete. This has continued since the sin of the tree of knowledge, for after the sin, his soul was divided into 600,000 souls, as explained in the writings of the ARI.

357- Abraham Begot Isaac

Heshvan, Tav-Shin-Yod-Het, November 1957

It is interpreted about the verse, "Abraham begot Isaac," that Isaac's features were similar to those of Abraham, and they all testified that Abraham begot Isaac.

We should ask, since the writing says, "These are the generations of Isaac son of Abraham," and it does not detail who are the generations. Rather, the verse explains about the generations of Isaac that "Abraham begot Isaac."

To explain the above-said, we should first present the *Mishnah*, "The world stands on three things: on the Torah, on work, and on doing *Hassadim* [mercies]." Abraham was called "a man of *Hesed*," dedicating his strength to do *Hesed* [mercy/grace] to people. Isaac is called "the pillar of the work," dedicating his soul to the altar. Jacob was called "the pillar of the Torah," as it is written, "Let truth be given to Jacob." The Torah is called "Torah of truth," and as it is written, "a complete man, dwelling in tents," and RASHI interpreted, "The tent of Shem and the tent of Ever, and engaging in the Torah."

Every person should achieve these three pillars. Previously, these three pillars were revealed one at a time through our patriarchs, each of whom revealed one pillar. After those three pillars were revealed, we have the power to also walk by the same ways that our fathers had paved for us.

For this reason, we are called by the name "a nation of *Segula* [virtue/power/cure]," for we have the *Segula* from the inheritance of our fathers to keep the three pillars by which there is existence to the world, meaning that by them the world will exist and achieve the goal for which it was created.

Hence, when the verse comes to clarify the generations of Isaac, meaning which quality of pillars Isaac bequeathed to his sons, the verse interprets "Abraham begot Isaac." That is, do not think that the generations of Isaac are only the quality of Isaac that he bequeathed to his sons, but rather also the quality of Abraham.

This is the meaning of the words, "These are the generations of Isaac," meaning those two attributes he placed in Jacob. Hence, from Abraham, whose own quality was only *Hesed*, emerged Ishmael, and from Isaac, who had his own quality, as well as inclusion with Abraham, emerged Esau. But when he had the three pillars, his complete measure could emerge, to have twelve tribes.

Since our fathers have already bequeathed us with those three pillars, we can easily follow in their footsteps. If a person sees that it is difficult for him to follow in their footsteps, he should pray to the Creator to deliver him. This is not help above nature, since these qualities are already clothed in our fathers.

Precisely in matters that are above nature, it is impossible to pray, as *The Zohar* explains about why Abraham did not pray for Sarah, who was barren, while Isaac did pray. It explains that Isaac, too, did not pray for Rebecca. The verse makes a precision, "Isaac pleaded on behalf of his wife," and not "on behalf of Rebecca," "for she was barren," since for a barren to have sons is above nature, and he did not pray for above nature, for the Creator to give him such big help.

It follows that once our fathers have extended these three pillars, we must do all that we can and pray to the Creator that we will also be rewarded with these three pillars, which are the existence of the world, meaning to achieve the goal for which the world was created.

358- And Isaac Was Forty Years Old

Heshvan-Kislev, Tav-Shin-Lamed-Tet, November-December 1978

"And Isaac was forty years old when he took Rebecca, the daughter of Betuel."

The Zohar interprets that Betuel means *Bat Bito Shel El* [the daughter of God's daughter]. We should interpret that it means that when a person is forty years old, it means that he has been rewarded with *Bina*, called "At forty, to *Bina*," and took upon himself to observe the Torah and *Mitzvot* [commandments].

"And Isaac pleaded with the Lord on behalf of his wife for she was barren," meaning he did not see any understanding in Torah and *Mitzvot*, namely with the same understanding he had had when he took upon himself the burden of Torah and *Mitzvot*, and he did not gain any understanding, yet he longed for *Banim* [sons], *Havanah* [understanding].

He thought that it could not be that he observed the Torah and *Mitzvot* with the same mind that he had had at the time of reception, when he had no knowledge or attainment in Torah and

Mitzvot. Rather, he took in the simplest way that was suitable for a little one when he grows up and continues with Torah and Mitzvot, for the Torah and Mitzvot to remain on the same level, and not a higher level, that is suitable for *Gadlut* of the Torah and Mitzvot.

Having no sons is regarded that "she was barren," meaning that he received no understanding, to understand and feel the greatness and importance of Torah and Mitzvot. "And Rebecca his wife conceived," meaning *Ibur* [impregnation], which is ideas and contemplations that he already began to put together thoughts regarding the greatness and importance of Torah and Mitzvot, and then she was glad that a son will be born out of these thoughts.

However, "The children strove within her, and she said, 'Why then do I ...' and the Lord said to her, 'Two nations are in your womb.'" We should ask what satisfied her in the fact that He told her "two nations."

We should understand that when she saw that "the sons strove," meaning that the understanding they received contradicted one another, and as RASHI interpreted, our sages explained it [the strife] as "running": When she passed by the doors of Torah of Shem and Ever, Jacob ran and struggled to come out; when she passed by the doors of idol-worship, Esau would struggle to come out.

They interpreted that when she was barren, the observation of Torah and Mitzvot was with wholeness and she did not feel any lack in their actions. When he did not have time to observe the orders of Torah and Mitzvot, he could always excuse himself and was righteous in his actions, and he could make every possible precision and did not have anything regarding observing Torah and Mitzvot.

But when he prayed for sons, he saw otherwise—that his situation grew worse than when she was barren, since now that she was passing by the doors of Torah of Shem and Ever, she agreed to work in Torah and Mitzvot in order to bestow, and when she passed by the doors of idol-worship, it means that he saw that people are working for their own sake, called "in order to receive," and the desire to follow them awakens.

In other words, she always has the striving between those two sons. Therefore, now he sees that he cannot work for the sake of the Creator whatsoever, since the minute he sees the door of the Torah, which is the view of Torah, called "the Torah exists only in those who put themselves to death over it," he agrees to walk in this way.

However, he promptly shifts to the door of people who are doing idol-worship, meaning for themselves, and then he sees that he cannot work for the sake of the Creator.

Thus, the current state is worse than when she was barren. So "Why then do I," why did I ask for sons? I wanted sons in order to have understanding in the work of the Creator, so I would ascend in degree. But now I see that I am worse than before.

"And she went to inquire with the Lord" what to do now—return to the previous path and remain barren without any understanding, or go forward on this path. "And the Lord said to her, 'Two nations are in your womb,'" meaning now you received the good inclination, too.

Previously, you only had the evil inclination, called "self-benefit," so there was no striving over self-benefit, since when he observed the Torah and *Mitzvot*, he did not have other thoughts at all and felt wholeness while observing them.

But now that he already has the good inclination, meaning that he is walking on the line called "in order to bestow," his body rejects, and from this comes the striving.

Therefore, do not say that now you are worse. Rather, previously the Torah and *Mitzvot* were in order to receive and it did not occur to you to work in order to bestow. Therefore, while observing Torah and *Mitzvot*, you had no objections and you felt that you were righteous.

But when you want to work in order to bestow, the body objects. Therefore, now you have ascended in degree, for you already know what is the good inclination. However, you must continue on the path, "and the elder will serve the young," and in the end, the good inclination, called "young," will succeed.

359- Isaac Sowed in That Land

Heshvan-Kislev, Tav-Shin-Mem, November 1979

"And Isaac sowed in that land, and he found on that year one hundred gates, and the Lord blessed him."

We should ask why specifically "one hundred gates." Why not one hundred and fifty, which is more important than one hundred? Also, if the verse wants to make a gross exaggeration, why does he find only one hundred gates? We should also ask about "And the Lord blessed him." It should have said it before "and he found one hundred," but from here it is implied that after he was awarded one hundred gates there is also room for the blessing of the Creator. But what was he missing? To have something for which to bless.

We should also ask about the verse, "he became very great." RASHI interpreted that it was said, "The manure and mules of Isaac, and not the silver and gold of Abimelech." Although there are many interpretations about this, in the literal, this remains perplexing.

It is presented in the "Introduction to The Study of the Ten Sefirot," that besides repentance from love there is also repentance from fear, at which time he is called "intermediate." He gives there an allegory about this, of two people who made a covenant of love between them because of the delight and pleasure that they bestowed upon each other.

There are two manners about this: 1) There was always love between them. 2) At first, they had grievances against each other, but after some time, love formed between them and they made a covenant.

By this he interprets that repentance from fear, when sins become for him as mistakes, means that only once they have repented is there love between them. But before this, he had sins. Hence, repentance from fear is called "intermediate," since there are two times here: before he repented, they did not have love. After he repented, they do have love.

But when he is rewarded with repentance from love, when sins become for him as merits, it follows that the part of the time before the repentance was also corrected, when they all became merits, see there. At that time, he is called "complete righteous," since he no longer has any sins.

This is the meaning of "And sowed ... and he found one hundred gates," meaning one hundred percent, since there aren't more than one hundred percent. This means that he corrected even the time before he repented, meaning the time when he had sins, which is called "manure and waste."

Baal HaSulam interpreted that *Predot* [mules] means *Perud* [separation], that during the concealment of the face, a person feels that he is separated from the Creator and must connect and adhere to the Creator, and this, too, was corrected in Isaac.

But when he makes repentance from fear, although after the repentance he has "silver and gold," from the words *Kisufim* [*Kesef* means longing] and *Ze-Hav* [*Zahav* means gold], that the Creator will give him love and fear because he already longs for the Creator, at that time the Creator is called *Avi Melech* [Abimelech, meaning "my father the king"]. However, this is a quality that is applied only after he has been rewarded with repentance.

Before he repents, there are still sins, called "manure and mules." This is the meaning of their saying, "The manure and mules of Isaac are more important than the silver and gold of Abimelech," since the manure and mules of Isaac, who is from repentance from love, are more important than repentance from fear, called the "silver and gold of Abimelech."

According to what is explained in the *Sulam* [Ladder commentary on *The Zohar*], before we are rewarded with the light of *Hochma*, we are still not rewarded with absolution of iniquities. Isaac, who is the quality of *Gevura*, the quality of *Hochma*, called "one hundred gates," all one hundred percent of his years were corrected. However, we still need a middle line, called "blessing," which is regarded as *Hassadim* that clothe the *Hochma*, as explained in the *Sulam*.

For this reason, the Torah begins with the *Bet* of *Beresheet* ["In the beginning"], since *Bet* means *Beracha* [blessing], which is *Hesed*. Hence, after all this, "And the Lord blessed him," meaning he was rewarded with inclusion in the middle line.

360- *I Did Not Find My Hands or Legs in the Seminary*

Hands and legs are two opposites. "Hands" means what we obtain, from the words, "for a hand obtains." *Raglaim* [legs] are *Meraglim* [spies], meaning that we still do not know what is there and we are now going to spy on the land.

Man's main advancement is through the legs, who walk from this place, implying that they always criticize the actions, to see if the land is good or not. Then, by overcoming, we come to the other end, which is regarded as "hands," meaning that the "hands of *Kedusha* [holiness]" are regarded as being above reason. Conversely, the hands of the *Sitra Achra* [other side] are "hands of knowledge." This is why we need both hands and legs.

361- *Your Good Treasure*

"Open the gates of heaven, and open for us Your good treasure." We should understand what is "Your good treasure."

Our sages said, "All that the Creator has in His world is the treasure of fear of heaven." This is the good treasure—a treasure of fear of heaven.

362- Jacob Saw that There Was Grain

Shabbat [Sabbath], Hanukkah, *Tav-Shin-Chaf-Vav*, December 25, 1965

It is written in *Midrash Tanchuma*, "And Jacob saw that there was grain," as the writing says, "Happy is he who asks Jacob for help." Why was it not said, "who asks Abraham," or "asks Isaac," but rather "asks Jacob"? It teaches that the Creator did not stand over Abraham, or over Isaac, but over Jacob, as it is written, "And the Lord stood over him."

Rabbi Simon said, "The King does not stand on his field when it is sown, or when it is ploughed, or when it is being hoed. When does He stand over it? When it is ripe. Thus, Abraham hoed, as was said, 'Arise, walk through the land'; Isaac sowed, and was said, 'And Isaac sowed.' He did not stand on it until Jacob came, when there was ripening of the crop, as was said, 'Israel are dedicated to the Lord, His first crop.' The Creator stood over him, as was said, 'And the Lord stood over him.' Thus, 'Happy is he who asks Jacob for help.'"

We should ask, 1) Why is specifically Jacob called "crop"? 2) What is the connection between the allegory and the lesson, that because of it we should say that the Creator stood specifically over Jacob and not over Abraham or Isaac? 3) What does it mean that the Creator stood over him? After all, Abraham and Isaac were also rewarded with the Creator speaking with them, as it is written about Abraham several times, "And the Lord said to Abraham... and He said to him, 'I am the Lord, who took you out of the land of the Chaldeans.'" Also, the Creator spoke with Isaac several times, "And the Lord appeared to him and said, 'Do not go down to Egypt.'"

Also, what is the importance that was said about Jacob during the dream, as it is written, "And he dreamed... and the Lord stood over him"?

363- Four Angels

Kislev, Tav-Shin-Mem, December 1979

The Zohar writes that there were four kings, and what one asked, the other did not ask. David said, "I will pursue my enemies and catch them, and I will not return until they are consumed."

Asa was very frightened ... he wanted to chase his enemies but not to fight them, and the Creator will kill them. Jehoshaphat, too, asked and said, "I cannot chase or kill them. Instead, I will sing and You will kill them," and the Creator did this for him.

Hezekiah King of Judah also said, "I cannot sing or chase or wage war..." and what is written? "And it came to pass that in the night, He struck the camp of Ashur," while Hezekiah was sitting in his home, the Creator was killing them (the *Sulam* [Ladder commentary on *The Zohar*], Item 121).

From this we see that a person cannot say that he lacks innate skills or ability to overcome, or strength to overcome, so he can win the war against the enemies.

Rather, even if one has no strength at all, not to wage wars like David, or chase them like Asa, or sing like Jehoshaphat, but he rather sits in his home doing nothing, like Hezekiah, but he must ask the Creator and then the Creator helps him.

This means that all we need is a desire, but it must be a strong desire. A strong desire means that this desire leaves no room for other desires to enter the body, and one walks with this desire all the time, and then the Creator helps him.

However, if there is no strong desire, but the desire that wants to win the war against the inclination leaves room for other desires to permeate the body, then the prayer he prays to the Creator, which is called "desire," is not a complete prayer.

This is similar to a story that is told about a *Hassid* [devout follower] who went to a righteous man who was famous as a maker of wonders, and asked for the righteous man's blessing for his livelihood. Since he was a shoemaker, he blessed him with success in shoemaking.

When the *Hassid* came home, the friends told him, "Can't you see that you are not successful as a shoemaker? We see that carpentry is a good craft; learn carpentry and be a carpenter." Yet, in his new profession, he was also unsuccessful.

Then, the *Hassid* went to the righteous man once more and told him that he is a carpenter but he cannot make a living, so the righteous blessed him with success in carpentry. When he returned home, the friends said to him, "You see that you are unsuccessful as a carpenter. Since a tinsmith's work yields more profits, learn this trade and be a tinsmith."

After some time, he did not succeed as a tinsmith so he went once more to the righteous man and told him that he had no sustenance. The righteous man blessed him once again with success. When he returned home, the friends said to him, "Since everyone succeeds as electricians, you should learn this trade."

But just as in the previous times, he did not find success in his work. Then, he went once more to the righteous man and asked him, "Why everyone whom the righteous blesses finds success in their livelihood and your blessings come true, while mine do not?"

The righteous man replied that he must think about this matter, so he should come the next day, and then he will answer him. The next day, when he came, the righteous man said, "Look, my son, when I blessed you with success in shoemaking, an angel came and wanted to give you success in shoemaking. He asked all the people in the town where Mr. so and so the shoemaker lived, but everyone said that there was no shoemaker by that name in town, so the angel went back up with the blessing and the success.

"Afterward, I blessed you with success in carpentry. An angel came with success in his hand in order to give it to you and asked all the people in the town where Mr. so and so the carpenter lived, but everyone said that there was no carpenter by that name in town, so the angel went back up. There was a man there by the name he mentioned, but he was not a carpenter but a tinsmith. Likewise, each time, the angel went back up after not finding that certain person who engaged in that certain craft."

Then the righteous man said to him, "What can I do for you if each time you work at a different craft? This is why my blessings are not helping, since you cannot receive the help for what you want because each time you want something else."

The lesson is that when a person prays to the Creator and is sent salvation for his prayer, by the time the salvation comes down, he has a different desire and a different lack. But when one has a strong desire, which does not let any other desire permeate the body, then he can receive salvation for the prayers and requests that he makes.

364- All Who Are Violent, Prevail – 1

"All who are violent, prevail." "If your wife is short, bend down and whisper to her" (*Baba Metzia* 59a).

In the work of the Creator on the path of truth, when one comes to take upon himself the burden of the kingdom of heaven above reason, there is no intellect there that he will be able to understand with his mind the benefits of accepting the work in order to bestow. Rather, "All who are violent," meaning that only by force can one subdue, and not with the mind.

This is so because when one has some reasoning that approves of doing this, it is already regarded as within reason. Hence, there must not be any intellect in this, only force. From this stems the judgment, in corporeal judgment, among people, it also happens that courthouses give the verdict, "All who are violent prevail."

But why must one's work be above reason? It is the reality. Since man is created with the *Kli* [vessel] of a body called "will to receive," the body cannot do anything against the will to receive. Therefore, he works within reason, and this is a sign that he is deceiving himself with respect to the truth. For this reason, he thinks that it is reason that obligates him to this.

365- And Judah Approached Him – 1
VaYigash, Tav-Shin-Mem-Bet, January 1982

It is interpreted in the *Sulam* [Ladder commentary on *The Zohar*], "'And Judah approached him,' for Judah is the *Nukva* [female] meaning a prayer, and Joseph is redemption." The text tells us that they approached each other for a *Zivug* [coupling] until, "And Joseph could not withhold himself" and revealed to them those *Mochin* [lights].

In regard to the above-said, we can interpret the verse, "And Judah approached him and said, 'My lord, may your servant please speak a word in my lord's ears, and do not be angry with your servant, for you are as Pharaoh.'" Here he brings an order by which to approach a prayer and ask the Creator to save him.

When a person wants to walk on the path of truth, and truth is called *Lishma* [for Her sake]—as Maimonides says in *Hilchot Teshuva*—he sees that he is far from the truth.

A prayer is *Malchut*, who is called Judah, who was a *Melech* [king], for Israel are sons of kings, the sons of *Malchut*. *Malchut* is called "the assembly of Israel," the collection of the soul of Israel. Hence, each one is called *Malchut*.

When he comes to pray to the Creator to bring him closer to His true work, which is called "truth," he says to the Creator, "Our sages said, 'I have created the evil inclination; I have created the Torah as a spice.' Thus, what I ask of You, to give me the light of Torah, is not because I need the *Gadlut* [greatness/adulthood] of the *Mochin*. Therefore, 'Do not be angry with your servant,' since all the light of Torah that I seek is not luxuries, but a necessity."

"You are as Pharaoh," since there are two kings in the world: 1) The King of all Kings, 2) An old and foolish king, called "Wicked Pharaoh."

Since "You are as Pharaoh," meaning I do not feel any greatness in the Creator and do not have importance of *Kedusha* [holiness], but it has the same taste and value as Pharaoh, and even at the most important time, when both are of the same value and I must determine whether for *Kedusha* or for *Tuma'a* [impurity]—and this is called "for You are as Pharaoh"—when they are of equal weight, this is the most important time. Sometimes, Pharaoh is more important than the *Kedusha*.

Hence, when he asks the Creator to show him the light of His Torah, it is a necessity and not because he wants *Gadlut*. This is why he said, "Do not be angry with your servant." This is the meaning of "And Judah approached him," for approaching is only a prayer, which is *Malchut*.

Joseph is redemption, as in "Joseph could not withhold himself," and revealed to him the *Mochin*. This is the meaning of "No man stood with him when Joseph made himself known to his brothers." When the Creator reveals Himself, "No man stood." That is, at that time a person annuls his being and begins to walk on the path of truth.

366- Hard on Himself and Easy on Others

Kislev-Tevet, Tav-Shin-Mem-Dalet, December 1983

Hard on himself and easy on others. That is, what others do, regardless of how much Torah and how many *Mitzvot* [commandments], he understands that others did not have the same understanding that he does. Hence, whatever they do is good because he is easy on them and everything that others do is fine in his eyes.

However, he is hard on himself. That is, everything he does, he sees that it is not alright because his intention while doing the good deeds is not the real intention. For this reason, he always sees that others are better than him because their actions are fine, and about his, he thinks the opposite. At that time, he can make an honest prayer about his situation, that he is in such lowliness.

367- To Benjamin He Gave Three Hundred Pieces of Silver

Kislev-Tevet, Tav-Shin-Mem-Dalet, December 1983

"To Benjamin he gave three hundred *pieces of* silver and five changes of gowns."

In the work, we should discern:

1) "Wealth" means an act of Torah and *Mitzvot* [commandments], and on the act, there is nothing to add, as our sages said, "Do not add and do not subtract." This is why it is called "wealth," meaning wholeness. This is regarded as "righteous," who walk on the path of the right [side].

2) Afterward, they must shift to the left. "Left" is regarded as something that needs correction, as our sages said, "And they will be a token on your hand," which is the weaker hand, left, where correction is missing.

In other words, once he is already on the right line in the work in Torah and *Mitzvot* [commandments], then begins the matter of intentions. That is, he begins to think what he wants in return for his work in Torah and *Mitzvot*, what reward he hopes to receive for his labor in Torah and *Mitzvot*.

At that time, he gets the "gowns," if he wants to work not in order to receive reward. At that time, the body comes and asks, "What is this work for you?" which is the wicked man's question.

3) Then he comes into answering, meaning to answer the question of the wicked one. That is, he wants to work above reason and above flavor.

This state is regarded as *Katnut* [smallness/infancy], meaning that his work is on *Katnut*. This means that the majority of his work is on the questions that the wicked one asks, that he must believe above reason that this is His will, and he wants to do His will, which is the manner of faith. This is called *Hassadim* [mercies], when he wants to work only in *Hesed*, which is in order to bestow.

4) After he has been rewarded with faith above reason, which is called *Katnut*, he is rewarded with the revelation of the secrets of the Torah, as Rabbi Meir said, "He who learns Torah *Lishma* [for Her sake] is rewarded with many things." This is also called "left," since here he should reveal once more the desire to bestow.

5) This is after he has been rewarded with the quality of receiving in order to bestow, when he can receive the *Kli* [vessel] of Torah in order to bestow. It follows that altogether, there are five changes of *Smalot* [gowns], from the word *Smol* [left]. The inversion of the "left" is called "right," and left is called "left." He does not say "right" because the "right," too, should replace the left, this is why they are called together, "five changes of gowns."

368- And Behold, the Lord Stood Over Him

Kislev, Tav-Shin-Mem, November 1979

"And behold, the Lord stood over him and said, 'I am the Lord, God of your father Abraham... This land on which you lie, to you I will give it and to your descendants.'"

RASHI interpreted about the question, Why are the four cubits where he lies important? He brings the words of our sages, "The Creator folded all of the land of Israel underneath him, implying to him that it will be as easy for his sons to conquer as four cubits, which is man's place."

We need to understand the words by intimation. *Eretz* [land] is called *Malchut*, which is the kingdom of heaven. The whole of the land of Israel, meaning the Creator folded the whole of the spiritual land under the kingdom of heaven, like the verse, "What does the Lord God require of you? Only fear." That is, we need nothing more than to accept the burden of the kingdom of heaven. By this we can be rewarded with the whole of the spiritual land, called "land of Israel," as our sages said, "Anyone who has fear of heaven, his words are heard" (*Berachot* 6b).

In other words, a person who has been rewarded with the kingdom of heaven can control all his thoughts and desires. This is regarded as his organs hearing the words. This is the meaning of the Creator folding all of the land of Israel underneath him, meaning beneath the land that is called "kingdom of heaven."

The Zohar interprets "And Jacob departed from Beer Sheba," meaning departed from the land of Israel "and went to Haran," meaning abroad. By this he comes to a state of "anger." In a person, there is the quality of "rising," when he stands upright, and there is the quality of "lying down," when he falls from his degree. The falling is called "lying down."

This is why he was told, "The land on which you lie," which you feel as lying on the ground, meaning that he could not take upon himself the kingdom of heaven as it should be. Know that this is not merely a land, which is only the quality of *Malchut*, which is a small degree. Rather, this land is a high degree.

Hence, one should make great efforts for it, since the whole of the merit of the land of Israel depends on this land. The Creator promised, "To you I will give it and to your descendants," and if you receive the land, everything will be in your hand.

They interpreted that this is why the Creator folded the whole of the land of Israel under the earth, to make it easy to conquer the land of Israel. As it is written (*Midrash Rabbah*, and presented in the "Introduction to The Study of the Ten Sefirot"), "The Creator said to Israel, 'Be sure, the whole of the wisdom and the whole of the Torah are easy. Anyone who fears Me and does the words of Torah, the whole of the wisdom and the whole of Torah are in his heart.'"

This is the meaning of the Creator folding the whole of the land of Israel underneath him, meaning under this land called "the kingdom of heaven." If the four cubits, meaning a person's height, is filled with fear of heaven, called "kingdom of heaven," it will be easy to conquer it. This is what He promised him, "This land on which you lie, to you I will give it and to your descendants."

369- Joy While Learning Torah

Kislev, Tav-Shin-Mem-Gimel, November 1982, Jerusalem

Question: If a person does everything in order to receive, meaning that all he does is only with the aim for his own benefit, then what is the difference between enjoying corporeal things or deriving pleasure from words of Torah?

We can understand this in the manner that a person eats fish, meat, and wine on weekdays and enjoys it. This eating is called "optional eating." But when he eats meat, fish, and wine on a Shabbat [Sabbath] meal, it is a *Mitzva* [commandment] of the delight of Shabbat.

Mitzvot [pl. of *Mitzva*] do not require intention, meaning to aim only in order to bestow. Rather, he should aim that he is doing this only because of a *Mitzva*. Thus, when he enjoys the Shabbat meal, he observes a *Mitzva* although this *Mitzva* is still *Lo Lishma* [not for Her sake], meaning that he cannot aim in order to bestow. Still, from *Lo Lishma* he will come to *Lishma* [for Her sake]. It follows that he is observing a *Mitzva*.

But when he eats an optional meal during the weekdays, it cannot be said that this optional meal will bring him to *Lishma*. It turns out that when he learns Torah and enjoys, although it is not in order to bestow, he observes the *Mitzva* of learning Torah with joy, since he enjoys it, so he is observing a *Mitzva*. It follows that from *Lo Lishma* he will come to *Lishma*. Thus, this is the right way to achieve *Lishma*. Conversely, other pleasures do not lead him to *Lishma*.

370- The Way of the Land Preceded the Torah

Kislev, Tav-Shin-Mem-Bet, December 1981

"What is light? Rav Huna said, 'light,' and Rav Yehuda said 'night'" (*Rish Pesachim*).

"Jacob went out from Beer Sheba and went to Haran and arrived at the place." "Jacob went out," *The Zohar* says, from Beer Sheba, from the land of Israel. "Went to Haran," abroad. Our sages said that Abraham and Isaac established the morning and afternoon prayers, which are mandatory, and Jacob established the evening prayer, which is optional (*Berachot* 26b).

We should understand why the prayer of Jacob—who is the senior among the patriarchs, and who is called "Jacob, a complete man," eliciting twelve tribes—is not mandatory like the prayers of Abraham and Isaac.

Normally, one who feels that his friend is doing him a favor feels a moral debt to bless him for the favor that he did for him and will return him favors henceforth.

But one who does not feel that his friend did him a favor, but thinks that perhaps he did him favors, he does not feel he should be grateful and that he should seek something from him. Rather, he has an option. In other words, the body does not feel indebted to ask of the other one, but this is an option, and he has the choice whether or not to do so. But if he feels that his friend has given to him, the body feels a debt to his friend.

Jacob, the complete man, wanted to correct the wholeness of the generations and the times and states. This is the difference between day and evening, since "day" is when he feels good and his heart is glad. That state is called "day." If it is to the contrary, he says, "the world has grown dark on me."

"Jacob went out from Beer Sheba," which is the land of Israel, a *Be'er* [well] from which water is pumped, when a person feels satiated and that he does not lack a thing, "and went to Haran," to a place where there is no satiation and there is *Haron Af* [anger/wrath]. This is called "evening." At that time, the body is not obliged to thank his friend and ask something of his friend. On the contrary, he has grievances against his friend.

"And he came to the place." This is a correction, for even in a place that is the evening prayer, when prayer is optional, meaning a choice, he should overcome and pray. But the body does not feel any obligation while it is dark for it.

Hence, Jacob, the senior among the patriarchs, established wholeness for the general public, so they can pray the evening prayer, at which time it is optional.

A person should make a choice so that the body will want to pray, since at that time it does not feel any obligation, as it is evening and not day. When it feels the state of "day," the body feels obliged. Through the optional prayer, which is evening, we come to a "day," and then it is a mandatory prayer.

Likewise, the blessing [grace] for the food is mandatory at a meal where there is satiation, as it is written, "And you shall eat, and be satisfied, and bless," to imply the above-mentioned, that when the body feels the state of "Beer Sheba," when it is *Save'a* [satiated], the body feels obliged to pray. But when he feels the state of "evening," the prayer is optional to the body and he needs the work of choice so he can pray.

By this we can interpret the dispute over the interpretation of "light to the fourteenth" [the night before the 14th of the month] when we examine the leaven. The Gemara asks, "What is light?" Rav Huna says, "light is light," and Rav Yehuda says, "Light is night." We should understand how come they are disputed. From the perspective of the *Kli* [vessel], being rewarded with the light requires that we first feel the darkness. Hence, light is mainly "night." When we speak from the perspective of the abundance, not from the perspective of the *Kli*, the abundance is called "light," which is day.

This is the meaning of "The voice is the voice of Jacob, and the hands are the hands of Esau." The body is regarded as the quality of Esau, since as soon as one is born, the evil inclination comes to him. Hence, it is regarded as Esau: It is complete and knows what is good and what is bad.

When the good inclination comes to him and tells him that there is a different good than what he knows to be considered good, he does not want to listen. The good inclination tells him, "The wicked in their lives are called 'dead.'" But he does not understand what it is telling him; he thinks that it is the complete opposite.

It was said about this, "The voice is the voice of Jacob, and the hands are the hands of Esau," meaning that through the voice of Jacob, which is the evening prayer, the *Kelim* [vessels] of Esau can receive correction, and the darkness will be turned to day, as it is written, "And it came to pass that when evening falls, it will become day."

371- A Ladder Set on the Earth

Kislev, Tav-Shin-Mem-Gimel, November 1982

"Behold, a ladder was set on the earth." What is a ladder? It is a degree on which all other degrees depend, meaning the *Nukva* [female], which is the rest of the degrees (*The Zohar*, p 29, and in the *Sulam* [Ladder commentary on *The Zohar*]).

"And behold, angels of God ascending and descending on it." These are the appointees of all the nations ascending and descending on this ladder. When Israel sin, the ladder comes down and the appointees ascend. When Israel improve their ways, the ladder ascends and all the appointees descend (Item 53 in the *Sulam*).

We need to understand all this, and to understand what people say, that there is nothing straighter than a crooked ladder, and nothing more crooked than a ladder when it is straight. *Malchut* is called "the assembly of Israel" and includes all the souls. Hence, according to the practices of the lower ones, so the bestowal from above appears to them.

For this reason, when Israel engage in acts of bestowal, there is a decline to the nations of the world, whose root is only reception of pleasure for themselves. But when Israel engage in reception, they give strength to the nations of the world, for the power of reception to control. When the power of reception governs, the power of *Tzimtzum* [restriction] governs and the abundance cannot be drawn from above.

It therefore follows that the ladder, which is *Malchut*, when the nations of the world ascend, *Malchut* descends, meaning that he cannot bestow upon the lower ones, and then there is concealment in the world.

But when Israel improve their practices through acts of bestowal, and the power of reception in order to receive declines, the ladder, which is *Malchut*, ascends in its importance, meaning it imparts upper abundance downward.

This is the meaning of what people say, "There is more crooked than a ladder when it is straight." In spirituality, "straightness" is called a "line" that has above and below, where *Malchut* is below and *Keter* is above.

This is called "In the beginning, He created the world with the quality of judgment. He saw that the world could not exist and associated with it the quality of mercy," which is regarded as a diagonal. It follows that when *Malchut* is associated with the quality of mercy, it is called "a ladder," and "crooked" means it stands diagonally. But when it is straight with the quality of judgment, the world cannot exist.

It is written about the verse, "He will command His angels over you, to keep you in all your ways," "His angels" are the good inclination and the evil inclination. There, in Item 2, "Rabbi Yitzhak started, 'It is written, 'The angel of the Lord camps around those who fear Him and will deliver them.' But elsewhere, it is written, 'He will command His angels over you,' meaning many angels. He explains, 'The words, 'He will command His angels over you' are angels as usual. And the words, 'An angel of the Lord' means the *Shechina* [Divinity].'"

We should understand why at one time he says "two angels," and another time he says "one angel," referring to the *Shechina*. That is, when does he have two angels and when does he have one angel?

We can interpret this as our sages said about the verse, "with all your heart," meaning with both your inclinations, the good inclination and the evil inclination.

Accordingly, angels as usual means that every person has two angels, the good inclination and the evil inclination, which are two hearts. But after a person is rewarded with fear of the Creator, he becomes among those who fear the Creator. At that time, he is rewarded with one angel, when his two inclinations become one, and by this he comes to love the Creator with both his inclinations, for they are both united within him. This is considered that he has been rewarded with the instilling of the *Shechina*.

372- It Came to Pass as That Day

Hanukkah, 28 *Kislev, Tav-Shin-Lamed-Bet*, December 16, 1971

It is written in *The Zohar, VaYeshev* (236), "'And it came to pass as that day, and he came home to do his work...' 'It came to pass as that day,' the day when the evil inclination rules the world... When a man comes to repent for his sins, or to engage in the Torah and to observe the commandments of the Torah."

In "The Soul of..." we say, "You hear the outcry of the poor, You listen to the shouting of the meager and You deliver. Who is like You, and who can be compared to You?" It seems as though we should ask why specifically the prayer of the poor and the meager? It seems as though he means that the outcry and the shouting are over what is written later, meaning "Who will be like," and "Who can be compared." But how can one even conceive of resembling the Creator?

We can interpret that there are three kinds in the work of the Creator, in each of which there is the matter of the evil inclination and the good inclination.

1) When he observes Torah and *Mitzvot* [commandments] with the intention *Lo Lishma* [not for Her sake], such as in order to be called "Rabbi." At that time, the intention is that in return for the work, he wants for the created beings to pay him for his labor in Torah and *Mitzvot*.

It follows that he is not working for the Creator to pay his reward, but for people to pay his reward. Hence, he works in public so that people will see that he is working for them, so they will pay him. If he acts in concealment, who will pay his reward?

The second kind is that he works *Lishma* [for Her sake], meaning for the Creator to pay his reward, to give him the good of this world or the good of the next world. At that time, he works in concealment, so people will not see his work, which is called "so the outer ones will not have control," when people on the outside see his work.

By this, he would fall under the governance of the outer ones, meaning to demand reward from people for his work, but he wants the Creator to pay his reward. This is called *Lishma*, since he wants the Creator to pay his reward. It follows that he is working for the Creator.

Conversely, one who wants people to pay his reward does not work for the Creator, but only for people. The evidence is that he wants people to pay his reward for the labor, and this is called *Lo Lishma*. *Lishma*, however, is when he works for the Creator. At that time, he does not want people to pay him, only the Creator.

The third kind is not in order to receive reward. At that time, the governance of the evil inclination comes and asks, "What is this work for you?" This is called "the question of the wicked one," for then there is nothing to answer him.

In *Lo Lishma*, the evil inclination has no control since he has what to answer, meaning that people will reward him, that they will pay his reward. In the evil inclination of the second kind, when he works *Lishma*, he still has what to answer—that the Creator will reward him, meaning that the Creator will pay his reward.

This is not so with the evil inclination of the third kind, which is not in order to receive reward. When it asks, "What is this work for you?" there is nothing to answer to this question. Hence, only then does it gain control.

This is why *The Zohar* says, "When is the day of the governance of the evil inclination? It is precisely when one wants to repent, to return to his source." That is, just as our source is only to bestow upon the creatures, we should also be only bestowing upon the Creator, as it says, to engage in Torah and observe the commandments of the Torah.

We should also interpret in the above manner that he wants to engage in Torah so he can observe the commandments of the Torah, as our sages said, "Great is the learning that yields action" (*Kidushin* 40b).

When one wants to work not in order to receive reward, there is the control of the evil and he cannot perform the *Mitzvot* of the Torah. This is, "I have created the evil inclination; I have created the Torah as a spice," meaning that through engagement in Torah, one can come to observe the *Mitzvot* not in order to receive reward.

This is the meaning of "the outcry of the poor and the shouting of the meager." What do they want? "Who is like You, and who can be compared to You?" meaning equivalence of form, "As He is merciful, so you are merciful."

They are called "poor and meager," meaning in knowledge, since they have nothing to answer to the evil inclination when it asks "What is this work?" while in the two previous kinds there is knowledge what to answer it. Hence, specifically then they are called "poor and meager," and only then is there control to the evil inclination.

373- He Saw that He Could Not Prevail Over Him

Kislev, Tav-Shin-Mem-Bet, December 1981

"He saw that he could not prevail over him." What did he do? He promptly "touched the hollow of his thigh," he schemed against him. He said that since the supports of the Torah were broken, the Torah will promptly become unable to strengthen further, and then what their father said, "The voice is the voice of Jacob, but the hands are the hands of Esau" will come true. And he did not know him.

"Supporters of the Torah" means that they support the Torah, that through them a wise disciple can learn, for without provision, it is impossible to learn; if there is no bread, there is no Torah. "Provision" means that which gives sustenance and enjoyment to the body. The body needs to be provided for, as through the provision, the body has sustenance. To the extent of the joy that a person has, to that extent he wants to exist.

Some people, whose sustenance is from money, meaning that if they are given money, this gives them all their joy, meaning they relinquish lust and honor and want only money. And the more money they have, the more they can work and enjoy life.

"So give honor to Your people." Can we ask the Creator to give honor? After all, our sages said, "Be very, very humble." The thing is that it is known that man is a small world comprised of seventy nations. This means that each nation has its own lust, which correspond to seven qualities, and each one consists of ten *Sefirot*, thus they are seventy. That is, man consists of seventy desires of the seventy nations and craves those desires that they want, meaning passion for money, respect, and so forth.

People respect the passions that they want, to the point that moralists said that we must loathe these lusts.

Conversely, "ordinary people," when the people of Israel must yearn to bring contentment to the Maker, this is not respectable, but to the contrary. When one does something that he does not see that it will yield any benefit to himself, and that it must be done only for the purpose of bestowal, at that time, a person feels himself in a state of lowliness, that he has no vitality from the work, since he does not see any self-benefit.

This is why we pray to the Creator, "Give honor to Your people," so we will respect the state of bestowal and not degrade it. This is called "the glory of the *Shechina* [Divinity]," "to raise the *Shechina* from the dust." This means that when we must act for the sake of the Creator, in order to bestow, this work tastes like dust. Hence, we pray that the people of Israel will be respected and the seventy nations will be only slaves serving the people of Israel, meaning that our engagement in corporeality, which is the desires of the seventy nations, will be only in order to thereby serve the quality of Israel within man.

374- He Touched the Hollow of His Thigh

Kislev, Tav-Shin-Mem-Gimel, December 1982

It is written in *The Zohar* (*VaYishlach*, Item 111) about the verse, "He touched the hollow of his thigh," meaning the supporters of the Torah, that he schemed against him. He said, "Since the supports of the Torah were broken, the Torah will promptly become unable to strengthen further." In Item 108 in the *Sulam* [Ladder commentary on *The Zohar*], it is written that because there is no one to support the Torah, which is *Zeir Anpin*, as it should be, the supporters of *Zeir Anpin* weakened, meaning *Netzah* and *Hod* of *Zeir Anpin*, which are called "supports," and cause that one who has no thighs or legs to stand on, namely the primordial serpent.

It is known that *Netzah* and *Hod* are called "two supports of the truth." We must know that everything one does must first have a reason that will oblige him to do those deeds. Without a reason, man is in a state of rest. But if he has reasons that will obligate him to do those deeds, he will try to do them according to the reason.

Esau's minister saw that he could not argue with the learners of Torah because they had the desire and the upbringing to learn Torah, and he could not distract them from learning the Torah. However, he could disrupt them through the reasons, meaning the reason why they learn, what they want in return for their labor in Torah and work, which are called "supports of the Torah," for through the reasons, he has the strength to learn Torah.

But if he has no reasons, it is regarded as having no support. Hence, since there are two supports to the truth, and his supports, meaning the reasons that obligate him to do things, will not be true reasons, as in "I have created the evil inclination; I have created the Torah as a spice," but rather false reasons, in this, the minister of Esau had a grip.

A lie has no legs. This means that he took the reason from the primordial serpent, who has no legs, as it is written in *The Zohar*, and therefore the real Torah cannot be drawn below, since the supports are false supports. In other words, the reasons that obligate him are false.

It follows that the main work on the path of truth is to see that he obtains supports for the Torah, meaning true supports by which he will have a foundation on which to build his Torah and *Mitzvot* [commandments], for here is the main grip of the *Sitra Achra* [other side].

On the rest of the things, it does not seem as though he has a grip. It is as the king of Sodom said, "Give me the soul and take the properties to yourself," as was said, "A prayer without an intention is like a body without a soul."

The spirit and the soul mean the intention in the matter. This is why the king of Sodom said, "Give me the soul," meaning the intention of a person, why he engages in Torah and *Mitzvot*, this will be for him. "And the property," meaning the Torah and *Mitzvot* that a person acquires, "Take for yourself." You can gain as much property as you want, but the intention will be for me. This is why this is the main thing that a person needs to overcome

375- *Jacob Sent*

Kislev, Tav-Shin-Mem, December 1979

"Jacob sent." RASHI interprets, "real angels."

We should interpret the meaning of "real angels" that Jacob sent to Esau. According to what is interpreted, Jacob is the quality of a person engaged in Torah and *Mitzvot* [commandments], and Esau is the evil inclination. How can it be said that he sent angels to the actual evil inclination?

We should understand this according to what Baal HaSulam said about why it is written about Laban, "And Laban answered and said to Jacob, 'The girls are my daughters, the boys are my sons, the flock is my flock, and all that you see is for me.'" Concerning Esau, the opposite is written, "And Esau said, 'I have much, my brother, let what is yours be yours.'" Jacob asked him, "Do take my blessing, which I have brought you... and he entreated him and he took."

Baal HaSulam explained that "Laban" means before the act, when the evil inclination claims that everything a person does is not for the sake of the Creator, so what value is there in his desire to engage in Torah and *Mitzvot* [commandments]? But a person must overcome and nonetheless do good deeds.

Once the act has been done, "Esau," who is called the evil inclination, claims that everything that the person did is for the sake of the Creator and wants to instill in him the quality of greatness so he will settle for his work.

With this we can interpret the words, "real angels." This is why it is called "evil inclination," for it argues that if he wants to engage in Torah and *Mitzvot*, he must first of all be completely white, without any stains or dirt, meaning that everything will be for the sake of the Creator. If he cannot aim for the sake of the Creator, it is not worthwhile to exert in vain.

Therefore, what will he gain by praying for another half an hour or learning for another half an hour? In any case, his work is worthless, so every bit of effort that he makes in Torah and work is a waste. By this, the evil inclination has the power to divert him from Torah and *Mitzvot*.

At that time, a person must overcome it through "And his heart was high in the ways of the Lord," and say "I believe above reason that I am doing everything for the sake of the Creator, and even the *Lo Lishma* [not for Her sake] that I do is a great thing because from *Lo Lishma* we come to *Lishma* [for Her sake]. Thus, by working *Lo Lishma*, I am still doing a *Mitzva* [commandment] and observing the words of the sages, who said, 'One should always engage in Torah and *Mitzvot Lo Lishma*, since from *Lo Lishma* we come to *Lishma*,' for the light in it reforms him."

But once he has done all that he could do, meaning the order of his times in Torah and *Mitzvot*, he must see the truth and criticize his work. Then, a person must say the opposite of what he said to the evil inclination. He should send messengers to the evil inclination, meaning tell the evil inclination that in his work, a person should be just like angels, meaning a *Kli* [vessel] for the sake of the Creator.

But since his work is not clean and compete, he says to the evil inclination that all his work was for him, for the evil inclination, and not for the sake of the Creator. This is regarded as a person sending all his work to the evil inclination.

At that time, the evil inclination says, "I have much, among other people who work for me. But you, my brother, let what is yours be yours, for it was all for the sake of your soul, and you do not need to be more complete in your work. Rather, continue with the same intention you have had thus far, until after great efforts "he entreated him and he took."

At that time, the evil inclination will agree to accept the work for itself. That is, he is convinced, and the evil inclination will not be able to send him thoughts that he is fine. Rather, he remains with the truth that they must be real angels, meaning completely for the sake of the Creator. And then his work begins anew in order to walk on the path of truth.

376- Jacob Was Very Frightened

The interpreters asked about the verse, "And Jacob was very frightened and distressed." After all, the Creator showed him in the vista of the ladder that He showed him, promised him to keep him wherever he may walk, as it is written, "And behold, I am with you and I will keep you wherever you walk, I will be with you." So why did he need to pray, "Save me please from the hand of my brother, from the hand of Esau"?

The *Zohar* interprets the angels' saying to Jacob, "And he is also walking toward you and four hundred men are with him." It asks, "Why did they tell him so?" It replies, "because the Creator always wants the prayers of the righteous and is crowned with their prayers," meaning that the Creator craves the prayers of the righteous (*Yevamot* 64a).

Baal HaSulam interpreted why the Creator does not give the created beings abundance without prayer, but rather wants them to ask of Him, and then bestows upon them. As our sages said, "More than the calf wants to suckle, the cow wants to nurse" (*Pesachim* 112). However, there is a rule that there is no light without a *Kli* [vessel]. A *Kli* is called "desire," since there is no coercion in spirituality because it is impossible to feel the taste of pleasure from something one does not want, since the sensation of pleasure depends primarily on the yearning and desire for the matter. Hence, the Creator does not bestow unless the creatures have a desire and yearning.

Man's desire is formed specifically by prayer, since by feeling the lack, a person begins to pray. By this, his prayer grows and multiplies until it comes to a level where he is fit to receive the upper abundance. For this reason, the Creator longs for the prayer of the righteous, for only by this can they receive His abundance.

It is known that we always discern two discernments in His abundance: *Ohr Makif* [surrounding light] and *Ohr Pnimi* [inner light]. *Ohr Makif* means that which a person is destined to receive, but he is not yet ready to receive the abundance. *Ohr Pnimi* means that a person is receiving in the present, meaning that the abundance comes inside of him.

According to what we said above, that we must precede everything we receive with a prayer, so as to have a *Kli* to receive the abundance, it follows that even after the Creator promised him in the vista of the ladder, it is regarded as *Ohr Makif*.

But when he met Esau, he needed salvation in the present. He had to pray and show the desire, regarded as the *Kli* for salvation, since without a *Kli*, it is impossible to receive *Ohr Pnimi*. The promise is regarded as *Ohr Makif*, but when we come to carry out the promise, we need a prayer. The *Ohr Makif* is an awakening from above, and the *Ohr Pnimi* comes by an awakening from below.

377- Better a Poor Child

Kislev, Tav-Shin-Lamed-Bet, December 1971

Rabbi Shimon said, "Come and see, 'A poor and wise child is better...' is the good inclination. But a child is better, as it is written, 'I was a youth, now I am old.'" Another thing: "He is a child, a poor child, who has nothing of his own. So why is he called 'child'? It is because he has renewal of the moon, which is constantly renewed, and he is always a child... and he is wise because wisdom dwells in him."

"'An old and foolish king' is the evil inclination... since the day he was born, he has not moved from his *Tuma'a* [impurity]. 'A child,' since he is with man from infancy, while he is from thirteen years and on."

We should ask, for it implies that in a person who is twenty years old, the evil inclination is twenty years old and is called "old." When a person is seventy, the good inclination is fifty-seven and is called "a child."

Yet, we should understand that we are dealing here with natural laws, which are just like the commandments that nature obligates us to follow. They divide into externality and internality. For example, when a person eats bread or other things, and drinks water or other drinks, the bread is called "externality," for the externality does not undergo any change in a person.

In each one, the matter appears in the same form, meaning he cannot say that a slice of bread has changed its form from one to another, but rather everyone sees the bread in the same external shape. Also, it is the same with other external things, such as water or wine. Everyone sees the external things without any change, and there is no difference between one person and another.

This is not so with the internality, which is clothed in the external things. It is known that in everything, a pleasure of a different flavor is clothed, which does not exist in another.

For example, the taste that is in bread does not exist in meat. Even in the meat itself there are quite a few discernments to make, since the taste of the meat of beef is not the same as in poultry. And in poultry, too, we should discern flavors, since the taste of chickens is not the same as in the meat of turkey or pigeons, and so forth.

This means that within the externality, a flavor is clothed, which is internal, and all the pleasure that delights a person is only from the internality, and not from the externality. Only in the internality can one discern between one person and another, for each one feels a different taste and pleasure from his friend. Even the same person does not always feel the same inner taste in food and drinks; it depends on one's health and mood.

But at the same time, we see that when a person cannot feel the inner taste and pleasure that is clothed within those things, a person must use external things. A person cannot say that since he does not feel the flavor of the food, he will not eat for a week or for a month.

Or as we see with little children, when they do not feel the taste and pleasure clothed in the food, they must eat against their will, without any flavor or pleasure, or they will not be able to continue to exist and will perish and die.

But when a grownup eats when he feels no taste, he will attribute it to some reason, such as an illness or melancholy and so forth. Concerning children, we say that they have not yet developed so as to understand and feel the taste in eating and drinking, and so forth.

It is likewise in *Mitzvot* [commandments]. The Torah divides into internality and externality. Here, too, the externality of the *Mitzva* [sing. of *Mitzvot*] is the same form for everyone, and there is no difference in the externality of the *Mitzva* between the righteous of the generation and a simple man off the street.

Here, too, the difference between man and man is only in the internality that is clothed in the *Mitzva*, as each one feels a different flavor in the same *Mitzva*.

Also, within the same person we should discern between one flavor and the next, since one does not always have the same understanding and the same mood so as to feel the internality of the *Mitzva*.

For this reason, if we take into account the externality of the *Mitzvot*, then every person is regarded as "continuously adding," since more or less each day a person performs *Mitzvot*. Hence, as long as he continuously adds, he has many *Mitzvot*, as our sages said, "The empty ones among you are filled with *Mitzvot* like a pomegranate."

But from the perspective of the internality of the *Mitzvot*, namely the flavor and pleasure that is clothed in the *Mitzvot*, and the purpose for which the *Mitzvot* came, as our sages said, "I have created the evil inclination; I have created the Torah as a spice," where the Torah and *Mitzvot* should cleanse and purify him so as to emerge from self-love and come to love of the Creator, a person might reach the age of seventy, and have many *Mitzvot* in externality, but in the internality, the intention clothed in the *Mitzvot*, he has still not achieved and is still in self-love.

The way for one who wants to be rewarded with internality is to say each time, "What happened, happened, and from now on, I will take upon myself to walk in the ways of the Creator, meaning to be rewarded with the desire to bestow."

It therefore follows that he is always a child. Even when he is seventy years old, he says, "Until now it was wrong; from now on, I begin." Thus, he is always in a state of "child." Even when he is a grownup, he is still in the quality of a child (such as the story about Rabbi Saadia Gaon).

378- Jacob Lived in the Land Where His Father Dwelled

Kislev, Tav-Shin-Mem, December 1979

"And Jacob lived in the land where his father dwelled." There is a question, Why does it not say, "the land where his fathers dwelled"? Why specifically the dwelling place of Isaac? We should interpret that it is known that Jacob is regarded as the middle line, whose role is to correct the left line, called "Isaac's fear." But as for the right line, it is not within Jacob's qualities to correct. It is explained in the *Sulam* [Ladder commentary on *The Zohar*] that the middle line leans toward *Hesed* [mercy], so we have nothing to add to the right line.

But Isaac is the quality of judgment, so Jacob comes and places himself in the left line in order to correct it with the quality of mercy.

RASHI explains in another place that the writing connects the generations of Jacob with Joseph for several reasons. 1) The very essence of Jacob worked for Laban only because of Rachel, and the image of Joseph was similar to his, and everything that happened to Jacob, happened to Joseph: One was hated, and the other was hated; one, his brother wanted to kill him, and the other, his brothers wanted to kill him.

We should understand the connection between the matters, that Jacob worked for Laban only because of Rachel. It is known that there is the quality of Leah, called "concealed world," and the quality of Rachel, called "revealed world."

As is written in *The Zohar* concerning Moses, it is written, "path," for only Moses could walk in the quality of a "path," called "concealed world," but the rest of the people can walk only in a manner of "way," for "way" means the "highway," where everyone can walk, since "way" means *Hassadim* [mercies], and where the *Hesed* [sing. of *Hassadim*] is revealed, all the people can walk. Hence, Jacob worked for Rachel, meaning for the *Hassadim* to be revealed.

The revealing is mainly from the *Chazeh* and below, the quality of *NHY*, and the most important is the middle line, called *Yesod*, which is the quality of Joseph. This is why it was said, "Israel loved Joseph."

There is a middle line above, called *Tifferet*, which decides between *Hesed* and *Gevura*, and a middle line from the *Chazeh* and below, called *Yesod*, which decides between *Netzah* and *Hod*. The work is mainly to submit the left line, for specifically the middle line subdues it.

Hence, the left line and those who are attached to the left line want to cancel the middle line, since the left line can fight with the right line and does not need to cancel it, since it is not afraid of the right line. But from the middle line, they are afraid because the middle line cancels the left line.

This is why there is a desire to cancel the middle line above, in *Tifferet* and the middle line below, called *Yesod*, which are Jacob and Joseph.

RASHI also brings, "Jacob sought to dwell in peace, and Joseph's anger jumped on him. The righteous seek to dwell in peace, said the Creator. The righteous do not settle for what has been prepared for them in the next world, but they also seek to dwell in peace in this world." This seemingly contradicts what our sages said, "If you do so, happy are you in this world and happy in the next world."

We should interpret that the "next world" is called "the quality of *Bina*," "concealed world," which is the quality of Leah. "This world" is the quality of *Malchut*, "the revealed world." Hence, the quality of Jacob is *Tifferet*, which is from the *Chazeh* and above, regarded as the next world.

The righteous want peace in this world, too, which is the revealed world. This is the meaning of "Joseph's anger jumped on him," meaning that he wanted to extend the degree of Joseph, which is this world, *Yesod*, from the *Chazeh* and below, regarded as the "revealed world."

Jacob worked for Laban primarily for Rachel, to have revealed *Hassadim*, as our sages said, "The righteous have no rest, neither in the next world nor in this world, as was said, 'They will go from strength to strength.'"

379- Miracle and Choice

"Rabbi Yitzhak said, 'If there are serpents and scorpions in it [the pit], why is it written about Reuben, 'In order to save him from their hands, to return him to his father'? Did Reuben not fear for him, that those serpents and scorpions might harm him? ...But Reuben saw that while he was in his brothers' hands, the harm was certain, for he knew how much they hated him...' Because of this, in a place of snakes and scorpions, if he is righteous, the Creator will make a miracle for him. And sometimes, the merit of one's fathers assists a person and he is saved from them. But once one is given to one's enemies, few can survive" (*The Zohar, VaYeshev*, Items 130-132).

We should understand why "once one is given to one's enemies" the Creator does not make a miracle for him. Concerning saving, we find two manners: 1) where harm is found, 2) where harm is not found, meaning that there are animals that harm only out of appetite, and when they are not hungry, they do no harm.

Some harm by nature, since they have a natural desire to harm people and their manner is to always prey. We also find that there is hatred for the human race in general, and sometimes there is hatred for a specific person and not to the whole collective, meaning that the animal feels that this person wants to harm it, so it intends to harm him.

But here we find that the bad animals, which are serpents and scorpions, have no hatred toward this specific person, but to the whole of the human race. Therefore, this is not regarded as harm that is found, so it is possible to rely on a miracle. But in the hands of his brothers, who have a specific hatred for this person, this is harm that is present, and then it is forbidden to rely on a miracle.

We can also say that there is a difference between animals and people, since man can choose. Animals do harm because it is their nature, since the Creator planted in them a nature for craving it. It follows that everything they do is from the Creator and they haven't the power to overcome it, meaning not to do harm.

Therefore, where the Creator wants to make a miracle, it is also from the Creator, so we can rely on a miracle.

This is not so with man, who has the power to choose between doing harm and doing good. It follows that if the Creator makes a miracle for that person and saves him so the other does not harm him, then the Creator has taken from him the power of choice, and where there is a conflict with free choice, we must not rely on a miracle.

380- Anyone Who Sanctifies the Seventh – 2

Bo, Tav-Shin-Mem-Gimel, January 1983

"Anyone who sanctifies the seventh as he should ... his reward is great, according to his work." We should understand the meaning of "according to his work." Also, what is the novelty, since in corporeality we also receive reward only according to our work, and one who works overtime receives a higher salary than one who does not work overtime. Hence, what is the novelty in saying "his reward is great," and then saying that he will be rewarded only according to his work?

Our sages said, "He who walks and does not do, the reward for walking is in his hand." We should understand the meaning of doing. Our sages said, "Great is the learning that yields action, and it is not the learning that is most important, but the action" (*Kidushin* 40b).

Baal HaSulam interpreted that "an act" is when a person turns his vessels of reception into vessels of bestowal, as our sages said, "Let all your actions be for the sake of the Creator." The *Midrash* says that this doing is the meaning of "I have created the evil inclination; I have created the Torah as a spice," that this is the doing to which one should come.

Our sages said, "Man's inclination overcomes him every day. If the Creator did not help him, he would not overcome it." We should understand why the Creator did not give us the power to defeat the evil inclination. But if this is not within man's hands, why does the Creator not do everything?

In other words, why must one fight with the evil inclination while the Creator only helps him, but if the person does not begin the war, the Creator does not help him? Also, why does the Creator need man to make the war and then He will come and help him, as our sages said, "One should always vex the good inclination over the evil inclination," and RASHI interpreted, "make war with it" (*Berachot* 5a)? This implies that first, one must begin the war and then the Creator helps him.

Baal HaSulam explained what Abraham asked the Creator, "How will I know that I will inherit it?" "And He said unto Abraham, 'Know for certain that your descendants will be strangers in a land that is not theirs, and they will be enslaved and tortured four hundred years ... and afterward they will come out with great possessions.'"

Baal HaSulam explained that when he saw the promise that the Creator had given him, saying, "to give this land to you to inherit it," he said, "How will I know?" since there is no light without a *Kli* [vessel], and he did not see that his sons would have a need for these attainments, but that they would be content with little.

Therefore, He said to him, "Know for certain" that they will be in exile and will want to emerge from the exile. Then, without the help, they will not be able to come out from the exile in Egypt. Therefore, by this they will have to receive His help. Also, each time, they will need more bestowals, and by this they will come to need the light of Torah, for only the Torah is the spice.

This is as was said in *The Zohar*, "He who comes to purify is aided." It asks, "With what?" and it answers, "With a holy soul. When one is born, he is given *Nefesh* [soul] from the side of a pure beast. If he is rewarded more, he is given *Ruach* [spirit]." It follows that by this they will come to need the Creator's help and will thereby have the *Kelim* [vessels] to receive the inheritance of the land.

By this we can interpret what we asked, What does it mean that he walks and does not do? It is one who begins to walk on the path of the Creator to achieve "action." This is the meaning of "Anyone who sanctifies the *Shevi'i* [seventh]," and Baal HaSulam interpreted that *Shevi'i* means *Shebi-Hu* [He is in me].

Accordingly, it means that when one properly sanctifies the point in the heart within him, he begins to enter the exile in Egypt. At that time, he begins to see each time how far he is from the act of bestowal. Then, *Kelim* form within him, meaning deficiencies, which the Creator will later be able to fill.

It follows that a person must begin the war so as to have *Kelim* and a need for salvation and the help of the Creator, as was said, "If the Creator did not help him, he would not overcome it." It follows that He did not give man the ability to win the war on purpose, since through the war one obtains the *Kelim* and need for the abundance.

Hence, we need both: to enter the war so as to obtain *Kelim*, and the help that is required is that specifically the Creator will help him, since through the help he obtains the inheritance of the land that the Creator promised to Abraham.

Accordingly, "according to his work" means the opposite of corporeality. In corporeality, each time we do a good job, we are paid according to the quality of the work. But here it is the complete opposite: The more one sees that he is incapable of anything in *Kedusha* [holiness], the more help he needs. Hence, each time he must be given more help from above, meaning greater attainment.

It follows that "his reward is great according to his work," meaning that when he sees his flaw, he can receive a greater filling. This is the meaning of "going and not doing." He went to war but did not do, meaning that he could not make all his actions be for the sake of the Creator. He is told, "The reward for walking is in his hand," meaning that specifically one who walks but does not do needs the help of the Creator, and specifically by this he receives the inheritance of the fathers.

381- *The Lord Hears the Poor*

13 *Shevat, Tav-Shin-Lamed-Bet,* January 29, 1972

"Rabbi Hiya said, 'I wonder about this text, which says, 'For the Lord hears the poor.' Does He hear the poor and not others?' Rabbi Shimon said, 'It is because they are closer to the King, as it is written, 'A broken and a contrite heart, O God, You will not despise...'" Rabbi Shimon also said, 'Come and see, all the people in the world are seen before the Creator in body and in soul, but the poor appears before the Creator only in a soul, for his body is broken, and the Creator is nearer to the soul than to the body.'"

The *Sulam* [Ladder commentary on *The Zohar*] interprets that a poor is seen before the Creator only in a soul because his body is broken, and the Creator is closer to the soul than to the body (*The Zohar, BeShalach,* Item 367).

To understand the above, we must know what is a "poor." It is known that normally, a person can do things that will yield him two things: 1) knowledge, meaning that he will understand with his intellect the work that he is doing, namely the benefit from this action. Conversely, if he must do something that his mind mandates the opposite of what he is commanded to do, it is difficult for him to do this. 2) Pleasure. A person can do things that will yield him pleasure. But if he does something and does not enjoy, it is difficult for him to do this.

Therefore, when the two conditions in the act are met, meaning knowledge and pleasure, this act is regarded as a state of "wealth," since this act imparts upon him knowledge and pleasure, and there is nothing more in reality for which the creatures yearn.

If only one condition is met, meaning that the act will not give him knowledge, meaning that the mind will not obligate him to do this, yet he derives pleasure from the act, this is still regarded as an act, and he overcomes the mind and does the deed because that act is still not regarded as poor, since it still has something to give, meaning that the act gives him pleasure.

Sometimes, the act does not give him pleasure but still gives him knowledge, meaning that the intellect affirms the action. Here he needs greater reinforcement to follow the intellect and not need the pleasure.

However, when an act has nothing to give him, neither knowledge nor pleasure, meaning above reason and above pleasure, this is called "poor and indigent," when the act has no reward to give him.

Man has a body and a soul. The body is called a *Kli* [vessel] of the will to receive pleasure and knowledge. The soul is regarded as the power of bestowal that exists in man. And man has a body and a soul.

Hence, when one prays to the Creator and expects the Creator to impart upon him abundance, but in his situation, he has a healthy body, meaning that the body can still find knowledge and pleasure in his work, or at least one of them, this is still not considered poor and indigent, since the body will receive reward for his work.

However, when one wants to walk on the path of truth, meaning above reason, and in order to bestow, the body has nothing to receive, and then the body is considered broken. Thus, at that time he prays for the Creator to help him go with the soul, meaning with the desire to bestow. But the body interrupts him because he sees that he has nothing to gain from this path where a person wants to walk on the path of truth.

The Creator, who is the giver, is close to the soul. That is, there is equivalence with the soul because the soul wants to walk on the path of bestowal, and from this is all of his prayer. Therefore, the Creator hears his prayer.

This is the meaning of "For the Lord hears the poor." But when a rich man, or when the act imparts upon him knowledge and pleasure, or at least one of them, then his prayer is only for the sake of the body, meaning for the will to receive. This is why it is not written that "He hears the prayer of the rich," but only that of the poor, for He is close only to the poor, as close means equivalence of form.

382- When Pharaoh Sent the People

BeShalach, Tav-Shin-Mem-Aleph, January 1981

"And it came to pass that when Pharaoh sent the people, God did not lead them by the way of the land of the Philistines, for it was near, since God said, 'The people might change their minds when they see war and return to Egypt.' So God led the people around by the way of the desert to the Red Sea."

We must interpret this according to the prevalent reality. When one wants to walk on the path of truth, each one asks, "Why?"

"And it came to pass that when Pharaoh sent the people," meaning that the body as a whole is called "Pharaoh," and he must choose to let the people come out, meaning all the powers and thoughts will be the Creator's and not under his control. This means that all his powers will serve the body, but he will use them for the sake of the Creator.

Why did the Creator let them walk to the holy land—a land flowing with milk and honey, which the Creator promised to give the inheritance of the land to our holy fathers—through the far away road and did not give them the near road, as it is written, "And

God did not lead them by the way of the land of the Philistines, for it was near."

"Near" and "far" mean that which is close to the mind, which the mind approves of doing. Also, it should be close to the heart, to coincide with one's heart, meaning what the will to receive feels is to its own benefit, as it was with *Adam HaRishon* before the sin, when the scrutiny was by bitter and sweet, as it is written in the "Introduction to Panim Masbirot."

383- They Stood at the Foot of the Mountain

Shevat, Tav-Shin-Yod-Het, February 1958

"'And they stood at the bottom of the mountain.' Rabbi Abdimi Bar Hama Bar Hasa said, 'This teaches that He forced the mountain on them like a cask and said to them, 'If you accept the Torah, very well; and if not, there will it be your burial.' Rabbi Aha Bar Yaakov said, 'This presents a strong protest against the Torah.' Raba said, 'Nevertheless, the generation received it in the days of Ahasuerus, for it is written, 'the Jews observed and accepted,' they observed what they had already accepted'" (*Shabbat* [Sabbath] 88a).

In the *Tosfot*, "He forced on them... although they already preceded 'We will do' to 'We will hear,' lest they would regret when they saw the great fire when their soul departed. This is as he said, 'Did You not force on us the mountain like a cask?'" (*Avoda Zarah*, 2b), meaning that had He not forced them, they would have repentance. But here he says that they protested against the Torah, meaning for not receiving it, but in that they did not observe it there is repentance.

We should interpret the meaning of forcing on them the mountain like a cask. We should know that as there is coercion by suffering, there is coercion by pleasure. One who wants his friend to do what he wants, his friend must comply in two ways: either because of suffering, when he is afraid of him that if he does not do his will, he will afflict him, or because of a pleasure that entices him to do what he wants.

384- Observing Shabbat [Sabbath]

20 Shevat, Tav-Shin-Lamed-Bet, February 5, 1972

What is the role of observing Shabbat in ethics?

A person must keep himself from what disrupts the revelation of the *Kedusha* [holiness] of the Shabbat. The weekdays are the place of work, when one must exert to annul his will to receive, on which there were *Tzimtzum* [restriction] and concealment so as not to feel the existence of the Creator. One may believe that "The whole earth is full of His glory," but he does not feel it due to the *Tzimtzum* that was done so as to avoid the bread of shame.

When one exerts over this and is rewarded with the aim to bestow, he begins to feel the *Kedusha* and is rewarded with the quality of Shabbat. Hence, on Shabbat we should observe the Shabbat, so the intruders, meaning the will to receive, do not come. Otherwise, the quality of Shabbat will promptly depart from him.

385- I Will Carry You on the Wings of Eagles

"And I will carry you on the wings of eagles and I will bring you to Me."

RASHI: "'On the wings of eagles,' as an eagle carries its nestlings on its wings, saying, 'Better the arrow hits me and not my sons.'"

The word *Hetz* [arrow] comes from the word *Hatzitza* [division], as was said about the verse, "Hezekiah turned his face to the wall," so that nothing will divide between him and the wall (*Berachot* 5b), and also from the word *Mehitza* [partition].

Division means separation, which separates two things. Concerning the partition, it is explained in *Baba Batra*, "The partners who wanted to make a partition in the yard build the wall in the middle."

He explains there that "Partition means 'a wall,' a wall that separates. And you say, 'A wall divides,' as it is written, 'And it parted the congregation.'" This means that a partition means a discernment that divides something into two. Also, it is written in Psalms, "Your arrows are sharp; nations will fall under You in the heart of the King's enemies" (45:6).

To understand all the above, it is known that the *Tzimtzum* [restriction] was in order to have equivalence of form. For this reason, a concealment was placed, which is called "unrevealed Providence," by which emerges a concealment of the face of the Creator, and for which there is work in choice. It takes a lot of work for one to believe that the Creator leads the world as The Good Who Does Good, and this is considered that a wall has emerged, which separates us from the Creator, as it is written, "He is standing behind our wall." When one prays, he should see that nothing parts, meaning he should unite himself with the Creator in equivalence of form, meaning that it will be for the sake of the Creator.

When a person is concerned with himself, he is in a state of separation. Hence, when thoughts of separation come, it is called "arrows" that kill the spirituality in man. This is called "Your arrows," of the Creator, are "sharp," killing the vitality of *Kedusha* [holiness]. All the arrows that one suffers stem only from the concealment, since the Creator concealed Himself.

It follows that the creatures slander Providence, and who caused it? The Creator Himself. This is the meaning of "He said, 'Better the arrow hits me,'" meaning the slander being said about Him, "and not my sons," since through the concealment He has made, there will be an opportunity and possibility that they will not be left with the arrows, meaning that they will not be in separation.

Precisely by overcoming at the time of concealment, they will come to equivalence of form. Otherwise, they will remain separated, called "partition," or "a separating wall," where precisely by this, "I will bring you to Me."

386- This Is the Day that the Lord Has Made

Shevat, Tav-Shin-Lamed-Het, January-February 1978

"This is the day which the Lord has made; we will rejoice and be glad in it." "This is the day" means that "this" is called "day," and not something else. What is it when the Lord "makes"? It is that each one will attain that "we will rejoice and be glad in it." "In it" means in the Creator, in *Dvekut* [adhesion] with the Creator, which is called "equivalence of form," which is that each and every one will understand that there is no greater joy than to bestow contentment upon one's Maker. This is what we hope for. When the general public achieves this degree, it will be called "the end of correction."

387- A Decent Judge and an Indecent Judge

Shevat, Tav-Shin-Mem-Aleph, January 1981

Baal HaTurim interprets the words, "The portion 'Judges' was placed adjacent to the portion 'Altar,' to tell you that one who appoints a decent judge, it is as though he built an altar." He learns this from what our sages said, "One who appoints an indecent judge, it is as though he built a stage by the altar" (Sanhedrin 7b). This means that if he appoints a decent judge, it is as though he built an altar.

To understand his words, we must interpret what is an altar, what is a judge, and why an indecent judge is as one who seemingly plants an Asherah next to the altar, and what is an Asherah.

A "judge" means as our sages said, "No calamity comes to the world but because of the judges of Israel" (*Shabbat* 139a). We should ask, Is there no one crueler than the judges of Israel, that because of them calamity comes to the world?

However, this is as we said several times about the verse, "You shall appoint judges and officers in all your gates." This means that in everything that one debates whether or not to do the act, he has judges, meaning he has thoughts and views that lean to this side or the other.

This is called "the judges of Israel." Within every person there are judges that judge everything, whether it is worthwhile. If the judge is honest, it is considered that he builds an altar, and *The Zohar* calls "an altar" *Malchut*, which is permanent.

It was said that by this he sacrifices the evil inclination, as our sages said, "He who wants to live will put himself to death," as well as "The Torah exists only in one who puts himself to death over it," since before he takes upon himself the burden of the kingdom of heaven, he is called a "gentile," and it is forbidden to teach Torah to idol-worshippers. As Baal HaSulam said, any place that is forbidden means that it is impossible even if he wants to.

Therefore, if he is a decent judge, it is as though he builds an altar, and if he is an indecent judge, it is as though he plants an Asherah, which is idol-worship, by the altar. In other words, where he should have built an altar, he builds idol-worship and says it is an altar.

Asherah comes from the word *Osher* [happiness]. That is, when he feels happy through his work in Torah and *Mitzvot* [commandments] in which he engages, meaning when the body and reason agree that the matter is worthwhile. But if reason does not agree, he cannot work above reason, so this is called idol-worship in the manner of Asherah.

Conversely, an altar must be acceptance of the burden of the kingdom of heaven above reason. This is called an "honest judge," who can rule that we must go above reason, and his external reason does not decide. But one who is dishonest, understands that everything must follow his own intellect, which is within reason.

388- *These Are the Ordinances*

Idol-worshippers have judges and Israel have judges, and you do not know the difference between them. There is an allegory about a patient that a doctor came to see. He told his family, "Feed him anything he wants." He went to another patient and told them, "Be sure that he does not eat this or that food." They said to him: "You said to the first one that he can eat whatever he wants, but to the other one you said that he should not eat this or that food." He replied, "The first one will not live; this is why I said that he can eat whatever he wants. But as for the one who will live, I said, 'Be careful with him.'"

Likewise, idol-worshippers have judges and they do not engage in Torah and do not do it, as was said, "And I also gave them laws that are not good and ordinances that they will not live in" (Ezekiel 20). But what is it written about the *Mitzvot* [commandments]? "The one who does them will live by them" (Leviticus 18).

We should understand: 1) The verse that the *Midrash* brings from Ezekiel refers to the judges of the idol-worshippers, but the verse concerns the people of Israel! 2) The allegory about the doctor who said, "Feed him anything he wants," meaning he has no limitations, but the verse, "laws that are not good and ordinances that they will not live in," implies that there are rules and limitations contradicting the allegory.

We should interpret that the intention of the *Midrash* when it says that idol-worshippers have judges, it is not the nations of the world. Rather, it concerns Israel. When he calls them "judges of idol-worshippers," it means that all the *Mitzvot* that they do and that the mind obligates them to, and which do not follow the path of faith, to achieve *Lishma* [for Her sake], that mind is called "a judge of idol-worshippers."

Since all that the judge obligates is on the path of *Lo Lishma* [not for Her sake], meaning that his aim is not to thereby achieve *Dvekut* [adhesion] in life, it follows that he is not intended to live.

To this one he said, "Feed him," meaning his nourishments of life is anything he asks, and he has no special conditions because he will not survive. Thus, what he does is of little consequence.

This is not so with the judges of Israel, when the power to judge is because of Israel, meaning because of faith to achieve *Dvekut*. At that time, he has special conditions, for not from everything is he permitted to receive vitality. Rather, with every thing, he must be careful not to eat this or that food. In other words, he must not receive vitality even of *Mitzvot* and good deeds, unless it brings him to *Dvekut*.

This is the meaning of the prohibition not to eat certain things, meaning not to draw vitality from something specific: from the will to receive.

This settles the two questions: 1) His intention is Israel and not the nations of the world. 2) Even in a state of *Lo Lishma*, there are *Mitzvot* and rules, but they are not good, as our sages said, "If he is not rewarded, it becomes to him a potion of death" (*Yoma* 72b). However, we must try to make the judge be from Israel, and then we will cling to the Life of Lives.

389- Raise a Contribution for Me – 1

Adar Tav-Shin-Mem, February 1980

"Raise a contribution for Me." RASHI interprets "for me" as "for My name." "From every man whose heart is willing." RASHI interprets, "Words of donation are words of good will. 'You shall raise My contribution.' 'Take' means against their will, which contradicts 'whose heart is willing,' which means voluntarily and not by coercion."

It is written in *The Zohar* that *Truma* [contribution/donation] means *Tarum* [raise] *Hey* [the letter], meaning we must raise the *Hey*, which is *Malchut*. It is also written in *The Zohar* that *Teshuva* [repentance] means *Tashuv* [return] *Hey* [the letter] to the *Vav*, meaning that a person must raise the *Hey*, which is regarded as the *Shechina* [Divinity] in the dust. We must raise the *Shechina* from the dust, meaning that the quality that is called "for the sake of the Creator" is in exile.

Since man is built from the desire to receive for himself—and the desire to bestow is under the control of the will to receive, and one cannot aim anything to be in order to bestow, since the will to receive controls him—one who wishes to walk on the path of truth must do everything where he does not see self-benefit, and he must overcome and do everything that is connected to *Kedusha* [holiness], which is called "you shall take my contribution," against your will, without the body's consent.

This is called "He is forced until he says, 'I want.'" When he says, "I want," this is called "repentance," meaning that he cannot do anything voluntarily until the Creator helps him and gives him the spirit of repentance. This is called "Let the *Hey* return," relating to his *Malchut*, which is the point of *Tzimtzum* [restriction], on which, namely on the will to receive, was the correction of the *Masach* [screen].

At that time, as the *Vav* of the name *HaVaYaH* is called a "Giver," so his will to receive achieves the quality of bestowal, and then he can make a contribution, meaning lower his *Hey*. When he is rewarded with this, "From every man whose heart is willing, you shall raise My contribution." This means that what was previously compulsory will not be voluntary, as RASHI interpreted concerning "his heart is willing."

It follows that "From every man whose heart is willing" means that now that you are about to take My contribution against his will, know that now it is in a state of "his heart is willing," that now he has a good will because his *Malchut* has already been lifted from the dust.

This is as it is written in *The Zohar*, "That *Yod* that Esau threw to the back, Jacob took to the head, since Jacob is at the head," referring to the point of *Yod* that was restricted; now it is in order to bestow.

390- Coercion and Inversion

Shevat-Adar Aleph, Tav-Shin-Mem-Aleph, February 1981

"Raise a contribution for Me; from every man whose heart is willing, you shall raise My contribution." RASHI interprets "for Me," "for My name." "Whose heart is willing," RASHI interprets, "meaning donation, good will."

We should understand the following:

1) "Taking" means by force. "His heart is willing" is good will. This contradicts "will take."

2) Why does it write, "My contribution"? This implies that it is the contribution of the Creator. It should have said, "Take the contribution of he whose heart is willing"; why does it say, "My contribution"?

3) What does it mean when it says, "for My name"?

4) We need to understand the common question about the verse, "Wherever I mention My name." It should have said, "You mention."

The thing is that there are two degrees: "coercion" and "inversion." Such as this we find in what our sages said in *Avot de Rabbi Natan*, "Who is a hero? He who makes his foe his friend."

"Hero" means one who conquers his inclination, who is regarded as "forced against his will." This is the meaning of "take," implying by force. Afterward, he promises that you will come to an inversion, where his foe becomes his friend.

This is the meaning of "from every man whose heart is willing," meaning that afterward he will have a good will. This is as Baal HaSulam said about the words of *The Zohar*, "When one is born, he is given a soul from the side of the pure beast." This means that his beastly soul will agree to follow the ways of the Creator.

He said, "When a man is born and enters *Kedusha* [holiness]," it is a sign that he has been rewarded with a soul of a pure beast, that his beastly soul agrees to walk in the ways of the Creator. This is called "inversion." It follows that first, one must take against his will although his body disagrees to walk on the path of truth which is called "for Me," "for My name."

When we are told to walk on a path where everything is for the sake of the Creator, the body resists. But later it will be rewarded with "his heart is willing," meaning that the body will agree. This is the meaning of "whose heart is willing, you shall take My contribution," meaning that the "for the sake of the Creator" that was there before, as in "You shall take My contribution," called "for the sake of the Creator," afterward we are rewarded with it being in the manner of "whose heart is willing," voluntarily.

Concerning his interpretation of "for Me" as "for My name," indeed, a person has nothing to give to the Creator, as it is written, "If you are right, what will you give Him?" All that one can give to the Creator is the intention, called "for My name." There is nothing more that he can give Him because the Creator has no deficiencies so He can be given something. Thus, all that we give Him is the intention.

Even the intention for the sake of the Creator is not for the Creator's benefit but for man's benefit, for by this, man will receive all the pleasures without the bread of shame, since through equivalence of form, he emerges from receiving to a state of giving. At that time, a person can receive all the pleasures.

This is called "for My name." If the Creator can say that this place is "My name," since the person said that he does not want anything for his own benefit, but everything is for the Creator, then the Creator can mention His name there, since the man has cancelled his own authority and made the place for the Creator.

At that time, "I will come to you and bless you." At that time, the blessing of the Creator can come there—all that the Creator wants to bestow upon His creations.

391- The Creator Did Not Try Job

Adar, Tav-Shin-Lamed-Bet, February 1972

"Rabbi Shimon said, 'The Creator did not try Job and did not test him as He tested the rest of the righteous, since it is not written about him, 'And God tried Job' ... and he was not told to give, but was handed over to the slanderer by the judgment of the Creator'" (*The Zohar, TeTzaveh*, Item 41).

We should understand the difference between Job, who is called "righteous gentiles," and Israel. With Job, we see that the Creator did not try him, whereas with Abraham He did try him.

We see here that there is an act and there is an intention, and in both, there is the matter of a test. That is, to Abraham, the test was given in both action and intention whether his work of the Creator was with joy, meaning if he were happy that he was now doing the Creator's will. With Job, he was tested only on the intention and not on the action, since it is implied that the Creator knew that he would not be able to endure a test on the action. For this reason, He tested him only with regard to the intention.

(We should also say that it is the same if we do not want to give and we believe that everything is guided by the Creator, so we should justify the Maker and not blemish our love for the Creator due to the absence of a few things that we think we need. That is... not receive from Him what one needs or give him what one needs.)

In this, there is a difference between the righteous gentiles and the righteous, since those two degrees exist in man. Before one achieves the degree of Israel, in the sense that man is a small world, he has the qualities of nations of the world, righteous gentiles, and Israel. When a person begins to walk on the path of the Creator, he is called "righteous gentiles." At that time, his tests are only on the intention and not on the action, since he is not given trials in the action but only in the intention.

That is, there is a rule that every person has grievances against the Creator that He does not give him what he wants. He understands that the Creator must give him everything he needs, as it is written, "His mercies are over all His works," and it is the conduct of the Good to do good. Thus, everything that one thinks he needs, it is as though he had it and the Creator took it away from him.

Thus, the act is not in his possession to say that he is tested not to do the action, since he was not given it to begin with. And as for the trial, it is as though he had these things that he is now demanding, and they were taken away from him, and all that he has in the trial is the intention. That is, we should say that all that the Creator does, He does for the best, and to be in joy and in love as though the Creator has given him all that he demands. This is called "trial on intention," as it was with Job, but the intention is whether he can justify the judgment.

But when one is rewarded with the quality of Israel, he is given the trial in practice, too. That is, he is given all the good things, and the person himself must be ready to return it all and not receive any more than he is certain that it will be only in order to bestow.

It is like Purim, where Baal HaSulam said that the meaning of the *Megillah* [Purim scroll/book of Esther] means that then was a time of *Hitgalut* [revealing]. Haman said about this that we must walk in the manner of knowing. This is the meaning of "and do not do the king's laws." Conversely, Mordechai argued that the revelation comes only in order to withstand the test and to take upon themselves the concealment, which is a trial in action.

392- A Hand on the Throne of the Lord – 2

Shabbat [Sabbath], 11 Adar, Tav-Shin-Tet-Vav, March 5, 1955

"And he said, 'A hand on the throne of the Lord; the Lord has war against Amalek from generation to generation.'" RASHI interprets, "The Creator swore that His name will not be whole and His throne will not be whole until He blots out the name of Amalek," meaning that the name is split in half.

To understand this, we must first present the verse, "In Yod-Hey [the Lord], the Lord is an everlasting rock." That is, He depicted the worlds with the two letters Yod-Hey.

"The world was created with ten utterances. What does that mean? After all, it could have been created with one utterance. Yet, it was created in ten utterances in order to avenge the wicked who are destroying the world" (*Avot*, Chapter 5).

There is a famous question: Does the Creator complain against His creations? It is like one who gives to his friend a cup that is worth one pound to watch over it. If he loses it, he must pay only one pound, but the landlord paid ten pounds. Should he have paid ten pounds for this?

The thing is that in the beginning, He created the world with the quality of judgment. When He saw that the world cannot exist, He associated with it the quality of mercy, for by this, man will be able to achieve completion. Conversely, when it was in the quality of judgment, it was impossible for man to be able to emerge from his evil inclination.

This is the meaning of "to give a good reward to the righteous." In other words, by the correction of the quality of mercy, called "ten utterances," there is existence to the world.

"And to avenge the wicked," meaning now that they have been given the chance to emerge from the control of the inclination, they still do not want to. For this they deserve to lose the world, although there is the correction of ten utterances there, which is easier than before the correction, meaning in one utterance.

393- Carrier of Iniquity

Adar, Tav-Shin-Lamed-Tet, March 1979

"Carrier of iniquity." The Creator snatches the bill of iniquities and by this, a sentencing to the side of merit takes place (presented in *Torah Temimah*).

We should understand that when one is half merits and half iniquities, how can one decide to the side of merit? The advice for this is prayer: One should pray to the Creator to snatch a bill of iniquities and by this he will be able to decide.

That is, seeing oneself as half guilty is not a matter of standing before the courthouse of above. Rather, it is about a person seeing on himself that the forces are equal and he can subjugate the good before the bad.

However, if there are equal forces in the body, and he must decide, who will give him more strength to decide to the side of merit, since they are equal forces? The advice is for one to pray to the Creator to carry the iniquity, meaning that the Creator will snatch the promissory note [debt], and thereby there will be a decision to the good side.

Thus, what is man's work when he is told he must decide? It is only prayer, and he has no strength for more than that. Since both the good and the bad are equal forces. Who decides? Through the prayer, by the Creator carrying the iniquity, there is already a decision.

394- When You Count the Heads of the Children of Israel to Number Them

Adar, Tav-Shin-Chaf-Vav, March 1966

"When you count the heads of the children of Israel to number them, each one of them shall give a ransom for his soul ... half a *Shekel* ... The rich shall not give more and the poor shall not give less."

We should ask, 1) What is the meaning of the word "head"? 2) "A ransom for his soul," what is the sin for which he must give a ransom for his soul, which is atonement? 3) Why specifically half a *Shekel*, why not give something complete, meaning a whole *Shekel*?

We should interpret this in ethics. There are two kinds of answers: in action, and in intention. "Head" means mind and knowledge, where there is the matter of intention, as it is written, "A prayer without an intention is like a body without a soul." The intention belongs to the soul and the spirit, whereas the action belongs to the body.

This is implied by the word "heads" of the children of Israel, a ransom for his soul." In other words, that which one sinned in the quality of the soul, meaning repentance in the intention, since this repentance applies to everyone, for man was created with a will to receive for himself, and in order to observe the Torah and *Mitzvot* [commandments] in order to bestow, this is repentance that each and every one must do.

In terms of the action, it can be said that he never sinned because since the day he was born he was given good upbringing and careful watch. But on the intention, there is the main choice that one must do, since on the intention there is no coercion. Only on the action can one force himself, but on the thought, meaning the intention, it is out of one's hands. Rather, this is a gift from above. It was implied about this, "Were it not for the help of the Creator, he would not overcome it."

We should interpret that half means that only the act is in man's hands, and not the aim. Hence, it is implied by the "half," meaning that if a person gives half, meaning the action, the Creator will give him the other half, namely the intention.

We should also understand that there is faith, which is charity, and there is Torah, which is a gift. A person must only give faith, which is charity, and this is called "the correction of creation." At that time, the Creator gives the other half, which is Torah. A gift is called "the purpose of creation," and the ransom for his soul pertains to the correction of creation.

395- The Quality of "Still" and the Quality of "Vegetative"

Adar, Tav-Shin-Lamed-Tet, March 1979

It is known that there is the quality of "general" and the quality of "particular." The general public in Israel are called "still." This is regarded as a "beast," which is the quality of *Nefesh*, from the word *Nefisha* [stillness/rest], which has only general movement, and each species has its own unique quality for everyone.

Conversely, the quality of "vegetative" has its own personal movement. This is called "man," "for man is a tree of the field." In the vegetative, there is always renewal, which constantly grows.

In the "still," it is not apparent how it grows. This is called "general movement," where in general there is growth in the "still." Hence, the general public are always generally fine.

Conversely, in the individual, those who belong to the quality "man is a tree of the field," there must always be renewals, meaning growth. They constantly grow because this is the manner of the manifestation of the upper abundance, as in "The Son of David [Messiah] does not come before all the souls in the body have been consumed" (*Yevamot* 62a).

Hence, there is no renewal of light that does not extend from *Ein Sof* [infinity], since in this manner the abundance expands one at a time. For this reason, when one constantly renews his work, he is always in a state of "walking." If he remains in his degree, he is brought down from above, and then he becomes "descending."

This is so in order for him to need to ascend once more to a new degree, since each time he rises back up, it does not mean that he ascends to his previous degree, but it is always a new state. It follows that either he ascends or descends, but "standing" does not pertain to the quality of man.

Conversely, people who belong to the quality of "still of *Kedusha* [holiness]," are regarded as "standing," meaning they do not need to fall from their degree. Rather, they are in the quality of "still," having only collective motion and not individual motion as in the vegetative.

396- Behold, the Lord Has Called the Name Bezalel

25 Adar Aleph, Tav-Shin-Lamed-Het, March 4, 1978

"And Moses said to the sons of Israel, 'Behold, the Lord has called the name Bezalel.'"

We should understand what it means that Moses tells the people of Israel, "Behold, the Lord has called the name Bezalel."

It is written in the *Midrash*, in the portion *Truma*, "Since the Creator said to Moses, 'Make Me a tabernacle,' He began to ask and said, 'The glory of the Creator is filled with upper ones and lower ones, yet He says, 'Make Me a tabernacle.'"

Moses said about this, "He dwells in the shelter of the Most High." What is, "Will abide in the shadow of the Almighty"? It does not say here, "in the shadow of God," "in the shadow of the

Merciful one," "in the shadow of the Gracious one," but rather "in the shadow of the Almighty," the shadow that Bezalel had made. This treatise is seemingly perplexing. How can it be said that Moses thought corporeal thoughts, since "The whole earth is full of His glory," so how will He enter the tabernacle that he has built?

Also, our sages said, "He constrained His *Shechina* [Divinity] between the curtains of the ark." Who can attribute a corporeal place?

We should ask similar to what perplexed Moses: Since "The whole earth is full of His glory," yet the creatures do not feel His glory, for if they felt His glory, there would not be wicked in the world, so how can it be that through the tabernacle they will feel His glory?

The *Midrash* replies to this, "Will abide in the shadow of the Almighty," meaning that the tabernacle that was made so they would feel that the *Shechina* is present in Israel was by the "the shadow of the Almighty."

As Baal HaSulam said, "Shadow" means that precisely where there is sun, we can speak of a shadow, which we create against the sun. "Sun" means knowing. That is, if the matter is as clear to you as the sun." "Shadow" means faith above reason, which is against knowing. So why must there be specifically faith? Why is it forbidden to serve the Creator with knowledge? It is that He said to His world, "Enough! Spread no farther."

It is explained in the words of the ARI that the name *Shadai* [Almighty] is that when the worlds expanded, He said to his world "*Dai* [enough], spread no farther." At that time, he interprets the *Yod-Dalet* [fourteen] discernments called "from *Chazeh* of *Yetzira* and below, and the world of *Assiya*, where there are fourteen *Sefirot*, where it is the section of the *Klipot* [shells/peels].

Klipa [sing. of *Klipot*] is the quality of receiving in order to receive. Until that place, we can feel *Kedusha* [holiness], but in the place of the fourteen, it is impossible to feel *Kedusha*. *Yod-Dalet* [fourteen/ *Yad* (hand)] means vessels of reception, from the words, "for a hand attains." Reception applies in both mind and heart, since where there is knowledge, we receive in vessels of reception.

For this reason, we must use *Kelim* [vessels] of faith where there is no grip to the vessels of reception, but only vessels of bestowal. Otherwise, the light of faith cannot be present. This is why it is called "by the shadow of the Almighty," meaning because *Shadai* [the Almighty] the shadow was made. By this, it becomes possible to feel His glory.

It therefore follows that the merit of the tabernacle is that we are able to feel that the *Shechina* is present in Israel specifically on vessels of bestowal. This is called "Constrained His *Shechina* between the curtains of the ark." "Constraining" means that specifically through vessels of bestowal and vessels of faith there is the ability to feel Him. But without these *Kelim*, although "The whole earth is full of His glory," we do not feel Him.

Moses said about this, "He dwells in the shelter of the Most High, will abide in the shadow of the Almighty." Moses said about this to the people of Israel, that precisely by the name Bezalel was the tabernacle made, meaning that precisely through the shadow, we will come to feel His glory.

397- *Take from Among You a Contribution to the Lord*

Adar Aleph, Tav-Shin-Mem-Aleph, February 1981

"Take from among you a contribution to the Lord; whoever is of a willing heart shall bring it."

The matter of taking from you means actual taking, from a person's actual body. *The Zohar* interprets that *Truma* [contribution] means *Tarum Hey* [to lift the (letter) *Hey*], where we must raise the *Hey* to the *Vav*.

Similarly, it is written in *The Zohar* that *Teshuva* [repentance] is called "the *Hey* will return to the *Vav*," which means, as he interprets in the *Sulam* [Ladder commentary on *The Zohar*] that *Hey* is called *Malchut*, which means that the *Kli* [vessel] that receives must be returned to the *Vav*, for *Vav* is called "the Giver." When one engages in matters of bestowal, by an act below, the act above is awakened.

At that time, it causes what will be included in the *Malchut* in the root of his soul, which will also be in order to bestow, like the man below engages in bestowal. This is called "the unification of the Creator and His *Shechina* [Divinity]."

With this we understand the contribution of the Creator, which is as it is written, "The Merciful one will *raise* for us the fallen hut of David." This is called "raising the *Shechina* from the dust." Concerning a fall in corporeality, we see that sometimes it becomes known that the gold fell in the world, meaning lost its value and it is not as valuable as it should be.

It is likewise with spirituality. If spirituality does not have the value it is supposed to have, we do not pay for it the required payment. And since one is demanded to work with devotion, if a person does not have the real value, to make it worthwhile to pay the price of devotion, this is considered that the *Shechina* is in the dust.

It is about this that we pray, "The Merciful one will raise for us the fallen hut of David," meaning that the Creator will give us the feeling of the exaltedness of the holy work. This is the meaning of "Take from among you a contribution to the Lord," meaning that the vessels of reception of a person will give to the Creator, which is called annulment in devotion to the Creator.

By giving the awakening to raise the *Hey* from the dust, the Creator will help from above, so it is "Whoever is of a willing heart shall bring it." This means that the whole heart will agree to the matter of devotion to the Creator. "Whoever is of a willing heart shall bring it" is called "He who comes to purify is aided."

But before this, we must begin the work with faith above reason in both mind and heart, meaning in order to bestow.

This is so because those people who have no work in corporeality, it is because they do not want to work for low wages. But if everyone agreed to work without reward, everyone would have work. But since they want a price for their work, the employer cannot always employ workers because he cannot pay for their work.

Hence, without payment, he does not want to work and therefore does not work. But in spirituality, when it is said that one must work without reward, this is because of *Dvekut* [adhesion], called "equivalence of form," so there will not be the bread of shame. All of one's work should be based on, "For He is great and ruling." Hence, when we come to a state where we do not receive anything for ourselves, this is all of our importance.

398- The Numbered Things of the Tabernacle – 2

"These are the numbered things of the tabernacle, the tabernacle of the testimony."

It is written in *Midrash Rabbah*, "Why does it write 'tabernacle' twice? Rabbi Shmuel said that it was mortgaged twice ['mortgage' and 'tabernacle' have the same root in Hebrew]. This is why the members of the great assembly say, 'We have acted very corruptly,' and corruption is mortgaging, as it is said, 'he will not corrupt [take mortgage].' What is the testimony? Rabbi Shimon said, 'It is a testimony to all the people of the world that there is forgiveness to Israel.'"

We should understand what is a mortgage. Normally, one who lends money to his friend and wants to be certain that he will repay his debt, receives from him a mortgage. Thus, what does a tabernacle mean here? that the Creator reclaimed the Temple?

What should Israel pay that they did not pay, and for which He took the tabernacle so He could be certain that we will pay the mortgage? Also, what is the testimony, and why does it immediately imply that the tabernacle was mortgaged twice?

It is written in *The Zohar*, "'These are the numbered things of the tabernacle.' Rabbi Shimon started, 'In the beginning God created.'" We should understand the conjunction between the "In the beginning" and the counted things of the tabernacle? It is written in *The Great Midrash*, "In the beginning... created... created from where?" We should understand the meaning of existence from absence.

But first we must understand what is "we," who must pay the debt and redeem the tabernacle. Creation is called "will to receive," and this is called "existence from absence," and the need for concealment is because of the bread of shame.

Rabbi Yohanan and Rabbi Elazar both said, "When one needs people, his face changes as chrome. It was said, 'as when vile things become high in the eyes of people.' What is 'become high'? There is a bird in the coastal cities whose name is *Ke-Rum* [become high]. When the sun shines on it, it changes into several colors" (*Berachot* 6b).

The sun refers to abundance. "The coastal cities" are those on the seashore. The "sea" is called *Hochma* [wisdom]. A "bird" is when a person lifts himself from worldliness, for it is the conduct of the bird that when it flies, it conceals its legs and spreads its wings. Legs means spies, and wings are covers for the head, as it is written, "And with two, it covers its face." "Covering" means faith.

When the abundance appears over it, he is ashamed, meaning he feels the bread of shame.

The Temple means the revelation of pleasures called the "instilling of the *Shechina* [Divinity]." The payments mean that it will be reception in order to bestow, and the reception of the mortgage, as is implied right in the beginning, is a testimony that there is forgiveness, for He took the Temple only as collateral, and He is destined to return it to us soon in our days, amen.

Thus, there is a testimony that there is forgiveness, meaning that He intends to return to us when we have paid our debt, meaning when we have the power of bestowal, at which time there will be *Dvekut* [adhesion], a certain measure of revelation of His Godliness to an extent that the lower ones can receive.

It follows that a soul is only a part of the *Shechina* [Divinity], which is called "The whole of the soul of Israel," meaning the full measure that the Creator wants to be attained. This is called "the desire to do good to His creations." A "soul" is regarded as a part of the *Shechina*, meaning a part that the lower one can attain according to the measure of the purity.

This is why our sages said, "Moses is tantamount to 600,000," meaning that Moses was rewarded with a measure of revelation of Godliness that was available to be revealed to the whole of Israel. This is the meaning of "The *Shechina* speaks from the mouth of Moses," meaning that Moses was rewarded with the general revelation called *Shechina*.

399- The Tabernacle of the Testimony

"These are the numbered things of the tabernacle, the tabernacle of the testimony." RASHI interpreted "the tabernacle of the testimony" as a testimony to Israel that the Creator forgave them the incident of the calf, for He "installed His *Shechina* [Divinity] among them." There, in *Daat Zkenim*, he brings another view, that it was a testimony to Moses. This is so because when he was suspected of stealing *Shekalim* from the work of the tabernacle, Moses said to them, "I want the tabernacle to be a testimony, and they recounted and found that they were placed in the hooks for the pillars."

Maimonides says, "How is repentance? Until He knows the mysteries will testify that he will not return to folly." The question people ask is if a person can ask the Creator to testify to him, so that by this he will know that his repentance is worthy. Baal HaSulam explained that if a person has achieved repentance, where his only aim is to bestow, the spirit of the Creator immediately lies upon him.

400- Half a *Shekel* – 1

Adar Aleph, Tav-Shin-Mem-Aleph, March 1981

It is written in *The Zohar* (*Pekudei*): "To give half a *Shekel*... stones to weigh with, this is Yod, Vav between the two *Heys*... the rich shall not give more and the poor shall not give less," etc.

We should discern that the manner of the work is to walk in the middle pillar. The "rich" is one who is happy with his lot. Whatever understanding he has in the *Mitzva* [commandment] is enough for him. For example, when he cloaks in *Tzitzit* [prayer shawl] and says the blessing for the *Tzitzit*, it suffices him and he is completely satisfied with observing the *Mitzva*, as though he kept it in all of its details and precisions.

He must say that he has no need for any addition or intention, but he suffices for the practice itself in order to feel in this that he is observing the *Mitzvot* [commandments] of the King. He will say, "There are several people in the world who were not given a desire and yearning to observe and do the *Mitzva*, while he was given a desire and thought."

For this reason, he is happy with his lot, that he has the ability to observe the commandments of the Creator. This is called "because he desires mercy," and he has no need for an intention in the *Mitzva*. At that time, he is called "rich."

This is called "the first *Hey*," which is the quality of *Bina*, which is "desiring mercy." Thus, he becomes a *Merkava* [structure/chariot] for the *Sefira* of *Bina*.

"Poor" means that he is poor in knowledge, that he has no intention in the *Mitzva* or knowledge or understanding about the connection between man and the *Mitzvot*. Also, it is a lot of work to feel that the intention we must aim is that it will be in order to bestow. He sees that he has already observed the *Mitzvot* many times, and the *Mitzvot* were given in order to cleanse people, but he has not moved a bit from the time he began to engage in *Mitzvot*.

At that time, he does not feel any ascent in degree. On the contrary, each time, he sees how far he is from the real intention.

It is written about it, "The rich will not give more than half," meaning that he will not have more than half the sensation of wholeness of one who is content with his lot, but only half and not more. In the other half in the order of the work, he should be as one who is poor and see his feeling from the perspective of his intention. At that time, he diminishes himself, meaning that there is absolutely no taste or feeling in his work.

However, he does not diminish himself more than half. He should leave the other half to work in the quality of "rich," meaning as one who is happy with his lot, and whatever portion of the work he has, even if it is in a manner of *Katnut* [smallness/infancy], he will still feel wholeness. This is called "the middle pillar." He must not deviate one way or the other; rather, he must always weigh so they are equal. At that time, we can achieve wholeness.

401- Hear, O Israel

Adar Bet, Tav-Shin-Mem-Aleph, March 1981

"Hear, O Israel, the Lord our God, the Lord is one." What is "one"? It is the assembly of Israel that is united in the Creator, who is *Zeir Anpin*. Rabbi Shimon said that the *Zivug* [coupling] of the *Dechar* [Aramaic: male] and *Nukva* [Aramaic: female] is called "one," since the place where the *Nukva* is placed is called "one."

What is the reason? It is because a male without a female is called "half a body," and half is not one. When the two halves of the body connect, they become one body, and then they are called "one" (*The Zohar*, *VaYikra*, Item 101).

It is written, "Here is a place with Me." Baal HaSulam interpreted that the acronym *Aleph-Tav-Yod* [letters of the words "with Me"] is *Emuna* [faith], *Tefillah* [prayer], *Yegia* [labor].

A person should begin the work of the Creator on the right, called "male," which is wholeness, called happy with his share, which is regarded as "desiring mercy." Whatever flavor and vitality he has in Torah and *Mitzvot* [commandments] is enough for him to labor in Torah and *Mitzvot* because he believes in private Providence, that such is the will of the Creator, and feels that he is a complete person, and thanks and praises the Creator for giving him a part in His work.

This is called a "male," when he feels himself as whole and he is always happy and observes, "Serve the Lord with gladness."

However, this is called "half a body"; he does not have the quality of female, which is a lack. From the perspective of the left, he begins to calculate to what extent his qualities and thoughts are whole, and then he sees the truth, that he is still immersed in the will to receive for his own benefit, and cannot work for the sake of others, whether between man and man or between man and the Creator.

To the extent that he has the recognition of evil, he can exert, meaning work, perform actions, as in "Everything that is in the power of your hand to do, that do." Also, he can pray from the bottom of the heart, since only to the extent that a person feels the bad, meaning feels that it is bad, to that extent he acts in order to be rid of the bad. This is called "female," meaning a lack.

It follows that he has room for two opposite qualities. On one hand, he is regarded as complete, which is the "right," *Hesed* [mercy], happy with his share. He can praise and thank the Creator for letting him into a place of Torah and good deeds. On the other hand, he can pray to the Creator for remaining outside of the work of the Creator because everything was built on the basis of self-love.

At that time, the person is called "complete," and otherwise he is not considered "man" because if he sees his deficiencies he will soon run from the quality of the "right," as well.

But once he has seen his bad state and yet reinforces himself above reason that he has wholeness, and the sign of this is that he can thank the Creator for this, then he is called "complete." This is "Right and left, and a bride between them." By having the quality of male and female, he can be rewarded with the quality of "bride," meaning the real kingdom of heaven.

This is the meaning of "Serve the Lord with gladness." He asks there in *The Zohar*: But he cannot be happy because his heart is broken due to his sins! We learn about this, "One always enters through two doors: mercy and fear."

We can explain this in the above manner. The "right hand side" door is faith above reason, when he is complete. This is private Providence, and it is "for he desires mercy." The other door is fear, meaning *Gevura*, "left." On this door we must give labor and prayer. This is called "man," since he has two discernments, male and female, complete and lacking, and then his work is considered whole.

402- If a Woman Inseminates – 1

29 Nissan, Tav-Shin-Lamed-Aleph, April 24, 1971

"If a woman inseminates. We learned that 'A woman who inseminates first, delivers a male child.' Rabbi Aha said, 'We learned that the Creator sentences whether a drop will be a male or a female, and you say, 'A woman who inseminates first, delivers a male child.' Rabbi Yosi said, 'Of course the Creator discerns between a drop of a male and a drop of a female. And because He has discerned it, He sentences whether it will be a male or a female'" (*The Zohar*, *Tazria*, Item 9).

The question is, if a woman who inseminates first delivers a male child, then we no longer need the Creator's sentence. But Rabbi Yosi explains that of course the Creator discerns it, and because He discerned it, He sentenced it. Yet, the explanation provides no clarification.

The *Sulam* [Ladder commentary on *The Zohar*] interprets that there are three partners in a person: the Creator, his father, and his mother. His father gives the white in him; his mother, the red in him, and the Creator gives the soul. This discernment, that the Creator discerns in the drop—that it is worthy of the soul of a male or a female, is regarded as sentencing, for had He not discerned it and did not send a soul of a male, the drop would not have been determined to be a male.

We should understand this in the work. "Sowing" means we take something and place it in the ground, where it strikes roots and then some being emerges from it. Hence, when a woman inseminates first, it means that a person places in the ground the will to receive, regarded as a female, and a male emerges from it, meaning that he is rewarded with the desire to bestow, which is called "a male."

Hence, Rabbi Aha's question was that if this depends on man's work, meaning on an awakening from below, then what we learned—that the Creator discerns the drop and sentences—what is this sentencing if the matter is determined by man's work below?

The *Sulam* interprets about this that there are three partners in a person. His father gives the white. That is, the discernment of father and mother is the thought, which is regarded as "parents" who engender the action. The father is his power of bestowal, which is the male, who gives the white, meaning whitens himself from being a receiver, removing from himself the will to receive. It follows that he is regarded as cleansed and that then he becomes truly as dust.

This is the meaning of "My soul will be as dust to all." That is, with regard to everything that is in the world, he is regarded as dust, meaning he has no need or desire, but he is annulled truly as dust.

The mother gives the *Odem* [red], as in *Adameh* [I will be like] *LaElyon* [the upper one], meaning she wants to be a giver.

We can discern in this that the quality of whiteness means "Turn away from evil," and the red of the mother is regarded as "and do good." "Good" means the quality of giving, as it is written, "My heart overflows with a good thing; I say, 'My work is for the King,'" meaning he wants to perform acts of bestowal upon the King.

But all this is only in potential, by coercion, since the body disagrees with all those things that are against the will to receive. Thus, all that he does has no spirit and vitality until the Creator sentences the drop and sends a soul of a male. Then he obtains the flavor of the desire to bestow, and all that he does contains spirit and vitality.

It follows that although from the perspective of the awakening from below, everything is as it should be, the soul is still missing. This is regarded as "He who comes to purify is aided." *The Zohar* asks, "With what?" and it replies, "With a holy soul." This is the meaning of the Creator discerning which drop has the quality of male or that of a female.

It is as Baal HaSulam interpreted what Maimonides says (*Hilchot Teshuva*), "Until He who knows the mysteries testifies to him," he asked if it was possible for man to rise up and ask the Creator so his repentance will be worthy and acceptable, and he explained that when a person's work is correct, he is rewarded with the revelation of the face, which is the attainment of the matter of reward and punishment.

In other words, he feels the wonderful delight while observing the *Mitzva* [commandment] and feels the affliction of a transgression. This is regarded that then His salvation, namely the revelation of the face, testifies to him that he will not sin. This is regarded as the one who knows the mysteries testifying that he will not sin, and by this we should interpret that the Creator sentences and gives him the soul of a male.

Accordingly, we can interpret that the Creator discerns whether the drop is a male, meaning that his repentance is worthy and good, and then the Creator testifies to him and sends him a soul. This is regarded as sentencing, from the word "decree" [in Hebrew], when he has no other choice but to walk on the straight path because of the revelation of the face with which he was rewarded.

Or He sends him a soul of a female, receiving and not giving. That is, it is intermittent, at times receiving an awakening from above, but then it departs. This is called "a lack," from the word "female," which is incomplete because it cannot be permanent.

Conversely, a soul of a male always extends a soul and vitality when he performs a *Mitzva*, since he has already been rewarded with the testimony of the Creator that "he will not return to folly."

By this we can interpret the verse, "There is the sea, great and broad, in which are swarms innumerable, animals both small and great. How many are Your works, Lord, in wisdom You have made them all; the earth is full of Your possessions."

"How many are Your works, Lord" refers to the whole of creation. "In wisdom You have made them all" means that the intention of creation is to do good to His creations, called "wisdom." "The earth is full of Your possessions" means that there are many discernments in the world. "This is the sea, great" refers to the sea of wisdom. "...and broad" refers to light of *Hassadim*, called "expansion."

Remes [swarms] from the word *Ramsa*, which is "night" [in Aramaic]. "Innumerable" means that they do not shine. "Animals both small and great" means there are many kinds of animals, the quality of *Katnut* [smallness/infancy] and the quality of *Gadlut* [greatness/adulthood].

403- This Shall Be the Law of the Leper

Nissan, Tav-Shin-Mem-Aleph, April 1981

"This shall be the law of the leper on the day of his purification, when he is brought to the priest." RASHI interprets, "Since the diseases come due to slander."

Slander is mainly when one wants to walk on the path of truth, meaning that the thought, speech, and action will be in order to bestow. At that time, the body comes and slanders that it is not worthwhile to work on this quality. That is, it does not pay to give all his work in order to bestow. This is the question of the wicked one, who asks, "What is this work for you?"

When the wicked comes with such questions, he finds himself in a bad state, which is called *Metzu-Ra* [Hebrew: found bad; English: leper]. As much as he wants to overcome his complaints, to that extent he feels that he is bad. Hence, if he wants to purify himself, which is "the day of his purification," then "he is brought to the priest."

In other words, if he wants to emerge from that state of "he is brought to the priest," it means that from above he is brought to the quality of *Hesed*, which is the quality of "priest." Through this quality, he is rewarded with vessels of bestowal.

This is the meaning of "He who comes to purify is aided," namely by the quality of "priest." This is why everything requires an awakening from below, which brings him a desire and yearning for the matter, since it is impossible to give someone something that he does not want. Even if he receives it, he will throw it away because he has no need for it. Hence, a person must have an awakening from below so he will need the matter.

Then, according to his need, so he values the gift that he is given from above. This is the meaning of "Everything that is in the power of your hand to do, that do," by which *Kelim* [vessels] form within him to receive the abundance, which is called "the quality of priest," which is the light of *Hesed*. And then, his only aim is to bestow upon the Creator.

However, before he has *Kelim* that need it, he cannot appreciate the gift that he is given and therefore does not keep the gift. Hence, he might lose everything, so we must wait for man's repentance. It follows that it is not within man's power to repent, but he can choose to have a desire to repent.

404- And Say a Matter

"'And say a matter.' Let your speech of Shabbat [Sabbath] not be as your speech of a weekday" (*Shabbat* 113a). Shabbat is called *Kedusha* [holiness], a Shabbat of holiness. *Hol* [weekday] means matters that are *Holanim* [sickly], which are the acts of the body. There is a time when we speak from the quality of the body, its bad thoughts, desires, and feelings, and how we must correct them so it is able to receive *Kedusha*, and this is called "the work on weekdays," namely the correction of the body.

Also, there is a time when we speak only of matters of *Kedusha*, which is generally called "the greatness of the Creator." The speech of Shabbat should come from this quality, from speaking from the perspective of wholeness and holiness, and not from the perspective of the body, which is secular and not holy.

405- When an Ox or a Sheep or a Goat Is Born

Iyar, Tav-Shin-Lamed-Tet, May 1979

"When an ox or a sheep or a goat is born." A day-old ox is called "an ox," since what he can achieve, he has already achieved on the first day. Hence, people who do not belong to the quality of "speaking" but to the quality of "animal" live their whole lives with the intellect that they had attained on the day they were born, meaning the day when they are initiated into *Mitzvot* [commandments].

The only addition that they have is in quantity, since it is a small intellect compared to the intellect that can be attained with the intellect of the Torah. Hence, what one achieves on the first day, with this he lives through the end.

Conversely, the speaking degree, which is the quality of "man," as in "You are called 'man' and not the nations of the world," is the opposite: "Man is born a wild ass" compared to what he can attain when he is rewarded with the quality of "man."

This is so because the spirit of the beast descends, meaning that all its actions are for the purpose of below, namely for one's own sake, while man's spirit ascends, meaning it is for the sake of the Creator, called "upward," as our sages said, "Know what is above you" (*Avot*, Chapter 1). At that time, he sees that he was born an uneducated person, and then his work to walk on the path of truth begins. At that time, it is said, "Even if the whole world tells you that you are righteous, be wicked in your own eyes."

406- Six Days You Shall Work

"Six days you shall work... Rabbi Yosi said ... and it does not write, 'On the six' ... the six upper days *HGT NH* from which all the works of creation emerged each day... Rabbi Yitzhak said... Rabbi Hiya said, 'Because it is permitted to work in them although they are regarded as *Zeir Anpin*, the *Havdalah* [separation] was established.' He asks, 'What is separation? Should they have been mingled in one another?' He replies, 'Holiness is something in itself, and separation is between secular and holy,'" etc. (*The Zohar, Emor*, 112).

Baal HaSulam asked why the six workdays that are regarded as *Zeir Anpin* are secular, and *Malchut*, which is the final discernment, is holy. He said that *Zeir Anpin* is called "six days of action" because on each day, they shine a small light on those days, and from them they extend each day. However, Shabbat means that at that time what is found in the six days of action is revealed. It follows that the revelation of *Zeir Anpin* is on Shabbat, but Shabbat itself has no quality so as to have something to give, since *Malchut* is called "poor and meager."

Accordingly, it follows that from Shabbat, which is *Malchut*, who has nothing, she has nothing to give from herself. For this reason, it is forbidden to work on Shabbat because *Malchut* has nothing to give from her own quality. Rather, *Zeir Anpin*, who is *HGT NH*, each *Sefira* [sing. of *Sefirot*] gives of its own quality to… opposite it. For this reason, the six days of action relate only to *Zeir Anpin* because only *Zeir Anpin* has what to give each day.

But the revelation of the lights of *Zeir Anpin* illuminate in *Malchut*, which is why Shabbat is called "holy," since then the abundance is disclosed. Conversely, on weekdays, it is necessary to work for the abundance of *Zeir Anpin* to be revealed in *Malchut*, who is Shabbat.

"From finding your wish and say a matter." Rabbi Yosi asked, "What is a lack for Shabbat if he is speaking something?" He told him it is certainly a lack for Shabbat because there is not a single word uttered by a person who has no voice, and it ascends and awakens another word.

And what is it? It is that which is called "secular," since anything that is not holy is secular, from those weekdays. When secularity awakens in the holy day, it is indeed a lack above, and the Creator and the assembly of Israel asked about it, who is it who wants to separate our coupling, who is it who needs secularity here (*The Zohar, Emor*, Item 294).

407- If You Buy a Hebrew Slave

Iyar, Tav-Shin-Yod-Tet, May 1959

In *The Zohar, BaHar*, Rabbi Elazar started, "'If you buy a Hebrew slave, six years he will work,' etc. This is so because everyone in Israel who was circumcised has a holy *Reshimo* [recollection] in him, and he has rest during a *Shmita* [a once-every-seven-years remission of land-cultivation], for this *Shmita* is his, to rest in it. This is called 'the Sabbath of the earth,' and there is certainly freedom and rest in it. As the Sabbath is rest for everyone, it is rest for everyone, rest for the spirit and rest for the body."

We should understand why specifically one who was circumcised has rest on the *Shmita*, and what it means that there is rest for the body, too, on the *Shmita*. We should also understand what is written in *Midrash Tanchuma*, "And who is like you, your brother, and a staff in his hand?"

This is the meaning of the words, "Do not rob a meager for he is meager, for the Lord will fight their quarrels." The Creator said, "Do not rob a meager for he is meager, for I have made him meager. One who robs him or scorns him despite his Maker, it is as though he scorns Me."

408- Count the Heads of the Whole Congregation of Israel

Iyar, Tav-Shin-Lamed-Het, May 1978

The matter of counting is that they count those who can come into the work of the Creator; it is from twenty years of age, from which he may be punished. Concerning the role that one must do in the work of the Creator, it is presented at the end of the *Haftarah* [final section of the Torah reading on Shabbat [Sabbath], where it is written, "And I will betroth you to Me forever."

The Creator takes into matrimony those who want to come into the work of the Creator forever, not those who want to be here today, and tomorrow follow the will to receive, but rather, specifically if one decides that he wants to adhere to the Creator forever. This is so because as the Creator is eternal, one who wants to adhere must also be adhered for eternity.

"I will betroth you to Me" means that one who wants to behave with Me above reason should say that however the Creator behaves with him in righteousness and in justice. Also, one should conduct himself with *Hesed* and *Rachamim* [mercy], meaning that precisely one who wants to engage in manners of bestowal, called *Hesed* and *Rachamim*, since "As He is merciful, so you are merciful," and this is the meaning of "And I will betroth you to Me in righteousness and in justice, in kindness, and in mercy."

Afterward, it can be, "And I will betroth you to Me in faith." One who has crossed the first two stages is rewarded with the light of faith.

Afterward, he is rewarded with "Then you will know the Lord," from the words, "They shall all know Me, from the least of them to the greatest of them." This is so because when a person works, there is a difference between *Katnut* [smallness/infancy] and *Gadlut* [greatness/adulthood], but when the abundance comes from the Creator, there is no difference between *Katnut* and *Gadlut* because the *Kli* [vessel] and the light come together.

409- Concerning Suffering – 2

"Israel are holy." He has but he does not want; he wants but he does not have. He does not want in order to bestow, he has Torah and *Mitzvot* [commandments] and fear of heaven. He wants in order to bestow, so he has neither Torah and *Mitzvot* nor fear of heaven. He does not want in order to bestow is regarded as "The whole world tells you that you are righteous." Wants in order to bestow, then he is regarded as "Be as a wicked one in your eyes."

"Count the heads of the whole congregation of Israel by their families ... according to the number of names, every male, head by head." RASHI interprets "A *Beka* [weight unit] per head, and such is the way of Torah... lead a life of sorrow and toil in the Torah," etc. Which is the suffering of love? One in which there is no cancellation of Torah. Happy is the man whom the Lord afflicts. He whom the Lord loves, He admonishes.

We should understand why we need the suffering, and why specifically "He whom the Lord loves, He admonishes," and what "Happy is the man whom the Lord afflicts" means, and what suffering without cancellation of Torah is there in the world, since the sufferings do not let a person exert in Torah. Also, what does the word *Beka* imply, from the word *Bekia* [fissuring] the *Gulgolet* [skull/head].

It is known that the whole *Kli* [vessel] that receives pleasure is the yearning, a lack for the thing, meaning for the thing to which he has a great desire. To the extent that he desires it, to that extent he yearns. And the desire, great or small, is measured by the amount of suffering that he would feel if he did not obtain the matter.

As it is explained (in the "Introduction to The Study of the Ten Sefirot," Items 96-97), Torah *Lishma* [for Her sake] means for the sake of the life that he finds in the Torah, since when one finds His face in the Torah, so he finds the life in the Torah, as it is written, "For by the light of the King's face is life."

Thus, when one learns Torah and does not find the life in the Torah, he regrets it, and this is called "You will lead a life of sorrow." That is, he will regret not finding the light of His face, yet he does not stop learning Torah, as it is written, "And in the Torah you toil" although he does not find Him.

It follows that to the extent that he learns Torah and intends to find Him, so his suffering increases. At a certain extent called "labored," you "find," as is explained there, that this is the meaning of the existence of the light of the King's face in the Torah.

It follows that through the suffering, a real desire to receive the "light of the King's face is life" forms within him, and this is called "pains of love," where there is no cancellation of Torah. This is so because the more he delves in Torah, the more he increases the suffering.

It follows that there is no cancellation of Torah in them because one who learns Torah, the suffering is born in him. It follows that if he has no Torah then he has no suffering. As said above, this is called "pains of love," since there is no cancellation of Torah in them.

This is called "He whom the Lord loves, He admonishes." It is so because in order for man to have these sufferings from not finding the Creator in the Torah, not every person is rewarded with suffering from this. This is why it was said, "Happy is the man whom the Lord afflicts."

Then a person must acquire the suffering so he will have a real desire and yearning, since precisely in the real desire appears the quality of suffering, for man has no other *Kli* in which to obtain the pleasure except for this desire.

Baal HaSulam interpreted the meaning of a "*Beka* per head" as foreign thoughts. When a foreign thought falls into a person's mind, it creates a fissure in his head. If he remembers all the fissures and regrets them then for every fissure appears a holy name.

We can interpret that "the number of names" means "according to the sorrow is the reward," meaning the number of names according to the number of fissures that he remembers and regrets. By them we are rewarded with "Count the heads of the whole congregation of Israel."

410- Self-Love and Love of the Creator

Iyar-Sivan, Tav-Shin-Mem, May 1980

There is self-love and there is love of the Creator, and there is a medium, which is love of others. Through love of others we come to the love of the Creator. This is the meaning of what Rabbi Akiva said, "Love your neighbor as yourself is a great rule in the Torah."

As Old Hillel said to the gentile who told him, "Teach me the whole Torah on one leg." He said to him, "That which you hate, do not do to your friend. And the rest, go study." This is so because through love of others we come to love the Creator, and then the whole Torah and all the wisdom are in his heart.

It is written, "The Creator said to Israel, 'Be sure, the whole wisdom and the whole Torah are easy. Anyone who fears Me and performs the words of Torah, all the wisdom and all of the Torah are in his heart'" ("Introduction to The Study of the Ten Sefirot," where he references *Midrash Rabbah*, portion *VeZot HaBracha*). Concerning fear, it is explained in the *Sulam* [Ladder commentary on *The Zohar*], that it is fear that he might not be able to bestow upon the Creator, since it is the conduct of love that he wants to bestow upon the Creator.

Hence, one who has love of the Creator wants to bestow, and this is called *Dvekut* [adhesion], as in "And to cleave unto Him." By this the Creator passes onto him Torah and wisdom. It follows that he taught him on one leg, meaning that through love of others he will achieve the degree of love of the Creator, and then he will be rewarded with Torah and wisdom.

When one is rewarded with the Torah of the Creator, meaning Torah from the mouth of the Creator, one sees that it is complete, that there is no lack in it.

"Sinai," since *Sinaa* [hatred] descended to the nations of the world. This is the sign of the Torah.

"In Your hand shall I entrust my spirit."

Isru Hag [after the holiday/festival], from the word "dial" [in Hebrew]. *Avotim* [thick] means *Aviut* [thickness], in the words of Baal HaSulam. "Until the corners" is *Malchut*. "Altar" is *Malchut*, meaning *Malchut* of *Malchut*. That is, a person should pray for the complete redemption, which is *Malchut* of *Malchut*.

A prayer of many means for the many. "Thanks," thanks to a person being able to pray for the many.

411- All Who Are Violent, Prevail – 2

Sivan, Tav-Shin-Lamed-Tet, May-June 1979

The origin of judgment extends from reality, since when the wicked comes and argues, "What is this work for you?" what do we tell him? "Blunt his teeth," meaning that we haven't the intellect to reply, but everything is above reason. This is regarded as "All who are violent, prevail," at times the good inclination and at times the evil inclination. Since the intellect has no concept by which to sort the good from the bad, it is only by force.

This is why that judgment was given concerning that Ishmaelite, for the body in this world is like a ship at sea, and each one wants to control it and assume ownership over the body. This is the meaning of the saying, "All who are violent, prevail."

412- The Vow of a Hermit, to Dedicate Himself to the Lord

Sivan, Tav-Shin-Lamed-Tet, May-June 1979

"The vow of a hermit, to dedicate himself to the Lord." RASHI interpreted "to the Lord" as for the sake of the Creator. The interpreters interpreted that he does not deny himself wine because wine is bad for his health or that it intoxicates him and costs him humiliations. Rather, he understands that by this he will bring himself closer to the Creator, and there, there is the judgment of *Tuma'a* [impurity], for then "The first days will fall," meaning he returns to the beginning and must start his work anew.

Interpretation: Wine indicates luxuries. The intimation to this is not necessarily in the wine, but rather in that wine symbolizes a person enjoying more than is necessary. When he denies himself this, he should say for what reason he wants to relinquish luxuries and settle for little—is it because he hopes for a greater reward, such as honor, or even that he hopes that thanks to this he will be rewarded in the next world.

For all those reasons, even though they make it difficult for a person to relinquish luxuries, still the *Tuma'a*, meaning the descent from his degree, is not so common because it is built on reward.

Conversely, for the sake of the Creator, then the *Tuma'a* is more commonplace, meaning the descent from his degree. When he falls, it means he is defiled. Sometimes the *Tuma'a* comes suddenly, as it is written, "But if a man dies very suddenly beside him and defiles his head."

This is commonplace because the body objects to the truth, since the body cannot understand working not in order to receive reward. At that time comes the commandment that he must begin his work anew, meaning not mind the place from which he stopped, since it shows that the acceptance of the burden of the kingdom of heaven is still not as it should be. Hence, he must begin anew to accept the burden of the kingdom of heaven again, as it is written, "The first days will fall."

413- The Difference between Books of Ethics and the Books of the Baal Shem Tov

Sivan, Tav-Shin-Mem, May 1980

When a person wants to buy an object and he must pay for it, a mediator between the seller and the buyer is required. The mediator lets the buyer understand that this object is worth more than the sum he is asked to pay, meaning that the seller is not asking for such a high price for merchandise that is worth a lot.

For this reason, ethics books help us understand what a person must relinquish in corporeality in order to attain spirituality. They teach that all the corporeal pleasures are but imaginary pleasures and are worthless. Thus, they do not yield such a great reward in order to attain spirituality.

The books of the Baal Shem Tov gave the primary weight to the merchandise, meaning they help understand the value and importance and greatness of spirituality. Hence, although there is merit to corporeality, something must be relinquished, but with regard to the merchandise, which is "for they are our lives," it is written, "nicer than gold and from much fine gold, and sweeter than honey."

414- The Rabble Who Were Among Them Had Greedy Desires

"The rabble who were among them had greedy desires ... we only see the manna."

We should ask the following:

1) What does it mean that they desired? Simply a desire? It should have said, "desired meat."

2) What is the connection between asking for meat and the fact that they ate fish?

3) What does "for free" mean?

4) They were not angry that they counted, but only about the meat, so why did they mention all the kinds?

5) RASHI interpreted, "Did they not have meat? Rather, they sought to slander." We should understand that it is not the conduct of one who abuses to ask for something that can be given to him right away, meaning meat, which was in their possession.

To explain all this, we must first bring the discernments that apply to transgressors: "To anger," and "for good appetite." There is also a medium, meaning although he has no lust, he woos cures and remedies so as to have lust and to enjoy.

Eats with good appetite means that he is unable to conquer the inclination because lust has stung him. The medium discernment is that he searches for lust in order to enjoy. This is worse than one who already has lust.

Conversely, "to anger" means that even though he has no lust, he does it in order to vex, as our sages said about King Amon who had intercourse with his mother. They asked him, "What pleasure did you derive from what you did?" He replied, "I do this only to anger my Creator."

It seems we should interpret the above words that they became lustful, meaning that they searched for things that would bring them lust, like the above-mentioned medium. Although they had meat, they did not have lust. Conversely, in Egypt they had acrid things that invoked in them the lust for eating.

This is why it is written, "fish for free," meaning that even though it was free, namely that they would throw them away because they were not good anymore, they could still eat it because through the garlic and the onions, such great lust awakened in them that they could eat anything. But now, "we only see the manna" (*Yesod HaTorah*, Rabbi Baruch Kasov).

415- When You Raise the Candles – 1

"When you raise the candles." It is as the writing says, "The Lord desires for the sake of His righteousness, He will make the Torah [law] great and glorious."

The Creator said to Moses, "It is not because I need the candles that I warned you about them, but in order to cleanse you, as was said, 'His light is a candle.'" It is written, "Even darkness will not make it dark for You, and the night will shine as day, the darkness as light." This teaches you that He does not need flesh and blood candles, so why did He command you? To cleanse you. This is why it was said, "When you raise the candles," the Lord desires for the sake of His righteousness (Midrash Rabbah).

We should understand this. Is there any fool in the world who would think that the candles of the Temple would shine to the Creator, to the point that it is necessary to bring proof from the Torah that He does not need our candles, and that only in order to cleanse us did He give us the Mitzva [commandment] of lighting candles?

We should interpret that this means that one should not think that the Creator cannot give us all the abundance that is concealed without work on our part, namely without labor. Rather, the Creator can bestow all of His abundance without any effort, since the purpose of creation is to do good to His creations. However, by reception of pleasures, a person grows thicker with Aviut [thickness/will to receive] of disparity of form.

Hence, in order for man not to come to disparity of form, we were given Torah and Mitzvot [commandments] in order to cleanse us. This is called "candles." That is, we must give the labor, but the Creator can give us even without an awakening from below, and He only gave us the Mitzvot in order to cleanse us from the Aviut.

416- This Is the Making of the Menorah [Temple Lamp] – 1

Sivan, Tav-Shin-Lamed-Tet, June 1979

"This is the making of the menorah." RASHI interpreted that the Creator showed him with the finger since he was perplexed about it. "One-piece work": "It was one talent [piece] of gold. He would strike with a hammer, etc., this is how he made the menorah." Elsewhere: "It was done by itself by the Creator." "He set it up outside of the curtain of the testimony."

We should understand what it means that Moses was perplexed about the making of the menorah, and what the talent of gold implies, and that he struck with a hammer, and also what it means that it was done by itself by the Creator.

By intimation, the menorah means man's body. When the light of the Creator is dressed in it, the man shines like a lamp. This is why Moses was perplexed, how a man's body could clothe the upper light when there is disparity of form between the light and the *Kli* [vessel], which is man's body.

To this came the answer that it was a talent of gold. The body is called "a talent of *Ze-Hav* [English: gold, Hebrew: give-this]," meaning the will to receive. Striking it refers to *Zivug de Hakaa* [coupling by striking] where through the striking, a person overcomes, for two opposite things are called "striking" where each strikes the other and wants to cancel it. This is the meaning of hammering his will to receive in order to cancel it.

However, "he was perplexed about it," meaning it is not within man's power to invert the will to receive so it works in order to bestow. To this comes the answer, "This is how he made the lamp," meaning that through the Creator, it was done by itself. This is the meaning of "He who comes to purify is aided." However, it is true what the body tells him—that it is not within man's power to invert it.

Thus, the difficulty to do the thing is called *Kli*, which is a lack. Afterward, the abundance, which is called "filling," can come and fill the lack. But if he has no questions then there is no place to receive the filling for the lack. This is called "assistance from above." Hence, it means that without questions, if a person does not begin, there is no place to fill the lack.

This is what the words "outside of the curtain of the testimony" refer to, that it is a testimony to the people of the world that the *Shechina* [Divinity] dwells in Israel. The question, "Does He need its light? After all, they walked by His light forty years," and what fool would think that the menorah would illuminate for the Creator, if one of the thirteen tenets is that He has no body? Thus, how can it be said that the menorah is for Him?

Rather, this refers to the light of the lower ones, meaning the awakening of the lower ones. He brings evidence to this that in the desert it was only by an awakening from above and not through the work of the lower ones. But there it is the testimony. Although he said that a deed was done, it was only a miracle, and a miracle means that it was not done by the lower ones. This is the meaning of "Rewarded, I will hasten it; not rewarded, in its time," that the whole of the "hastening" is for the lower ones, so they will think that they are doing something.

417- And Aaron Did So

Sivan, Tav-Shin-Mem, May 1980

"And Aaron did so, he mounted its candles at the front of the lampstand, just as the Lord had commanded Moses." RASHI interpreted, to praise Aaron for not changing. The interpreters ask, "What would I say so he would not observe the commandment of the Creator, etc.?"

"Our sages said, 'When Rabbi Yosi Ben Kisma fell ill, Rabbi Hanina Ben Tardion went to visit him. He said to him, 'Hanina my brother, do you not know that this nation was crowned from above? Its house was destroyed, its hall burned down, its followers were killed and it lost its best sons, and still it exists. I heard about you that you sit and engage in Torah and make assemblies out in the open with a book of Torah placed in your bosom.'"' RASHI interpreted and they declared a judgment about it.

"He said to him, 'From heaven there will be mercy.' He said to him, 'I am telling you meaningful words and you are telling me, 'From heaven there will be mercy'? I wonder if they do not burn you and the book of Torah in the fire.' Rabbi said to him, 'Where am I with regard to life in the next world?' He said to him, 'Has an act come into your hand?' He replied, 'I mistook coins of Purim with coins of charity and handed them to the poor.' He replied, 'In that case, of your share will be my share and of your fate will be my fate.'"

RASHI interprets that coins of Purim, which I placed for the Purim meal, I accidentally replaced them and I handed them out to the poor. I thought that my wallet was for charity, but I did not pay off my wallet of charity (*Masechet Avodah Zarah* 18a).

Indeed, it is hard to understand concerning Rabbi Yosi Ben Kisma, a man who dedicated himself to the sanctification of the Creator and who sits and engages in Torah, is it still not enough that he should have the next world? If he performs an act that any uneducated person can do, to be generous with his wealth, as he said about it, "of your share will be my share," doing such an act does not require devotion. So why after he heard about the matter with the *Tzedakah* he said, "Of your share will be my share"?

According to the way of Baal HaSulam, it follows that the most important is to emerge from self-benefit, meaning that a person can perform acts of devotion also on the basis of self-benefit.

Hence, when he saw that he was relinquishing self-benefit through an act of *Tzedakah*, he knew that all his dedication was on the basis of the intention to bestow. This is why he said, "of your share will be my share," etc. This refers not only to the act of charity, but also to the act of sitting and engaging in Torah, and gathering assemblies out in the open, since everything was on the basis of the intention to bestow.

This is the meaning of "It teaches that Aaron did not change," since the making of the Menorah is a high degree, and the pleasure is immense, and the greater the pleasure, the harder it is to work in order to bestow. This is the meaning of not changing, and that everything was on the basis of "just as the Lord had commanded Moses."

418- Poverty Becomes Israel

Tammuz, Tav-Shin-Mem, June-July 1980

It is written, "For the poor will never cease from the land." Also, our sages said, "Poverty becomes Israel" (*Hagigah* 9b).

We should understand this, for it is known that there is no *Kli* [vessel] to receive the pleasure except yearning, for the lack and the yearning for the thing are the gauge that can receive the pleasure from the matter. This is as our sages said, "One who drinks when he is thirsty, blesses for the pleasure," for one does not enjoy eating if he has no appetite, as in "Sweet is the worker's sleep."

Accordingly, in the matter of poverty, that "there is none who is poor except in knowledge," it follows that the yearning for knowledge is discerned according to how a person feels that he has a desire for knowledge. Accordingly, we should ask if when a person has been rewarded with the quality of Israel and feels that he has no lack, and he is not poor, from where will he take the *Kli* [vessel] called "yearning," since he has already been rewarded with the quality of Israel?

The Torah comes and says about this, "For the poor will never cease." Rather, the Creator will provide him with deficiencies and emptiness and poverty, so he will have *Kelim* [vessels] to receive the abundance. It follows that "For the poor will never cease" is a promise that the Torah gave to Israel that they will always have room to ascend in the upper degrees. This is the meaning of "Poverty becomes Israel," etc., for by this they will always ascend in degrees.

This is the meaning of "A poor is as important as the dead." If one feels his deficiency as though he is dead, that he has no life without the filling, that he needs to be filled, this is called "a *Kli* of yearning," and by this he will receive the filling for his poverty.

419- Spies

"Send," RASHI interprets, "I do not command you ... for certain, I am giving them room for error." Why? The spies told the truth, but we must believe above reason that it is good.

If we want to go within reason, I will give room for error so they will not inherit it within reason. Above (reason) is needed because only by this will they be able to receive in order to bestow, and within reason there is no free choice.

Kaleb went to Hebron so he could believe above reason, and Joshua, who was adhered to Moses, Moses prayed for him.

420- Send Forth

Sivan, Tav-Shin-Mem, June 1980

"Send forth," RASHI interpreted, "To your reason."

It is known that sending the spies to tour the land of Israel is a matter of acceptance of the kingdom of heaven, for man has spies that always see if it is worthwhile to walk on the path of the Creator, on the path of truth, called "for the sake of the Creator."

The Torah promises us that it is a land flowing with milk and honey, but the body, which sent spies to tour the land, sees that there is no self-benefit there, and then the body does not agree to walk to the land called "kingdom of heaven."

It is written that the Creator tells them, "Go up in the Negev," meaning exert in Torah, "See what the land is like," meaning see the world from it, that it is an inheritance and a lot. "The people who live in it" are the righteous in the Garden of Eden (in *The Zohar*, Items 56-57).

It is also written there, "When they return from touring the land..." return from the path of truth and say, "What did we get out of it? To this day, we have not seen good in the world. We have toiled in Torah and the house is empty. Who will be awarded that world? Who will come into it? It would have been better had we not toiled so" (Item 63).

421- Concerning the Spies

Sivan, Tav-Shin-Lamed-Tet, June 1979

"If a wise disciple is loved by all the townspeople, it is because he does not rebuke them on spiritual matters."

When man's body respects the wise disciple of himself, meaning that it is important to him that he engages in Torah and Mitzvot [commandments], it is because he does not rebuke it on spiritual matters, meaning that his wise disciple is not telling the body that we must work in order to bestow.

When the wise disciple tells him that all his actions should be with the aim not for his own benefit, then the townspeople, meaning the body, called "small town" (Ecclesiastes 10), hate the wise disciple, since if he says to the body, meaning the will to receive, not to work for its own sake, it objects.

In other words, if his own body agrees to his work, it is a sign that he is not walking on the path of truth. Then, when he sees that the body disagrees and argues, "What is this work for you?" to this comes the answer, "What does the Lord your God require of you? Only to fear Me." At that time, a person becomes needy of the

Creator's help so he can walk on the path of truth. And when he makes an honest prayer then "He who comes to purify is aided."

The Zohar says that by being given a soul from above, he has the strength to walk on the path of truth. It follows that by this he has the qualification of the *Kelim* so he can be rewarded with the soul of the Creator shining within him, for only by this can we walk on the path. Thus, when he walks on the path of Torah and *Mitzvot* and does not have interferences from the body, he has no need to be rewarded with the soul of the Creator from above.

"All are people," meaning they were all righteous and the heads of Israel, but they took a bad counsel. They said, "If Israel entered the land, we will be overthrown from being heads, and Moses will appoint other people" (*The Zohar, Shlach Lecha*, Item 30).

Thus, the question is, If they were righteous, why did they take a bad counsel? According to what is explained in several places, Israel walking in the desert and eating bread from the sky is regarded as "covered *Hassadim* [mercies]." When they are heads, they will influence the general public to walk on the straight path.

But the land of Israel is the quality of *Malchut*, which is "revealed *Hassadim*," and they cannot be the heads. Moses will appoint such heads that belong to revealed *Hassadim*, and since revealed *Hassadim* are received in vessels of reception, he says that they will be utterly unable to receive in order to bestow. This is why they thought that this was a dangerous path to walk in—to use the vessels of reception.

This is called "slander," when they said the truth. Thus, what is their sin? It is that they only had to believe that although by nature it is impossible for man to be able to receive in order to bestow, the Creator can help them be rewarded with it. Thus, within reason, the spies were truthful, but the above reason was missing—that the Creator could help them merit it.

This is why slander is so difficult, for although it is true, since it extends from the root of the spies, that a person thinks that he cannot walk on the path of truth, what derives from this is that he cannot walk above reason.

422- From Afar the Lord Appeared to Me

Sivan, Tav-Shin-Lamed-Tet, June 1979

"Far" means that there is a difference in the importance between one and the other.

Hence, when a person feels no difference between speaking to a minister or a judge, and when he speaks to the Creator, when he does not consider or discern with whom he speaks or whose law he is uttering, then a person cannot see the Creator, meaning achieve true recognition of the Creator. When he feels the distance and importance that there is to spirituality, then he can come to feel.

423- Three Lines – 2

"Right" is called *Hesed*, as in "Because he desires mercy." This is regarded as being happy with one's share, meaning he settles for little.

This is as Baal HaSulam explained what our sages said about the verse, "who will not lift up the face or take a bribe," etc., that they are strict on themselves even as much as an olive and as an egg, he said, "as much as an olive," like the dove that said, "I would prefer my nourishments to be as bitter as an olive from the hand of the Creator," etc.

"As much as an egg," although a chick comes out of the egg, an animal, while it is still an egg, it has no life. Still, they were strict, although the rule "and you shall eat, and be satiated, and bless," meaning eating that is satiating, this is called "happy with his share."

However, with this quality, he will remain in his *Katnut* [smallness/infancy] and will have no need for the Torah, since the Torah is required for the evil inclination, as in "I have created the evil inclination; I have created the Torah as a spice." Hence, there is the left side, which is introspection as to the greatness of the reason that obligates him to Torah and *Mitzvot* [commandments], and what reward he expects in return for these works, and how much understanding he has in the true Torah and *Mitzvot*.

At that time, he sees only negativity and not positivity. He should include that negativity in the right [side] and settle for little and be happy with his share as though he had a satiating meal.

It follows that the left always brings him diminution so as to know what to install into the right and settle for little. Through both of them, we achieve the middle line. This is called "Father gives the white," for he is always in a state of "white," without any deficiencies, since he is happy with his share.

"Mother gives the red," meaning that he is not as he should be, but only red. This is the quality of Esau, called "red." At that time, the Creator, who is called "middle line," gives the soul, and then he is rewarded with the quality of Torah.

424- The Dispute between Korah and Moses

We need to explain the dispute between Korah and Moses. Moses said that everything that Korah argued was not against Moses but against the Creator. Korah argued that he believed in the Creator, as it is written, "The whole congregation are holy," and what our sages said, "Everyone heard in Sinai, 'I am the Lord your God,'" but he did not want to believe in Moses.

However, before he had personal interest, meaning that he had to make a big concession, he believed in Moses. But once he saw that Eltzaphan became president, while he understood according to his mind that he deserved the presidency, and he had to believe Moses that this was the Creator's commandment, his faith in Moses was not so great anymore.

It was not enough that he believed in the Creator and that the Torah was given through Moses and he must believe in him, since with the intellect, it is impossible to understand the Torah, since the view of landlords is opposite from the view of Torah, and we need only faith in the sages, for without Torah it is impossible to know what is the view of Torah and fear of heaven, for it is not the uneducated who is pious, as it is written, "I wish they left Me and kept My Torah [law]."

A person cannot tell his friend that he trusts him only concerning something small, but not concerning something great. If a person does not trust his friend concerning great things, he certainly does not trust him concerning small things, too. The reason why it seems as though he trusts him concerning something small is only that the thing is not important to him, so he thinks that even if he is not telling the truth, it does not matter.

For this reason, when Korah did not want to trust Moses with regard to the presidency, it immediately became revealed that with regard to the rest of the matters he also had no faith. This is why he immediately asked about a *Talit* [Jewish prayer shawl] that is all azure and a house that is full of books.

Rather, we must be strong in faith in the sages and submit ourselves, and be lowly in our eyes compared to the righteous. The matter of lowliness becomes revealed primarily when one must do something that his friend obligates him to do, while his own view indicates the opposite of his friend's view, and yet he subjugates himself. This is called "lowliness," when he lowers his own view.

This is the meaning of Datan and Aviram. "Datan" means that they wanted the *Dat* [religion] to be in the form of *Avi*, meaning "desire," as in "He did not *Ava* [wanted] to let them go." This is the meaning of *Avi-Ram*, that religion is *Ram* [high], suitable for his intellect.

Conversely, Moses gave a religion of lowliness, which does not befit his intellect, as it is written, "A *Talit* that is all azure," etc. This is why "They descended alive to Sheol," meaning that even though they had life because they were all at the occasion at Mt. Sinai, without Torah with faith in the sages we descend to Sheol. There is no other way but faith in the sages.

425- Korah Took

Sivan, Tav-Shin-Mem, June 1980

"Korah took, he took a bad counsel for himself, for 'The counsel of the Lord forever stands.'"

Normally, a person does what his intellect determines will be good for him, and this is what he can do. But what the intellect does not confirm is hard for him to do, much less if it is against the intellect. This is why he asked, if a *Talit* [Jewish prayer shawl] that is all azure still requires *Tzitziot* [fringes] or if a house full of books still requires a *Mezuzah* [a case containing a piece of parchment inscribed with specified verses from the Torah].

This is called a "bad counsel," that which is clothed within the reason. Conversely, above reason is called "the counsel of the Lord," and this "forever stands."

It is as Baal HaSulam said, that since the Creator chose that the creatures will walk by the way of above reason, He must have known that this was the best way. This is called "the counsel of the Lord," and precisely by this can one achieve the completion of the goal.

426- The Prayer of a Righteous, Son of a Righteous, and a Righteous, Son of a Wicked

Sivan, Tav-Shin-Mem-Aleph, June 1981

"The prayer of a righteous, son of a righteous is unlike the prayer of a righteous, son of a wicked."

An act that one does is called the "father," and the intention in the act is called the "offspring," meaning that first we do and then we hear.

We should make two discernments in the action: An act of bestowal is called "an act of a righteous," and an act of reception is called "wicked." When a person comes to pray to be given the strength to always be able to aim to act for the sake of the Creator, this is called "righteous son of a righteous." If he prays to be given the strength to aim for the sake of the Creator with vessels of reception, this is called "the prayer of a righteous son of a wicked."

This is the meaning of the prayer of a righteous son of a righteous being accepted, while the prayer of a righteous son of a wicked is not always accepted, as our sages said, "Not every person is rewarded with two tables," as our sages said, that for Rabbi, there were Torah and greatness in the same place.

We should understand this, since he said that he did not enjoy this world even with his little finger, so for what purpose did the Creator give him the Torah and the greatness? According to the above-said, we should interpret "Not every person is rewarded with two tables." One table means that he can bestow in order to bestow, which is called "righteous." This is called "Torah." "Greatness" means *Gadlut* [greatness/adulthood], which is a righteous son of a wicked, when he receives in order to bestow, when all his vessels of reception, called "wicked," are not for his own sake but in order to bestow.

427- This Is the Constitution of the Torah [Law] – 1

Adar, Tav-Shin-Mem, March 1980

It is written in *The Zohar* about the verse, "This is the constitution of the Torah," why it is written, "And this is the Torah." It explains that "and this" means unification of general and particular together. "And" is regarded as *Zeir Anpin*, which is general, and *Malchut* is the particular.

However, "this" without the added "and" is the constitution of the Torah, which is *Malchut*, called "constitution." It comes from *Zeir Anpin*, who is called "Torah," and not the Torah itself, which is *Zeir Anpin*, but only the judgment of the Torah, the decree of the Torah, which is *Malchut*. This is what is explained in the *Sulam* [Ladder commentary on *The Zohar*].

We should understand why *Zeir Anpin* is called "general" and *Malchut* is called "particular," and why *Malchut* is called "judgment" and "the decree of the Torah." The thing is that it is known that the heart of the work is faith, meaning above reason. We must go above reason because there was a judgment on *Malchut*, called "will to receive," that it is forbidden to receive in order to receive because there must be *Dvekut* [adhesion], which is equivalence of form. Otherwise, there is separation. Hence, wherever there is a lack of *Kedusha* [holiness], it is because there is judgment on this place, meaning a prohibition on self-reception.

When one takes upon oneself the burden of the kingdom of heaven above reason, there is no room for reception there. This is called "the decree of the Torah," since the receiver cannot agree to work above reason, for man's view asserts that one must not make a single move without profits. When one wants to walk on the path of truth, meaning only in order to bestow, the body disagrees with it.

For this reason, he must take upon himself the work in this manner only above reason, and this is called "particular," and this work is regarded as "righteousness," as it is written, "And he believed in the Lord and He regarded it for him as righteousness."

However, once he has taken upon himself the work above reason, he is rewarded with the quality of the Torah. Torah is regarded as "general" because it contains two things—faith and Torah—for it is forbidden for idol-worshippers to learn Torah, as it is written, "They have not known the ordinances."

Hence, the first quality with which one must be rewarded is faith. Afterward, he comes to the quality of the Torah, and this is called "The unification of *Zeir Anpin* and the kingdom of heaven," male and female.

When one engages in acceptance of the burden of the kingdom of heaven, he is still deficient. However, when he is rewarded with the quality of the Torah, he is called "male" because the Torah bestows upon him the light of Torah, and then there is no longer judgment because he can already work in order to bestow.

By this we will understand what is written in *The Zohar*, that a red cow is called *Malchut* in the first state, called "the left line of *Bina*," meaning that it is complete with respect to *Hochma*.

This is called "in which there is no flaw and on which a yoke has not been placed." He interprets there that "yoke" means *Hesed*, and this is why there is a need to burn the cow, which is regarded as the diminution of the moon, and she is rebuilt into the second state, and in the second state is all of her existence... (in the *Sulam* [Ladder commentary on *The Zohar*], Item 20).

428- *This Is the Constitution of the Torah [Law] – 2*

"This is the constitution of the Torah." RASHI interprets, "Since Satan and the nations of the world count Israel, saying, 'What is this *Mitzva* [commandment] and what is the point about it?' He wrote about it, 'a constitution,' a decree before Me and you have no permission to doubt it."

We should understand this, for this implies that this is why it is written about it, "a constitution," since the nations of the world ask for the reason. Conversely, regarding the rest of the *Mitzvot* [commandments] of the Torah, of which the nations of the world do not ask, He does write the reasons for the *Mitzvot*. Yet, the reasons for the other *Mitzvot* are not explained, and it seems as though it should have been the opposite—precisely where we seek a reason for the matter, we should give the reason, and not where no one is asking.

We should also understand the connection to the allegory that RASHI brings about a handmaid's child who soiled a king's palace. They said, "Let his mother come and wipe clean the faces." Likewise, let the cow come and wipe clean the calf. This implies that this is the reason for the cow.

About the verse, "They shall take to you," RASHI interprets that it is always named after you, the cow that Moses had made in the desert. We should understand why specifically the cow is named after Moses and not other *Mitzvot*, since there were more *Mitzvot* that he did in the desert.

To understand all the above, we first need to introduce the purpose of Torah and *Mitzvot* [commandments] and what they mean. It is written in *Midrash Rabbah* about the verse, "And you shall offer from your cattle and from your flock." Rabbi asks, "Why should the Creator mind whether he slaughters at the throat or at the back of the neck, for it was said, 'The Torah and *Mitzvot* were given only in order to cleanse Israel through them.'"

The thing is that since the creatures were created with a nature of being receivers, and this is called *Av* [thick], and since it is impossible to go against nature, we were therefore given the advice that through Torah and *Mitzvot* we will be able to invert our nature and walk in the ways of bestowal. Only then will we be fit to receive the King's gift without any lack, meaning without the bread of shame.

The discernment by which one can know if he is receiving only for the purpose of *Mitzva* is if he feels that he could relinquish the pleasures although he has a desire and yearning, and he receives only provided that such is the will of the Creator. This is considered that he is receiving only because of a *Mitzva*, and only when he can relinquish the pleasures can he achieve the state of receiving in order to bestow.

The rule is that to accustom himself in concessions, he must accustom himself with smaller pleasures and then with greater pleasures, since we always go from light to heavy.

It is accepted by us that the greatest pleasure in the world is to be in *Dvekut* [adhesion] with the Creator in the manner of attainment of Godliness. For this reason, it is written in *The Zohar* that the matter of the *Tzimtzum* [restriction] was done, which is a correction of the issue of the bread of shame.

A *Tzimtzum* means concealment, where as long as one is still under the authority of the will to receive, he cannot feel any attainment of Godliness because the pleasure of attainment of Godliness is so intense that it is utterly impossible to relinquish it. This means that even if this would not be a *Mitzva*, he would still receive the pleasure, and this is called "separation" and *Lo Lishma* [not for Her sake].

In order for one to be able to act because of a *Mitzva*, which is in order to bestow contentment upon his Maker, there had to be the matter of the *Tzimtzum*, which is concealment, for during the concealment there is the matter of work in Torah and *Mitzvot* by way of faith, meaning that he takes upon himself the burden of Torah and *Mitzvot* because it is a decree before Him. This is called a "constitution."

The rule is that when do we feel that it is a law and not a reasoning? It is only when a desire and yearning awaken in a person to feel the reason, but he does not feel. Then, when he takes upon himself the burden of Torah and *Mitzvot*, he accepts it as a law.

Conversely, when there is no demand for reasoning, how does he know that there is no reason to it, but it is rather a law?

This is the intimation, "This is the constitution of the Torah," for the laws of Torah seem as laws only when Satan asks, meaning the evil inclination, as our sages said, "He is Satan, he is the evil inclination, he is the angel of death" (*Baba Batra* 16a).

The order is that during the question, when he asks about the reason for it, this is called the "evil inclination." Afterward, it obstructs him from observing, and then it is called "Satan" because it stands as Satan on his path.

Afterward, it puts him to death, and then it is called "the angel of death," since it takes away from him all the vitality of *Kedusha* [holiness] that he had, and in return gives the vitality of this world. In other words, he finds no taste of life except in corporeal things, which is the vitality of the wicked, whose lives are regarded as death.

It follows from all the above that only when Satan comes with a complaint and asks about all the work, we should prevail over this Satan and reply to him, "This is the constitution of the Torah"; I am observing the Torah only because it is a "law, a decree before Me, and there is no permission to doubt it."

This is what we received from Moses and we believe in him, for the meaning of the cow is "faith," which is a law. This is why the cow is named after Moses, who is called "Moses, the loyal shepherd," who brings the faith to all of Israel.

This is the meaning of what our sages said, that the cow is named after Moses. The cow that Moses made in the desert, where "desert" is regarded as prior to entering the settlement that is the land of Israel, as it is written in the books that the land of Israel is the permanent installing of the *Shechina* [Divinity], in complete attainment, called "the revealed world," while where it writes "desert," it means "concealed world," meaning a law.

The meaning of the calf is presented in *The Zohar* in the introduction about the verse, "Raise your eyes to heaven and see who created these." "Who" means light of *Hassadim*, and "these" means light of *Hochma* without *Hassadim*.

The matter of "who" means that when Satan comes and asks "Who is the Lord that I should obey His voice?" we should take everything upon ourselves as a constitution, which is *Hassadim*, meaning bestowal, where everything is only above reason, called "faith," the quality of "Moses, the loyal shepherd."

Conversely, "these" are called "knowledge," and it was said about it, "These are your gods, Israel," meaning that the name of the making of the calf is called wisdom and knowledge, and it is the opposite of the cow, which is called "faith." For this reason, when we accept "the constitution of the Torah," it is a correction of the making of the calf.

This is the meaning of "Let the mother come and wipe clean her son," and this is the meaning of "on which a yoke has not been placed." Baal HaSulam interpreted that we must accept the faith with joy and not as a burden, which means that he wants to get rid of it and waits for the opportunity when he can throw this burden off of him, and as it is written, "because you did not serve the Lord your God with joy."

It follows from all the above that faith is primarily in order for man to be able to work in choice, meaning even where he does not feel the delight and pleasure in Torah and *Mitzvot*, yet he observes them because he believes that such is the will of the Creator, to serve Him with faith.

He does not want to receive in a different manner, and he is as inflexible as steel about the matter, as our sages said, "Any wise disciple who is not as hard as steel is not a wise disciple" (*Taanit* 4a).

This means that even if one is proficient in Mishnah and Gemara, yet is not as hard as steel, he is not a wise disciple. That is, one must be as hard as steel concerning receiving the pleasure, whether in mind or in heart, until he has it in his own mind that his intention is only that this is the Creator's will. And precisely he is called "a wise disciple," since the Creator is called "wise," and the Creator only gives.

Hence, if a person walks with the quality of the Creator, meaning that he also bestows, it is considered that he is a wise disciple, learning the quality of the Wise, meaning the quality of the Creator, and only then can we receive all the delight and pleasure that the Creator had contemplated in our favor.

429- Make Everything in Order to Bestow

"This is the constitution of the Torah [law]." RASHI interprets, "Since Satan and the nations of the world count Israel, saying, 'What is this *Mitzva* [commandment] and what is the point about it?' He wrote about it, 'a constitution,' a decree before Me and you have no permission to doubt it."

A red cow, an allegory about a handmaid's child who soiled a palace. They said, "Let his mother come and wipe clean the faces." Likewise, let the cow come and atone for the calf. This means that they made everything be in order to bestow.

The words, "Since Satan and the nations of the world count," etc., mean that to them it is a constitution, meaning that one should reply to them that it is a decree before Me and you have no permission to doubt it. But for Israel, it is not a constitution. There is a verse by our sages: "To you, a reason; but for others, a constitution."

Concerning the question, "What is this *Mitzva* [commandment] and what is the point about it?" In the way of The Secret, this pertains to the intention we should have, that everything will be in order to bestow. At that time, Satan and the nations of the world ask, "What is this *Mitzva*?" Is the Creator deficient that we should impart upon Him delight and pleasure? On the contrary, He desires to do good to His creations, and not for the created beings to do good to Him. Also, they ask, What is the reason about it?

What reason can there be to a person if he is told that he is forbidden to work for his own benefit, called receiving in order to receive? That is, a person must achieve a degree where no pleasure is for the sake of man's enjoyment, but only in order to delight the Creator.

What flavor can one derive from such work that will oblige him to engage in Torah and Mitzvot [commandments]? After all, they do not see in it a good enough reason to make them engage in Torah and Mitzvot "with all your heart and with all your soul."

On the contrary, he understands that he is relinquishing self-benefit from corporeal things, from which he would obtain greater pleasures for his self-benefit, but what flavor can there be in a vessel of bestowal?

To this comes the answer that it is written about it, "a constitution, a decree before Me and you have no permission to doubt it." This means that we should not give any answer to the body while it asks the question of Satan and the nations of the world. Rather, we should tell the body that this is so, a decree from heaven that the aim to receive is forbidden for us. Only then can we avoid arguments, and then we can win.

However, when he acquires the quality of Israel it is to the contrary—he has no pleasure or flavor unless he can work in order to bestow. When he cannot aim in order to bestow, he feels himself as bad and as dead, for then he feels that "The wicked in their lives are called 'dead,'" since then he is rewarded with feeling the taste of Dvekut [adhesion] with the Creator, and the opposite of it when he is separated from the Creator.

This is the meaning of "Since Satan and the nations of the world count Israel," etc. But when they acquire the quality of Israel, when they emerge from the control of the nations of the world, it is to the contrary: They feel all the flavor in life precisely in the aim to bestow, which is called Dvekut.

This is the meaning of "Let the mother come and wipe clean her son." The event with the calf was that they fell into a state of receiving in order to receive. At that time, the cow erases the incident with the calf. The cow is regarded as the intention *Lishma* [for Her sake], which is regarded as annulment of his self, regarded as the burning of the cow.

It is explained in the *Sulam* [Ladder commentary on *The Zohar*] that it is regarded as "Go and diminish yourself," which was said about the moon, who returns to being a dot, having lost all of the left line, called *Hochma* [wisdom]. Naturally, the sin of the calf passes away and he walks only with the aim to bestow.

430- A Higher Soul

"This is the constitution of the Torah [law] that the Lord had commanded to say," etc. "Come and see, when this dead departs from the world without children, the daughter of that prince does not gather him to her." (*The Zohar*, *Hukat*, Item 10). In other words, if the will to receive departs from him and he has no need for himself, but his intention is only for the sake of the Creator, he still has no sons because he has still not been rewarded with understanding in the Torah, as in "If you do not know, O fairest among women."

It was interpreted in the new *Zohar* that "Although you are the fairest among women, if you do not know the secrets of the Torah, 'Go forth by the footsteps of the flock,'" and you can learn the secrets of Torah from people "who trample it with their heels." This is the meaning of "the daughter of that prince does not gather him to her."

"The Creator takes pity on him and commands his brother to redeem him." That is, the soul, which is a brother to the body in the same manner as Esau, who is called the "will to receive," and Jacob is called "desire to bestow," the soul, as in "He who comes to purify is aided." *The Zohar* interprets that it is with a holy soul, meaning that he is given a higher soul, called "greater forces," which can win the war of the inclination.

"To return and be corrected in another dust," meaning another body. In other words, through an incarnation, when a higher soul incarnates into his body and is called "other" with respect to the new soul, which is clothed in this body.

"If this redeemer does not wish to revive his brother," meaning if the new soul cannot redeem the body that is called "her brother," "Does not wish" means "cannot."

"A shoe must be tied to his leg," meaning we must add in the matter of faith.

"That woman," meaning the *Shechina* [Divinity], "shall release him and take that shoe to her." In other words, the *Shechina* takes the shoe that man has made for her, meaning she accepts the work that he has done, which is a *Masach* [screen] that he has placed on the will to receive.

"To show that that dead returns to being among the living by this act," and by this the dead is incarnated into the newborn son. In other words, through one's work of placing a *Masach* on the will to receive, he is rewarded with a son, meaning with the secrets of Torah called "son."

"It is the opposite of that shoe which the dead takes from the living" (*The Zohar*, *Hukat*, Item 12), for then that kept shoe, which is on faith, takes the will to receive, meaning those who want to walk with the external intellect.

Conversely, when the *Shechina* takes the shoe, he is rewarded with the inner intellect, meaning that now he has the sensation of Godliness through *Dvekut* [adhesion], for the Creator has given him the knowledge and feeling of Godliness. Before the dead receives the shoe, it is considered that he wants knowledge and reception for himself. But through the *Dvekut* he is rewarded with all the knowledge and feelings.

This is called that the Creator has given him the gift without an awakening on the part of the lower one, and this is called "I have given help to one who is mighty." Yet, for himself, a person wants to be a servant of the Creator unconditionally, and this is considered that he is receiving everything because it is the will of the Creator.

431- A Shoe for His Foot

"That shoe places... Hence, everything that the dead gives to a person in a dream is good. But if he took an object from the house, it is bad, such as taking his shoe. What is the reason? It indicates that he has moved his leg" (*The Zohar*, *Hukat*, Item 8).

We should interpret that "dead" means the will to receive. All the efforts he makes in the work for *Kedusha* [holiness] are because the will to receive gives the strength to bestow. But if the will to receive takes, it is bad because there are only two domains: the domain of bestowal or the domain of reception. Reception is called "death" and bestowal is called "life," since by this we adhere to the Life of Lives.

Hence, if the dead takes, it means that he takes forces from the domain of bestowal and transfers them to the domain of the *Sitra Achra* [other side]. And the reason he says precisely "shoe" is that *Naal* [shoe] comes from the word *Man'ul* [lock], namely a place that should be locked from the external mind. Instead, it should be in the manner of faith above reason. The dead takes this shoe and wants it to be open so that the intellect will permeate it and make its inquiries.

This is the meaning of the shoe being specifically on the feet, since *Raglaim* [legs] comes from the word *Meraglim* [spies]. In that place—in the Providence of the Creator—we must go with faith above reason, meaning there must be a shoe on one's foot, a prohibition to enter with the intellect.

If the will to receive, which is called "dead," takes it, it means that he has entered the domain of the *Sitra Achra*. This is the meaning of

"Do not inquire in that which is beyond you." Only in this manner do we adhere to the Life of Lives.

"This is when the dead takes him. But when the live one removes his shoe and gives it to another, to keep the possession, he affects the decree of above" (Item 9). That is, if a person takes off his shoe and wants to know and understand with his intellect not because he wants to walk in the ways of the external intellect, but in order to see Providence, how it is hidden from him, and that he is full of contradictions to the external mind, and he does it in order to keep the possession, meaning for his faith to be sustainable, then he will be able to do everything by the decree of above. In other words, he will be able to observe the Torah and *Mitzvot* [commandments] as a constitution, which is "I have given a decree and you have no permission to doubt it" or comprehended with the intellect. Instead, he should accept everything with faith above reason, meaning understand that faith contradicts reason.

If he has no reason that will understand otherwise, it is not regarded as "against reason," but rather this, too, is regarded as "within reason." But when he takes off the shoe and spies there to see what the intellect has to say about such places where the intellect sees otherwise than faith, then faith lies over the "against reason."

Yet, this is called "simple faith," for only simple faith obligates him to be a servant of the Creator and not the intellect. It follows that he took off his shoe only to observe the faith and to be certain that all his work is only because he works because of the decree from above, called "constitution," and this brings him eternal life.

432- *The Making of the Calf*

Miron Village, *Tammuz, Tav-Shin-Chaf-Hey*, June 1966

The matter of the purity of the cow comes before the month of *Nissan*, for in *Nissan* they were redeemed. The cow is regarded as faith, as RASHI interpreted, an allegory about a handmaid's child who soiled a king's palace. They said, "Let the mother come and wipe clean her son."

Likewise, the cow atones for the making of the calf. The issue of the calf was that they said "these," as it is written in *The Zohar*, and "cow" is regarded as a constitution, as RASHI interpreted, "It is a decree before Me, I have made a constitution." Therefore, we need preparation for redemption, which is the matter of acceptance of faith.

433- The Lord Your God Was Unwilling to Listen

2 Heshvan, *Tav-Shin-Lamed-Bet*, October 21, 1971

"The Lord your God was unwilling to listen to Balaam, and the Lord your God turned the curse into a blessing for you."

We should understand the wonder of the Creator being unwilling to listen to an unworthy man. Also, what does it mean that He turned the curse into a blessing, if He did not hear Balaam at all?

The thing is that there are those who slander to find a place of iniquity in Israel. This means that when one wants to walk in the ways of the Creator, the body slanders and seeks iniquities in Israel. Iniquity means a place of deficiency, where he finds that by wanting to be in the quality of Israel, there are many questions, meaning he has tough questions and issues regarding the quality of Israel.

With this power, it detains a person from walking in the ways of the Creator, meaning from being in the quality of Israel, as it is written, "My son, My firstborn, Israel." By the body's slandering Israel and finding iniquities, meaning faults, it obstructs him and detains him.

The verse comes and says about this that He was completely unwilling to listen, for although it came with an argument that cannot be defeated through reasoning, its words are not heard or accepted whatsoever. In other words, one who wants to walk on the path of the Creator—that "the Lord will be your God," and not other things—should not listen whatsoever to the complaints and grievances of the body, which come from the intellect.

Thus, the meaning of being "unwilling to listen" is that he did not want to reply to it within reason, but rather went above rhyme and reason.

At that time, "The Lord your God turned the curse into a blessing for you." That is, of all the slandering that it slanders through the complaints and grievances, when it overcomes the complaints by going above reason, they cause him to be rewarded with faith above reason. Otherwise, he would walk in the path of the Creator within reason, but the real *Kli* [vessel] to be rewarded with the light of the Creator is specifically above rhyme and reason, and this *Kli* is called a *Kli* of bestowal.

Conversely, within reason, it is called "a *Kli* of reception," and on that *Kli* there was the *Tzimtzum* [restriction]. It follows that by wanting to be rewarded with "the Lord will be your God," and not other gods, he "was unwilling to listen" whatsoever. That is, he says to it, "I do not want to hear what you are saying." By this, the Creator turns the curse into a blessing.

434- *How Good Are Your Tents, Jacob – 2*

Tammuz, Tav-Shin-Lamed-Tet, July 1979

"How good are your tents, Jacob, Your dwellings, Israel."

By the blessings of that wicked one, what was in his heart becomes apparent. Balak has the letters of *Kabel* [receive], whose quality is self-reception. Balaam has the letters of *Lev-Am* [heart of the nation], a nation that belongs to the stony heart.

He sent to him, "Behold, a nation has come out from Egypt," meaning that the people of Israel has emerged from the *Klipa* [shell/peel] of Egypt, which is self-reception. Therefore, from this day onward there will not be dominance to those who are placed in self-reception.

Since Balaam is an *Am* [nation] of the stony heart, he wanted to spoil the method of Israel, who emerged from the control of the *Klipot* [pl. of *Klipa*] of self-reception. This is why he was compelled to bless, as our sages said, "A bad angel will say 'Amen' against his will."

This is why he said, "How good are your tents, Jacob," for "tent" means Torah, which is *Katnut* [smallness/infancy], Jacob. Afterward, we are rewarded with the quality of "Your dwellings, Israel," by which comes the tabernacle of the whole of Israel.

Each time, there are *Katnut* and *Gadlut* [greatness/adulthood], as Baal HaSulam said, "And it came to pass when the ark journeyed, that Moses said, 'Arise...' and when it rested, he said, 'Return.'" In other words, during the work there is rising, and at a time of rest, there is the quality of "returning."

On one hand, Torah is *Katnut*, since when we feel a deficiency, we learn Torah, and through the deficiencies we achieve fillings, for where there is no lack, there is nothing to fill.

But when a person is filled in the tent of Torah, he shifts to "Your dwellings, Israel." Yet, when he dwells in the tabernacle, it is called "when it rested, he said, 'Return,'" meaning that there is no ascent in degree there, since "journeying" means walking from degree to degree.

Hence, when he achieves wholeness, he should immediately try to find a deficiency, and then he shifts to the state of "How good are your tents, Jacob," which is the tent of Torah. At that time, he is in the degree of "Jacob," which is *Katnut*. When he completes the filling through the Torah, he shifts to wholeness, which is regarded as a tabernacle, and so forth until he achieves complete wholeness. The beginning of the exit is from the exodus from Egypt.

The exodus begins not necessarily when he has departed, but even if he merely wants to emerge from Egypt, or even if he wants to emerge but cannot, and he has the strength to pray to the Creator to deliver him from Egypt, then he already begins to walk on the path of truth.

435- When Balak Took Counsel

Tammuz, Tav-Shin-Lamed-Het, July 1978

When Balak took counsel, he said, "and I will drive it out from the land." He said, "That degree to which Israel grip is from the land for certain," for it is *Malchut*, which is called "land." This is the meaning of "For it is mightier than I, for certain, who can fight and stand up to Israel," for their degree is stronger than his.

For this reason, "I will drive it out from the land," meaning from their degree, which is *Malchut*. If I drive them out from that land, meaning he can make them sin, he will be able to do with them everything he wants (*The Zohar*, Balak, Item 264).

We should interpret why he says that the degree of *Malchut* is stronger than his degree. *Malchut* is called "above reason," as our sages said, "One should not say 'impossible' about pork, but rather 'possible' but the Torah forbade."

This is called "above reason," when the reason of the created being cannot agree to go against the will to receive, since man's nature is that when he must relinquish the pleasure, he must know and understand why, meaning why I am making a concession, what does my body gain from preventing myself from enjoying.

At that time, it should be replied that it is either because of fear, meaning that by relinquishing pleasure, he denies himself the afflictions of Hell, meaning that when he weighs the value of the flavor of pleasure compared to the taste of suffering he will suffer for that pleasure, he sees that it does not pay because the suffering is far greater and it is not worthwhile to endure great suffering in return for a short-lived pleasure while the suffering is eternal suffering in Hell.

Or from the perspective of love, meaning that in return for relinquishing a fleeting moment of tasting pleasure, he will receive a greater pleasure and more prolonged, namely the pleasures of the next world.

For those two reasons, if a person compares the commandment to the transgression, he has the power to overcome the pleasure. Yet, in that state, although the body understands this, the evil inclination might come and confuse his calculations because everything follows the calculation of the will to receive, so the evil inclination has the power to confuse him and blur the depiction of heaven and hell.

But when one is rewarded with all his power of detaining being because of the kingdom of heaven, meaning that he is rewarded with not having to work for himself at all, but only in order to bestow, the evil inclination cannot argue with him because it has nothing to give him.

This is the meaning of the words, "and I will drive it out from the land," from the degree of the kingdom of heaven, and then I will be able to make them sin. But a "land," which is the kingdom of heaven, is stronger than him, and with this degree, it is utterly impossible to make them sin, and this is with respect to the heart.

It is likewise with respect to the mind: He must believe that the Creator hears the prayer. That is, if a person avoids everything and wants to adhere to the Creator, the Creator connects to him and brings him closer, as in "He who comes to purify is aided," as *The Zohar* writes, "with a holy soul." In other words, the Creator is revealed to him, and then he naturally forgets about the whole world and remembers only the Creator.

Come and see that the "The Lord, when you came out from Seir as you marched from the field of Edom, the earth quaked..." When the Creator wanted to give the Torah to Israel, He went and summoned the children of Esau but they did not accept it, as you say, "the Lord came from Sinai, He shone on them from Seir," who did not want to receive it. He went to the children of Ishmael but they did not want to receive it, as it is written, "appeared from Mount Paran." Because they did not want it, He returned to Israel.

We should understand why He went first to the children of Seir and Ishmael and did not go to the children of Israel straight away, if Israel would receive the Torah. Afterward, He would go to the children of Esau and Ishmael so that they, too, would receive the Torah. Also, if Israel would receive the Torah, there would be no place for the children of Esau and Ishmael to also receive the Torah.

We should interpret this according to the path of truth, according to the order of the reception of the Torah, as in "I have created the evil inclination; I have created the Torah as a spice" (*Baba Batra* 16), by which we are rewarded with the Torah of the Creator, in the sense that the Torah is the names of the Creator. In other words, the Torah is not a sorting of *Tuma'a* [impurity] and *Tahara* [purity], but rather the whole of the Torah is the names of the Creator.

When one begins to observe Torah and *Mitzvot* [commandments], he thinks that the Creator invited the children of Seir, as well, meaning he thinks that he can observe the Torah together with the children of Esau, since man consists of all seventy nations, and Esau and Ishmael are the roots of the nations of the world because the *Klipa* [shell/peel] of Esau is the quality of the "left," corresponding to the mind, and the *Klipa* of Ishmael is the quality of the "right," corresponding to the heart, while the rest are branches.

Hence, a person agrees to observe Torah and *Mitzvot* but does not want to relinquish the quality of the children of Esau.

Afterward, he sees that they do not agree to receive the Torah if he does not relinquish them, so he realizes that with the children of Esau, this will not go well. This is considered that they did not want to receive it, meaning that the person sees that with them he will never come to the real Torah.

Afterward, he thinks that perhaps together with the children of Ishmael he will be able to observe the real Torah, but then he sees that if he does not relinquish the children of Ishmael, he will never achieve the real Torah.

This is considered that a person thinks that the Creator gave the Torah to the children of Ishmael, that even if he did not relinquish them, the Creator intended to give them the Torah, meaning together with them. But when he truly understands, he sees that even with them He did not give the Torah.

This is considered that "they did not receive it," meaning they do not agree. Once a person has come to a complete resolution that the children of Esau and the children of Ishmael do not want the Torah, this is considered that a person has achieved the recognition of evil.

At that time, a person returns to the quality of Israel, called *Yashar-El* [straight to the Creator], where everything he does must be aimed directly for the sake of the Creator, and this is the meaning of *Yashar-El*.

Then he has a choice: He can relinquish everything and take upon himself the quality of *Yashar-El*, or stay as he is, observing Torah and *Mitzvot* with the aim he has had since childhood, or accept above reason, called "We will do" before "We will hear," meaning "for the Lord alone."

This is the meaning of the words, "Then he returns to Israel," meaning that then a person returns to Israel because the Torah was given only to the discernment of the name "Israel." This is called "Who has chosen us from among all the nations." Only when one has come to a state of *Yashar-El* is he capable of receiving the Torah. It follows that the real Torah is given to a person only when he is in the quality of Israel.

Prior to this, he can observe the Torah in practice, but not with an intention that is in order to bestow contentment upon his Maker, and then he receives the Torah as a means, which is "I have created the evil inclination; I have created the Torah as a spice." Afterward, when he becomes Israel, he is rewarded with the internal Torah called "the names of the Creator."

436- Three Prayers

Tammuz, Tav-Shin-Lamed-Het, July 1978

"But three are called 'prayer': a prayer for Moses, the man of God, a prayer such as which exists in no other person; a prayer for David, such as which exists in no other king; a prayer for the poor. Of those three prayers, which is the most important? It is a prayer for the poor. This prayer precedes the prayer of Moses and precedes the prayer of David and precedes all other prayers in the world."

"He asks, 'What is the reason?' It is because the poor is brokenhearted, and it is written, 'The Lord is near to the brokenhearted.' The poor always quarrels with the Creator, and the Creator listens and hears his words, since when the poor prays, he opens all the windows of the firmament, and all the other prayers that rise up, the brokenhearted poor delays them, as it is written, 'A prayer for the poor when he envelops.'"

It should have said, "when he is enveloped." What does "when he envelops" mean? It means that he causes a delay, delaying all the prayers in the world, which do not enter until his prayer enters. *Atufa* means delayed, from the words, "the *Atufim* [enveloped] for Laban" (*The Zohar*, Balak, Items 187-188).

We have the prayers of Moses, David, the rest of the prayers, and the prayer for the poor. What is the difference? What are the answers that the poor quarrels with the Creator? What does it mean that he delays, as though there is a queue and one follows the other, or is there a mess before Him? 1) The difference between the prayers of Moses, David, the rest of the prayers, and the prayer of the poor. 2) What is the relation toward the poor because he quarrels with the Creator? 3) What does it mean that he delays all the prayers until his prayer is accepted, as though when the poor prays, only he should be treated, and it is impossible to answer the prayers of the rest of the people at that time?

Prayer is called "work in the heart," meaning a lack—that which the heart feels that it is missing. Sometimes, a person feels that he lacks Torah, which is the quality of Moses, and sometimes he feels that he lacks the quality of the Messiah, meaning that he is concerned that redemption has not yet come to the whole of Israel, called "David, the King Messiah." So it is with the rest of the prayers, each according to what he feels.

But there is a prayer when a person feels that he has nothing and he is just like a beast, without faith or fear of heaven, which are the whole basis of Judaism. For this reason, he quarrels with the Creator over why He created him as man, meaning making calculations about himself and he is worried and concerned over his situation, namely that he has no lack other than his self-benefit, and that he has no feeling of others except where it concerns his own benefit.

He is seemingly angry with the Creator about this, why He created him a man with a mind and heart that must yield some benefit to the world, while both the mind and the heart are preoccupied only with his own benefit. And if He did create him a man, why does he not feel the existence of the Creator?

He wants to believe but his heart is numbed and his faith brings him no sensation so he can know or feel, as our sages said, "Know before whom you stand." When he speaks to people, even to beasts and animals and birds, he feels that he is speaking to someone, but when he speaks to the Creator or when he learns the teaching of the Creator, he does not feel the existence of the Creator.

It follows that he has nothing because he lacks the very basis, namely faith in the Creator, so he cannot aim in order to bestow for he does not feel the greatness of the Creator to make it worthwhile for him to annul himself and all his possessions before the Creator.

He is always angry and quarrels with the Creator over why the Creator hides Himself from him so he will not feel Him, and he is always angry over why the Creator has left him, meaning why the Creator allows him to say as though the Creator created him.

Afterward, when he comes to a state of birth, meaning when he comes to his own authority, when he feels that he is a separate being from the Creator and stands in his own right, he should believe that the Creator is standing near him but there is no such faith over him, and then he has grievances over why the Creator made it so he would not have the power of faith so he can believe that the Creator is standing next to him, as it is written, "For the matter is very close to you; it is in your mouth and heart to do it."

Hence, before one is answered for this prayer of the poor, how can it be said that He will answer him the prayer of Moses, which is the Torah, before he has faith, which is the primary foundation? Also, when he prays for redemption, it is also impertinent to answer him, and likewise with the rest of the prayers before he has the basis that the Creator even hears a prayer. Hence, no prayer can be answered if the prayer for the poor has not been answered.

This is considered that it delays all the prayers, which means only that no prayer is accepted before his prayer is accepted, for it is the basis. Afterward, it is possible to be saved on other things, as well.

437- Great Priesthood

Tammuz, Tav-Shin-Mem-Aleph, July 1981

The *Zohar* explains what should have been a commandment for great priesthood, as it is written, "for he was zealous for his God," since any priest who kills a soul is forever disqualified for priesthood, for he clearly disqualifies the degree of those.

The *Sulam* [Ladder commentary on *The Zohar*] interprets that priesthood is *Hesed* [mercy], and killing a soul is its opposite. And because Pinhas killed Zimri and Cozbi, he was disqualified by law from being a priest. And because he was zealous for the Creator, He had to give him once again everlasting priesthood, to him and to his descendants (Item 21).

We should understand this. If a priest is the degree of *Hesed*, because he should engage in sacrifices, to bring atonement for each and every one from Israel, since all the sins come from the vessels of reception. Hence, the priest, who is the quality of *Hesed*, whose interest is only to bestow, for this reason, he has the power to install nearing, called "equivalence of form," so the sinner will acquire for himself the quality of *Hesed* through the acts of sacrificing. This is not so when a priest kills a soul, since any murder comes specifically by wanting to take revenge on someone who afflicts him.

Moreover, death is the opposite of life. *Kedusha* [holiness] is called "life." When one performs an act that is the opposite of life, he is attached to the *Klipa* [shell/peel]. Thus, how can he bring a sinner close to *Kedusha*, which is life?

Since all the atonement that one brings is only to adhere to the Life of Lives, which is the matter of equivalence of form, we should understand why then was he later given the priesthood because he was zealous for the Creator, though the quality of *Hesed* was blemished in him.

We should interpret that here, for he was zealous for the Creator, he knew that he was meant to be a priest, for he was the son of Eliezer, son of Aaron the priest, and the importance of the priest is something very high, for we see that the priest can make an intention for the Name in the Holy of Holies, unlike any other person.

This is the unification of ASHAN—*Olam* [world], *Shanah* [year], *Nefesh* [soul]. It is known that *Olam* is a place, which is precisely the place of the Holy of Holies. *Shanah* means "time," which is specifically the Day of Atonement. *Nefesh* is the high priest. Precisely by uniting *Olam, Shanah, Nefesh*, he could make an intention for the explicit Name. There are also many advantages to the high priest.

When Pinhas saw what was happening in Israel, he engaged in the quality of *Hesed*, which is the quality of "priest," whose aim was only to bestow, although he knew that he would lose the priesthood. Even his physical life was in danger, but he performed an act of bestowal for the sake of the general public so the public will be saved from the danger it was in at the time.

It therefore follows that precisely then he engaged in acts of bestowal and not of reception. This is why he was given it back, since the killing was not an act of disparity from the Life of Lives. Rather, through the act of *Hesed*, everyone would see and learn from him to adhere to the Life of Lives. This is the meaning of "for he was zealous for his God."

438- Save Your Servant, You, My God

Tammuz, Tav-Shin-Mem-Aleph, July 1981

"Save Your servant, You, my God; delight the soul of Your servant; give Your strength to Your servant." Three times David became a servant in this praise, corresponding to three times that the authors of the Mishnah said that a person should be a servant in the prayer.

"In the first blessings, he should be as a servant praising his rav [great one/teacher]. In the middle ones, as a servant seeking a gift from his rav. In the final blessings, as a servant thanking his rav for the gift he has received from him, and he walks away" (*The Zohar*, Pinhas, Item 180).

Here lies the order of man's work. First, one must believe in the Creator above reason and praise his rav, meaning feel completely and utterly whole, for it is known that to the extent that a person feels that his friend is giving him gifts, to that extent he praises him. Also, to the extent that he feels his friend's greatness, to that extent he can praise. In other words, if he feels that he is lacking something and his friend can satisfy it, he immediately loses the power to praise and glorify his friend.

Therefore, when a person begins his work, he must go with faith above reason that he is not lacking anything, and that his rav has satisfied all his wishes. At that time, he is called "whole," and then the whole can connect to the whole. Conversely, when he is deficient, the deficient does not connect to the whole.

Afterward, he can establish deficiencies like a slave seeking a gift from his rav, when he asks for his needs, meaning that the judge has only what his eyes see and he must not ignore any deficiency that he has. On the contrary, to the extent that he feels his deficiency, so he can pray that his rav will satisfy his wishes. And then, the more the student asks, the better.

Finally, he must not stay deficient. He must go again on the path of faith above reason, that he is utterly and completely whole. This is the meaning of the words, "as a servant thanking his rav for the gift he has received from him, and he walks away." He should believe above reason that he has already received all his wishes, called a "gift."

He thanks his rav for this, for one must not live in separation, meaning that he has complaints against his rav that he is not giving him what he asks. For this reason, it is forbidden for man to be deficient and he must always be in joy. However, in order to have *Kelim* [vessels] to receive, he must evoke the deficiencies.

In the offering, this is regarded as ascending and descending, "Knowing in the beginning and knowing in the end, and concealment in between." That is, between knowing and knowing it is permitted to see the concealment, meaning that he has no revelation with respect to the truth, to feel that his work is desirable to his rav.

It follows that one must not disclose any lack in Torah and work for himself. Rather, he must always go above rhyme and reason that he is utterly and completely whole. In between, he can ask his wishes as his eyes see, that he has only faults. But afterward, he must believe as though he has already received all his wishes and he thanks his rav for this.

At that time, he can be happy that he is whole. It follows that all his wholeness is built on faith, and his deficiencies are built on knowledge, since "the judge has only what his eyes see."

439- Why Was Pinhas Awarded the Priesthood?

Tammuz, Tav-Shin-Mem-Aleph, July 1981

The evil inclination and the good inclination are not a matter of intellect, but a matter of feeling. If a person does not see any benefit for himself while engaging in Torah and *Mitzvot* [commandments], he feels bad. This is called "the evil inclination." The measure of the evil inclination is according to the measure of the sensing of the evil, if he regrets not having grace in the work if he does not see that he will derive from this something for his own benefit.

To the extent of the sensation of suffering from such a state of lowliness, this is considered that he has a big evil. However, if he understands with his intellect that he is not fine in spiritual matters but it does not hurt him, this is not regarded as having an evil inclination, since he does not feel bad.

This is the meaning of "If you encounter this villain, pull him to the seminary," for precisely when he wants to pull him to the seminary, he sees that he is a villain. However, the advice to be rid of him is precisely through faith above reason, and prayer above reason.

440- Pinhas Saw

Tammuz, Tav-Shin-Lamed-Tet, July 1979

"Therefore, say, 'Behold, I give him My covenant of peace.'"

We should understand in the way of intimation what is the meaning of "a covenant of peace." What is it about that covenant for which it is called "a covenant of peace"?

At the end of the portion Balak, it is written, "And Pinhas saw." RASHI interpreted that he saw an act and remembered a rule. He said to him, to Moses, "Thus I have received from you: He who has intercourse with an Aramean, zealots hurt him ... meaning that the courthouse does not instruct him to do." This means that he saw an act, that there was only an act here, and remembered a rule, meaning that the rule is that the courthouse does not instruct him to do.

By the way of intimation, the courthouse is as our sages said, "No calamity comes to the world but for the judges of Israel" (*Shabbat* [Sabbath] 139a). This means that each one in Israel has a courthouse, meaning that within a person there is a mind that decides to do or not to do that thing. This is regarded as the courthouse of each and every one.

It follows that if his judge is an unworthy judge, it is as though he plants an Asherah. Before one is rewarded with repentance, his courthouse are judges who are unfit to cast verdicts in Israel.

This is the meaning "he saw an act," that a servant of the Creator who wants to walk on the path of truth can see only actions and not laws. The law that his mind should determine, his intellect will never obligate him to work in order to bestow, since this is against his will. Hence, his courthouse will not agree for him to do and to aim in order to bestow.

However, if he overcomes and says "I am zealous," meaning that although his court does not instruct this, he will act without intellect, this is called "above reason."

On the action, one should always be in a state of overcoming. This is considered that he is always at war, as our sages said, "One should always vex the good inclination over the evil inclination" (*Berachot* 5a), and RASHI interpreted, "make war with it."

If a person always walks in a state of above reason, the Creator says, "Behold, I give him My covenant of peace," as it is written, "I will hear what God the Lord will say, for He will speak peace to His people and to His followers and let them not return to folly" (Psalms 85).

This means that after the Creator makes a covenant of peace with a person, he has no more wars, as it is written, "When the Lord favors man's ways, even his enemies will make peace with him."

441- Avenge the Vengeance of the Children of Israel

Tammuz, Tav-Shin-Lamed-Tet, July 1979

"And the Lord spoke to Moses ... 'Avenge the vengeance of the children of Israel on the Midianites' ... and Moses spoke to the people ... to execute the Lord's vengeance on Midian."

The interpreters ask about this, "Why did Moses change the words of the Creator in telling the people 'the Lord's vengeance,' and not 'the vengeance of the children of Israel,' as the Creator said?" They also asked about changing the phrasing, that the Creator said, "on the Midianites," in plural form, and Moses said, "on Midian," in singular form.

We should interpret that it is known that the purpose of creation from the perspective of the Creator is to do good to His creations. It follows that the Creator said that all the wars that we should make are in order to achieve the delight and pleasure, so the creatures will receive it.

When Moses spoke to Israel, if he told them that the war would be for their own sake they would fall into self-love called "receiving in order to receive." But on this there was a *Tzimtzum* [restriction], and they would never achieve the goal in this manner.

This is why he told them, "Avenge the vengeance of the Lord," for they need to aim that the war against the inclination will be for the sake of the Creator and not for their own sake. By this they would achieve the purpose of creation, to do good to His creations.

In truth, there are many qualities to fight against, so when the Creator said to Moses, "Avenge the vengeance of the children of Israel on the Midianites," it means that there are many judgments that must be subdued. This is why it was said in plural form, which is what should be, namely to subdue many Midianites, which are called *Dinim* [judgments], who interfere with achieving the purpose of creation.

When Moses said to the people, "Avenge the vengeance of the Lord on Midian," he thereby implied that should they walk on the path where they need only one correction, which is the vengeance of the Creator, from that perspective there is not more than one judgment, which contains within it many judgments. In other words, a person does not need to fight against all the judgments, meaning all the bad qualities. Instead, if he walks on a path that we must aim all our actions to the Creator, meaning for the sake of heaven, if this is all of our intention, then all the qualities will be cancelled by themselves and we do not need to work specifically on each quality.

The more the aim is for the sake of the Creator, if one is rewarded with this, with winning this war, so it is in order to bestow upon the Creator, then all the qualities are cancelled and revoked. This is why he spoke in singular form, "Avenge the vengeance of the Lord on Midian."

442- Your Children, Whom You Said

Av, Tav-Shin-Lamed-Tet, July 1979

"And your children, whom you said would become a prey, and your sons, who this day have no knowledge of good or bad, shall come there. To them I will give it and they shall inherit it."

The heart of the Torah and *Mitzvot* [commandments] that we were given is in the manner of "I have created the evil inclination; I have created the Torah as a spice." The Torah and *Mitzvot* qualify a person to come into the King's palace and obtain the hidden light that is called "the quality of the land of Israel."

A person always values the best states, which he perceives as worthy of being qualification to enter the domain of *Kedusha* [holiness], called "the land of Israel," meaning the times when he has a desire and yearning to learn Torah, as well as the times when he has excitement during prayer and good intentions while doing good deeds.

However, the times when there is no desire for Torah and *Mitzvot* and the understanding and reasoning interfere with Torah and *Mitzvot*, at that time, a person needs much work to overcome them. At that time, everything he does in the work of the Creator is compulsory, since the thoughts of separation push him away.

And the more he overcomes, the more he sees that he is far, and all his prayers are bodies without souls, filled only with dryness. Although he cries out to the Creator to help him, he sees that his heart is not with him. A person despises these states and regards them as lowliness, since he has no appreciation, to think about them that they should do him some favor or bring him closer to the goal.

The verse implies about this, "Your children," meaning the little ones, which is your state of *Katnut* [smallness/infancy], "whom you said would become a prey."

"Your sons," which are the understandings you have in Torah and *Mitzvot*, "this day have no knowledge of good or bad," meaning the times when you saw that you could not tell good from bad, when all your work is in a form where there is no distinction between good or bad, meaning the times when you feel that there is no feeling. Whether you engage in Torah and *Mitzvot* or you are not, you have the same feeling that you have no inspiration. At that time, you do anything that you can think of to emerge from these states; they "shall come there." These states are the real *Kelim* [vessels] required for the Creator to give them the land of Israel.

"To them I will give it and they shall inherit it," the inheritance of the fathers, which the Creator had promised to give the land of Israel. Specifically, they are the real *Kelim* that need the salvation of the Creator.

Conversely, the states that are important to you, do not need My help, since according to a person's opinion, only when he has excitement in the prayer, and desire and yearning and pleasure while studying Torah, this is what he appreciates because in this there is self-love. Yet, there is no connection between this and nearing the truth.

443- The Writing Is in the Labor

"What is your work? ... I am even afraid that a fly might come and sit on the coronet of a *Dalet*, erasing it, and turning it into a *Reish*" (*Iruvin* 13).

A "fly" means foreign thoughts. As for the *Dalet* (see the beginning of the "Introduction of The Book of Zohar"), the *Dalet* is in *Kedusha* [holiness] and *Reish* is in the *Sitra Achra* [other side]. He wrote that it could erase, meaning the faith. *Kankantom* [black ink] means *Ken* [*Kof-Nun*, 150 in *Gematria*] reasons, which is knowing. "Writer" means "Write them on the tablet of your heart." "Lacking and surplus" are the lack of the right [side] or the lack of the left.

Kankantom means two times *Ken*—a pure *Ken* and an impure *Ken*. When they are equal, he has room for faith.

"Into the ink," meaning blackness, which is work, for the writing is mainly in the labor. When he writes, he already has two discernments, called *Kan-Kan-Tom* [*Tom* (Hebrew: end)], for precisely then he has room to recognize it, and with this he writes.

444- Darkness Precedes Light

"If the rav [teacher/great one] is like an angel," etc. "Who is rich? He who is happy with his share." "Eating materializes a man."

Food has no taste unless it moves through the tongue and the palate. It is likewise with spiritual foods. If the Torah and *Mitzvot* [commandments] do not pass through faith in the Creator, they have no taste, the same as with physical food.

There is the purpose of creation and the correction of creation. Unlike eating them, there is no pleasure, which are the palate and the tongue. In Torah and *Mitzvot*, they are for the sake of the Creator and *Lo Lishma* [not for Her sake]. The night follows the day because any light lies on its unique darkness, just as every answer lies on its unique question. For this reason, there cannot be light, or day, prior to the darkness and the night.

445- No *Masach* [Screen] in *Keter*

It was said in several places that there is no *Masach* in *Keter* so it can make a *Zivug* [coupling], since it is completely pure. Thus, why did he write that in the new *Partzuf* MA there is a *Masach* of *Behina Hey*, which is called *Keter* (see in *Panim Meirot*, p 221 [in Hebrew]).

Afterward, it emerged, etc., and in the second *Behina*, the *Melech* of *Gevura*, whose level of ten *Sefirot* reaches *Hochma de Bina* (*Panim Meirot*, p 165 [in Hebrew]). It seems as though it should have been written, only up to *Bina*.

When the *Kelim* [vessels] of *Aleph-Vav-Chaf-Lamed Mem-Samech-Peh-Reish-Tav* are in *Gadlut* [greatness/adulthood], then below, the *Kelim* of *Bet-Dalet-Kof Het-Yod-Hey*, the *Ketarim* [pl. of *Keter*] stand in two lines, right and left. ZA is in *Hesed* of *Gevura*, except for the rest of the *Behinot* [discernments], which stand in *Hesed* and *Netzah*. The ARI writes explicitly that even the *Ketarim* stand in *Hesed* and *Netzah* (*Panim Meirot*, p 253).

446- The Meaning of Dry Land

Now we will explain the meaning of dry land, where there is no danger, but on the contrary, a great sweetening. However, it is like taking in without letting out, since it cannot elicit food and nourishment, and what falls in it burns and is lost by its heat and dryness, as in "when the sun grew hot, it would melt."

This is the meaning of "Vapor went up from the land and watered the face of the earth," since the power of the land is mainly its face, from which come all the sweetenings. Also, "vapor" comes from the words, "vapor and shattering," which is the opposite of the desire and the earth.

Indeed, know that this vapor takes from the abyss in the water, but not in a stormy wind, but only through the pillars of cloud, which is regarded as "earth" and "dry land," which is completely blocked by the light of the sun and covers the sun. It brings darkness and mist to the dwellers of the earth, and those clouds themselves, which are vapor and shattering and darkness, are dipped in the waters of the sea and suck from the mingling of the seawater with the sky, and the water becomes sweetened in the clouds and waters the earth.

The land elicits because the dry land becomes hardened by the *Kli* [vessel] of the abyss, and then she yields fruits. This is the meaning of the twofold "it was good" in it, meaning both for the great abyss in the water and also for the small abyss. This happened because first, all the water gathered into one place, to the quality of mercy and life. Hence, they were also cured as one, as in "And they delighted for they were silent."

The third day. You see that the light of the first day is *Keter*, the light of the second day is *AB*, and that of the third day is *SAG*, and that *SAG* contains *Galgalta* and *AB* and subdues them both in the waters in the sea, and in the fruits that the earth yields.

Do not be perplexed, since it is also written about the first day, "evening and morning," for "evening" indicates joining, so how does he say that there it is *Behina Dalet* [fourth phase] without joining?

However, the Torah spoke of creation and of *Beresheet* [in the beginning], which is the verse that associates the quality of mercy with the root of the *Bet* of *Beresheet*. However, we start from *Ein Sof* [infinity] to the nine utterances, which is the meaning of "one day" ... and creation ... from the second day.

A twofold "it was good." Since all the water gathered into one place, the quality of mercy, *Malchut de Bina* of the great abyss, and the corruption was attributed to the upper one, they were also healed as one, as in the land that was revealed. Then the two chasms become good for drinking and for yielding fruits. Understand the preceding of the revealing of the dry land, as it is written, "And the dry land appeared," and the subsequent making of the *Segula* [power/virtue/remedy] of eliciting bread and fruits from the earth.

The *Bet* of *Beresheet* is RADLA. One day is *Behina Dalet*, as in the skies within her from the inner *Zivug* [coupling], which is *Behina Dalet* without association. The second day is *Malchut de AB* prior to the dry land, and the third day is *Malchut de SAG*, in which there is dry land.

447- *Peace with the Creator*

"I heard of You and I was frightened." It was interpreted that because of what she underwent, he extends fear although now he is in complete wholeness and has nothing to add. But it was from what she underwent, meaning from the time of *Katnut* [smallness/infancy], when all his work was incomplete. It follows that for a long time, he was not at peace with the Creator.

Now he wants to correct this, for he cannot calm himself because of how he once was in such a state. He is ashamed about it and now he extends the fear and the shame.

"You have given those who fear You a banner to wave because of adornment, Selah" (Psalms 60). "Adornment" means decoration at the point of desire. By wanting to walk in a manner of bestowal, a person is rewarded with a miracle because it is against nature and reason, and man is incapable of it. Rather, we need a miracle from heaven. According to the miracle, we are rewarded with fear. It follows that precisely those who fear His name are rewarded with the miracle.

This is "a banner to wave," and it is precisely to those who want to walk in a manner of decoration at the point of the will to receive. Conversely, those who do not walk in a manner of decoration, and all their work is in the will to receive corporeality or spirituality, they are not on the path of *Kedusha* [holiness] and miracle. This is the meaning of what our sages said, "A miracle does not happen every day."

That is, not all that is regarded as day—when he learns and prays and has enthusiasm and high spirits—is regarded as a miracle, since his structure is only the will to receive, whether in heart or in mind. Rather, specifically the work that is on the basis of adornment is regarded as a miracle, and not that which is within reason.

"Before the face of the lamp, the seven candles will illuminate." RASHI interpreted that it is so it will not be said that he needs its light.

We should ask, "Would you think to say so?" Even more perplexing, our sages said in *Masechet* Shabbat [Sabbath], "Does He need its light? After all, all forty years when Israel were in the desert, they walked only by His light. Rather, it is a testimony to the people of the world that the *Shechina* [Divinity] dwells in Israel." What is a testimony? Rav said, "It is a western candle, which places in it oil such as the measure of the others, and from it he would light, and in it he would conclude."

"His light" are lights of *Hassadim* [mercies], regarded as vessels of bestowal. "Needing" means that the Creator must lead them on the path so they will walk in the ways of the Creator. Otherwise, they will not continue with their holy work. "Does He need its light?" meaning does the Creator want and need, and has no other way if there is an upper desire that they will walk in the way of the Creator only through light of *Hochma* [wisdom] that is received in vessels of reception, called "the light of the lower ones," which is received in vessels of reception?

They bring evidence to this, that the forty years that Israel walked in the desert, they walked only by His light, meaning a concealed world, which is from the *Chazeh* and above, called "light that is clothed in vessels of bestowal," which exist only in the Emanator.

However, although the light of the lamp illuminated below, the oil means light of *Hochma* that shines in the *Kelim* [vessels] of the lower one. Still, "before the face of the lamp" means that everyone, both the right side and the left side, turn toward the middle line.

448- The Sensation of Wholeness

It is said about the verse, "'The eyes of the Lord are always on her, from the beginning' (Deuteronomy 11), sometimes favorably, sometimes unfavorably. Sometimes favorably, how so? Israel were complete wicked in the beginning of the year and were sentenced to few rains. In the end, they repented. It is impossible to add, since the sentence has already been given, but the Creator brings them down in their season on the land that needs them." It is all according to the earth.

"Sometimes unfavorably, how so? In the beginning of the year, Israel were complete righteous. Therefore, they were sentenced to much rain. But in the end, they went astray. It is impossible to take away from them, since the sentences has been given, but the Creator brings them down not in their season and on a land that does not need them. At any rate, can the decree be rescinded and the rains increased? There it is different, for it is possible this way" (*Rosh Hashanah* 17b).

In other words, if a person is not rewarded, then during the eating he feels his wholeness, and during Torah and *Mitzvot* [commandments] he feels his faults and lowliness. But the truth is that it should be to the contrary: When he engages in corporeality, he should be lacking, and during Torah and *Mitzvot*, he should be in wholeness, and then he will be happy with his share.

449- The Drop Is Declared

"Israel, who were worthy at that time... in the right place." RASHI interpreted, with fruits and things (*Rosh Hashanah* 17b). The drop is declared that it will be a drop of, etc., and he becomes worthy. What should be done? He is given the powers in a place that will yield fruits, meaning he learns in books that lead to *Lishma* [for Her sake], and in an environment that do the work *Lishma*. And if not, then to the contrary.

450- Forces that Induce the Development of the Heart and the Mind

"If a wise disciple gets into a rage, it is because the Torah inflames him." RASHI interpreted, that he has a big heart due to his Torah, and he becomes more attentive than other people. This means that we must sentence him to the side of merit" (*Taanit* 4a).

We should interpret that because of his big heart, he is moved by everything and he is sensitive to everything.

"Lust" is a demand from his own internality. "Envy" means that for himself he has no demand, but his externality invokes in him a demand. This is why it is considered a demand from his externality. Therefore, there are two forces in man that cause him to develop: the mind and the heart.

451- Pure Eyed

The Creator is called "Pure Eyed" after the action, like "Healer of the Sick" and "Freer of the Imprisoned," since He purifies man's eyes as in the descent of the bottom *Hey* from the *Eynaim* [eyes] down. When the Creator removes the vessels of reception from a person's eyes, that person is rewarded with seeing the good.

452- Just as I Am Dancing before You

Av, Tav-Shin-Lamed-Tet, July-August 1979

"Just as I am dancing before You but I cannot touch You, so will all my enemies not be able to harm me." "May ... we fill the blemish of the moon so there is no diminution in it ... as it was prior to its diminution," etc. We should understand why one should care that there is a flaw in the moon and what he loses by this.

The moon implies *Malchut*. *Malchut* means the kingdom of heaven, which means that we must aim all the actions to be in order to bestow upon the Creator and not in order to receive for oneself. There are two discernments in the *Sitra Achra* [other side]: 1) the grip of the *Klipot* [shells/peels], 2) the suckling of the *Klipot*.

When a person does not feel taste in the work and does everything in a compulsory manner, the *Klipa* [sing. of *Klipot*] shows a person the flaw in spirituality, namely that spirituality is tasteless. By this, it gains a grip and does not let a person engage in Torah and *Mitzvot* [commandments] because spirituality is lowered. This is called "*Shechina* [Divinity] in the dust."

When a person grows stronger in Torah and *Mitzvot* and is rewarded with obtaining some flavor in the work, the *Klipa* comes and wants to suckle from the *Kedusha* [holiness]. That is, it makes a person think that he should engage in Torah and *Mitzvot* not for the purpose of a *Mitzva* [commandment] but because of the personal pleasure he is feeling now. Thus, all the taste and pleasure move to the *Sitra Achra* and not to the *Kedusha* [holiness]. This is called "the suckling into the *Klipot*."

For this reason, in order not to avoid the suckling into the *Klipot*, the moon was diminished. In other words, the taste and the pleasure in *Kedusha* were reduced and therefore it has nothing to suck. However, because of this there is room for a dance, since "dancing" means that a person goes up and down intermittently, and at times falls forward, and at times backward.

Hence, during the concealment of the light, when a person should overcome above reason, there is the matter of dancing, which means ascents and descents in spirituality. It was said about this, "But I cannot touch You," meaning that there is nothing to suck. "So will all my enemies not be able to harm me" during the filling, for then we pray for the filling of the blemish of the moon, that there will not be any diminution in it, meaning that it will be filled. The prayer is that then, too, the enemies will not be able to harm it, meaning to suck from it.

The prayer is over this, so that just as during the diminution there is no room for suckling, during the filling of the moon, the enemies will not have a place to suck from it.

Hence, we pray for the filling of the blemish of the moon, meaning that the light and pleasure will be revealed, and then we pray that there will be no diminution in it, meaning that the *Sitra Achra* will not be able to come and suck from it, since through the suckling, the diminution happens. This is why we say, "that there is no diminution in it."

453- The Eyes of Both of Them Opened

Av, Tav-Shin-Mem-Bet, July 1982

It is written in *The Zohar* (*VaEtchanan*, Item 35) about the verse, "And the eyes of both of them opened," "In the future, it is written, 'And I will lead the blind in a way that they do not know ... for the Creator is destined to open eyes that were not wise, so they will look in the high wisdom and attain what they did not attain in this world, so they will know their Master.'"

It is written in Isaiah 42, "The deaf will hear and the blind will look and see. Who is blind but My servant, or deaf like My messenger whom I send? Who is so blind as he that is at peace, and as blind as the servant of the Lord?"

We should understand this. Does the Creator have only blind servants and deaf messengers? Could He not pick for Himself people without blemishes?

In the way of the work of the Creator, the path of truth, there are always two opposites, as is explained in several places in the *Sulam* [Ladder commentary on *The Zohar*]. Also, here we should interpret that one who can be a messenger of the Creator is precisely one who is "deaf," since he does not want to hear slander. When a person wants to work *Lishma* [for Her sake], the body resists him with all kinds of arguments, and he pretends not to hear what the body tells him.

It follows that he can always be in wholeness, since the reason why one falls from one's degree is only because he listens to slander from his body about work not in order to receive reward. It follows that he could always be in wholeness.

On the other hand, he should see that he is "blind," meaning that he has no opening of the eyes in the Torah, since the whole Torah is the names of the Creator, yet he does not see.

At that time, he has *Kelim* [vessels], called "deficiencies for the light of Torah," since he feels deficient because the whole of the

Torah is concealed from him, and he feels that he is blind. Precisely he can be a servant of the Creator, meaning that the Creator will open his eyes in His Torah [law], as it is written, "Open our eyes in Your Torah."

However, we see that there are many people who are blind because their eyes were sealed to the light of Torah, and not just anyone is rewarded with opening the eyes. Our sages said about that, "A blind is as important as the dead; the poor is as important as the dead; he who has no sons is as important as the dead."

This means that if one considers himself "dead" when he feels that he is blind, meaning feels that by this he becomes poor in knowledge, that he has no understanding in the Torah, which is regarded as having no sons, he regards himself as though he were dead, that he has no taste in life because his eyes are sealed from the Torah. Yet, he is called "a servant of the Creator," as it is written, "as blind as the servant of the Lord," and he is rewarded with opening the eyes in the Torah.

This is the meaning of the words, "the deaf will hear." It means that afterward, when he is rewarded with the light of Torah, he who was previously deaf and did not want to hear the slander of the body concerning work in order to bestow, afterward he hears, observing "And you will love the Lord your God with all your heart," meaning with both your inclinations, since "When the Lord desires man's ways, even his enemies make peace with him." At that time, the body, too, agrees to the work of the Creator.

454- He Who Prays for His Friend

Said in a meal, 29 *Av*, *Tav-Shin-Lamed-Tet*, September 1, 1978

"He who prays for his friend is answered first" (*Baba Kama* 92b).

This is seemingly a deceit. We should understand "answered first," as in "Before they call, I will answer." It means that for a person to be able to ask for his friend, one first needs assistance from above. Otherwise, the body does not agree.

"To You Lord is the righteousness, and to us is the shame." "And he believed in the Lord and He considered it for him as righteousness." Concerning shame, it must be felt over the Giver, and then the shame comes by itself, as our sages said, "afraid to look at his face." However, when he does not feel the Giver, from whom will he be ashamed? Therefore, "To You Lord is the righteousness," meaning that he gives Him the faith. Then it can be said, "and to us is the shame."

This is as it is written in *The Zohar*: "It is known that no quality can rise above its degree before upper illumination is lowered down to it, so that afterward it will be able to grow and rise up" (Song of Songs).

455- Because You Hear

Av, Tav-Shin-Lamed-Het, August 1978

"And it came to pass because you hear these sentences and observe and do them, the Lord your God will keep for you the covenant and the kindness that He has sworn to your forefathers."

RASHI interpreted that if you observe minor *Mitzvot* [commandments] that a person tramples with his heels, the Lord your God will keep for you, etc., will keep His promise to you.

We should understand that "minor *Mitzvot*" imply contempt, referring to the intention to bestow, which is something that the body despises. But if a person observes, the Creator will keep His promise. Otherwise, there is a *Tzimtzum* [restriction] over a person's actions, so the light of the Creator cannot be on them.

456- Small Talents

Concerning choice: If a person is born with small talents, how can it be said that he will be a wise disciple? After all, his brain is too small to understand words of Torah.

Midrash Rabbah says about this (portion, "This Is the Blessing"), "The Creator said to Israel, 'Be sure, the whole wisdom and the whole Torah are easy. Anyone who fears Me and performs the words of Torah, all the wisdom and all of the Torah are in his heart.'"

He interpreted this in the "Introduction to The Study of the Ten Sefirot" as follows: There is no prerequisite for excellence here, for only by the *Segula* [merit/power/cure] of fear of heaven and observance of the *Mitzvot* [commandments] we are rewarded with all the wisdom of the Torah. This is the meaning of "Everything is in the hands of heaven but the fear of heaven," for only in fear of heaven is there choice, and everything else, the Creator gives.

457- The Counsel of the Lord Ever Stands

In the verse "The counsel of the Lord, ever stands," we should understand that it is a rule that a person uses a counsel in order to obtain something. However, once he has obtained the matter, he no longer uses the counsel. Thus, what does "ever stands" mean?

We should ask, for because man was created after the *Tzimtzum* [restriction], there is concealment on him. Thus, how can he achieve the goal called "to do good to His creations"? For this reason, the Creator gave an advice—to aim to bestow. This advice stands forever, for it is impossible to receive any abundance if one does not use the counsel of "in order to bestow." When one cannot work with this intention, he loses what he has obtained.

"Delight them with a complete structure." What is completeness? It is when he has two things in his hand: 1) abundance, 2) reception of the abundance. If he cannot give the aim to bestow then there is no completeness because the abundance departs from him.

Or we can interpret "complete structure" to mean *Hochma* and *Hassadim*, for only by those two will he be able to keep the abundance in his hand.

458- And It Came to Pass because You Hear

Av, Tav-Shin-Lamed-Tet, August 1979

"And it came to pass because you hear..." RASHI interpreted, if you obey the minor *Mitzvot* [commandments], which a person tramples with his heels. Also, it was said, "Be mindful with a minor *Mitzva* [commandment] as with a major one."

The *Mitzvot* to which a person is accustomed by upbringing, he knows he should be mindful of them. However, things that do not come to him by education are hard for him to keep because he does not know the seriousness of the matter, since he is not used to them or knows he should be mindful of them.

Therefore, if a person receives the *Mitzvot* by upbringing, he calls them serious. Therefore, he knows how to keep himself with all the care as much as possible. But as for the intention, it is impossible to give this to a person in the beginning of his work. Hence, when he grows, when he is told that he must aim for the sake of the Creator, this work is not so important to him because he did not receive it through education.

Therefore, he tramples with his heels, meaning he does not pay attention to them because they are minor and insignificant. Conversely, regarding practical *Mitzvot*, he knows that it is worthwhile to observe them, and even be stricter than the law and judgments dictate.

Yet, regarding the intention, he does not pay attention to this because he is not used to it. Hence, a person can observe the Torah and *Mitzvot* without knowing the reason that obligates him, but education itself is a good enough reason for which to observe Torah and *Mitzvot*.

But most important, once a person has grown up, he should know why he observes Torah and *Mitzvot*, meaning for what purpose he exerts—since man's purpose is to achieve *Dvekut* [adhesion] with the Creator, which is called "repentance." The imperative "because you hear" relates to this, meaning the thing that one tramples with his heels and pays no attention to it. This is the meaning of "Be mindful with a minor *Mitzva* as with a major one," meaning that if one cannot aim for the sake of the Creator, it will be in his eyes as though he has committed a grave transgression. At that time, he will be able to achieve the wholeness required of him.

Kalah [minor] comes from the word *Kalon* [disgrace] and degradation.

459- Because of Humbleness and Fear of the Lord

"And it came to pass because you hear these sentences and observe and do them." "The Lord your God will keep with you the covenant and the kindness that He swore to your forefathers." "Because of humbleness and fear of the Lord."

When a person walks in the ways of the Creator, he feels that each day he acquires a certain measure of Torah and *Mitzvot* [commandments], and he always adds, at times more and at times less. But during the week, he acquires a possession of Torah and *Mitzvot*. When Shabbat [Sabbath] comes, on the eve of Shabbat he has what he toiled. Thus, he feels that on Shabbat, he eats from what he toiled during the rest of the weekdays, called "six workdays."

At that time, he knows that he needs lowliness, so he searches for some fault in himself in order to be able to say that he is still in lowliness. But the verse says, "Do not bring abomination into your home." It is also written, "Anyone who is proud is an abomination to the Lord." Also, here Rabbi Yochanan said in the name of Rabbi Shimon, "Anyone in whom there is crassness of spirit, it is as though he commits idol-worship" (*Sotah* 4b).

We should understand why one in whom there is crassness of spirit, it is as though he commits idol-worship. "Because of humbleness" means that the end of humbleness is fear of the Creator [*Ekev* means "because" and "heel"]. We should understand what is humbleness.

When a person feels that he has no Torah or good deeds, when he feels that he is the worst, it means that he sees that everyone engages in Torah and *Mitzvot* [commandments] and they are satisfied with their lives, while he is living without satisfaction in Torah and *Mitzvot*.

Because the general public is built in the quality of "surrounding," and there is a difference between the whole of Israel and the individual, since in the whole of Israel the surrounding lights shine, so in general, each one from the public can mourn over the ruin of the Temple and await the revelation of Elijah and the complete redemption and the coming of the Messiah soon in our days, Amen, for in the quality of "surrounding," each one has some sensation in these words, "exile" and "redemption."

But when an individual asks himself and introspects, he sees that he has no clue about these matters. In this, there is a difference between the general public and the individual. That is, it is impossible for an individual to obtain inner light before one is rewarded with repentance.

Hence, when one wants to walk in the way of the Creator personally, namely not as part of the general public, engaging in Torah and *Mitzvot* the way the general public engages in Torah and *Mitzvot*, but rather individually, he sees that he has nothing. On the contrary, each day becomes worse for him, for the more he engages in Torah and *Mitzvot* on the path of truth, the more he sees that he is far from the truth.

At that time, he comes into humbleness, since he feels that he is worse than everyone, for everyone has at least an illumination in the form of "surrounding," while he cannot go with the surrounding because he has already begun to work in the way of the individual, so he has nothing of the way of the general public.

So with his humbleness, with the afflictions he suffers from having no possessions, from being completely empty, he must make an honest prayer for the Creator to give him fear of the Creator. This is called "The Lord your God will keep for you the covenant and the kindness," that the Creator will bring him closer to Him.

Conversely, one who has crassness of spirit, who thinks that he has more possessions than everyone, will never be able to achieve fear of the Creator. For this reason, it is as though he commits idol-worship, since he does not need the Creator to bring him closer.

460- Will Keep His Promise to You

Av, Tav-Shin-Mem-Bet, August 1982

"And it came to pass because you hear ... the Lord your God will keep for you the covenant and the kindness that He has sworn to your forefathers."

RASHI interpreted that if you observe the *Mitzvot* [commandments] that a person tramples with his heels, "The Lord your God will keep for you," etc., will keep for you His promise.

We should understand the novelty that if he observes even the minor *Mitzvot*, the Creator will keep what He promised, since it is known that one who does not observe even one *Mitzva* [sing. of *Mitzvot*] is regarded as wicked, and even one who breaches a slight prohibition of the words of authors is called "wicked" (as said in Chapter 2 in *Yevamot*).

Thus, what is the innovation that by observing the minor ones, it is a condition that one who is wicked does not receive the reward that the Creator promised?

We can interpret that this means that, as our sages said, the intention of creation was to do good to His creations. In order to receive His abundance, we must have equivalence of form. This means that everything we do must be in order to bestow. This is called "minor *Mitzvot*," for one does not think that it is important that the *Mitzvot* will be with the aim to bestow, and this is the meaning of a person "tramples with his feet."

When a person does something and does not see that it will yield benefit for himself, but that it will be only in order to bestow, the body loathes such work. Instead, all of one's measurements are about how much self-benefit he will derive from this. Hence, the aim to bestow—namely *Mitzvot* that one does when he does not see self-benefit—are considered "minor," that one tramples with his feet.

The verse tells us about this that precisely the *Mitzvot* that one does when he does not see self-benefit, but does them with the aim to bestow, then the Creator will keep His promise. In other words, by this he will achieve equivalence of form, which is called *Dvekut* [adhesion], and then he will be able to receive the delight and pleasure.

461- "See" in Singular Form

Av, Tav-Shin-Lamed-Het, August-September 1978

"See" is in singular form. "Before you" is in plural form [in Hebrew]. "The blessing that you will hear." Why does it not say "If you hear," meaning that the blessing is contingent? He explains that "see" pertains to every individual, meaning when it comes to seeing, everyone is equal.

According to his interpretation, that the whole collective should come to a state of seeing, meaning "See, I place before you today," the Creator gives the blessing. What is the blessing? He says, "The Torah that you will hear," this is the whole blessing.

However, according to this we should ask, If the Creator gives the blessing, which is out of man's hands, what is the choice of which we can say that to one He gives the blessing, and to another He does not? This is explained at the end of the portion *Ekev* [Because], where it says, "If you surely listen to all of this commandment that I am commanding you to do," 1) "to love the Lord your God," 2) "to walk in all His ways and to cleave unto Him."

In other words, one who observes all three things in practice, the Creator will give him hearing, as it is written, "We will do and we will hear." By taking upon themselves the practice, the Creator gives the hearing, as it is written, "the blessing that you will hear the commandment of the Lord that I am commanding you today."

462- Blessed Is the Place [Creator]

Av, Tav-Shin-Mem-Bet, July-August 1982

We normally say, "The Place [Creator] will fulfill your need," "The Place will comfort you." Our sages said, "He is the place of the world, and the world is not His place."

"Place" refers to the place of creation, which the Creator created. By His desire to do good to His creations, He created existence from absence a place for them to receive the delight and pleasure that He wants to impart upon them. It follows that this place, meaning creation, should be filled with the light of the Creator, which is to do good to His creations. It follows that "Blessed is the place" means that we bless Him for creating the place.

It therefore follows that if the place has not yet been filled, and there is concealment of the face in this place, we say that this place must be filled with the light of the Creator. Although it is still not revealed to us, we must believe that "The whole earth is full of His glory," and "His servants ask one another, 'Where is the place of His glory?'"

Accordingly, the meaning of "The Place will fulfill your need" means that this lack, the concealment of the face, which causes all the lacks, will be filled, namely that it will be in revelation of the face.

Also, we say, "The Place will comfort you among the mourners of Zion and Jerusalem." That is, because all the afflictions that exist in the world derive from the concealment of the face, we say "The Place will comfort you." In other words, this place called "creation," which He created with the intention to do good to His creations, will be in revelation of the face, and then "They shall all know Me, from the least of them to the greatest of them."

This is the place of the world, meaning that He fills the lack of the world, but the world is not His place. In other words, the world does not fill His lack because He has no lack that needs to be filled. That is, the only reason we need to work in order to bestow is only for our sake, so as to have equivalence of form, and not that He needs anything.

463- You Became Rich; You Are in the Evening; Light the Candle

Elul, Tav-Shin-Mem-Gimel, August 1983

"You became rich; you are in the evening; light the candle." The king had two books of Torah—with one he comes out, and the other he leaves in his treasury.

It is known that there are two opposites in the work of the Creator: 1) A person must be happy in any state that he is in, even if it is the lowest possible state. He should praise and thank the Creator for letting him be among those who sit inside the seminary, as our sages said, "He who walks and does not do, the reward for walking is in his hand." This is called "You became rich," as in "wealth," for on the eve of Shabbat [Sabbath] he should be as one who is wealthy who does not lack a thing.

Afterward, one must shift to the other side, to see what he has—how much fear of heaven and greatness of the Creator he has, and how many good deeds and how much Torah, and understanding in the Torah. At that time, he sees that he is deficient. This is called "evening," as in "And there was evening and there was morning," and this is called "you are in the evening."

Once one has those two, then "Light the candle" of Shabbat. At that time, the middle line comes, namely the light of Shabbat.

In this manner, we can interpret the meaning of the two books of Torah that the king had, one with which he would go out and in, meaning it was for using in the states that he was in, and one was that he had to believe that there is Torah from a higher degree, which is still concealed from him, and he will be rewarded with attaining it later on.

This means that in any degree that he is in, in which he comes in and out, there is always Torah that is still concealed from him, and which he must attain. By this, he goes from degree to degree. Also, "king" means that he can reign over his body.

464- If You Go to War – 2

Elul, Tav-Shin-Lamed-Het, September 1978

"If you go to war." RASHI interpreted that the verse speaks of optional war. We must understand the "optional war" in the work. That is, in a place of commandment or in a place of transgression, it is called "mandatory war," where a person must observe the Mitzvot [commandments] to do and the Mitzvot not to do. Only in permitted things, the war is "optional."

The option pertains to the intention, meaning for whose benefit he is observing Torah and Mitzvot, whether this will enhance man's authority, meaning that his reward will be that his will to receive will be rewarded with delight and pleasure, meaning that he takes everything into his own possession, or his reward is that he can engage in Torah and *Mitzvot* for the sake of the Creator, which is in order to bestow and he wants everything to go into the singular authority, meaning the authority of the Creator, and wants to cancel his own authority.

This is what RASHI means by "The verse speaks of optional war." At that time, the verse promises us, "And the Lord your God delivers them into your hands," meaning that he will have the strength to subdue the *Sitra Achra* [other side].

Afterward, the verse clarifies the order of the work: "And you see among the captives a beautiful woman," meaning the soul, which is the quality of bestowal, is in captivity. Before he began the work on the optional, he did not see that man's soul was captive among the *Klipot* [shells/peels]. "And you desire her," meaning to elicit the soul, that his intention will be that he will have the strength to work in order to bestow. This is the meaning of "and you take her for yourself as a wife and bring her into your home."

As RASHI interpreted, the Torah speaks only against the evil inclination, as our sages said, "I have created the evil inclination; I have created the Torah as a spice." Hence, "Your home" means a place of Torah, as in "In wisdom shall a house be built," since the evil inclination controls only a heart that is vacant of wisdom, as our sages said, "One does not sin unless a spirit of folly has entered him."

"She shall shave her head." The hair on the head is regarded as judgments, for *Se'ara* [hair] comes from the word *Se'ara* [storm], which are foreign thoughts that come into the head, and he must cancel all the foreign thoughts he had.

"She shall do her *Tzipornaim* [nails]," from the [Aramaic] word *Tzafra*, meaning "day." "Days" are states in which one was satisfied. "Doing" means that he extolled them, meaning looked at all the days he had been through and found satisfaction in them, and now he sees that it was all nothing but false imagination, since all the measurements were only by what satisfied the will to receive, and how those days pushed him away from the truth.

By this, "She shall remove her gown of captivity," meaning from the soul, "and dwell in your home," meaning a home of Israel, and not in her captivity among the *Klipot*, which is called "*Shechina* [Divinity] in exile."

465- The Work of the General Public and the Work of the Individual

Elul, Tav-Shin-Lamed-Tet, August 1979

"When you go to war against your enemies, and the Lord your God delivers them into your hands and you take them away captive. And you see among the captives a beautiful woman, and you desire her and take her as a wife for yourself ... And if it came to pass that you do not want her, you shall let her go where she wishes." RASHI interprets that the verse speaks of "optional war."

We should interpret this by the way of intimation. It is known that there are two kinds of work: the work of the general public and the work of the individual. In both, there is the war against the inclination. The work of the general public is called "a war of commandment," or "mandatory." In other words, we must fight in order to observe the *Mitzvot* [commandments] and not commit transgressions.

The work of the individual is called "optional war" and concerns things that are neither transgressions nor *Mitzvot*. The work is to do them with the intention to bestow.

When a person is in this optional war, the verse tells us "delivers them into your hands," meaning that he will succeed in the war. "And you take them away captive," and then you are rewarded with "And you see among the captives a beautiful woman." The *Shechina* [Divinity] is called "a beautiful woman," as in "Who will find a woman of valor," since when a person fights, he is a man of valor, and the *Shechina* is called "a woman of valor."

Concerning beauty, it is written in *The Zohar*, "a good world," since the light of *Hochma* [wisdom] is revealed there, and the light of *Hochma* is called "beauty." "And you desire her" means that you will have a desire and yearning to receive her.

In that case, we should know that we must perform corrections so we can receive not because of the desire but in order to bestow. "And if it came to pass that you do not want her," meaning perform the corrections in order to bestow, then "you shall let her go where she wishes," meaning that it is forbidden to use that quality with which he has been rewarded because it is forbidden to receive without a *Masach* [screen].

Precisely if his war is "optional war," meaning in things he wants to do in order to bestow, then he is rewarded with a woman of valor, and then begins the work of the *Masachim* [pl. of *Masach*].

466- Optional War and a War of *Mitzva* [Commandment]

Elul, Tav-Shin-Mem-Bet, August 1982

"When you go to war." RASHI interpreted that it is optional. But concerning a war of *Mitzva*, it is written, "You shall not keep alive any soul."

We should divide between "optional war," when one engages in war against the inclination, and a war of *Mitzva*, where there is no thinking, meaning that a person does not need to introspect whether he is working *Lishma* [for Her sake] or *Lo Lishma* [not for Her sake].

This is so because even an act of *Mitzva*, such as observing Shabbat [Sabbath], if a person has the power to force his neighbor not to desecrate the Shabbat, or he will deny him provision, and so forth, for which he would be observing Shabbat not because it is a *Mitzva* but because his neighbor forced him not to desecrate the Shabbat, in this, too, one must force his neighbor to observe the Shabbat. This is the meaning of "You shall not keep alive any soul."

Conversely, in an optional war, meaning in things that are permitted, when it is neither a *Mitzva* nor a transgression, there is the work of *Lishma* or *Lo Lishma*, to thereby see how much faith he has in observing something permitted in order to bestow. But when it concerns a war to do a *Mitzva* or a transgression, there are no calculations whatsoever, and we must observe the practices even without intentions.

467- All the Peoples of the Earth Shall See

Elul, August-September

"All the peoples of the earth shall see that the name of the Lord is called upon you and they will fear you."

Rabbi Eliezer the Great says "these are the head *Tefillin* [phylacteries] (*Minchot* 35b)." The *Tosfot* interpret that because the head *Tefillin* are more visible than the hand, "see" pertains to them. Conversely, the hand *Tefillin* should be covered, as was said "a token on your hand, for you as a token and not for others as a token."

Also there, the *Shin* [Hebrew letter (ש)] of the *Tefillin*, a law given to Moses at Sinai. He writes in the *Tosfot* that in the [book] *Shimusha Raba*, in *Tefillin* there are three heads in the *Shin* of the right [side], and four heads on the left.

Placing on the left, from where does it come? Rav Ashi said, "from Your hand," written with an unpronounced *Hey*. RASHI interpreted that when it is written with an unpronounced *Hey*, it implies a female form. From this you learn that when he says "left," she is as powerless as a female. Another explanation: "your hand," the weak hand, with him without strength.

Assorted Notes

We should understand the following:

1) Why is the head [*Tefillin*] exposed and that of the hand concealed?

2) Why are there three heads on the right, and four heads on the left?

3) We do not see that uneducated people fear the head *Tefillin*.

Our sages said, "Rabbi Helbo said, 'Rav Huna said, 'Anyone who has fear of heaven, his words are heard, as was said, 'In the end, after all is heard, fear God and keep His commandments, for this is the whole of man'''" (*Berachot* 6b).

We should ask the following: 1) We see that although there were many sages and righteous in Israel whose words were not heard. 2) What evidence do the words "In the end" provide that one who fears heaven, his words are heard?

We should interpret this in the work, that the verse pertains to the individual himself. That is, if a person sees that the organs disobey him, and although he engages in Torah and work, he is still standing still and is not moving whatsoever toward being rewarded with spirituality, our sages give him advice and say that the main reason is that he lacks fear of heaven.

In other words, to the extent that he has fear of heaven, to that same extent his organs will submit to him. This is implied in the words, "In the end," since the body is called "end" and "boundary," as our sages said, "Man's end is to die," whereas the soul in the body is eternal and unlimited.

This is the meaning of the words, "In the end, after all is heard." One way or the other, the body will obey the advice of the good inclination. "Fear God," for you lack nothing but fear of heaven. At that time, you will be rewarded with "Keep His commandments," meaning you will be able to observe His commandments, "for this is the whole of man." What is "for this is the whole of man"? Rabbi Elazar said, "The Creator said, 'The whole world was created only for this.'"

Creation is called "existence from absence." Fear of heaven is a matter of choice, and there is choice only where there is darkness, which is the matter of concealment. Otherwise, there is no such thing as choice. Creation is darkness, since before the world was created, it was all light, for "You are until the world was created." This is the meaning of "the whole world," meaning that the concealment was done only so as to have room for choice, called "for this."

Concerning the hand *Tefillin* being covered and the head *Tefillin* being exposed, I heard from Baal HaSulam that the head *Tefillin* imply Torah, and the one on the hand implies faith. Accordingly, we should interpret that the head *Tefillin*, which are regarded as Torah, the Torah should be revealed, which is "seeing," called "the eyes of the congregation," for seeing means *Hochma* [wisdom].

It is the opposite with faith, which means covered, for precisely during the concealment is there the matter of faith, for then it can be said that although he does not understand or see the truth of the matter, he still believes. Hence, the hand *Tefillin* must be covered.

This also explains why the hand *Tefillin* should be put on the left hand. Rav Ashi brings evidence from "your hand," which is the weak hand, which means attainment, from the words, "If a hand attains." Attainment is female, for "his strength has become as weak as a female," since it is a matter of faith and not of knowledge. The Torah is to the contrary: specifically knowledge. Otherwise, it is not considered Torah.

Concerning the *Shin* having to be with three heads on the right, and four heads on the left, the ARI says that *Mochin*, which is the upper abundance, bestows upon the four *Sefirot* called *Hochma*, *Bina*, and *Daat*, which contains two *Sefirot* called *Hesed* and *Gevura*.

Hochma is the abundance itself, which is bestowed upon the lower ones. *Bina* is called "the forces that the lower ones want to impart upward." When there is an awakening to extend *Hochma*, the awakening is called *Hesed*, which is the carrier for the extension of *Hochma*. At the same time, we must place a *Masach* [screen], called "forces," so the intention will be only to bestow contentment upon his Maker.

Sometimes the desire to extend abundance already exists, but the power of the *Masach* on the abundance has not been completed. This is considered that *Hesed* and *Gevura* are not united. Hence, this is called "the *Shin* of the four heads." When the power of the *Masach* is suitable for the abundance, it is called "*Hesed* and *Gevura* united." This is why it is called a "*Shin* of three heads."

Also, there is the matter of the *Hochma* not being able to shine due to the amount of the abundance. At that time, there is a correction that the *Hochma* will not shine, and then the *Hesed* and *Gevura* are disunited. Hence, only *Hassadim* illuminate there. This is called "right," since the place where *Hochma* illuminates is called "left," for there is a need for corrections there, as in, "a weak hand."

468- *This Day, the Lord Your God Commands You*

Elul, Tav-Shin-Lamed-Het, September 1978

"This day, the Lord your God commands you to do these statutes and ordinances, and you shall keep and do them with all your heart and with all your soul." RASHI interprets, each day they will be as new in your eyes, as if you were commanded them that day.

We should understand how one can make them be as new, as though he were commanded them that day, for it has been sworn and standing since Mt. Sinai. To understand this, we first need to know the rule that everything is measured by the greatness of the one who commands. That is, according to the greatness and importance of the giver of the Torah, so is the greatness of the Torah.

Hence, each day when one takes upon himself the kingdom of heaven, according to the measure of the faith in Him, the merit of the Torah increases. Therefore, according to what a person attains in the greatness of the Creator, so the Torah is renewed in him. It therefore follows that each time, he has a new Torah, meaning that each time he has a different Giver. Then, naturally, the Torah that extends from Him is regarded as a new Torah.

However, this was said about the Torah in relation to the names of the Creator, meaning in relation to "The Torah, Israel, and the Creator are one."

That is, when Israel attains the greatness of the Creator each day, according to his faith, to that extent the Torah grows within him. At that time, he becomes a different Israel because in spirituality, everything that has a different form is a new quality. Hence, if a person receives greater faith each day then the Torah is regarded as new.

This is the meaning of "as if you were commanded them that day," since each day he has a different *Mitzva* [commandment]. Thus, "as if you were commanded them that day" means that on the day when a person takes upon himself the kingdom of heaven more intensely, he has a new *Mitzva*, a new Torah, and a new Israel.

469- Each Day They Will Be as New in Your Eyes

Elul, Tav-Shin-Mem-Aleph, September 1981

"This day, the Lord your God commands you to do these statutes and ordinances, and you shall keep and do them with all your heart and with all your soul." RASHI interprets, "Each day they will be as new in your eyes, as if you were commanded them that day."

We should understand the commandment that each day they will be as new in your eyes. Clearly, this does not mean that each day he should buy new *Tefillin* [phylacteries] or a new *Tzitzit* [prayer shawl]. For this reason, it is interpreted, "as if you were commanded them that day." However, we should still understand why they need to be "as if you were commanded them that day."

The thing is that there are those who observe Torah and *Mitzvot* [commandments] in the manner of the general public, and there are those who observe Torah and *Mitzvot* in the manner of individuals. Those who want to work in the manner of individuals should engage in Torah and *Mitzvot* not in order to receive reward. Rather, they want to bestow contentment upon their Maker. Then, to the extent that they attain the greatness of the Creator, to that extent they want to bestow.

As is written in *The Zohar* about the verse, "Her husband is known at the gates," each one according to what he assumes in his heart. It follows that the whole aim of their engagement in Torah and *Mitzvot* is in order to bring them to recognize the greatness of the Creator.

It therefore follows that a person who grows needs greater recognition of the Creator every day. Thus, each day he has a commandment from "the Lord your God." "Your God" means that he knows the Creator in person, as it is "your God" in singular form.

This is the meaning of "Each day they will be as new in your eyes, as if you were commanded them that day," since each day he must receive a commandment from a higher degree, which means that there, the greatness of the Creator is more apparent.

470- When You Come

Elul, Tav-Shin-Lamed-Tet, September 1979

"And it shall come to pass that when you come to the land that the Lord your God gives you as an inheritance, and you inherit it and dwell in it." RASHI interpreted, "They were not obliged to give the first fruit until they conquered the land and divided it."

By intimation, we should interpret that man's work is to engage in the way of the Creator throughout the day as much as possible. When one reflects on how his day went by, this is called "conquering the land," and then he begins to divide the order of the work—for whom he worked, meaning for whose favor. At that time, it is written, "And you shall take some of the first of all the produce of the *Adamah* [land]," from the words *Adameh la Elyon* [I will be like the Most High].

This means that first, one must see if his fruits have given him the quality of equivalence of form, since first we must see if our work has yielded the fruits, since "I have created the evil inclination; I have created the Torah as a spice."

If one is rewarded with the "spice," which is equivalence of form, one should see what extent of equivalence of form he had during his work and what remains with him after his work.

If he sees that his work is not as it should be, then "You shall answer and say ... 'Aramean serving my Father.'" That is since there is the evil inclination in him, who is a fraud, deceiving a person each time in a different way, and mainly showing him that he does not need to correct his ways, this is why it is written, "And you will answer."

RASHI interpreted this as raising the voice. That is, we must yell out loud so he will hear well that he still has the deceiver in his heart. Yet, he should be happy about one thing: that nevertheless, he has reached the truth, to see his true state.

This is the meaning of "You will rejoice with all that good that the Lord has given you." "Good" means once he has been rewarded with real fruits.

"All the good" means he should be happy that nevertheless, he was rewarded with seeing the bad, whereby recognition of evil he can achieve the good. Thus, "all the good" means the bad, which is the *Kli* [vessel] for the good. From this he should be happy, meaning that one should always be happy because otherwise, he is attached to the *Sitra Achra* [other side].

Yet, a person can feel the joy only through some actual reality, or if he has still not come to see the truth then he has joy from thinking that he has wholeness. When he begins to see the truth, he should be happy that he has been rewarded with seeing the truth. Afterward, he is rewarded with real joy that he has been rewarded with the truth, and then he brings the first fruits.

The first fruits are the fruits that are revealed through the work, as in "They who sow in tears will reap in joy." "Sowing" means that he places everything he has in the ground until it decays and he has nothing. That is, he loses even the small bit that he had.

Hence, at that time he has tears because he has nothing to hold on to, and the suffering he feels for the negativity within him are the *Kelim* [vessels] that can later be filled. This is called, "They who sow in tears will reap in joy." They are *Kli* [vessel] and light, lack and filling, negativity and positivity. It follows that when he is rewarded with the light, he returns to the deficiencies he had.

This is why he says, "Aramean serving my Father and went down to Egypt." This is as Baal HaSulam said, "At the time of *Gadlut* [greatness/adulthood], we must receive fear from what we experienced before (see "Introduction of The Book of Zohar" in the essay, "A Prayer for Havakuk").

471- You Stand Today – 2

Elul, Tav-Shin-Lamed-Tet, September 1979

"You stand today ... from the one who chops your wood to the one who draws your water ... that you may enter into the covenant ... that the Lord your God has made with you today."

The interpreters ask, it begins in plural form and then in singular form. Also, to understand the meaning of the covenant, the interpreters bring the *Midrash* [interpretation] that individuals are like thin reeds, which are weak. But if they are turned into a bundle, they are strong.

Concerning the covenant, Baal HaSulam said why two people who love each other need the covenant if there is love and friendship between them. However, the covenant is because as now the love between them is complete, it is possible that after some time there will not be the same love and each one will imagine that the other is causing him harm. At that time, the covenant comes so that each one will keep the covenant that they had made while there was true love between them.

Thus, now, too, although they do not feel so, they will maintain the friendship between them as though now, too, they feel love.

Likewise, when a person feels the love of the Creator, he understands that it is worthwhile to leave other loves for the love of the Creator. But later, when the awakening passes away from him and he no longer feels the love of the Creator, he will want to return to the other loves that he had already decided to toss away.

At that time, a person needs the covenant and maintain the same conduct that he had while he felt the love of the Creator, although now he has no feeling whatsoever. Then, the work must be compulsory, to enslave himself to the covenant that he had made before. This is called "that you may enter into the covenant."

472- The Concealed Things Belong to the Lord Our God

Elul, Tav-Shin-Mem-Aleph, September 1981

"The concealed things belong to the Lord our God, and the revealed things belong to us and to our children forever, to do all the words of this Torah [law]."

By intimation, we should interpret that "revealed" means "practiced," and "concealed" means "intention." The intention—which is the reason that obligates a person to do the act—is concealed from people, for one does not know what is in one's friend's heart.

A person might even deceive himself with regard to the intention and think that the reason that obligates him to do the deed is the benefit of the Creator, when perhaps it is his own benefit that obligates him to do the deed. This is why "concealed" implies the intention.

We should make two discernments in regard to this: 1) the general public, 2) the individual. The general public normally thinks mainly about the action and not about the intention, since it is impossible to force the public to aim the true aim during the act. But with regard to the individual, we speak mainly about the intention. Hence, perhaps with respect to the general public, he is righteous, but with respect to the individual, he is wicked.

In that regard, it can be said, "Even if the whole world tells you that you are righteous, be wicked in your own eyes." That is, he should aim that it will be only for the Creator, meaning not in order to receive reward, and he is still regarded as wicked.

And when one sees that in terms of the concealed, he is completely removed from the goal, he must not despair. Rather, he must believe that "The concealed things belong to the Lord our God." This means that He will give the concealed part, and we will do the revealed part, namely the actions.

According to the increase in actions, so grows the need to increase intentions, meaning for the concealed part. Since there is a rule that there is no light without a *Kli* [vessel], meaning a desire, through increasing the actions we increase the lack until it reaches a certain measure, and then "The concealed things belong to the Lord our God," meaning that then He gives the concealed.

473- Sins Become for Him as Merits

It is written in the "Introduction of The Book of Zohar" (Item 126) that in the end, a great light will appear in all the worlds, by which every flesh will repent in complete repentance and love.

It is known that our sages said that one who is rewarded with repentance from love, sins become for him as merits (*Yoma* 86b), as the prophet said about those wicked who said and were using curses among them saying "It is vain to serve God, and what profit is it that we have kept His charge?"

Earlier in Item 126: A book of remembrance that is introduced in Malachi (3:16), as it is written, "You said, 'It is vain to serve God ... doers of wickedness were built, and also tested God and escaped. Then those who feared the Lord spoke to one another and the Lord listened and heard, and a book of remembrance was written before Him for those who fear the Lord and who esteem His name. 'They will be Mine,' said the Lord of hosts, 'for the day when I make a *Segula* [cure/miracle/virtue].'"

We should understand the words when they spoke to one another and said such despicable words, and the prophet said about them, "Then those who feared the Lord spoke to one another." He explains about this that in the great day of the end of correction, when the light of repentance from love is revealed, these sins will also turn to merits.

We should understand the meaning of sins becoming as merits. Although the interpretation is literal, we should interpret this the way we learn that when a person wants to engage in Torah and *Mitzvot* [commandments] not in order to receive reward, the body objects and argues, "What is this work for you?" which is "What profit is it that we have kept His charge?"

Those who work in the manner of the general public have no questions of "What is this work," since the questions begin mainly when one wants to work only in not in order to receive reward. And the more a person overcomes, the more the body resists.

It follows that those who fear the Creator, who want to work only not in order to receive reward, speak to one another. If he works all day, the body argues all day "What is this work?" Through these complaints, a desire forms within a person to be rid of these questions.

When these questions complete their quota, He gives him from above the spirit of repentance, and it turns out that the only cause of the spirit of repentance was those sins, meaning the questions. It follows that sins, meaning the questions, have become as merits, for were it not for these questions, he would not have a *Kli* [vessel] to receive the spirit of repentance.

474- And the Canaanite, King of Arad, Heard

Elul, Tav-Shin-Mem, September 1980

"Aaron is the right arm of Israel, as it is written, 'And the Canaanite, king of Arad, heard.'" It is written in the *Sulam* [Ladder commentary on *The Zohar*], "It means that when it is written, 'The Canaanite, king of Arad ... heard that Israel was coming by way of Atarim, and he fought against Israel and took some of them captive.'"

"By way of Atarim" means that Israel were as a person walking without an arm and supporting himself in every place. *Atarim* means places [in Hebrew]. And then, "He fought against Israel and took some of them captive." Come and see, Aaron was the right arm of the body, which is *Tifferet*. For this reason, it is written, "Walking at the right side of Moses, the arm of his glory [*Tifferet*]. Who is he? It is Aaron, who is the right arm of *Tifferet*" (*The Zohar*).

It is known that Aaron is called "the queen's best man." In order to take upon themselves the burden of the kingdom of heaven, they needed the quality of Aaron, called *Hesed* [grace/mercy], as in "because he desires mercy." This means that whatever situation one is in, he is content because the acceptance of the burden of *Malchut* is from the side of *Hesed* and not from the side of *Hochma* [wisdom], but above reason.

The vessels of bestowal, whether in mind or in heart, are considered "because he desires mercy," when he has no need for any support or solid basis on which to build his kingship [*Malchut*]. Rather, without any support on any place or seeing, with this quality he goes and fights the war against the inclination.

At that time, the *Sitra Achra* [other side] cannot harm him because she has nowhere to grip in a place where he has support, and cancel his support, since he has no support anywhere. For this reason, the *Sitra Achra* cannot conquer any spots where he has acquired his support, since this discernment is called "the earth hangs on nothing."

Hence, when they did not have the quality of Aaron, which is *Hesed*, but they rather came by way of Atarim, meaning that they came to *Kedusha* [holiness] through support in many places, for this reason, the *Sitra Achra* could fight against Israel, as it is written, "He fought against Israel and took some of them captive."

But in the quality of Aaron, which is *Hesed*, there is no place, so there is no grip. This is called "the earth hangs," meaning his quality of *Malchut*, "on nothing," without any place.

475- Lend Ear, O Heavens

Tishrey, Tav-Shin-Mem, September 1979

"Lend ear, O heavens, and let me speak, and let the earth hear the words of my mouth."

The interpreters asked why concerning the heavens it is written, "Lend ear," and concerning the earth it is written, "hear." Also, why is it written in terms of speaking with regard to the heavens, and "words" when it comes to the earth?

The "heavens" are people whose engagements are all spiritual, and "earth" are those who engage in earthly matters. "Lend ear" implies closeness, as though standing close to someone and telling him, "Listen to what I'm telling you." But "hearing" implies distance, as it is written, "We heard a rumor from afar."

"Lend ear" pertains to people who engage in spiritual matters, who are not far from the truth. "Speaking" also pertains to them, as our sages said about the verse, "Thus shall you say to the house of Jacob, and tell the children of Israel." To the men, you shall say words as hard as tendons, but to the women—soft speaking.

Maimonides says that it is forbidden to reveal the "truth," which is *Lishma* [for Her sake], to women and children and uneducated people until they gain knowledge and acquire much wisdom. Then, that secret is revealed to them little by little.

For this reason, the body does not agree to "speaking," which is words that are as hard as tendons, meaning *Lishma*, working not in order to receive reward. But the body can agree to "soft speaking," meaning *Lo Lishma* [not for Her sake]. For this reason, uneducated people and women need soft speaking.

Therefore, working people, who engage in spirituality, are permitted to be told to work *Lishma* because they are not far from the matter of *Lishma*. This is why it is written, "Lend ear," implying closeness, unlike those who are far from the matter of *Lishma*.

476- The Rich Shall Not Give More and the Poor Shall Not Give Less

Shevat, Tav-Shin-Mem-Het, February 1988

"The rich shall not give more and the poor shall not give less than half a *Shekel*, to make a contribution to the Lord."

"Poor" and "rich" mean poor in knowledge or to the contrary. *Shekel* means "scales," which is stones with which to weigh. In other words, a person must reflect on the way that he is in. He must know that he is always in a state of half and half, as our sages said, "One should always see oneself as half guilty" (*Kidushin* 40b).

One should not think that there is someone who is rich, who has more Torah and good deeds, so he is no longer in a state of "half." Rather, it is as in "Anyone who is greater than his friend, his inclination is greater than him" (*Sukkah* 52b).

It therefore follows that between rich and poor, we can weigh for ourselves the good path or the bad one. To weigh means to decide to give the contribution to the Lord. This is like the allegory about a person who walks into a grocery store and the merchant weighs the goods. If there are many customers in the shop, each one thinks that the merchant is weighing for him.

It is likewise here: The *Sitra Achra* [other side] wants him to weigh for her and the *Kedusha* [holiness], for her. It is about this that the verse says, "to give the contribution to the Lord," meaning he is weighing for the Creator. Also, "half" means a lack, which is the *Kli* [vessel], for you have no light without a *Kli*. Hence, the *Kli* and the light are regarded as one discernment. The light is one half, and the *Kli* is one half, and the two of them make the discernment of truth—from the lack and the revelation.

This is the meaning of his saying "half a *Shekel*," meaning that one should see that he has half, meaning a lack, and also that he is fit to receive the filling, namely that he should also be fit to receive the lack.

477- What Do You Have in the House?

"What do you have in the house?" "It is forbidden to bless on an empty table." "The blessing on eating is not present on an empty place" (*The Zohar*, *Yitro*, Item 487).

It is known that "The blessed adheres to the Blessed." Hence, an empty place is regarded as "cursed." For this reason, the cursed does not adhere to the Blessed. Hence, when a person asks for his deficiencies, he is called "cursed." For this reason, one must find within him a place where he has something, meaning he should find within him something for which he can be grateful to the Creator, and on this place the blessing can later come.

478- What Was the Sin of Korah?

We must understand what was the sin of Korah. After all, our sages said that he was clever.

Korah did not sin against the Creator. On the contrary, he said that "The whole congregation are all holy," and all that he said about Moses was that he said that Moses fabricated from his heart, and not from the Creator. If he were certain that it were from the Creator, he would not dispute.

Thus, why did he deserve such a harsh punishment that they had to create a special punishment specifically for him, to the point that the punishment is against nature, when the earth opened its mouth and he went down to Sheol alive?

It is known that the Creator repays an eye for an eye. Since the sin was against Moses, who is the loyal shepherd, and this quality comes from the lower one, for faith, meaning concealment, comes from the lower one—while only revelation comes from the upper one—when Moses wanted to show that we must walk in the ways of faith, which is above reason, and Korah did not agree, for this reason, Moses had to extend a punishment that is also above reason, a new creation, something that is unnatural.

This was in order for everyone to know that the punishment came to them not because of some other sin, but specifically because of the sin of not wanting to go above reason. It follows that the new punishment comes as an eye for an eye, as the verse says, "for he did not fabricate from his heart, but only from the mouth of the Creator."

479- You Shall Not Distort Justice

Portion, *Shoftim* [Judges]

"You shall not distort justice; you shall not be partial, and you shall not take a bribe, for a bribe blinds the eyes of the wise and perverts the words of the righteous."

There are three discernments here: 1) justice, 2) partiality, 3) bribe.

The Torah explains only bribe but does not give any reasoning to justice or partiality. We should understand the difference between justice and partiality.

According to the work, first we should understand justice, and the dispute, who are the litigators, and who is the judge. The thing is that when a person wants to walk in the way of the Creator, he must believe that the Creator is good and does good. Hence, the question is, Why does man feel suffering? At that time, he has a litigation with Providence, since "a judge has only what his eyes see."

If one feels suffering, it is hard for him to overcome and say that it is all mercies, since he sees and feels unpleasantness, and he must not lie—that this is not suffering, meaning that he understands that Providence is concealed. This is the meaning of "You shall not distort justice."

At the same time, one should believe above reason that this is absolute benefit, and that "You shall not be partial," meaning not to want the state of "face," namely knowledge, called "wisdom" and "face."

Rather, "You will see My back, and My face shall not be seen." This is precisely by not taking a bribe, since a "bribe" means that a person wants to receive pleasure for himself, meaning he wants to exert only where he sees self-benefit.

At that time, he is unfit to see the truth, "for a bribe blinds the eyes of the wise," since only when he is in a state of "You shall not take a bribe," but everything will be for the sake of the Creator, he will be able to be rewarded with wisdom, meaning open

Providence. Otherwise, it "blinds the eyes of the wise," meaning that he will only have concealment, since the light is present only in a place of bestowal.

480- The Place Where the Lord Will Choose

"And it shall come to pass that the place where the Lord your God chooses for His name to dwell, there you shall bring all that I command you: your burnt offerings and your sacrifices, your tithes and the contribution of your hands, and all your choice vows, which you will vow to the Lord" (Deuteronomy 12:11).

We should ask about this: Since the Torah is eternal, what is the place where the Lord has chosen for His name to dwell today? We should also ask what this place that the Lord has chosen means, since "I fill the heaven and the earth."

A blind man asked Rabbi Meir that question (*Beresheet Rabbah*, Portion No. 4). He said to him, "Is it possible that it is written about it, 'I fill the heaven and the earth?' He was speaking with Moses from between the two curtains of the ark. He said to him, 'Bring me big mirrors.' He replied, 'See Your image in them.' He saw it big. 'Bring small mirrors.' He said to him, 'See your image in them.' He saw it small.

"He said to him, 'As you, who is flesh and blood, change yourself however you want, he who said, 'Let there be the world' is much more so. When He wants, 'I fill the heaven and the earth.' And when He wants, He speaks with Moses from between the two curtains of the ark.'"

We should understand the answer in this allegory, for it seems as though the allegory does not fit the lesson. The image in the mirror is something outside of him. But in the person himself, of course he has a size: He is either big or small.

The thing is that "The place where the Lord will choose" means bestowal in mind and heart. "There you shall bring" means the whole *Mitzva* [commandment], for one must bring the *Mitzvot* [commandments] and good deeds that one has. Conversely, in the rest of the place, the Creator is not present, meaning that there is no revelation. This is specifically from between the two curtains of the ark.

The "two curtains of the ark" are regarded as love and fear, which is "do" and "do not do" as in "I" and "You shall not have." Specifically on those two, the *Shechina* [Divinity], who is called "ark," was revealed.

This is "the ark carries its carriers," meaning that a person does not receive the face of the *Shechina* unless the *Shechina* brings the person closer, and then he can do everything in bestowal.

The meaning of the mirror is the revelation of the Creator, which is called "in sight, and not in riddles."

481- The Whole World Is Nourished by My Son Hanina – 2

15 *Shevat*, *Tav-Shin-Tet-Vav*, February 7, 1955

"The whole world is nourished by my son Hanina, and Hanina my son suffices himself with 102 carobs [meager food] from one eve of Shabbat [Sabbath] to another" (*Taanit* 24b).

We should interpret this in the work. One who walks in the ways of the Creator, during the work, called "weekdays," as in "He who did not toil on the eve of Shabbat [Sabbath]," "suffices," meaning settles for feeling the taste of carobs in his work. Yet, through the exertions he makes in that he has no taste in his work, but only that of carobs, and it is known that "If you labored and did not find, do not believe," so he wants that through his work and labor, abundance and blessings will be drawn out to the whole world, meaning that all the vitality and attainments of the light of Torah will reach the entire world.

This is the meaning of the words, "The whole world is nourished by my son Hanina." Why does he do this? It is because he has the grace of *Kedusha* [holiness]. This is why he is called Hanina, from the word *Hen* [grace]. Therefore, he is rewarded with the state of Shabbat. This is why "He who did not toil on the eve of Shabbat, what will he eat on Shabbat?"

Hence, we could ask, If Hanina extended the light of Torah to the whole world, why are they not obtaining the light of the pleasure and only Hanina was rewarded with the state of Shabbat? This is so only because they have no *Kelim* [vessels] to receive. The labor is the *Kelim* in which the lights pour.

It is about this that they said (*Avoda Zarah* 3a), "He who did not toil on the eve of Shabbat, what will he eat on Shabbat?" Although Hanina extended the light of Shabbat to the whole world, they haven't the *Kelim* to receive. However, the servant of the Creator himself should walk on the path of not receiving anything, which is called "carobs."

482- *This Is the Path of Torah – 2*

18 *Sivan*, Tav-Shin-Tet-Vav, June 8, 1955

"This is the path of Torah: Lead a sorrowful life," etc.

This is so because when one works for the sake of the Creator, the body derives no pleasure because it is not receiving anything. However, when one is accustomed to work in a manner of bestowal, one is later rewarded with "Then will you delight in the Lord." In other words, when we work for the sake of the Creator, we receive pleasure. This is called "Her ways are ways of pleasantness."

483- A Hedge for Wisdom – Silence – 2

23 Sivan, May-June

"A hedge for wisdom - silence." That is, in order to be rewarded with *Hochma* [wisdom], one must first correct the *Kelim* [vessels] so they have the quality of bestowal. Hence, the correction is "silence," meaning that in every matter, he shall answer himself as in "Silence! Such was My thought."

484- He Whom the Lord Loves He Admonishes

"He whom the Lord loves He admonishes." That is, the Creator sends suffering to those He loves, meaning that they will suffer that they are not walking on the path of the Creator. Conversely, one who does not feel any suffering at not walking on the path of the Creator never received any counsels how to be saved from it.

485- The Fear of You and the Dread of You Shall Be upon All the Animals of the Earth

"The fear of you and the dread of you shall be upon all the animals of the earth."

RASHI interprets that "as long as a day old infant is alive, there is no need to guard him from the mice. When Og, King of Bashan, is dead, he must be guarded" (Sanhedrin 98).

Vitality means that all the war against the inclination is only in that it shows a person that there is vitality in corporeal matters in this world. It argues that it is not worthwhile to relinquish them in order to be rewarded with the next world. When a person is rewarded, all the corporeal animals become annulled before him because all the corporeal vitality is that which pertains to the will to receive, but when a person is rewarded with walking in the desire to bestow, they are naturally annulled.

It is a rule that the will to receive is called "death," and the desire to bestow is called "life," since it is adhered to the Life of Lives. Hence, if a person is rewarded with walking in the ways of bestowal, even though he is still an infant, he is nonetheless considered alive, and the animals of the earth surrender before him, meaning all the bad animals are vitality that is dependent on the will to receive.

486- The Beginning of Speech Is from *Ein Sof*

According to the rule, we begin to speak only from the place of the connection between the Creator and the created beings, called *Ein Sof* [infinity], which is the desire to do good to His creations, and not before. It therefore follows that we should not ask why the Creator wants to do good, meaning about the reason that caused it, since we begin from the desire to do good and downward, and not from before the desire.

If you ask about the point, namely the reason that the quality of bestowal emerged from Him, then we are asking about prior to the connection, and here we do not attain. Even the quality of doing good that we attain is in the manner of "By Your actions we know You," meaning that by receiving the benefit, we understand that there is a desire to do good.

487- Concerning the Will to Receive

The will to receive is man's essence, which is called something innovated existence from absence. However, the rest of the things, meaning all the fillings, extend existence from existence. Every kind of fulfillment in the world extends existence from existence since the Creator contains them. But the negative things, meaning deficiencies and suffering, are something new.

488- The Garments of the Soul

Southport, 1 *Adar Bet, Tav-Shin-Yod-Zayin*, March 4, 1957

Concerning the garments of the soul, "To the extent that a person exerts in observing Torah and *Mitzvot* [commandments], a garment is made for him above in that palace (the palace of the essence of heaven, *Hod*), to wear in that world" (*The Zohar, Pekudei*, Item 166).

We should understand the meaning of clothing. It is known that nothing can be attained in spirituality except by clothing, which is like a *Kli* [vessel] that is suitable for revealing light. Hence, if a person exerts, the exertion makes the *Kli* for him, meaning the desire and the need for the filling of light, since nothing is given from above before there is a need for that illumination.

The labor that a person exerts causes him a need and a desire, meaning he becomes needy of the Creator's help to emerge from the strait in which he finds himself during the labor. Were it not for the labor, he would have no need for His help. It follows that precisely the labor provides him with the clothing of the soul, so there will be revelation of Godliness.

489- Against Your Will – 2

"Against your will you live." If a person does not want to receive life for himself, then he is alive.

"Against your will you die." If a person does not want to die, as in, "The wicked in their lives are called 'dead,'" the more he does not want to be wicked, the more he is dead. That is, he achieves recognition of evil, which is called "dead." Otherwise, he is in the life of the wicked.

490- Adornments of the Bride

Pinhas, p 212 (*The Zohar, Sulam* [Ladder] Commentary [in Hebrew])

The adornments of the bride are MAN of the lower one that ascends upward. That is, the lower one lacks the *Masach* [screen] meaning vessels of bestowal, which are called "adornment" with regard to the upper one, for any lower one induces a deficiency in its root.

Concerning the upper one, this is regarded as adornments because the upper one does not feel these deficiencies as such, but rather as adornments on which the upper one extends the upper light for the sake of the lower one. For this reason, the MAN of the souls in *Malchut* is regarded as "adornments of the bride" on which the light of *Hochma* [wisdom] is revealed. With respect to the upper one, the light of *Hochma* is regarded as a decoration and not as a lack, whereas with regard to the lower one, it is regarded as a lack.

491- Raising MAN – 2

Question: Raising MAN is regarded as raising a deficiency upward. Thus, why does he write that raising MAN is called *Mitzvot* [commandments] and good deeds?

MAN is called "a deficiency." But what does the lower one lack by which to add abundance in the world? When one engages in Torah and *Mitzvot*, the Torah and *Mitzvot* first create MAN in a person, meaning he receives a deficiency and sees that he is lacking Torah and fear of heaven because of the concealment and hiding in the world due to the *Tzimtzum* [restriction]. At that time, a person receives a lack and raises that lack upward so as to be filled. It therefore follows that through the Torah and *Mitzvot*, a person receives MAN, and he elevates that MAN and causes revealing in all the worlds.

492- The Reward for a *Mitzva*

"The reward for a *Mitzva* [commandment] is not in this world." This means that it is absent in the will to receive because there was a *Tzimtzum* [restriction] and concealment. Rather, it is in the next world, meaning the *Kelim* [vessels] of *Bina*, which is called "the next world," which are vessels of bestowal.

493- A Righteous Son and a Wicked Son

"Come see, it is written about Abraham, 'I shall indeed return to you,' and not to her, but indeed, I will connect to you and not to the *Nukva* [female]" (*The Zohar, BeShalach*).

We should interpret this according to what RASHI interpreted concerning, "And the Lord granted him." It is said, "To him and not to her, for the prayer of a righteous son of a righteous is unlike the prayer of a righteous son of a wicked."

It is seemingly bewildering that a righteous son of a righteous is a higher degree, for the opposite makes more sense, according to the rule, "According to the labor, so is the reward," and it is harder for a righteous son of a wicked to be righteous because he does not learn from the practices of his fathers, and each time, he overcomes by himself until he becomes a righteous. Thus, on the face of it, his prayer should have been more accepted.

We should interpret that "righteous son of a wicked" is called *Nukva*, which is faith. That is, initially, he was wicked, but then he became a righteous. In other words, before he is rewarded with faith, he is still wicked, and afterward he becomes a righteous.

The quality of faith is called *Malchut*, who has nothing of her own. Hence, there is still no life from her quality. Only when one is rewarded with the Torah, called "tree of life," is he called "male," namely a giver, for the Torah gives life. One who has been rewarded with the Torah is called "righteous son of a righteous," since in his previous degree, before he was rewarded with the Torah, he had faith, which is called "righteous." Hence, "The Lord granted him," since through the quality of a male, which is the quality of "righteous son of a righteous," the son will have existence.

494- There Is Fear Only in a Place of Wholeness

"There is fear only in a place of wholeness, for when there is fear there is no lack" (*The Zohar*, Yitro, Item 248).

We should understand why fear means wholeness and no lack.

Answer: Fear is called "terrible," which is the middle line. There is fear there that it is forbidden to receive *Hochma* without *Hassadim*. It follows that in the right line, where there are *Hassadim*, there is no wholeness because *Hochma* is missing. Likewise, the left line has no wholeness due to lack of *Hassadim*, and without *Hassadim*, the *Hochma* cannot illuminate.

It follows that we should interpret that Jacob, who is called "terrible," is *Masach de Hirik*, meaning that he awakens *Malchut* of the quality of judgment, and in the quality of judgment, she cancels the GAR of *Hochma* to the point that the light departs, and you do not have great fear.

However, Jacob is called "the quality of mercy," and mercy indicates wholeness. That is, through the departure of the GAR of *Hochma*, he will now receive wholeness, meaning *Hochma* that is clothed in *Hassadim*.

This is called "wholeness," where there is no lack of *Hassadim* or *Hochma*. This is the middle line, which consists of *Hochma* and *Hassadim*. This is why Jacob is called "terrible," meaning fear, and he is also called "mercy" and "wholeness," for there is no lack here.

495- The Creator Ascended

The Creator ascended, as it is written, "God ascended with a shout" (*The Zohar, Yitro*, Item 250).

We should understand what it means that the Creator ascended; are there ascents and descents in the Creator?

Answer: All the ascents and descents that unfold in the created beings come from the created beings. But in Godliness, there are no changes. However, if the lower ones are worthy, God is ascended in them during the ascent, meaning they see the importance of Godliness, and this is called "God ascended with a shout."

496- The Path of Truth

Concerning the path of truth, there is a path of falsehood, and there is the path of truth concerning the reason that obligates a person to engage in Torah and *Mitzvot* [commandments]. There is a reason called "the benefit of the body," where by engaging in Torah and *Mitzvot* he will be rewarded in this world, as well as in the next world. To the extent that he believes in reward and punishment, he can observe them because it benefits the will to receive, which is called "body."

This is called "the path of falsehood," since he cannot achieve the purpose of creation, which is to do good to His creations because of the bread of shame. For this reason, we need equivalence of form, for if his engagement is only for his own sake, how can this lead to equivalence of form?

Therefore, the path of truth means that the reason that obligates him is the aim to bestow, which is not in order to receive reward. Hence, only this is the path of truth, since by this the bread of shame will be corrected.

By this we will understand what is written in *The Zohar*, "To the extent that one appreciates, one is allotted" (*The Zohar*, Pinhas, Item 506). The *Sulam* [Ladder commentary on *The Zohar*] interpreted that he is given to the same extent that he mentions. This is as it is written, "Wherever I mention My name, I will come to you and bless you." It should have said, "You mention My name." However, this means that to the same extent that I mention My name, to that same extent I will come to you.

It seems as though there is no answer to what he explains. But according to the above, it is thoroughly clear that to the same extent that he mentions, meaning what a person wants, this is what he is given. Those who walk on the path of truth, who want to bring contentment to the Maker, see that everything they do is not for the sake of the Creator, so they pray to the Creator to see that they can work for the sake of the Creator.

At that time, the Creator says, "Wherever I mention My name," meaning that you will give me the possibility to attribute My name to your actions. In other words, there will be an awakening from below, where I, says the Creator, will attribute My name to the actions. So how will you know that I am already attributing My name to them? You will see this if I "come to you and bless you."

In other words, the whole purpose of creation, which is to do good to His creations, cannot be revealed before you correct the matter of the bread of shame, meaning that you work in order to bestow. At that time, the purpose of creation will come true, which is to do good to His creations.

This is the meaning of what is written, "Wherever I mention My name," where I attribute My name to them, meaning that all your actions will be only to bestow. Then you will know if I "come to you and bless you." This is as Maimonides says, "How is repentance? Until He who knows the mysteries testifies to him."

497- Blessed Are You

"Blessed are you in the city; blessed are you in the field." One should not say, "Had the Creator given me a field, I would pay tithing from it. Now that I have no field, I am giving nothing."

The Creator said, "See what I wrote in the Torah, 'Blessed are you in the city,' to those who dwell in cities, and 'Blessed are you in the field' to those who have fields."

498- It Shall Come to Pass That If You Surely Hear

"And it shall come to pass that if you surely hear." If you hear in this world, you will hear in the next world from the Creator. "And it shall come to pass that if you surely hear the voice of the Lord your God, be careful to do all His commandments that I command you today, the Lord your God will set you high above all the nations of the earth." Rabbi Levi said, "What is as high as this upper one? If you are rewarded then you are above four fingers. If not, below four fingers."

We should understand what being above four fingers implies. It is written, "One gold pan of ten, full of incense." In other words, a person should have a pan, meaning a *Kli* [vessel] in which to receive the upper abundance, called *Zahav* [gold], from the words *Ze-Hav* [give this]. Likewise, out of the light of Torah, the pan, meaning the five fingers, must be dedicated to this.

The *Zohar* says that a cup of blessing should be held with five fingers. These are its words in the "Introduction of The Book of Zohar": "'As a rose among the thorns.' As a rose of five hard leaves surround the rose, these five leaves are called 'salvations,' and this is the meaning of 'I shall raise a cup of salvations,' which is a cup of blessing. This is the meaning of the five times that 'light' is mentioned in the work of creation."

This light was created and concealed. This is the meaning of what our sages said (*Hagigah* 12), the light that the Creator created on the first day, Adam was observing in it from the end of the world to its end. The Creator looked into the generation of the flood and the generation of Babylon and saw that their practices were corrupt. He stood and concealed it from them.

The five fingers are *KHB ZON*. If a person observes "to keep and to do," the Creator makes the *Keter* above all of them, meaning that the Creator gives the power for the control of *Keter* or *Hesed*, which is called "a *Kli* [vessel] of bestowal." If the control is given to the quality of below, namely to *Malchut*, which is reception without *Hassadim*, there is separation and it is not considered "one pan."

499- "I" is the *Malchut*

"He who learns Torah before an uneducated person, it is as though he has intercourse with his fiancé in front of him."

An "uneducated person" is called the "will to receive." "Intercourse" means unification. "Before an uneducated person" means that the quality of the uneducated still controls him, where it should surrender before him, as our sages said, "The uneducated person, the fear of Shabbat [Sabbath] is on him."

Concerning engagement and matrimony: "A bride without a blessing is forbidden to her husband like menstruation." "Blessing" means bestowal, which is in order to bestow, when a person unites with the *Shechina* [Divinity].

The month of *Elul* means repentance, "I am for my beloved, and my beloved is for me." This is the intimation of repentance. It is written in *The Zohar*, "The *Hey* shall return to the *Vav*, to unite there the *Yod-Hey* with *Vav-Hey* in complete unity. The Lord is not complete, and His throne is not complete until He uproots the descendants of Amalek.

To understand all this, we must precede with the purpose, what is our role in life, and with the Torah and the *Mitzvot* [commandments]. The purpose of creation is to do good to His creations. Creation is existence from absence, meaning I from nothing, where "I" is the *Malchut*.

500- When You Raise the Candles – 2

"When you raise the candles." The Creator said to Moses, "It is not because I need the candles that it is written about them, but rather in your favor, as was said, 'His light is a candle.'" It is also written, "Even darkness will not make it dark for You, and the night will shine as day, the darkness as light." This teaches you that He does not need flesh and blood candles (*Midrash Rabbah*).

"Outside the veil of testimony, He will establish. Does He need its light? After all, all forty years when Israel were in the desert, they walked only by His light. Rather, it is a testimony to the people of the world that the *Shechina* [Divinity] dwells in Israel." What is a testimony? Rav said, "It is a western candle, which places in it oil such as the measure of the others, and from it he would light, and in it he would conclude" (*Shabbat* [Sabbath] 22b).

To interpret this, we should understand that the purpose of creation is to do good to His creations. At the same time, the Creator gave us practical *Mitzvot* [commandments]. This means that without the actions of the created beings, He cannot impart the abundance.

He brings the evidence that Israel walked forty years in the desert only by His light, meaning that there was only an awakening from above, called "bread from the sky," for the abundance came to them without preparation on the part of the lower ones.

"Bread from the earth" means that the abundance comes through the work of the lower ones. This is called "spoiled bread," meaning without labor, and our soul has grown loathsome of this bread, since when something comes without labor, we feel very little taste in it compared to something that comes through labor.

www.ingramcontent.com/pod-product-compliance
Lightning Source LLC
Chambersburg PA
CBHW051706160426
43209CB00004B/1045